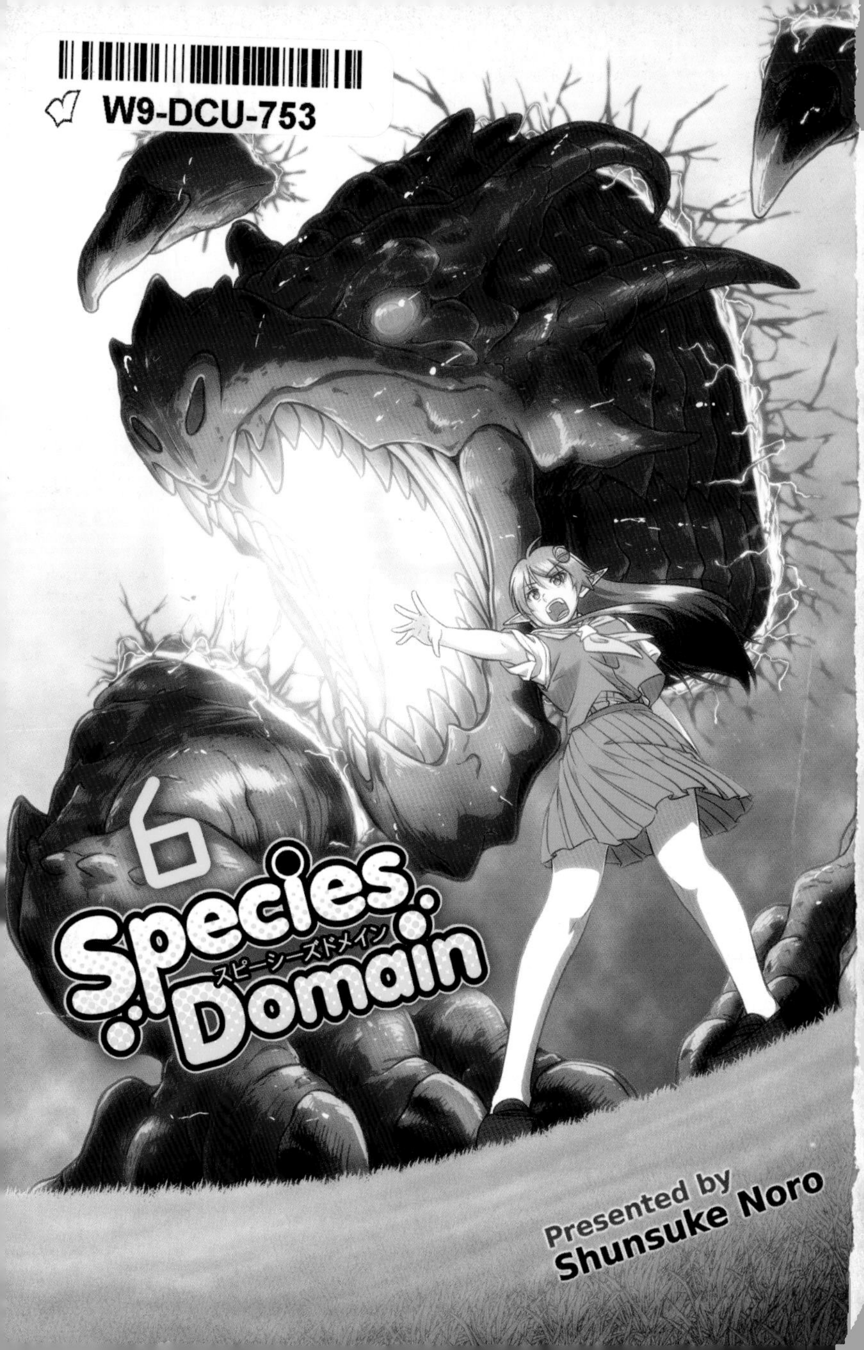
6
Species Domain
スピーシーズドメイン
Presented by
Shunsuke Noro

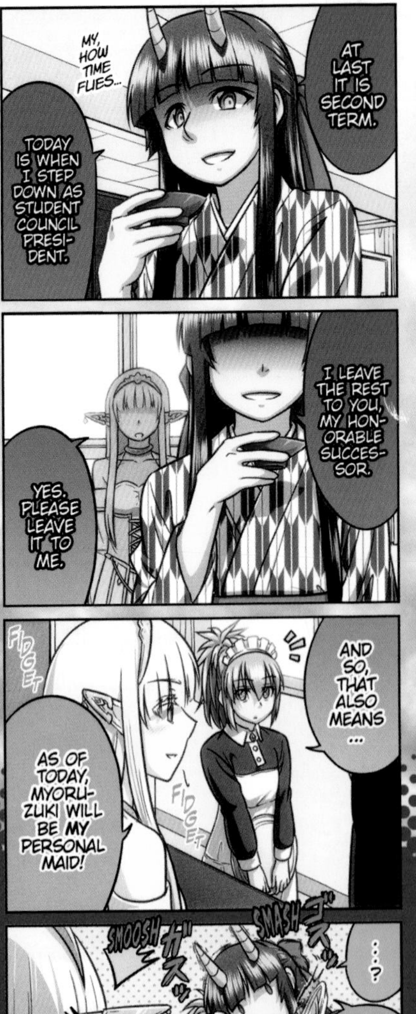
AT LAST IT IS SECOND TERM.
MY, HOW TIME FLIES...
TODAY IS WHEN I STEP DOWN AS STUDENT COUNCIL PRESIDENT.
I LEAVE THE REST TO YOU, MY HONORABLE SUCCESSOR.
YES. PLEASE LEAVE IT TO ME.
AND SO, THAT ALSO MEANS...
FIDGET
AS OF TODAY, MYORUZUKI WILL BE **MY** PERSONAL MAID!
FIDGET
...?
SMASH
SMOOSH
BUT MYORUZUKI-SAN BELONGS TO **ME**, SEE?
GET LOST.
DID YOU NOT SAY SHE WAS THE **STUDENT COUNCIL PRESIDENT'S** PERSONAL MAID ROBOT?!

She even took her home for summer break.

Species Domain

スピーシーズドメイン

6

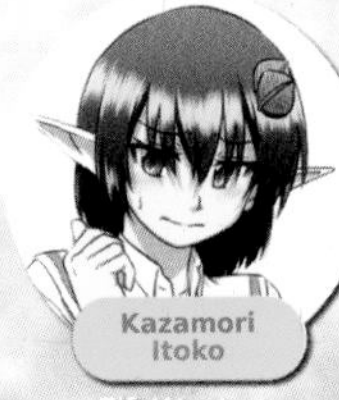

Kazamori Itoko

Elf. Wants to use magic but can't.

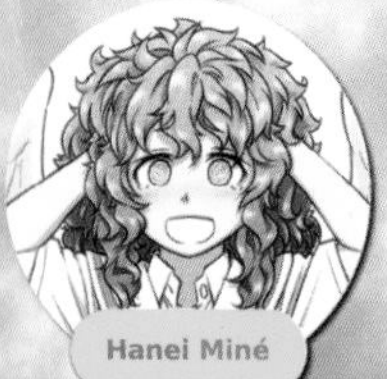

Hanei Miné

Icarus. Kind-hearted and large-breasted.

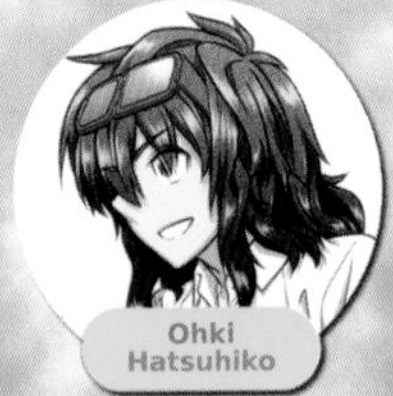

Ohki Hatsuhiko

Human. Science nut.

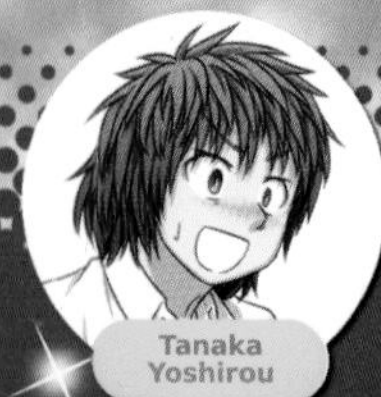

Tanaka Yoshirou

Human. Life of the party.

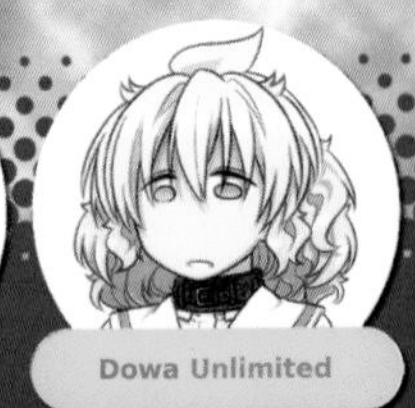

Dowa Unlimited

Dwarf. A girl with a beard.

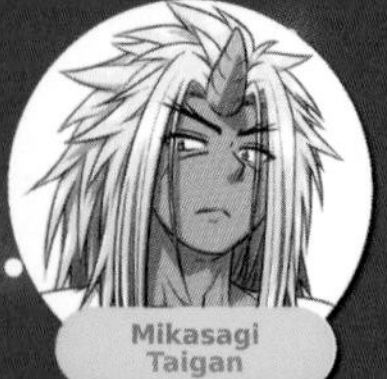

Mikasagi Taigan

Ogre. A young tough guy.

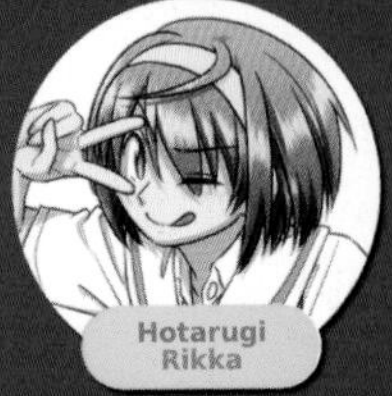

Hotarugi Rikka

Human. Tanaka's childhood friend.

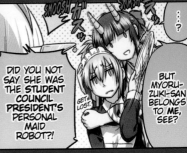

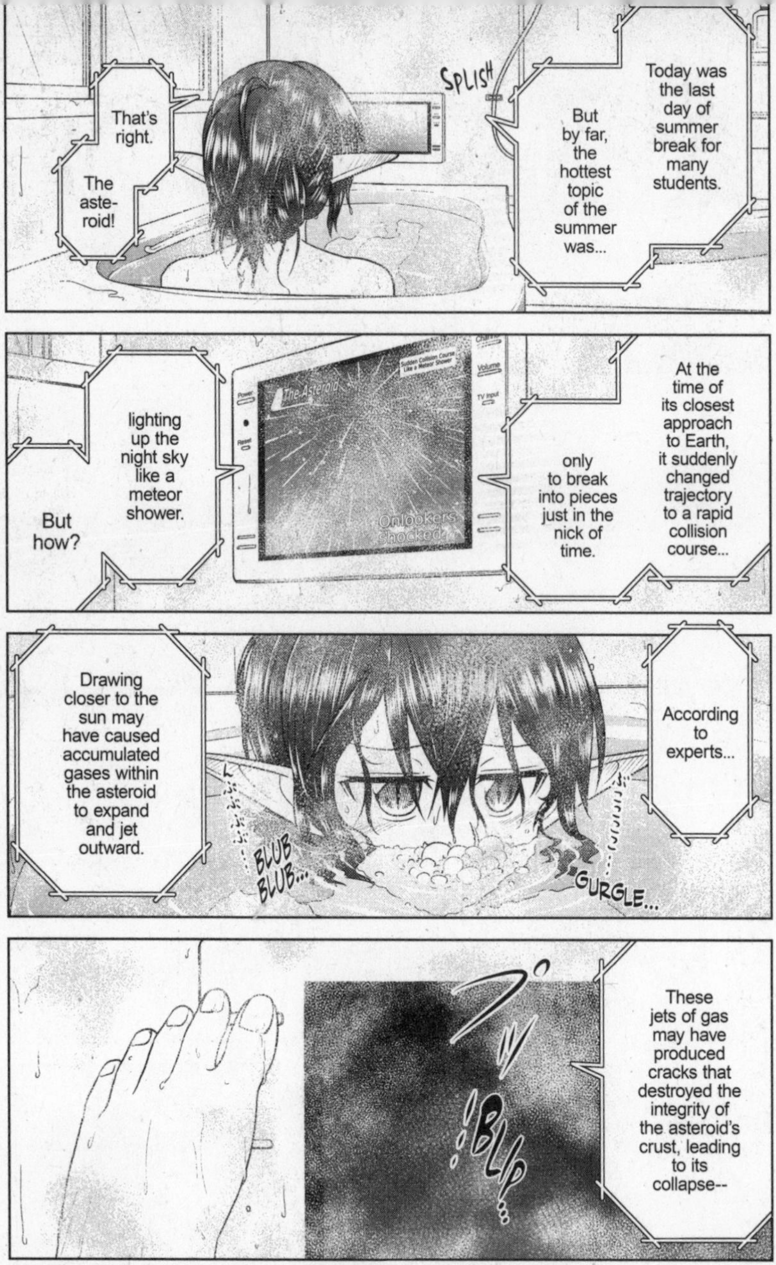
Today was the last day of summer break for many students.
But by far, the hottest topic of the summer was...
SPLISH
That's right.
The asteroid!
At the time of its closest approach to Earth, it suddenly changed trajectory to a rapid collision course...
only to break into pieces just in the nick of time.
Sudden Collision Course Like a Meteor Shower
The Asteroid
Onlookers shocked
Power
Reset
Volume
TV Input
lighting up the night sky like a meteor shower.
But how?
According to experts...
GURGLE...
BLUB BLUB...
Drawing closer to the sun may have caused accumulated gases within the asteroid to expand and jet outward.
These jets of gas may have produced cracks that destroyed the integrity of the asteroid's crust, leading to its collapse--
BLIP...

Chapter 36: Kazamori-san Writhes

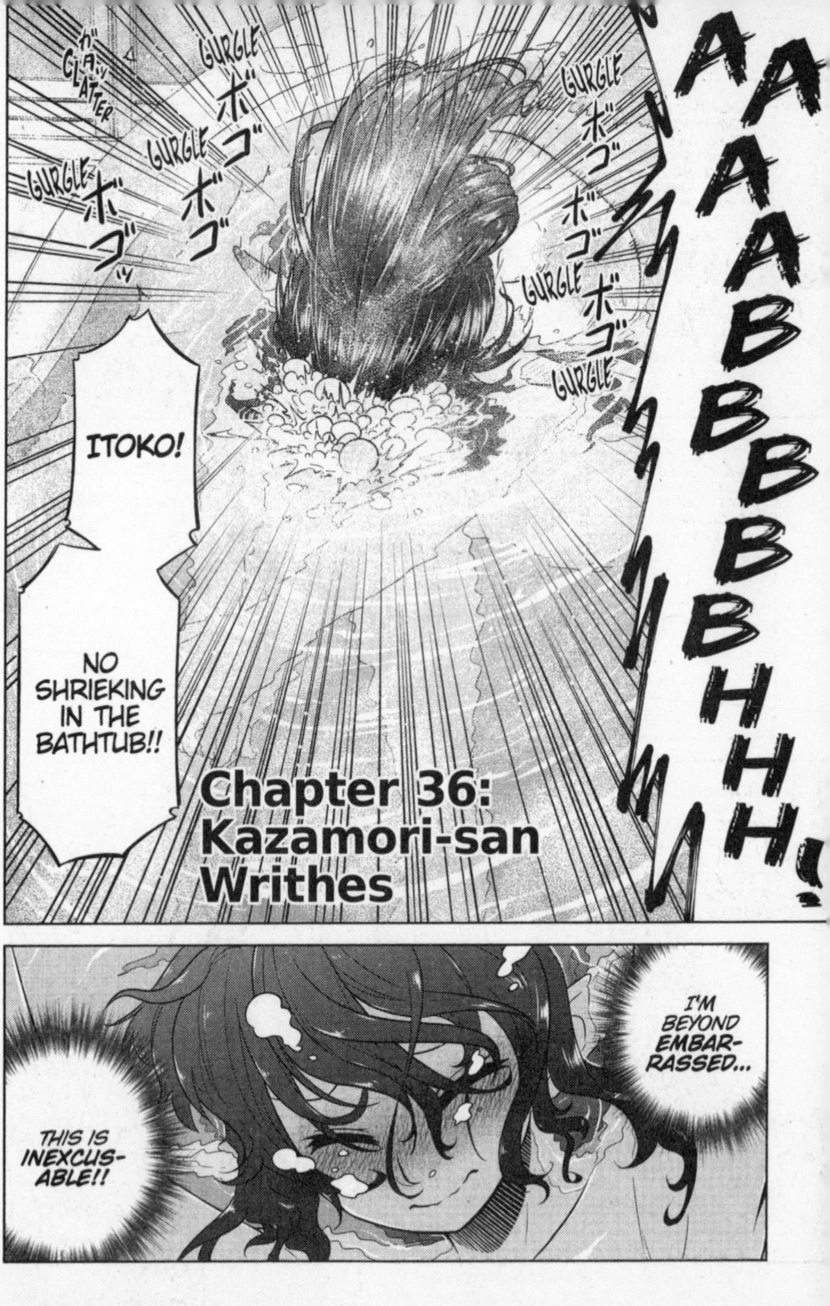
AAAABBBBBHHH!
GURGLE
GURGLE
GURGLE
GURGLE
CLATTER
GURGLE
GURGLE
ITOKO!
NO SHRIEKING IN THE BATHTUB!!
Chapter 36: Kazamori-san Writhes
I'M BEYOND EMBARRASSED...
THIS IS INEXCUSABLE!!

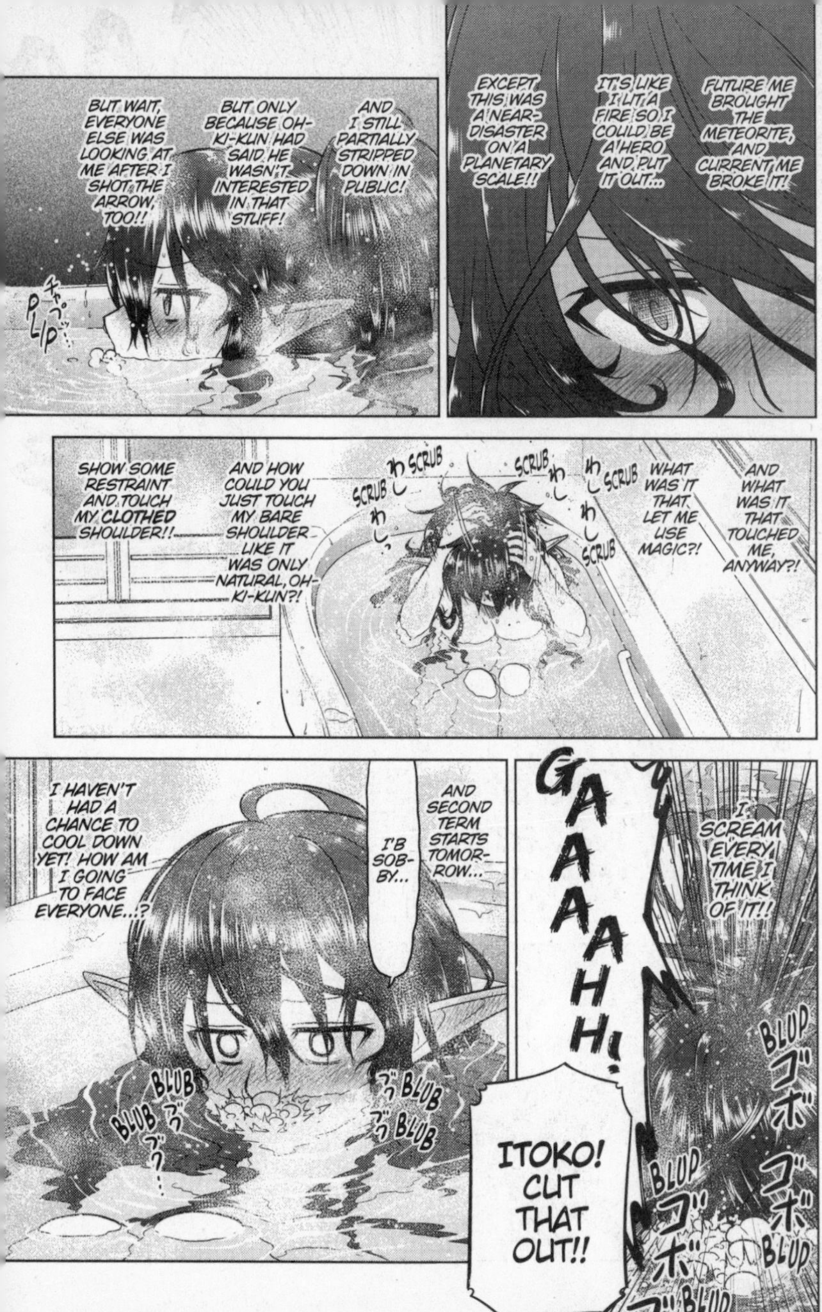
FUTURE ME BROUGHT THE METEORITE, AND CURRENT ME BROKE IT!!
IT'S LIKE I LIT A FIRE SO I COULD BE A HERO AND PUT IT OUT...
EXCEPT THIS WAS A NEAR-DISASTER ON A PLANETARY SCALE!!
AND I STILL PARTIALLY STRIPPED DOWN IN PUBLIC!
BUT ONLY BECAUSE OH-KI-KUN HAD SAID HE WASN'T INTERESTED IN THAT STUFF!
BUT WAIT, EVERYONE ELSE WAS LOOKING AT ME AFTER I SHOT THE ARROW, TOO!!
チャプッ… PLIP
AND WHAT WAS IT THAT TOUCHED ME, ANYWAY?!
WHAT WAS IT THAT LET ME USE MAGIC?!
わし SCRUB
わし SCRUB
わし SCRUB
わし SCRUB
わしっ SCRUB
AND HOW COULD YOU JUST TOUCH MY BARE SHOULDER LIKE IT WAS ONLY NATURAL, OH-KI-KUN?!
SHOW SOME RESTRAINT AND TOUCH MY **CLOTHED** SHOULDER!!
GAAAAAHH!
I SCREAM EVERY TIME I THINK OF IT!!
BLUP ゴボ
BLUP ゴボ
BLUP ゴボ
BLUP ゴボ
ITOKO! CUT THAT OUT!!
AND SECOND TERM STARTS TOMORROW...
I'B SOBBY...
I HAVEN'T HAD A CHANCE TO COOL DOWN YET! HOW AM I GOING TO FACE EVERYONE...?
ブク BLUB
ブク BLUB
BLUB ブク
BLUB ブク…

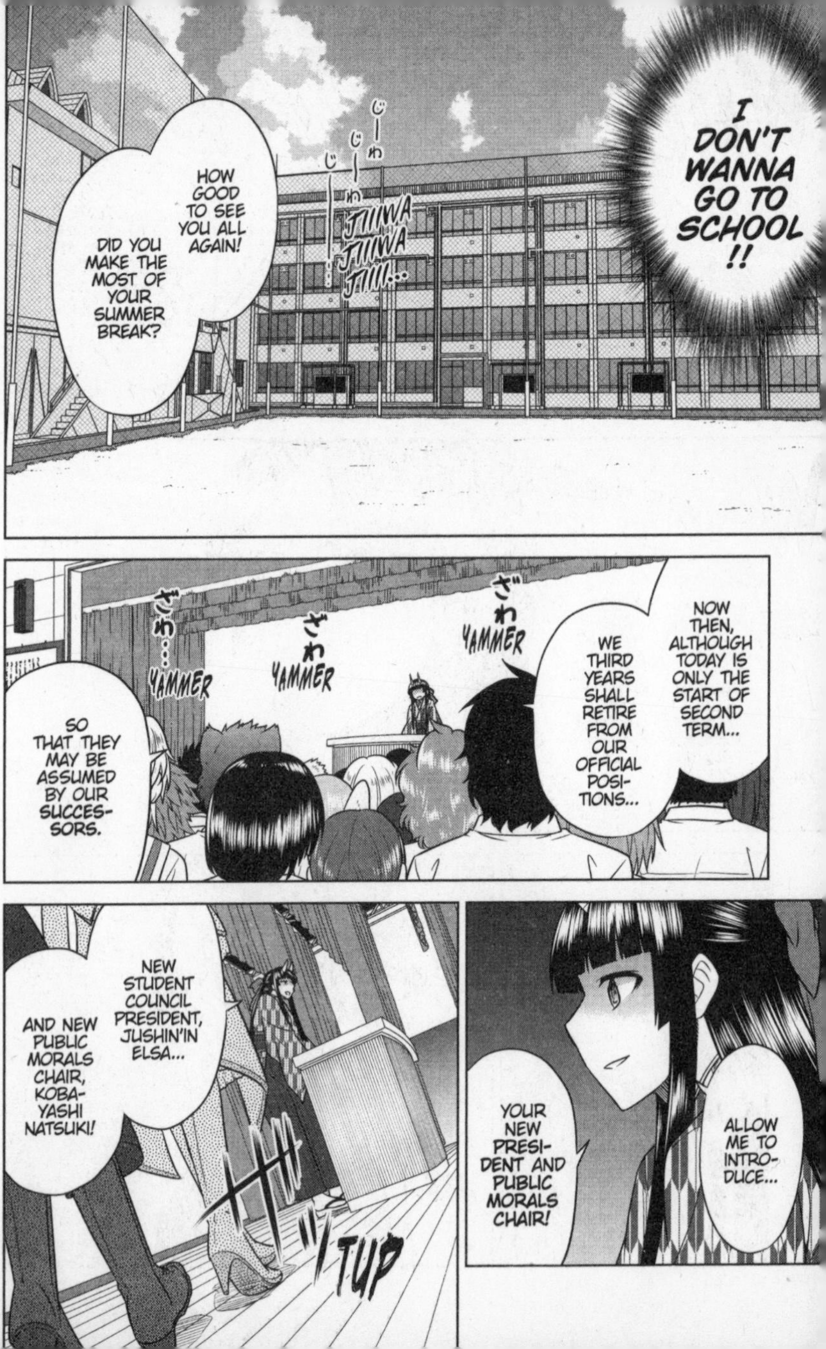
I DON'T WANNA GO TO SCHOOL!!
じーわ じーわ じー…
JIIIWA JIIIWA JIIII...
HOW GOOD TO SEE YOU ALL AGAIN!
DID YOU MAKE THE MOST OF YOUR SUMMER BREAK?
NOW THEN, ALTHOUGH TODAY IS ONLY THE START OF SECOND TERM...
WE THIRD YEARS SHALL RETIRE FROM OUR OFFICIAL POSITIONS...
ざわ YAMMER
ざわ YAMMER
ざわ… YAMMER
SO THAT THEY MAY BE ASSUMED BY OUR SUCCESSORS.
ALLOW ME TO INTRODUCE...
YOUR NEW PRESIDENT AND PUBLIC MORALS CHAIR!
NEW STUDENT COUNCIL PRESIDENT, JUSHIN'IN ELSA...
AND NEW PUBLIC MORALS CHAIR, KOBAYASHI NATSUKI!
TUP

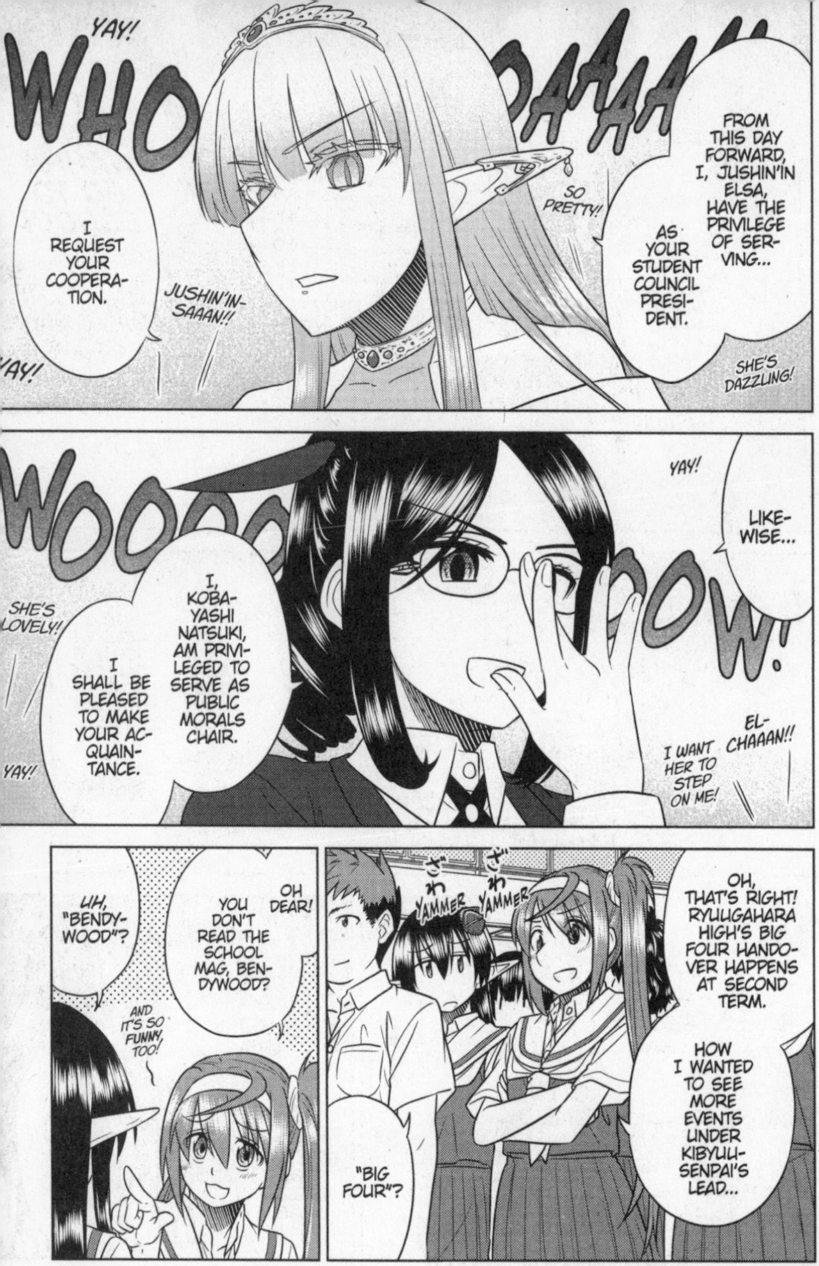
WHO
OAAAA
FROM THIS DAY FORWARD, I, JUSHIN'IN ELSA, HAVE THE PRIVILEGE OF SER-VING...
AS YOUR STUDENT COUNCIL PRESI-DENT.
SO PRETTY!
SHE'S DAZZLING!
YAY!
I REQUEST YOUR COOPERA-TION.
JUSHIN'IN-SAAAN!!
YAY!
WOOO
OW!
LIKE-WISE...
YAY!
I, KOBA-YASHI NATSUKI, AM PRIVI-LEGED TO SERVE AS PUBLIC MORALS CHAIR.
I SHALL BE PLEASED TO MAKE YOUR AC-QUAIN-TANCE.
EL-CHAAAN!!
I WANT HER TO STEP ON ME!
SHE'S LOVELY!
YAY!
OH, THAT'S RIGHT! RYUUGAHARA HIGH'S BIG FOUR HANDO-VER HAPPENS AT SECOND TERM.
ざわ YAMMER
ざわ YAMMER
HOW I WANTED TO SEE MORE EVENTS UNDER KIBYUU-SENPAI'S LEAD...
"BIG FOUR"?
OH DEAR!
YOU DON'T READ THE SCHOOL MAG, BEN-DYWOOD?
UH, "BENDY-WOOD"?
AND IT'S SO FUNNY, TOO!

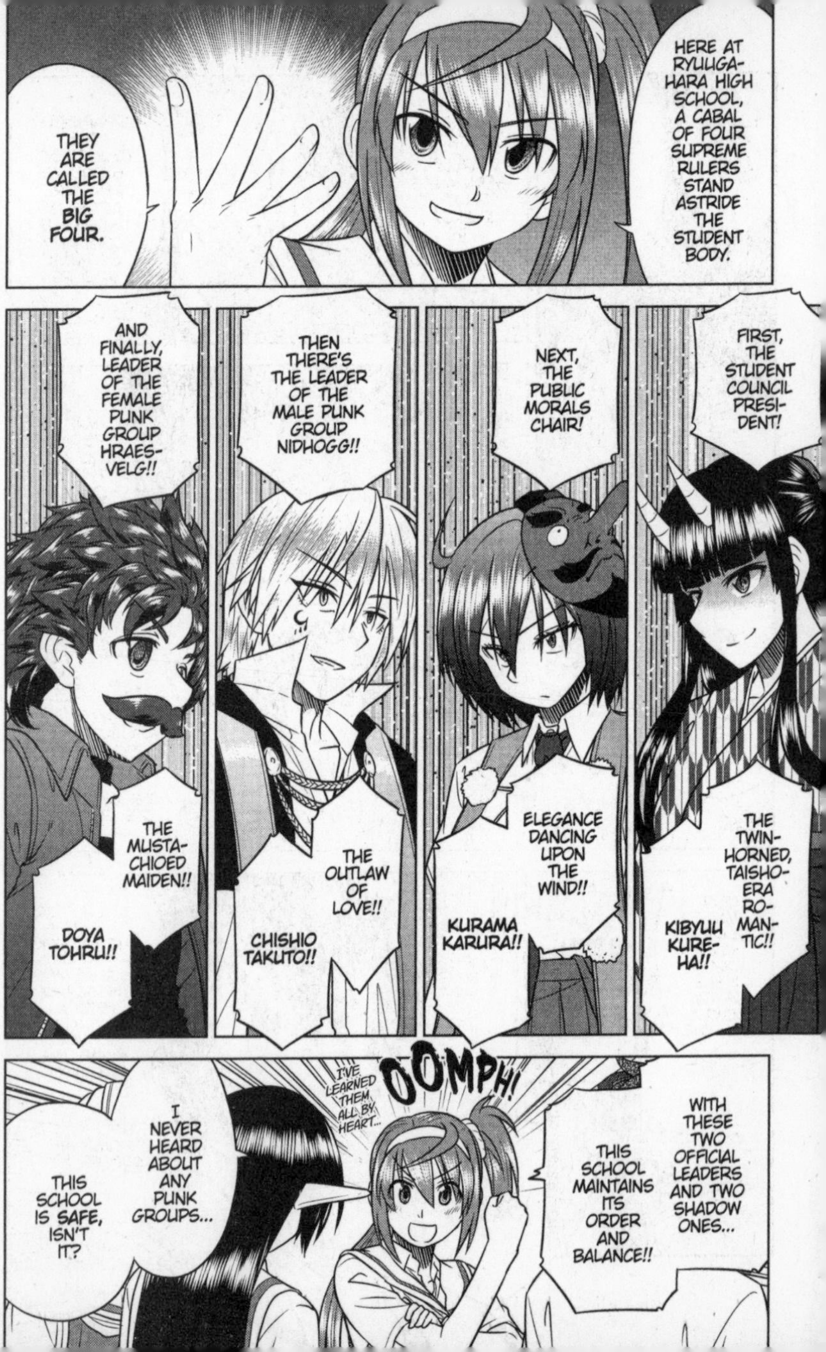
HERE AT RYUUGA-HARA HIGH SCHOOL, A CABAL OF FOUR SUPREME RULERS STAND ASTRIDE THE STUDENT BODY.
THEY ARE CALLED THE BIG FOUR.
FIRST, THE STUDENT COUNCIL PRESI-DENT!
THE TWIN-HORNED, TAISHO-ERA RO-MAN-TIC!!
KIBYUU KURE-HA!!
NEXT, THE PUBLIC MORALS CHAIR!
ELEGANCE DANCING UPON THE WIND!!
KURAMA KARURA!!
THEN THERE'S THE LEADER OF THE MALE PUNK GROUP NIDHOGG!!
THE OUTLAW OF LOVE!!
CHISHIO TAKUTO!!
AND FINALLY, LEADER OF THE FEMALE PUNK GROUP HRAES-VELG!!
THE MUSTA-CHIOED MAIDEN!!
DOYA TOHRU!!
WITH THESE TWO OFFICIAL LEADERS AND TWO SHADOW ONES...
THIS SCHOOL MAINTAINS ITS ORDER AND BALANCE!!
OOMPH!
I'VE LEARNED THEM ALL BY HEART...
I NEVER HEARD ABOUT ANY PUNK GROUPS...
THIS SCHOOL IS SAFE, ISN'T IT?

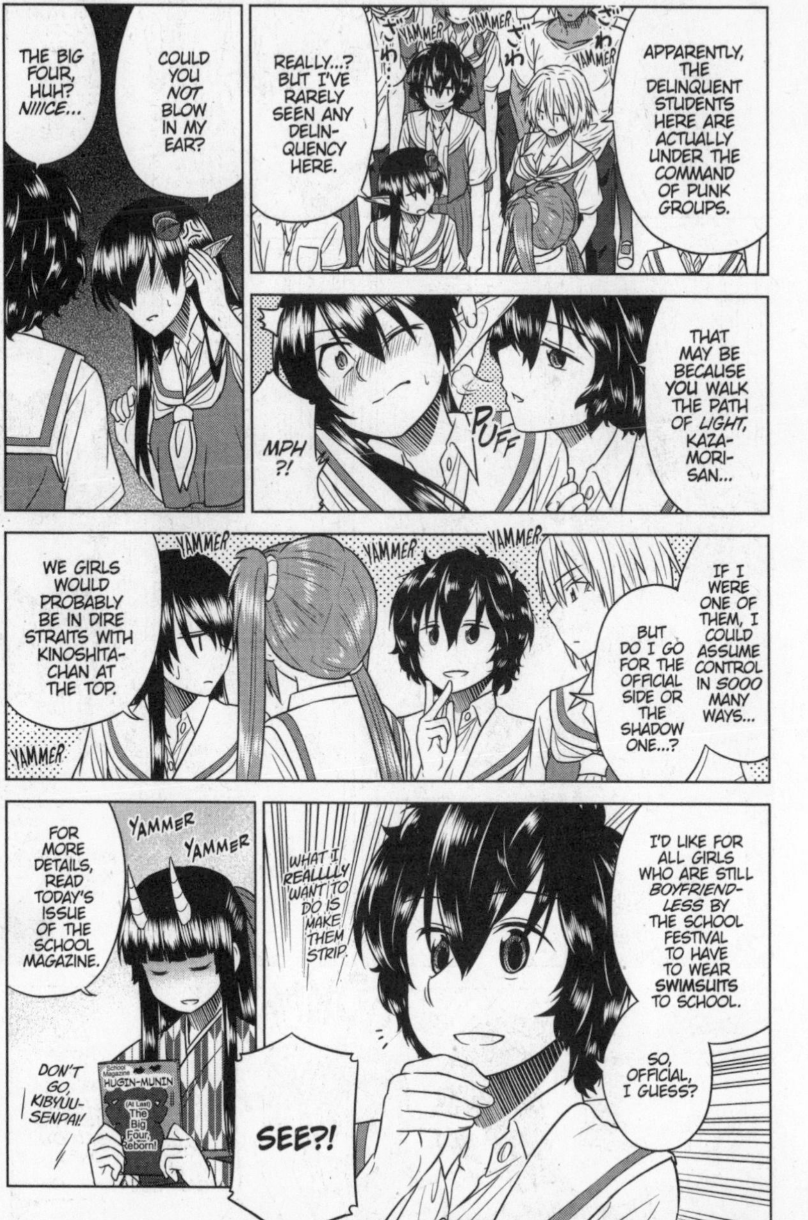
YAMMER
YAMMER
YAMMER
APPARENTLY, THE DELINQUENT STUDENTS HERE ARE ACTUALLY UNDER THE COMMAND OF PUNK GROUPS.
REALLY...? BUT I'VE RARELY SEEN ANY DELINQUENCY HERE.
THAT MAY BE BECAUSE YOU WALK THE PATH OF LIGHT, KAZAMORI-SAN...
PUFF
MPH?!
COULD YOU NOT BLOW IN MY EAR?
THE BIG FOUR, HUH? NIIICE...
YAMMER
YAMMER
YAMMER
IF I WERE ONE OF THEM, I COULD ASSUME CONTROL IN SOOO MANY WAYS...
BUT DO I GO FOR THE OFFICIAL SIDE OR THE SHADOW ONE...?
WE GIRLS WOULD PROBABLY BE IN DIRE STRAITS WITH KINOSHITA-CHAN AT THE TOP.
YAMMER
I'D LIKE FOR ALL GIRLS WHO ARE STILL BOYFRIEND-LESS BY THE SCHOOL FESTIVAL TO HAVE TO WEAR SWIMSUITS TO SCHOOL.
SO, OFFICIAL, I GUESS?
WHAT I REALLLLY WANT TO DO IS MAKE THEM STRIP.
SEE?!
YAMMER
YAMMER
FOR MORE DETAILS, READ TODAY'S ISSUE OF THE SCHOOL MAGAZINE.
School Magazine
HUGIN-MUNIN
(At Last) The Big Four, Reborn!
DON'T GO, KIBYUU-SENPAI!

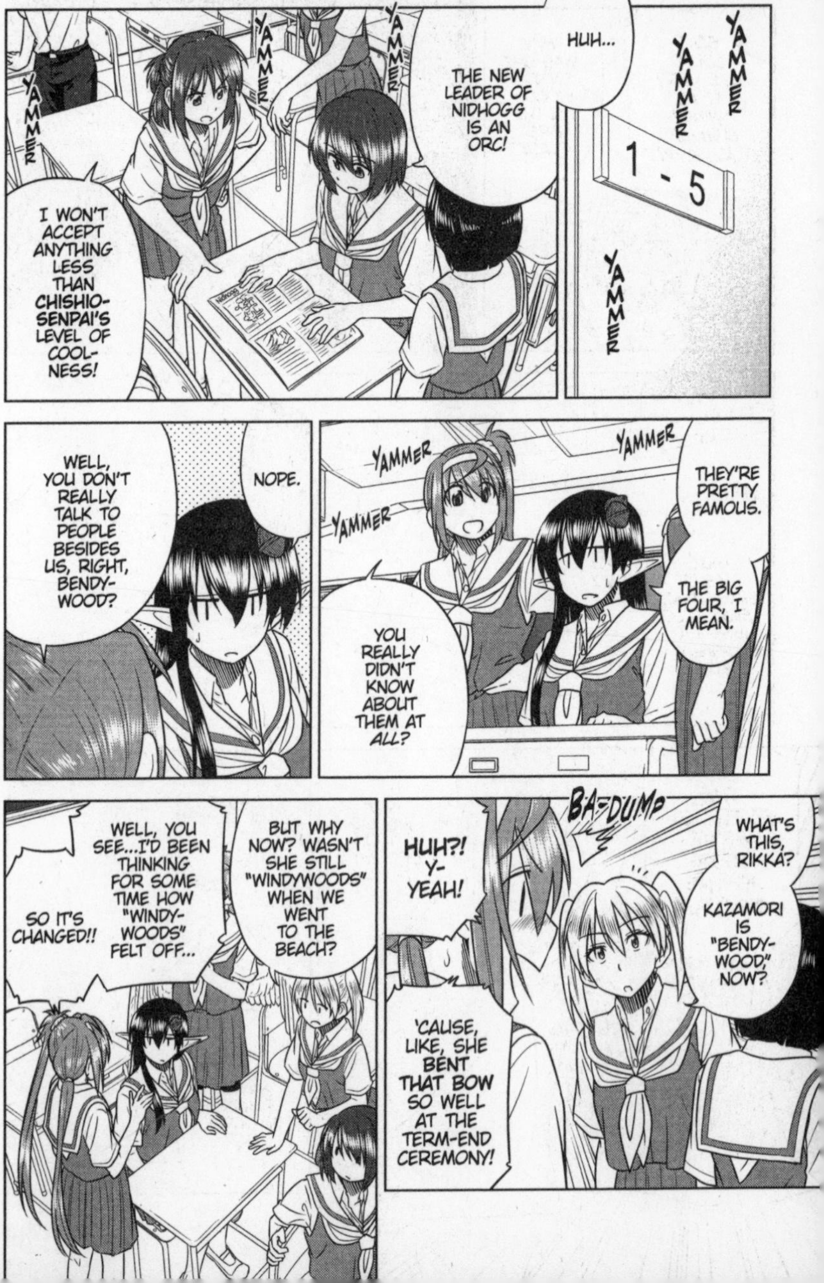
YAMMER
YAMMER
YAMMER
1 - 5
HUH...
THE NEW LEADER OF NIDHOGG IS AN ORC!
YAMMER
YAMMER
I WON'T ACCEPT ANYTHING LESS THAN CHISHIO-SENPAI'S LEVEL OF COOL-NESS!
YAMMER
YAMMER
YAMMER
THEY'RE PRETTY FAMOUS.
THE BIG FOUR, I MEAN.
YOU REALLY DIDN'T KNOW ABOUT THEM AT ALL?
NOPE.
WELL, YOU DON'T REALLY TALK TO PEOPLE BESIDES US, RIGHT, BENDY-WOOD?
BA-DUMP
WHAT'S THIS, RIKKA?
KAZAMORI IS "BENDY-WOOD," NOW?
HUH?! Y-YEAH!
'CAUSE, LIKE, SHE BENT THAT BOW SO WELL AT THE TERM-END CEREMONY!
BUT WHY NOW? WASN'T SHE STILL "WINDYWOODS" WHEN WE WENT TO THE BEACH?
WELL, YOU SEE...I'D BEEN THINKING FOR SOME TIME HOW "WINDY-WOODS" FELT OFF...
SO IT'S CHANGED!!

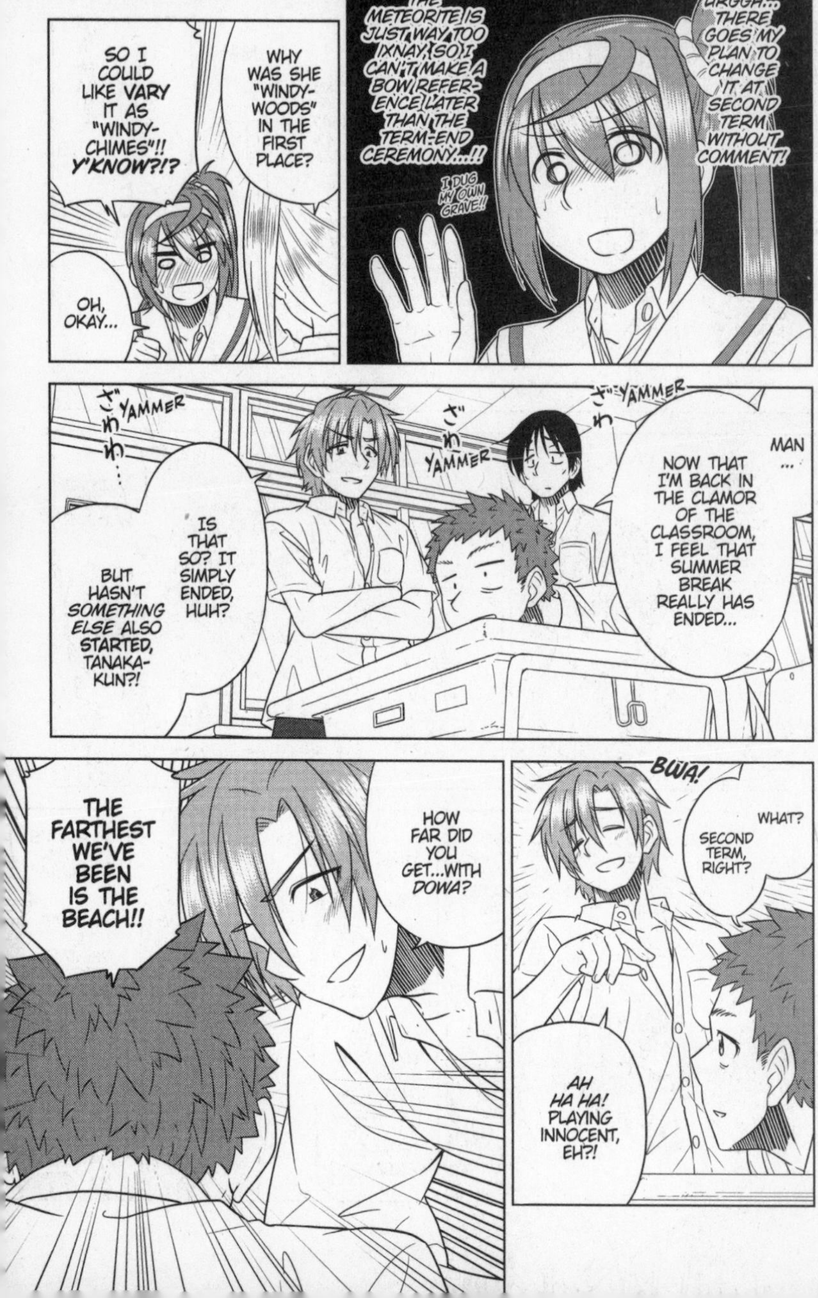
URGGH... THERE GOES MY PLAN TO CHANGE IT AT SECOND TERM WITHOUT COMMENT!
THE METEORITE IS JUST WAY TOO IXNAY, SO I CAN'T MAKE A BOW REFERENCE LATER THAN THE TERM-END CEREMONY...!!
I DUG MY OWN GRAVE!!
WHY WAS SHE "WINDY-WOODS" IN THE FIRST PLACE?
SO I COULD LIKE VARY IT AS "WINDY-CHIMES"!! Y'KNOW?!?
OH, OKAY...
ざわ YAMMER
MAN ...
NOW THAT I'M BACK IN THE CLAMOR OF THE CLASSROOM, I FEEL THAT SUMMER BREAK REALLY HAS ENDED...
ざわ YAMMER
ざわ YAMMER
IS THAT SO? IT SIMPLY ENDED, HUH?
BUT HASN'T *SOMETHING ELSE* ALSO STARTED, TANAKA-KUN?!
BWA!
WHAT?
SECOND TERM, RIGHT?
AH HA HA! PLAYING INNOCENT, EH?!
HOW FAR DID YOU GET...WITH *DOWA*?
THE FARTHEST WE'VE BEEN IS THE BEACH!!

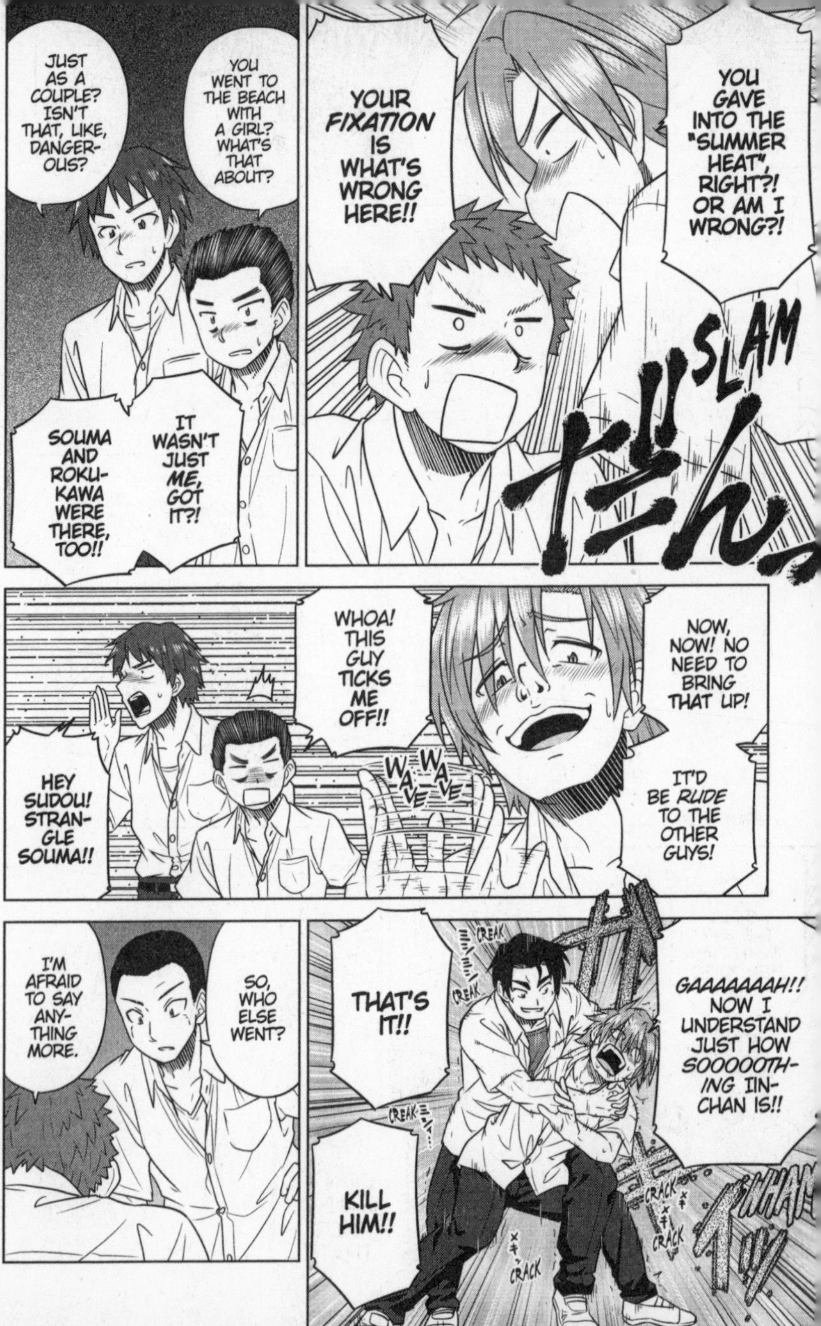
YOU GAVE INTO THE "SUMMER HEAT", RIGHT?! OR AM I WRONG?!
YOUR *FIXATION* IS WHAT'S WRONG HERE!!
SLAM
YOU WENT TO THE BEACH WITH A GIRL? WHAT'S THAT ABOUT?
JUST AS A COUPLE? ISN'T THAT, LIKE, DANGEROUS?
IT WASN'T JUST *ME*, GOT IT?!
SOUMA AND ROKUKAWA WERE THERE, TOO!!
NOW, NOW! NO NEED TO BRING THAT UP!
WHOA! THIS GUY TICKS ME OFF!!
IT'D BE *RUDE* TO THE OTHER GUYS!
WAVE WAVE
HEY SUDOU! STRANGLE SOUMA!!
GAAAAAAAH!! NOW I UNDERSTAND JUST HOW *SOOOOOTHING* IIN-CHAN IS!!
THAT'S IT!!
CREAK
CREAK
KILL HIM!!
CREAK
CRACK
CRACK
CRACK
SO, WHO ELSE WENT?
I'M AFRAID TO SAY ANYTHING MORE.

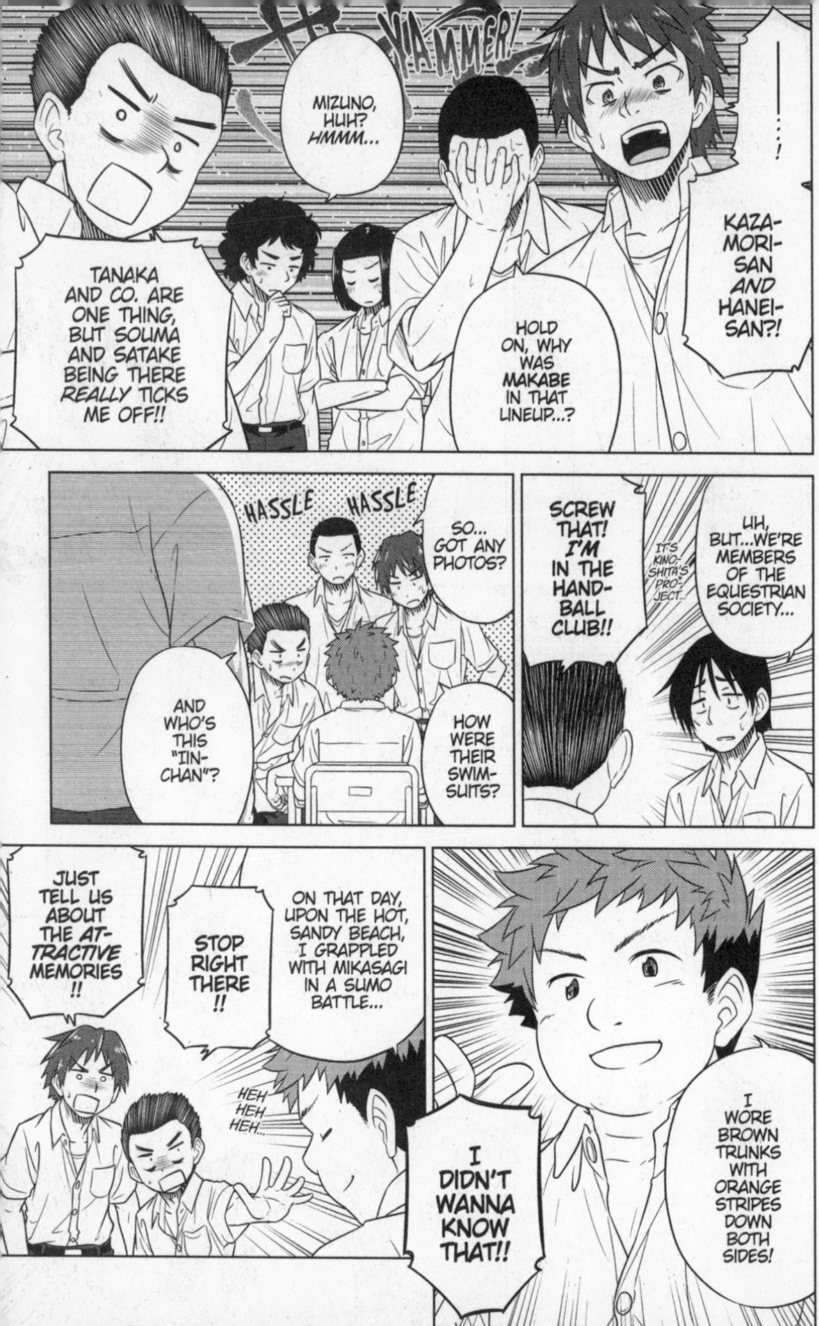

......!
KAZAMORI-SAN AND HANEI-SAN?!
YAMMER!
MIZUNO, HUH? HMMM...
HOLD ON, WHY WAS MAKABE IN THAT LINEUP...?
TANAKA AND CO. ARE ONE THING, BUT SOUMA AND SATAKE BEING THERE REALLY TICKS ME OFF!!
UH, BUT...WE'RE MEMBERS OF THE EQUESTRIAN SOCIETY...
IT'S KINOSHITA'S PROJECT...
SCREW THAT! I'M IN THE HANDBALL CLUB!!
SO... GOT ANY PHOTOS?
HASSLE HASSLE
HOW WERE THEIR SWIMSUITS?
AND WHO'S THIS "IIN-CHAN"?
I WORE BROWN TRUNKS WITH ORANGE STRIPES DOWN BOTH SIDES!
I DIDN'T WANNA KNOW THAT!!
ON THAT DAY, UPON THE HOT, SANDY BEACH, I GRAPPLED WITH MIKASAGI IN A SUMO BATTLE...
STOP RIGHT THERE!!
JUST TELL US ABOUT THE ATTRACTIVE MEMORIES!!
HEH HEH HEH...

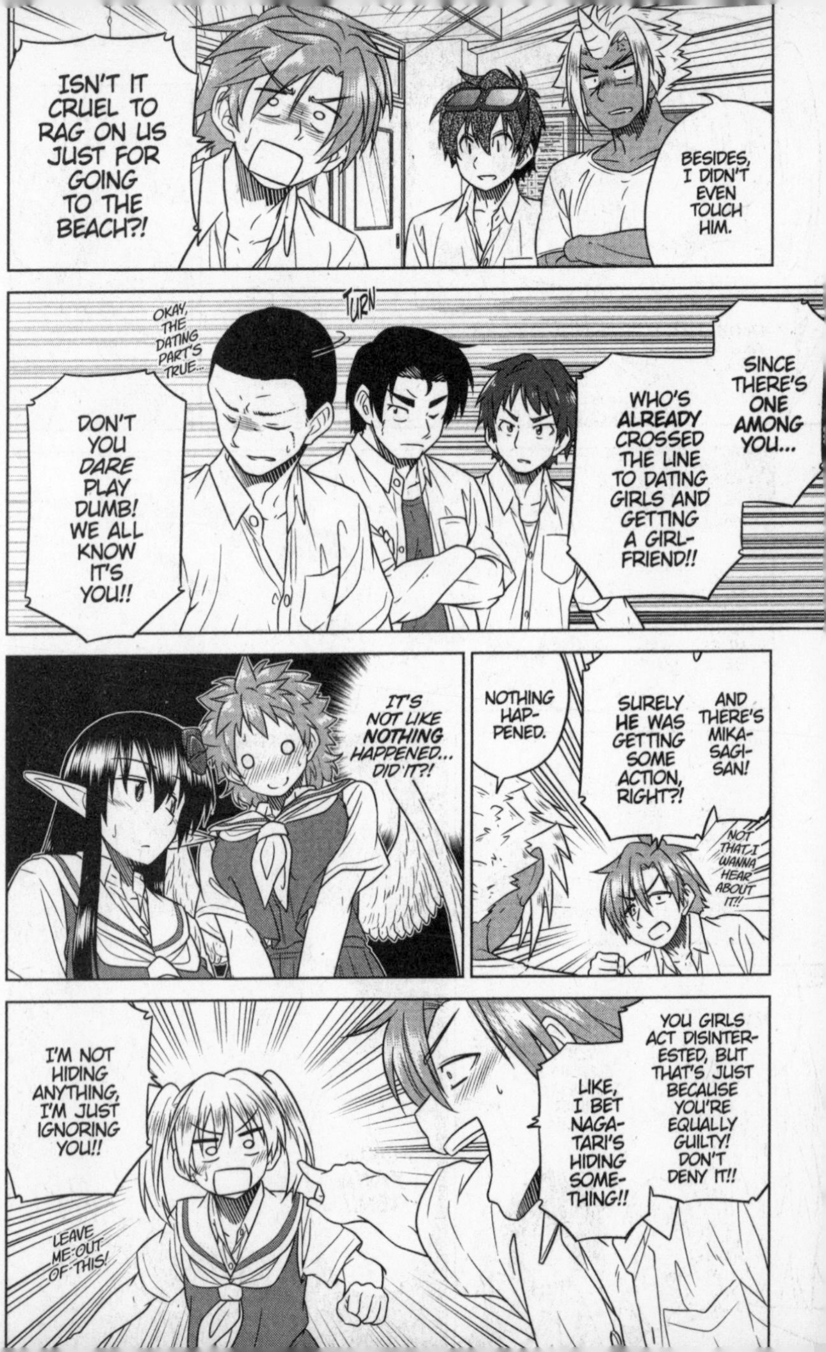
BESIDES, I DIDN'T EVEN TOUCH HIM.
ISN'T IT CRUEL TO RAG ON US JUST FOR GOING TO THE BEACH?!
SINCE THERE'S ONE AMONG YOU...
WHO'S ALREADY CROSSED THE LINE TO DATING GIRLS AND GETTING A GIRL-FRIEND!!
TURN
OKAY, THE DATING PART'S TRUE...
DON'T YOU DARE PLAY DUMB! WE ALL KNOW IT'S YOU!!
AND THERE'S MIKA-SAGI-SAN!
SURELY HE WAS GETTING SOME ACTION, RIGHT?!
NOTHING HAP-PENED.
NOT THAT I WANNA HEAR ABOUT IT!!
IT'S NOT LIKE NOTHING HAPPENED... DID IT?!
YOU GIRLS ACT DISINTER-ESTED, BUT THAT'S JUST BECAUSE YOU'RE EQUALLY GUILTY! DON'T DENY IT!!
LIKE, I BET NAGA-TARI'S HIDING SOME-THING!!
I'M NOT HIDING ANYTHING, I'M JUST IGNORING YOU!!
LEAVE ME OUT OF THIS!

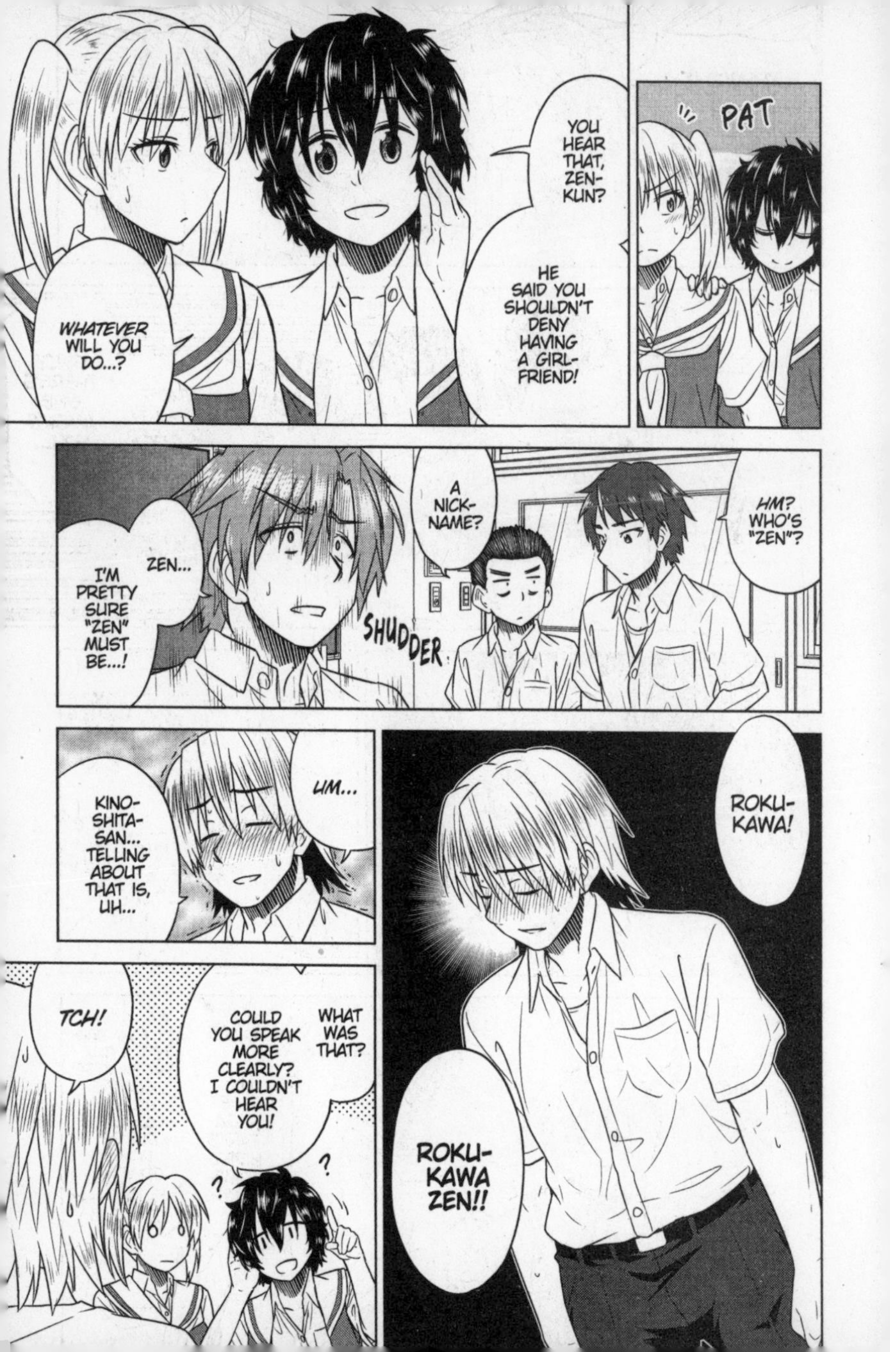
PAT
YOU HEAR THAT, ZEN-KUN?
HE SAID YOU SHOULDN'T DENY HAVING A GIRL-FRIEND!
WHATEVER WILL YOU DO...?
HM? WHO'S "ZEN"?
A NICK-NAME?
SHUDDER
ZEN...
I'M PRETTY SURE "ZEN" MUST BE...!
ROKU-KAWA!
ROKU-KAWA ZEN!!
UM...
KINO-SHITA-SAN... TELLING ABOUT THAT IS, UH...
WHAT WAS THAT?
COULD YOU SPEAK MORE CLEARLY? I COULDN'T HEAR YOU!
TCH!

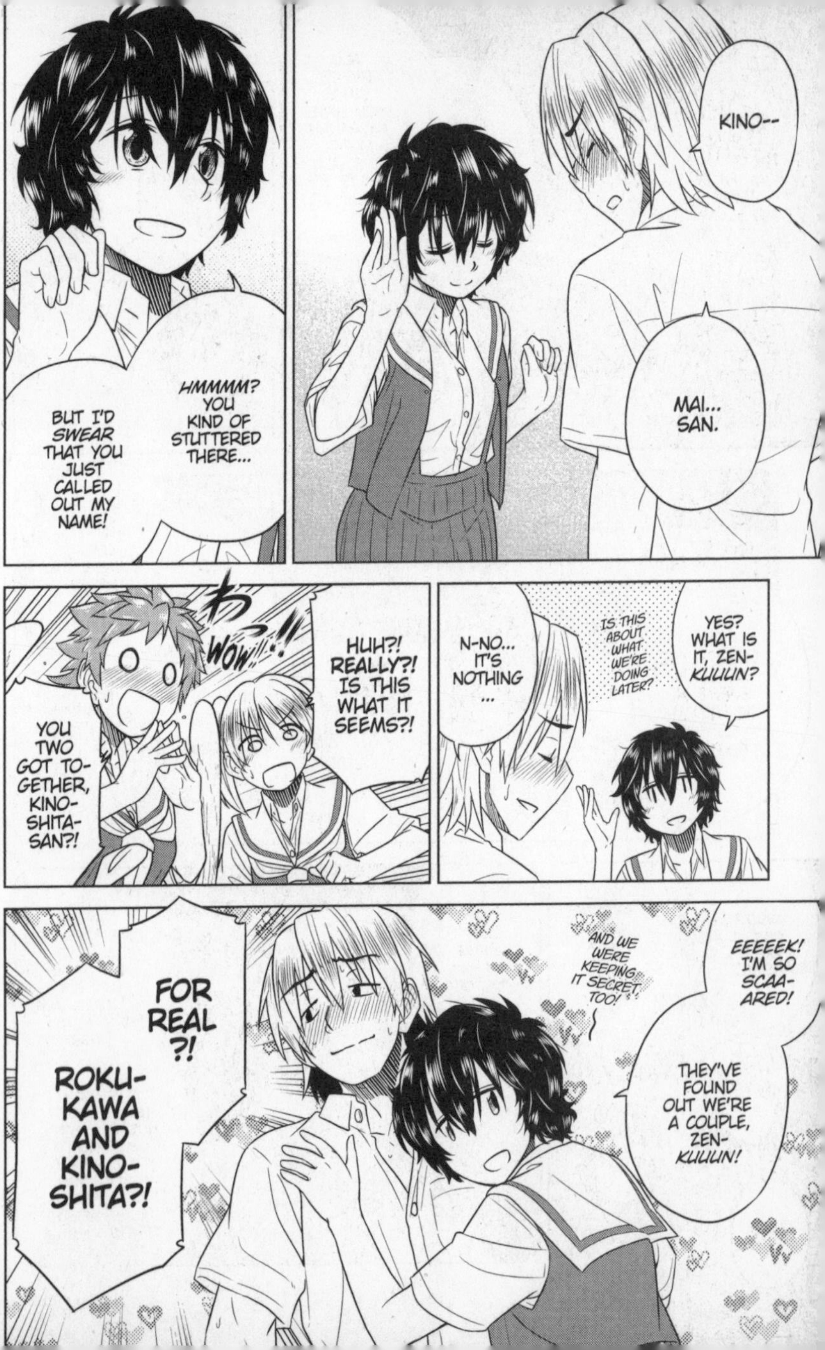
KINO--
MAI... SAN.
HMMMM? YOU KIND OF STUTTERED THERE...
BUT I'D SWEAR THAT YOU JUST CALLED OUT MY NAME!
YES? WHAT IS IT, ZEN-KUUUN?
IS THIS ABOUT WHAT WE'RE DOING LATER?
N-NO... IT'S NOTHING ...
HUH?! REALLY?! IS THIS WHAT IT SEEMS?!
わっ
WOW!!
YOU TWO GOT TO-GETHER, KINO-SHITA-SAN?!
EEEEEK! I'M SO SCAAARED!
AND WE WERE KEEPING IT SECRET, TOO!
THEY'VE FOUND OUT WE'RE A COUPLE, ZEN-KUUUN!
FOR REAL?!
ROKU-KAWA AND KINO-SHITA?!

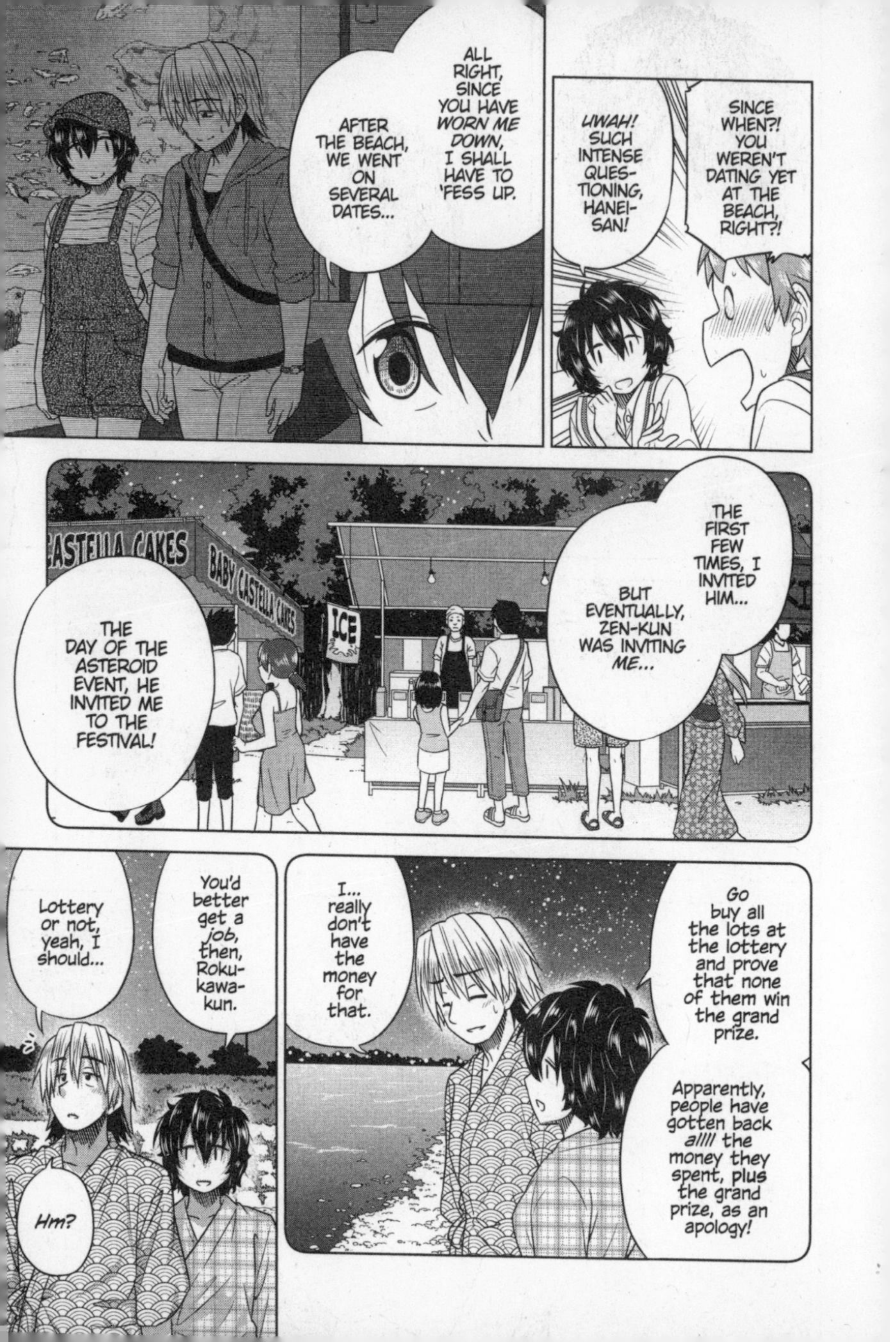
SINCE WHEN?! YOU WEREN'T DATING YET AT THE BEACH, RIGHT?!
UWAH! SUCH INTENSE QUESTIONING, HANEI-SAN!
ALL RIGHT, SINCE YOU HAVE *WORN ME DOWN*, I SHALL HAVE TO 'FESS UP.
AFTER THE BEACH, WE WENT ON SEVERAL DATES...
THE FIRST FEW TIMES, I INVITED HIM...
BUT EVENTUALLY, ZEN-KUN WAS INVITING *ME*...
CASTELLA CAKES
BABY CASTELLA CAKES
ICE
THE DAY OF THE ASTEROID EVENT, HE INVITED ME TO THE FESTIVAL!
Go buy all the lots at the lottery and prove that none of them win the grand prize.
Apparently, people have gotten back *allll* the money they spent, plus the grand prize, as an apology!
I... really don't have the money for that.
You'd better get a *job*, then, Rokukawa-kun.
Lottery or not, yeah, I should...
Hm?

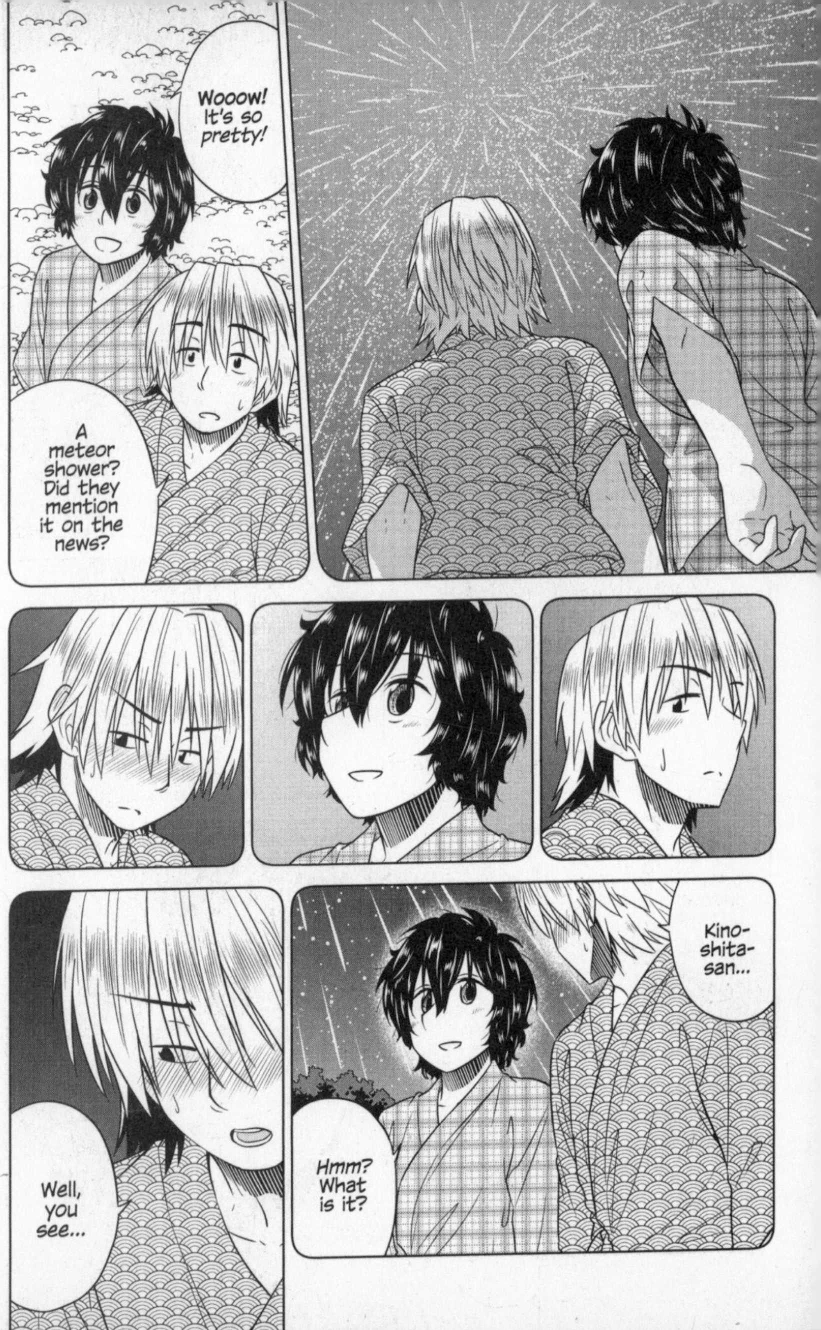
Wooow! It's so pretty!
A meteor shower? Did they mention it on the news?
Kino-shita-san...
Hmm? What is it?
Well, you see...

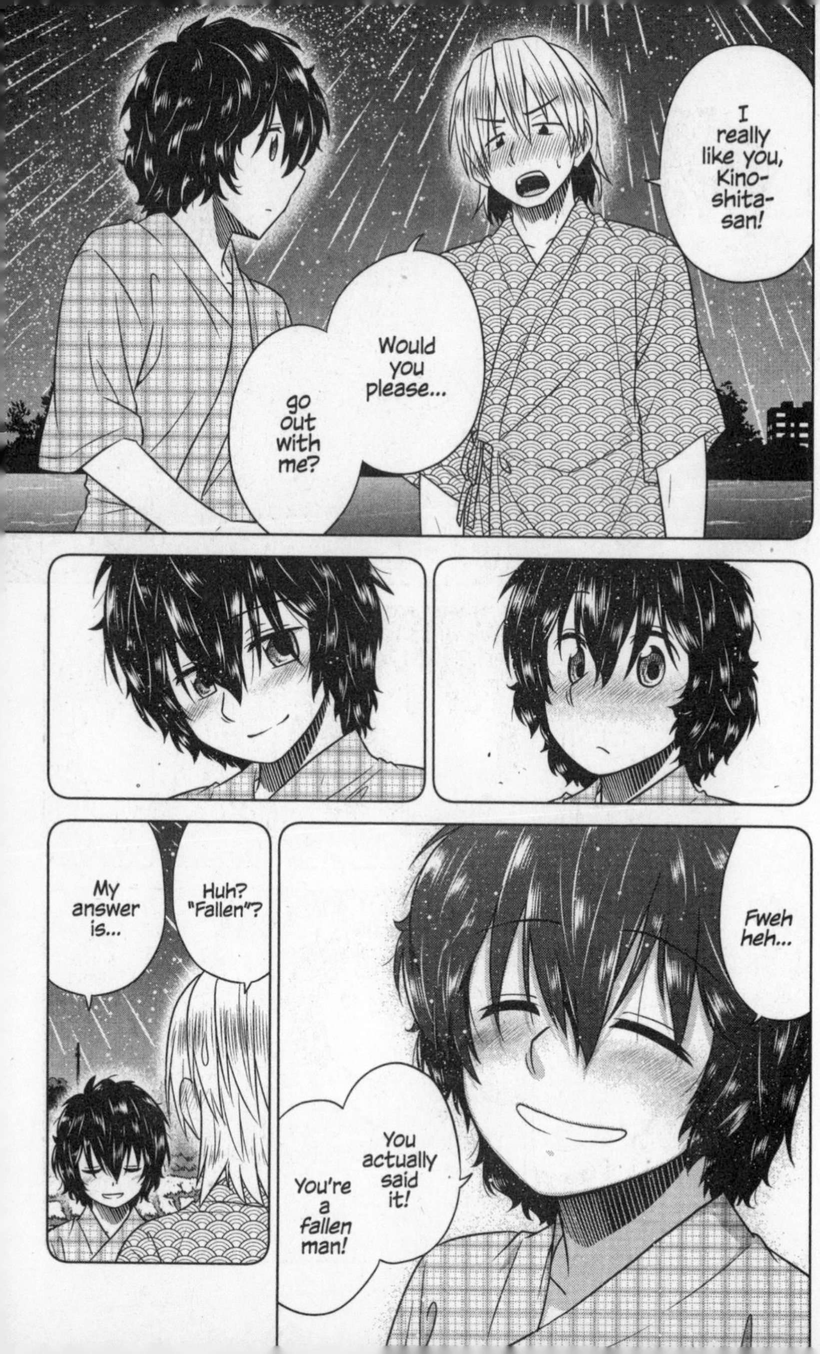
I really like you, Kino-shita-san!
Would you please...
go out with me?
Fweh heh...
You actually said it!
You're a fallen man!
Huh? "Fallen"?
My answer is...

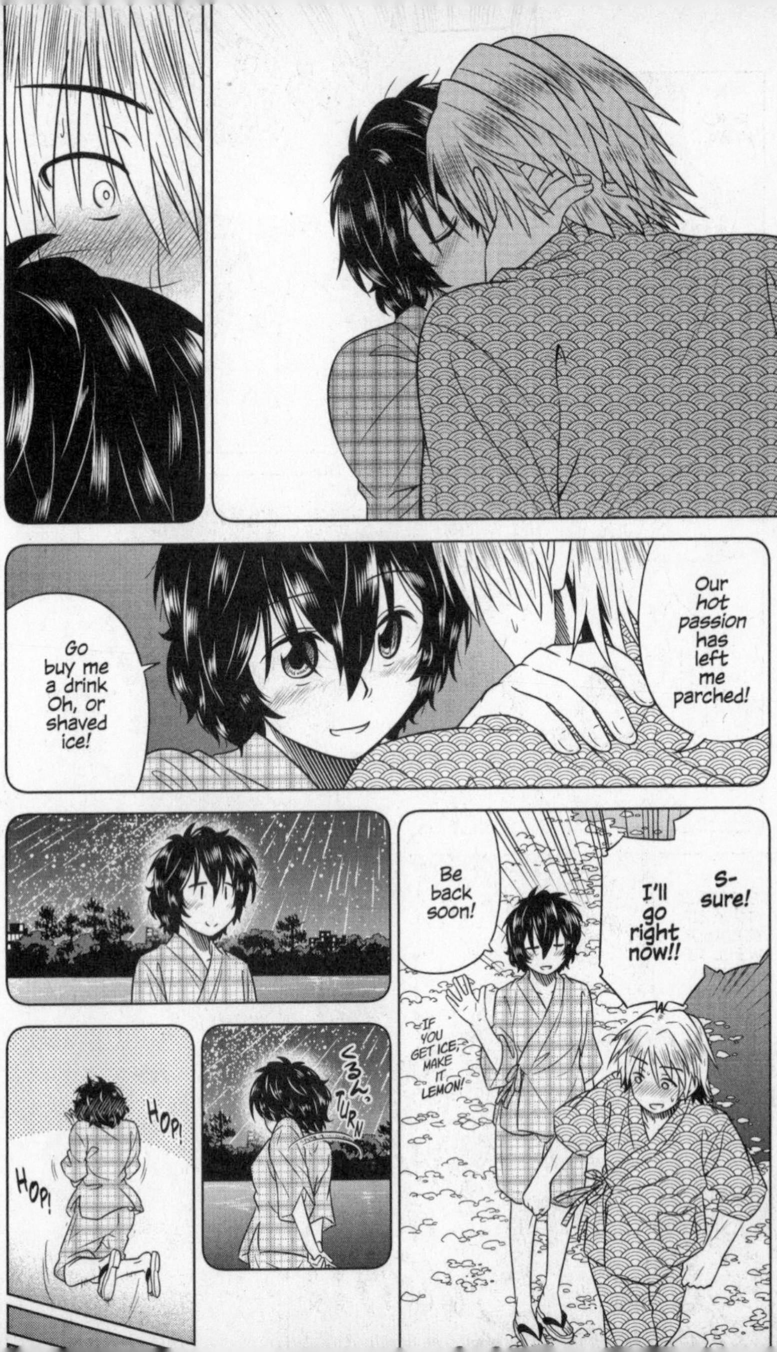
Our hot passion has left me parched!
Go buy me a drink Oh, or shaved ice!
S-sure! I'll go right now!!
Be back soon!
IF YOU GET ICE, MAKE IT LEMON!
くるん TURN
HOP!
HOP!

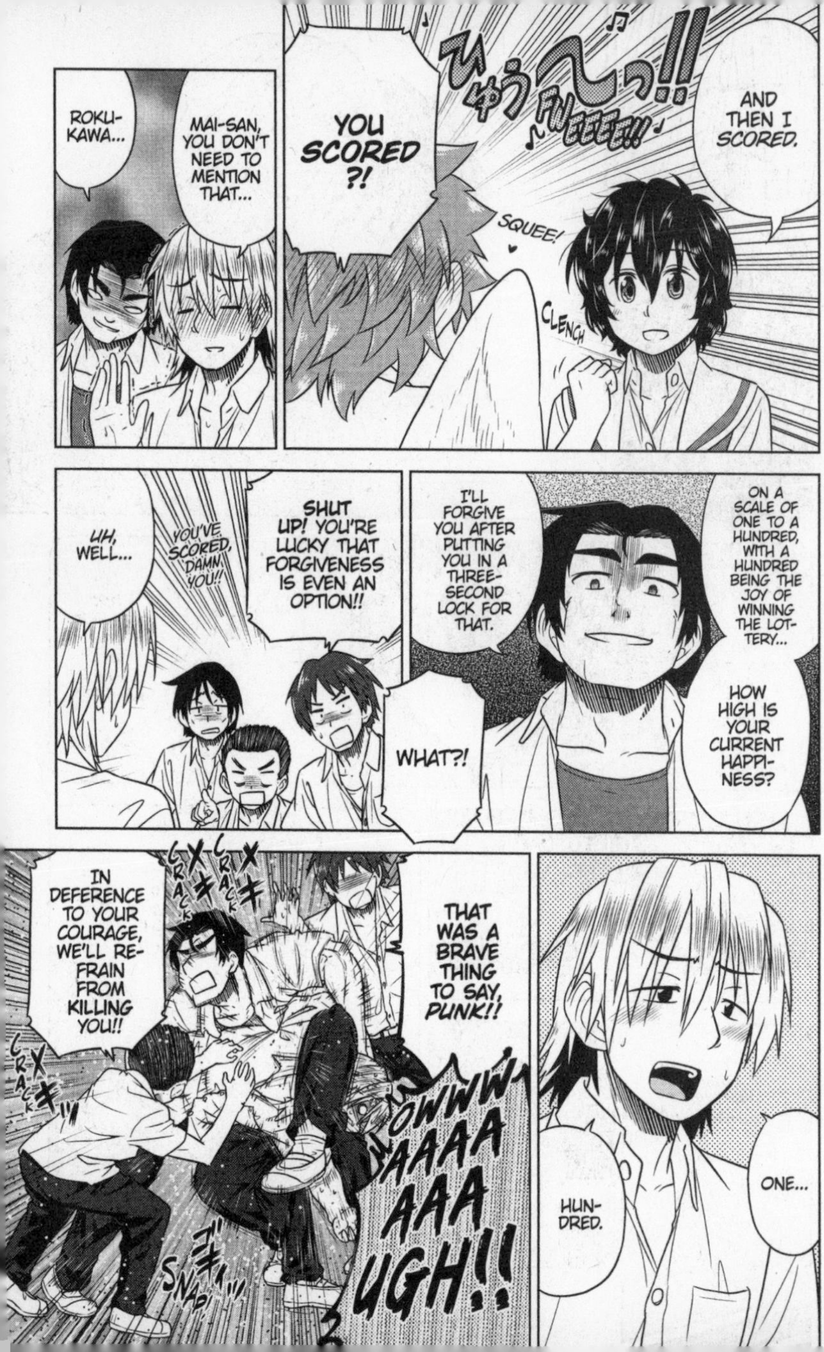
AND THEN I SCORED.
FWEEEE!!
SQUEE!
CLENCH
YOU SCORED?!
MAI-SAN, YOU DON'T NEED TO MENTION THAT...
ROKU-KAWA...
ON A SCALE OF ONE TO A HUNDRED, WITH A HUNDRED BEING THE JOY OF WINNING THE LOTTERY...
HOW HIGH IS YOUR CURRENT HAPPINESS?
I'LL FORGIVE YOU AFTER PUTTING YOU IN A THREE-SECOND LOCK FOR THAT.
WHAT?!
SHUT UP! YOU'RE LUCKY THAT FORGIVENESS IS EVEN AN OPTION!!
YOU'VE SCORED, DAMN YOU!!
UH, WELL...
ONE...
HUN-DRED.
THAT WAS A BRAVE THING TO SAY, PUNK!!
IN DEFERENCE TO YOUR COURAGE, WE'LL RE-FRAIN FROM KILLING YOU!!
CRACK
CRACK
CRACK
OWWWAAAAAAAUGH!!
SNAP

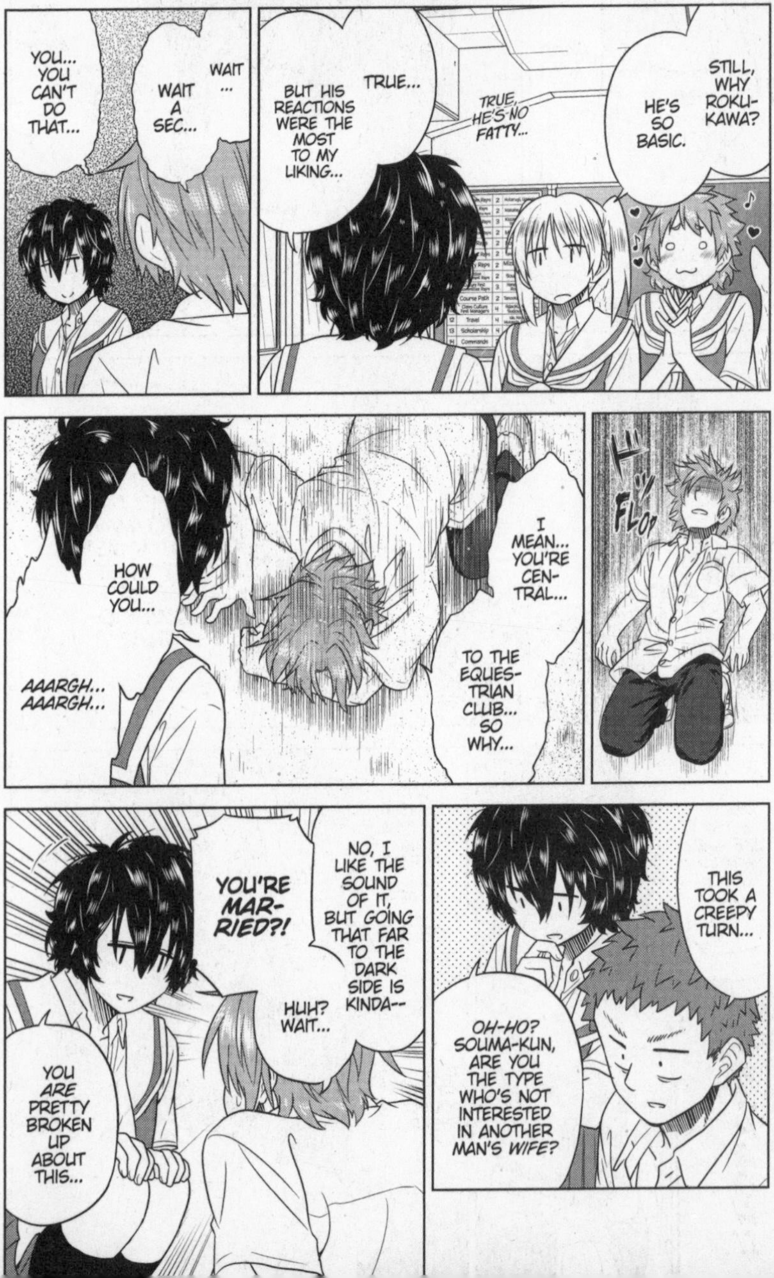
STILL, WHY ROKUKAWA?
HE'S SO BASIC.
TRUE, HE'S NO FATTY...
TRUE...
BUT HIS REACTIONS WERE THE MOST TO MY LIKING...
WAIT ...
WAIT A SEC...
YOU... YOU CAN'T DO THAT...
FLOP
I MEAN... YOU'RE CENTRAL...
TO THE EQUESTRIAN CLUB... SO WHY...
HOW COULD YOU...
AAARGH... AAARGH...
THIS TOOK A CREEPY TURN...
OH-HO? SOUMA-KUN, ARE YOU THE TYPE WHO'S NOT INTERESTED IN ANOTHER MAN'S WIFE?
NO, I LIKE THE SOUND OF IT, BUT GOING THAT FAR TO THE DARK SIDE IS KINDA--
YOU'RE MARRIED?!
HUH? WAIT...
YOU ARE PRETTY BROKEN UP ABOUT THIS...

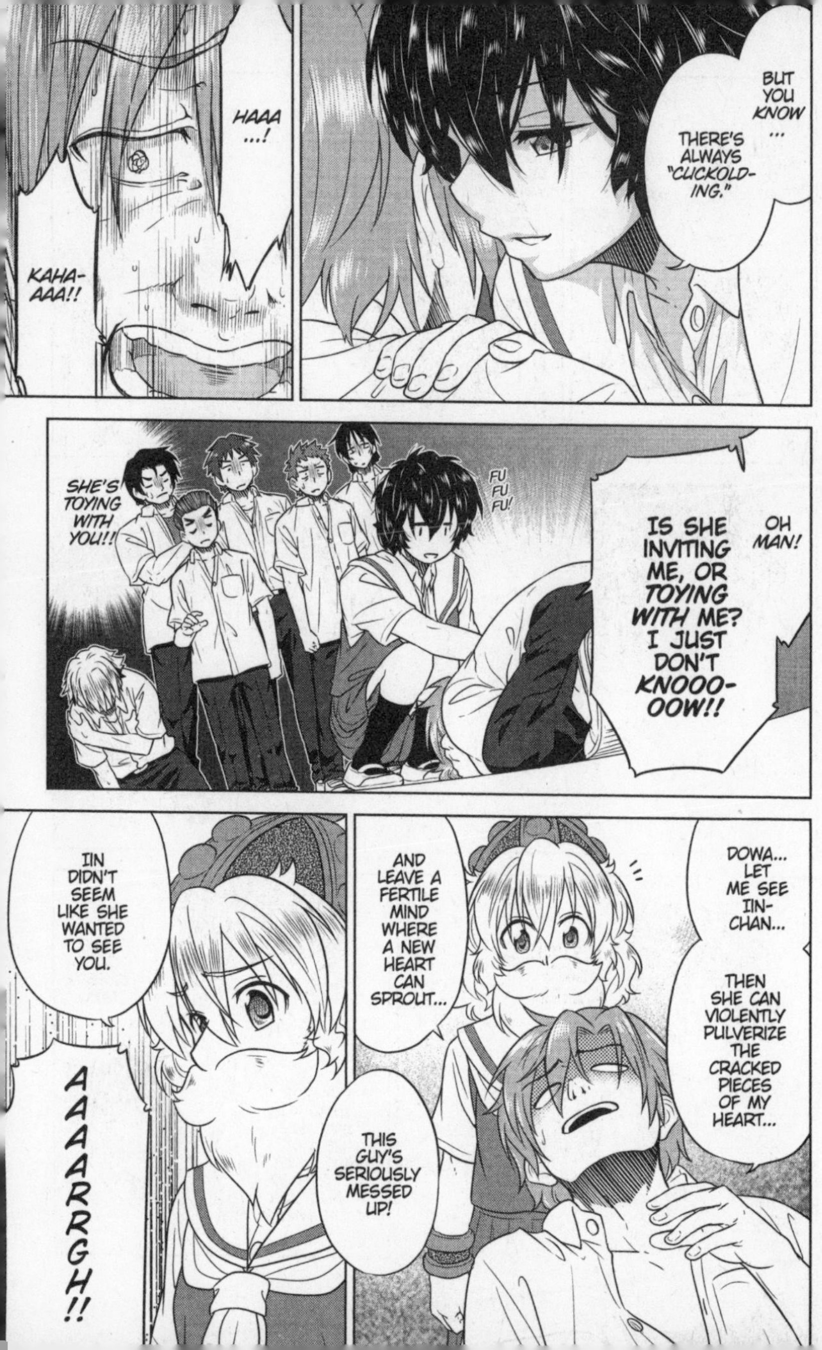
BUT YOU KNOW ...
THERE'S ALWAYS "CUCKOLDING."
HAAA ...!
KAHA-AAA!!
OH MAN!
IS SHE INVITING ME, OR TOYING WITH ME? I JUST DON'T KNOOO-OOW!!
FU FU FU!
SHE'S TOYING WITH YOU!!
DOWA... LET ME SEE IIN-CHAN...
THEN SHE CAN VIOLENTLY PULVERIZE THE CRACKED PIECES OF MY HEART...
AND LEAVE A FERTILE MIND WHERE A NEW HEART CAN SPROUT...
THIS GUY'S SERIOUSLY MESSED UP!
IIN DIDN'T SEEM LIKE SHE WANTED TO SEE YOU.
AAAAARRGH!!

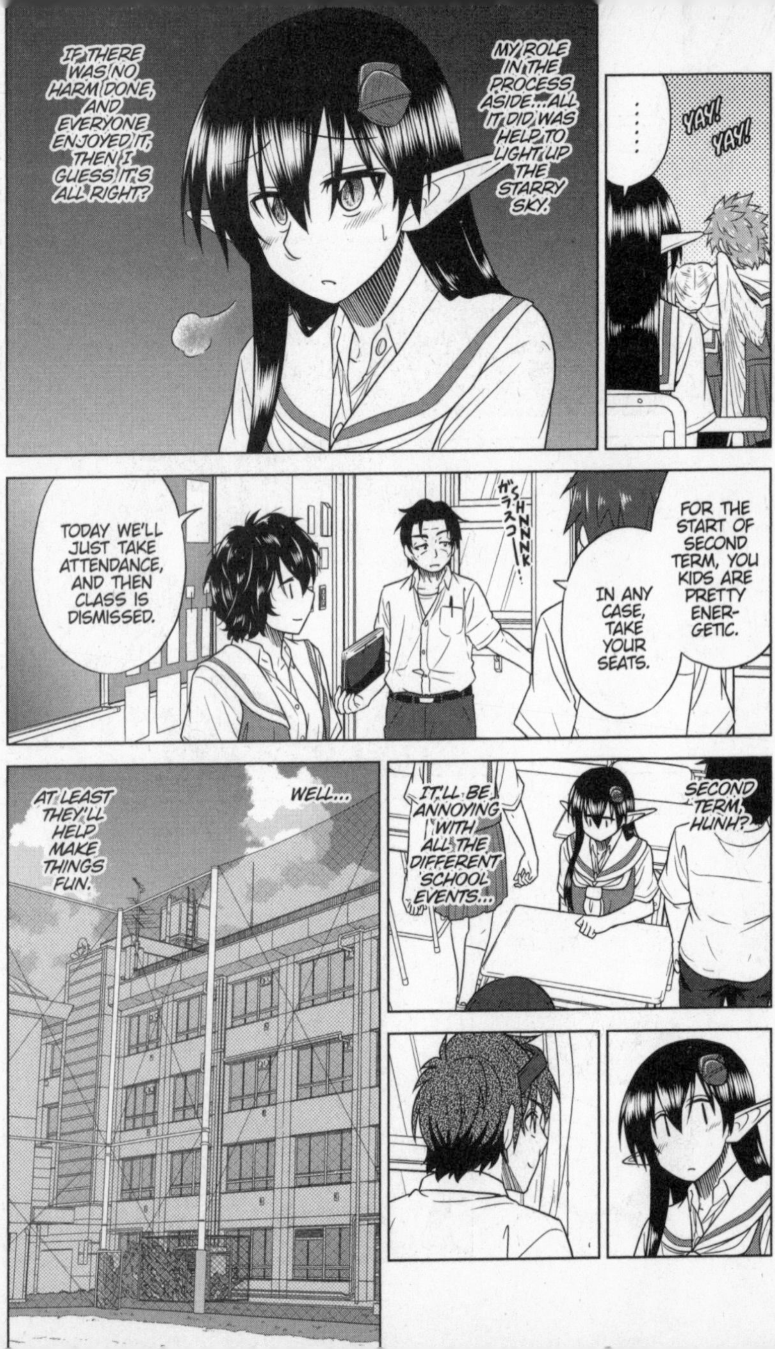

......
YAY! YAY!
MY ROLE IN THE PROCESS ASIDE... ALL IT DID WAS HELP TO LIGHT UP THE STARRY SKY.
IF THERE WAS NO HARM DONE, AND EVERYONE ENJOYED IT, THEN I GUESS IT'S ALL RIGHT?
FOR THE START OF SECOND TERM, YOU KIDS ARE PRETTY ENER-GETIC.
IN ANY CASE, TAKE YOUR SEATS.
SHNNNK...
TODAY WE'LL JUST TAKE ATTENDANCE, AND THEN CLASS IS DISMISSED.
SECOND TERM, HUNH?
IT'LL BE ANNOYING WITH ALL THE DIFFERENT SCHOOL EVENTS...
WELL...
AT LEAST THEY'LL HELP MAKE THINGS FUN.

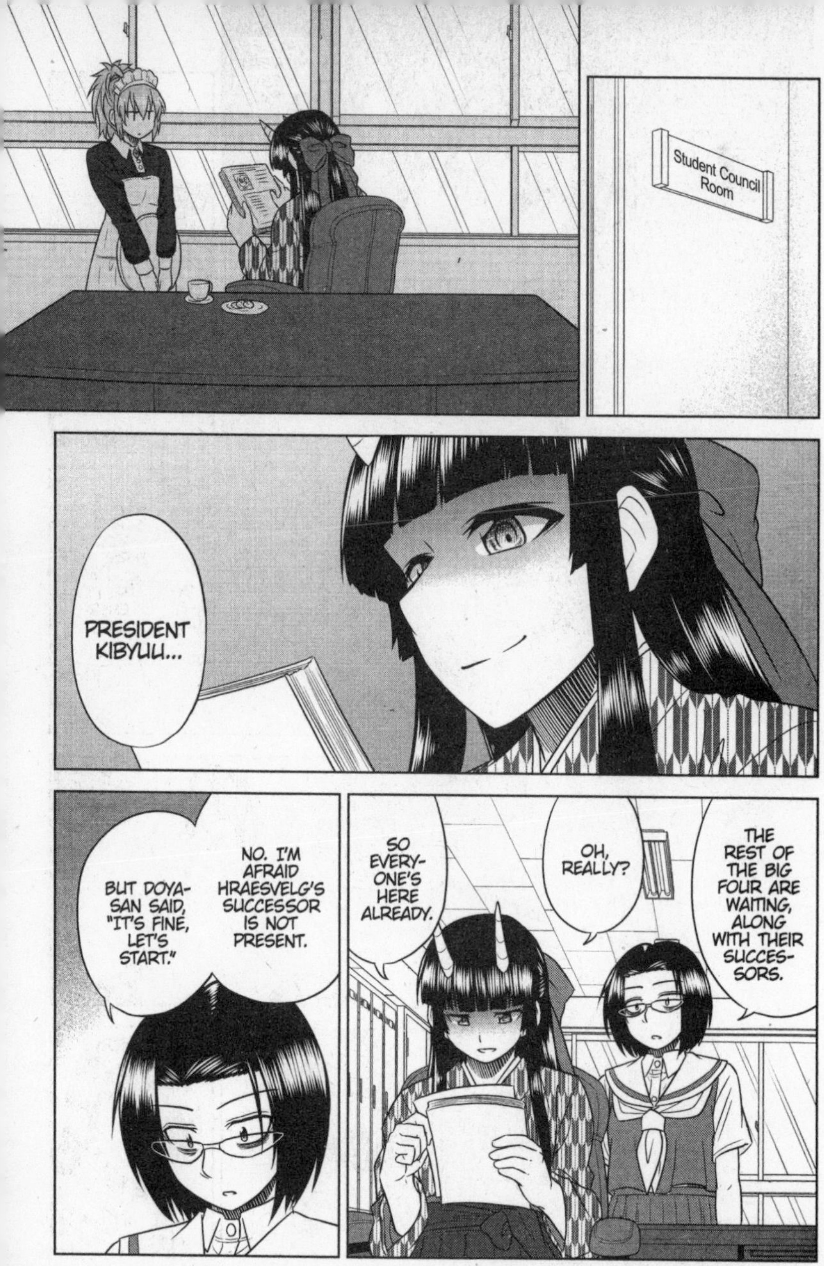
Student Council Room
PRESIDENT KIBYUU...
THE REST OF THE BIG FOUR ARE WAITING, ALONG WITH THEIR SUCCES-SORS.
OH, REALLY?
SO EVERY-ONE'S HERE ALREADY.
NO. I'M AFRAID HRAESVELG'S SUCCESSOR IS NOT PRESENT.
BUT DOYA-SAN SAID, "IT'S FINE, LET'S START."

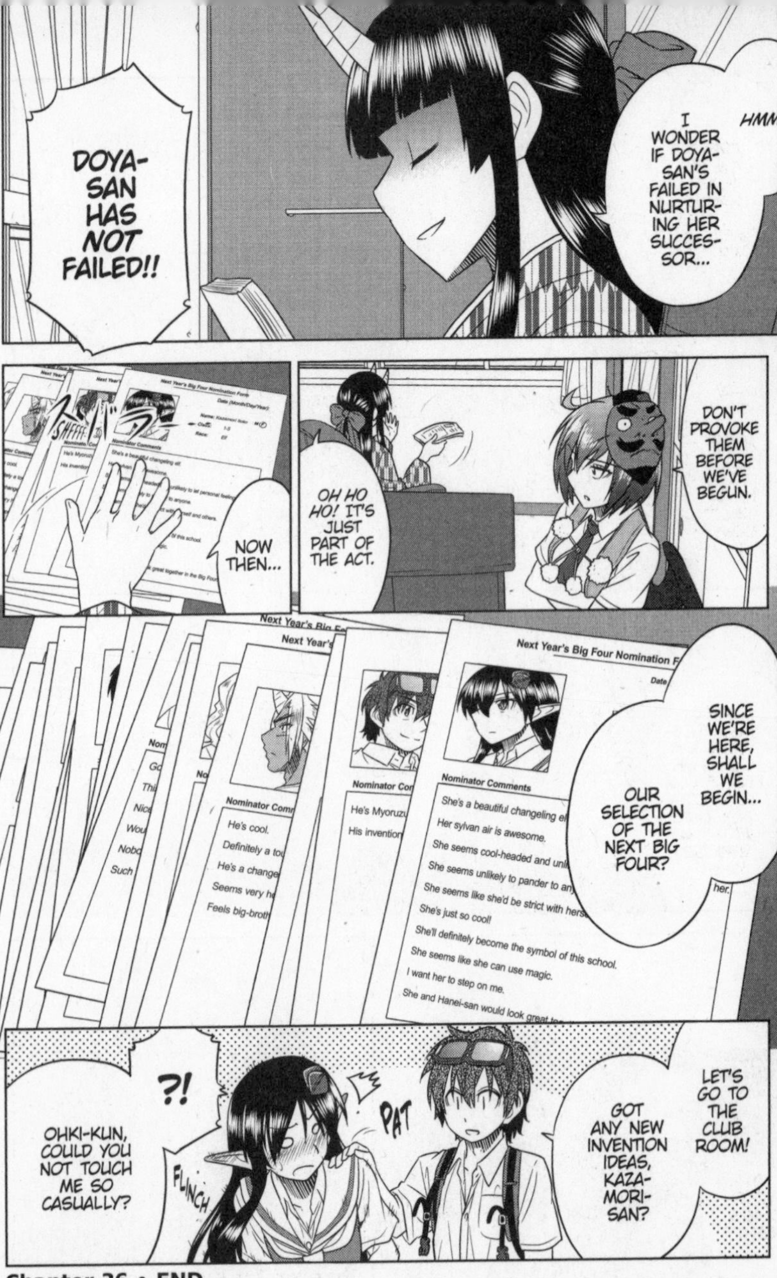
HMM...
I WONDER IF DOYA-SAN'S FAILED IN NURTURING HER SUCCESSOR...
DOYA-SAN HAS *NOT* FAILED!!
DON'T PROVOKE THEM BEFORE WE'VE BEGUN.
OH HO HO! IT'S JUST PART OF THE ACT.
NOW THEN...
SHFFF
SINCE WE'RE HERE, SHALL WE BEGIN...
OUR SELECTION OF THE NEXT BIG FOUR?
Nominator Comments
Her sylvan air is awesome.
She's just so cool!
She'll definitely become the symbol of this school.
She seems like she can use magic.
I want her to step on me.
He's cool.
LET'S GO TO THE CLUB ROOM!
GOT ANY NEW INVENTION IDEAS, KAZAMORI-SAN?
PAT
?!
OHKI-KUN, COULD YOU NOT TOUCH ME SO CASUALLY?
FLINCH

Chapter 36 • END

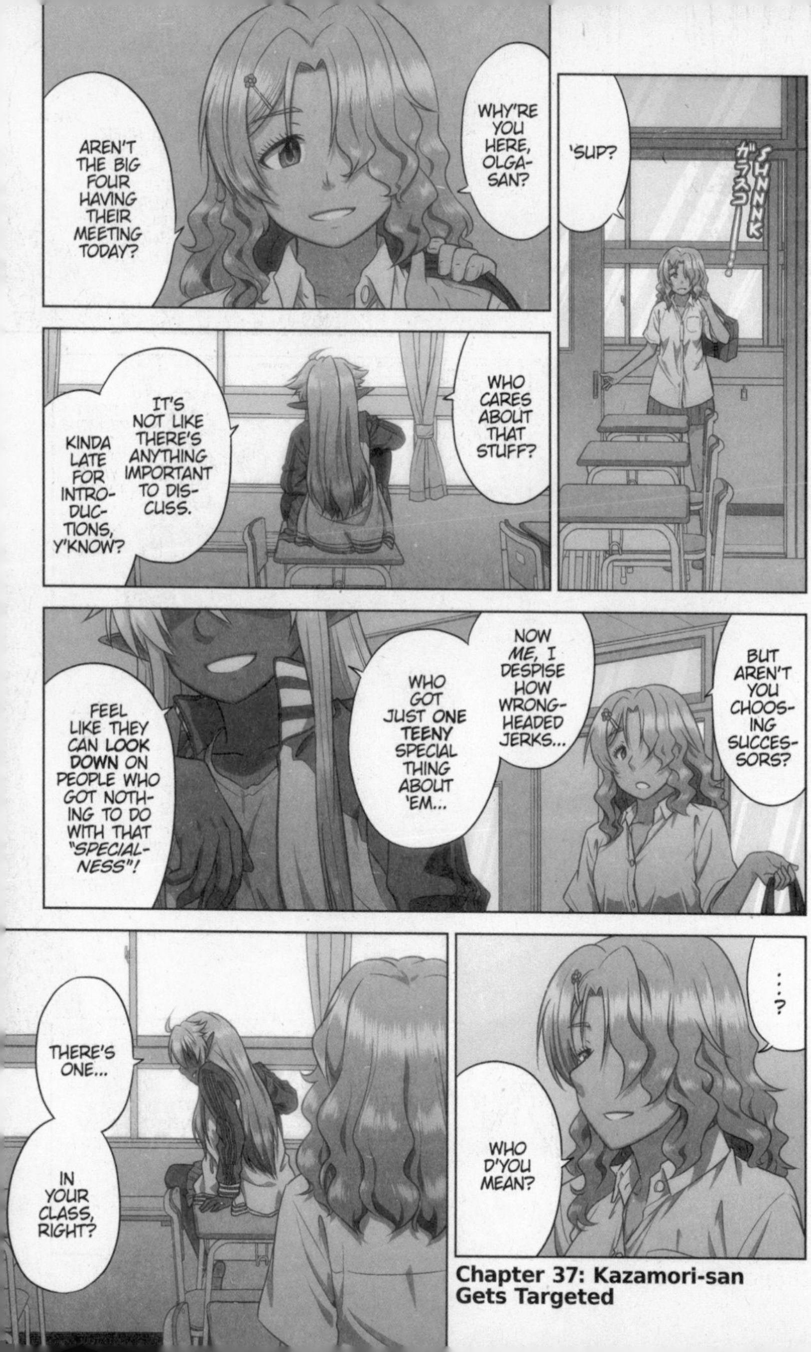
SHNNNK ガラスー
'SUP?
WHY'RE YOU HERE, OLGA-SAN?
AREN'T THE BIG FOUR HAVING THEIR MEETING TODAY?
WHO CARES ABOUT THAT STUFF?
IT'S NOT LIKE THERE'S ANYTHING IMPORTANT TO DISCUSS.
KINDA LATE FOR INTRODUCTIONS, Y'KNOW?
BUT AREN'T YOU CHOOSING SUCCESSORS?
NOW *ME*, I DESPISE HOW WRONG-HEADED JERKS...
WHO GOT JUST ONE TEENY SPECIAL THING ABOUT 'EM...
FEEL LIKE THEY CAN LOOK DOWN ON PEOPLE WHO GOT NOTHING TO DO WITH THAT "SPECIALNESS"!
...?
WHO D'YOU MEAN?
THERE'S ONE...
IN YOUR CLASS, RIGHT?

Chapter 37: Kazamori-san Gets Targeted

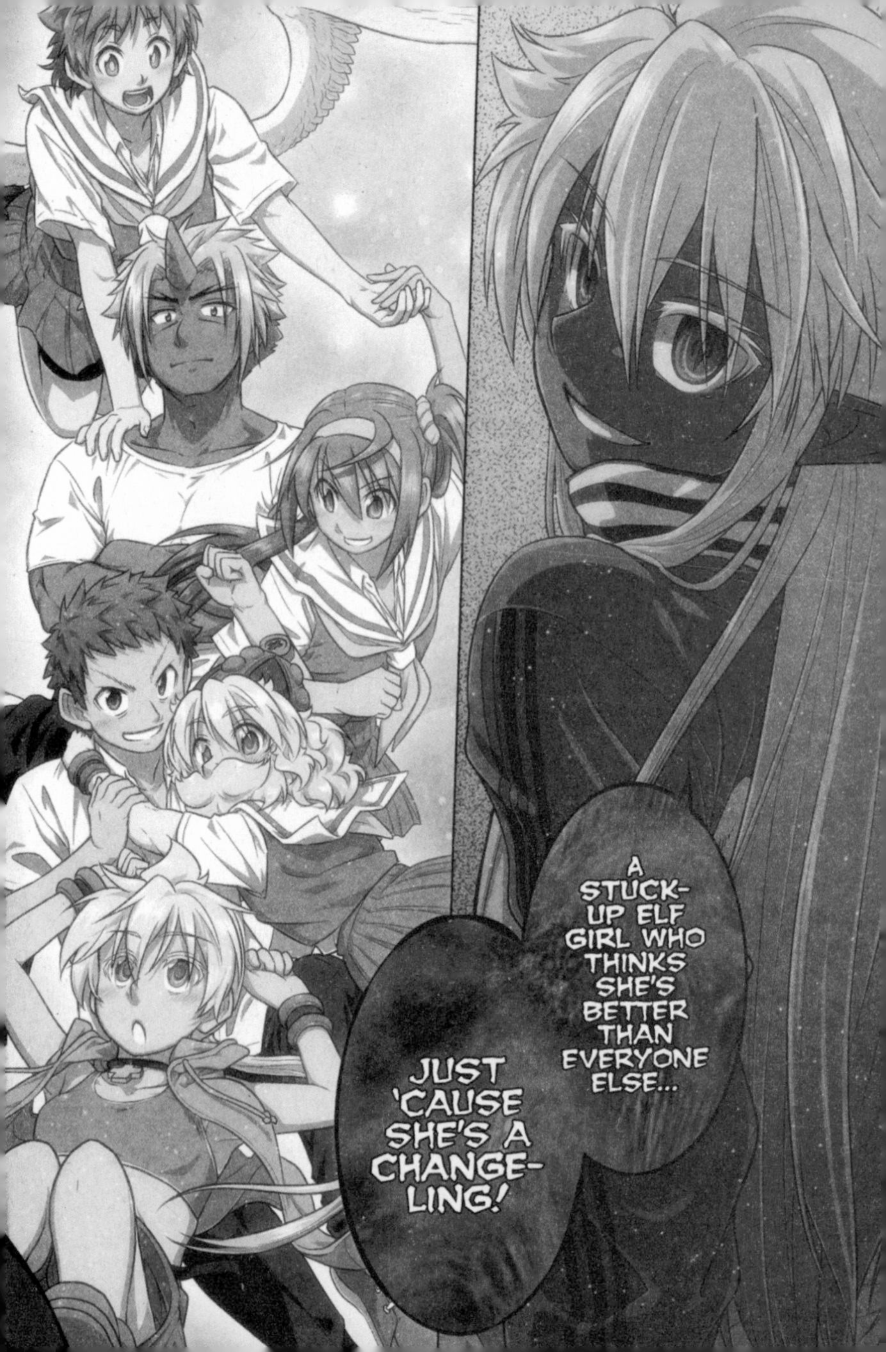
A STUCK-UP ELF GIRL WHO THINKS SHE'S BETTER THAN EVERYONE ELSE...
JUST 'CAUSE SHE'S A CHANGE-LING!

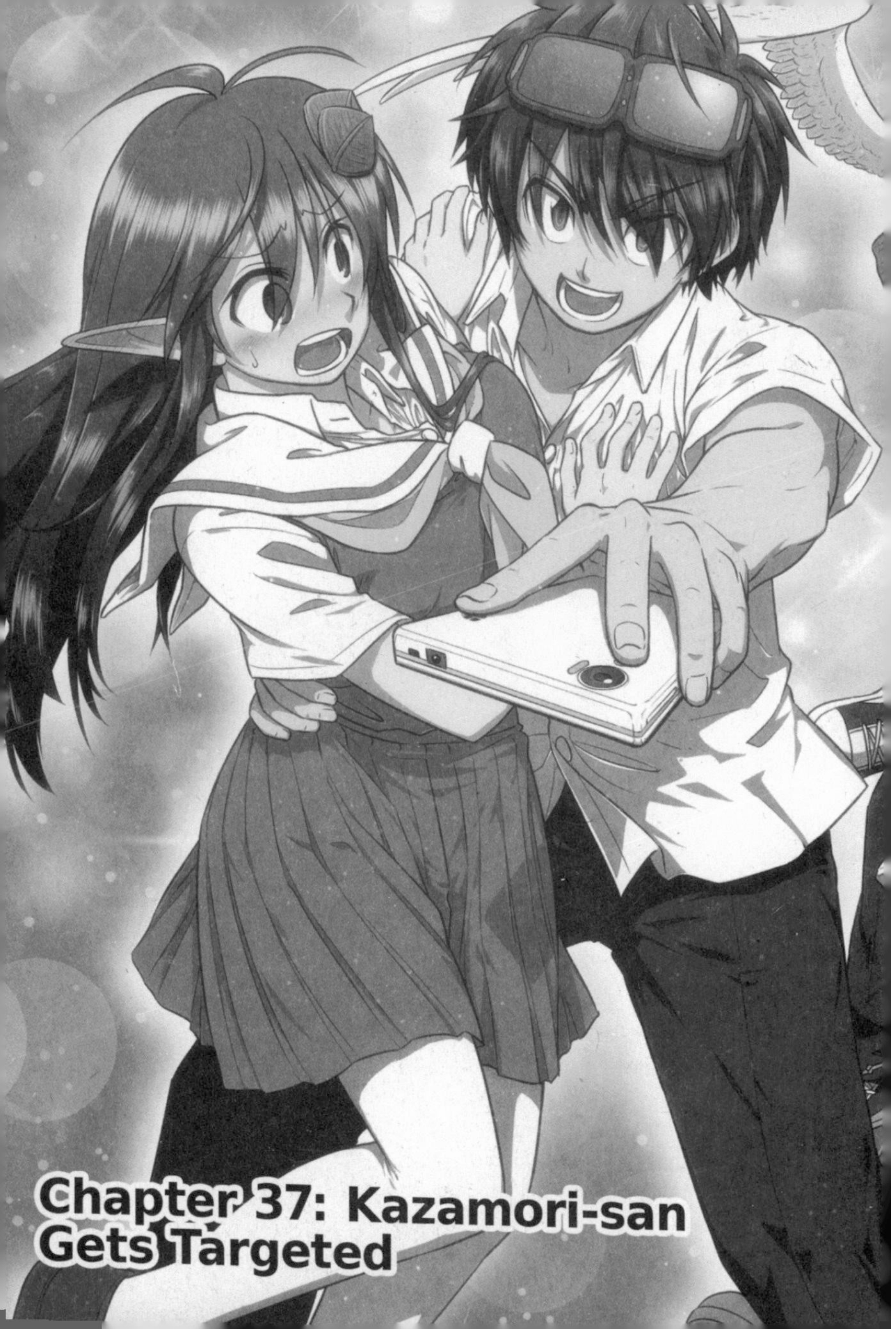

Chapter 37: Kazamori-san Gets Targeted

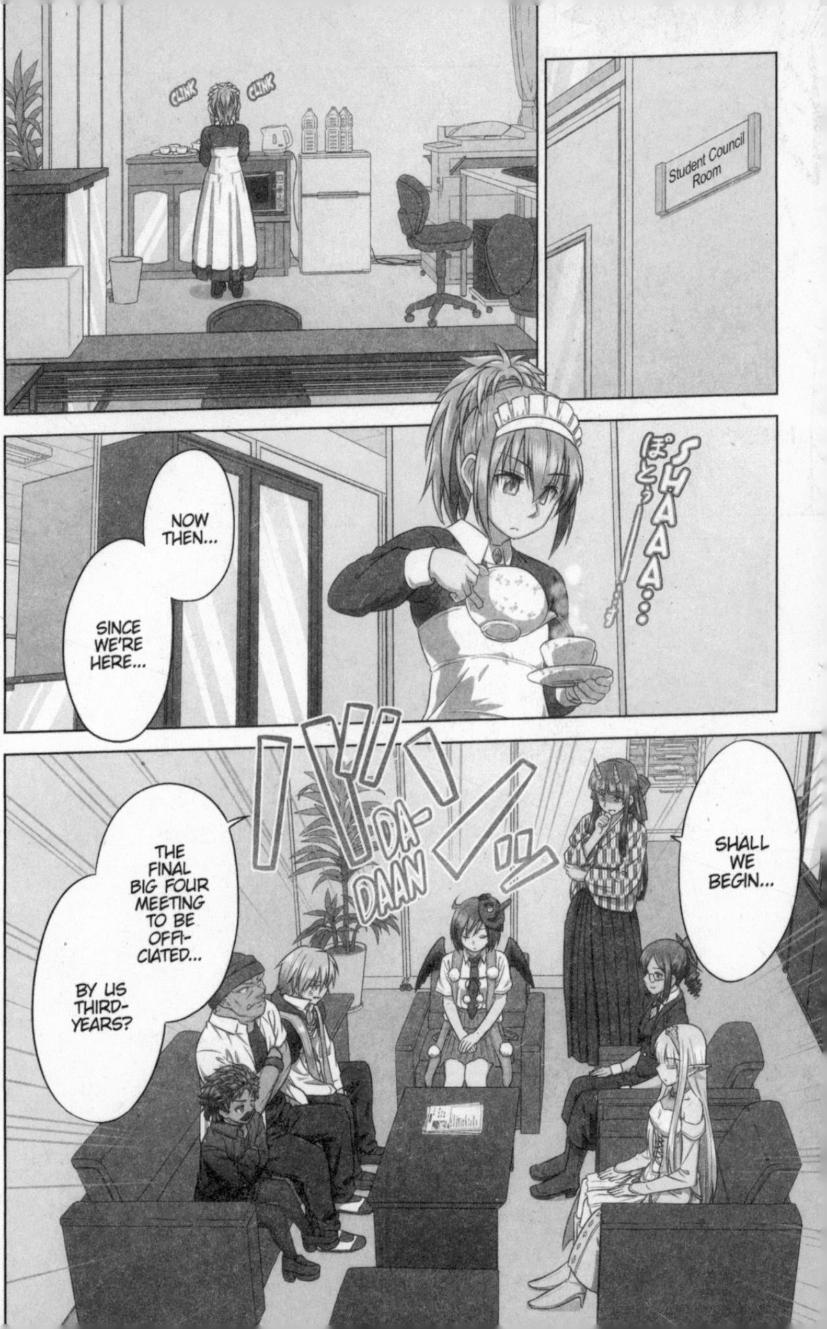
Student Council Room
CLINK
CLINK
HAAAA...
NOW THEN...
SINCE WE'RE HERE...
SHALL WE BEGIN...
DA-DAAN
THE FINAL BIG FOUR MEETING TO BE OFFI-CIATED...
BY US THIRD-YEARS?

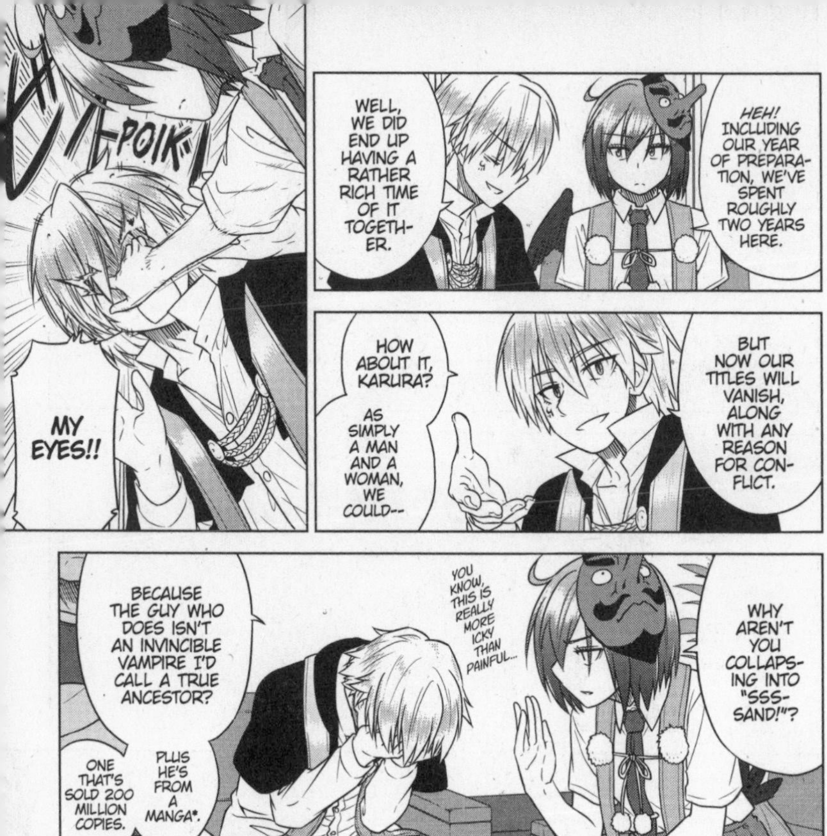
HEH! INCLUDING OUR YEAR OF PREPARATION, WE'VE SPENT ROUGHLY TWO YEARS HERE.
WELL, WE DID END UP HAVING A RATHER RICH TIME OF IT TOGETHER.
BUT NOW OUR TITLES WILL VANISH, ALONG WITH ANY REASON FOR CONFLICT.
HOW ABOUT IT, KARURA?
AS SIMPLY A MAN AND A WOMAN, WE COULD--
POIK
MY EYES!!
WHY AREN'T YOU COLLAPSING INTO "SSS-SAND!"?
YOU KNOW, THIS IS REALLY MORE ICKY THAN PAINFUL...
BECAUSE THE GUY WHO DOES ISN'T AN INVINCIBLE VAMPIRE I'D CALL A TRUE ANCESTOR?
PLUS HE'S FROM A MANGA*.
ONE THAT'S SOLD 200 MILLION COPIES.

This is a reference to Kyuuketsuki Sugu Shinu (The Vampire Dies in No Time).

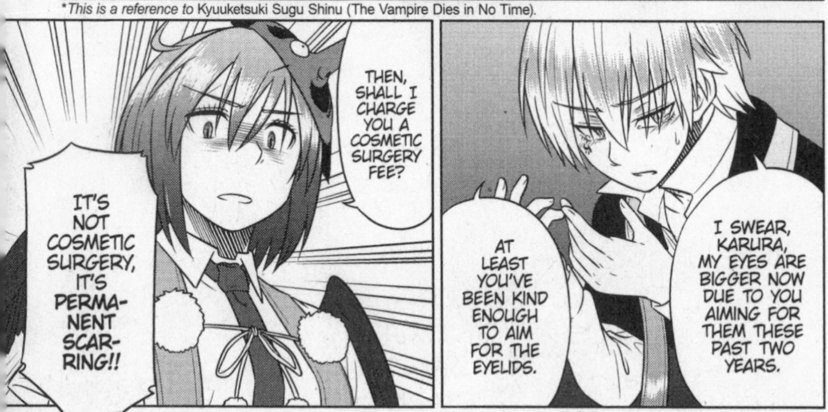
I SWEAR, KARURA, MY EYES ARE BIGGER NOW DUE TO YOU AIMING FOR THEM THESE PAST TWO YEARS.
AT LEAST YOU'VE BEEN KIND ENOUGH TO AIM FOR THE EYELIDS.
THEN, SHALL I CHARGE YOU A COSMETIC SURGERY FEE?
IT'S NOT COSMETIC SURGERY, IT'S PERMANENT SCARRING!!

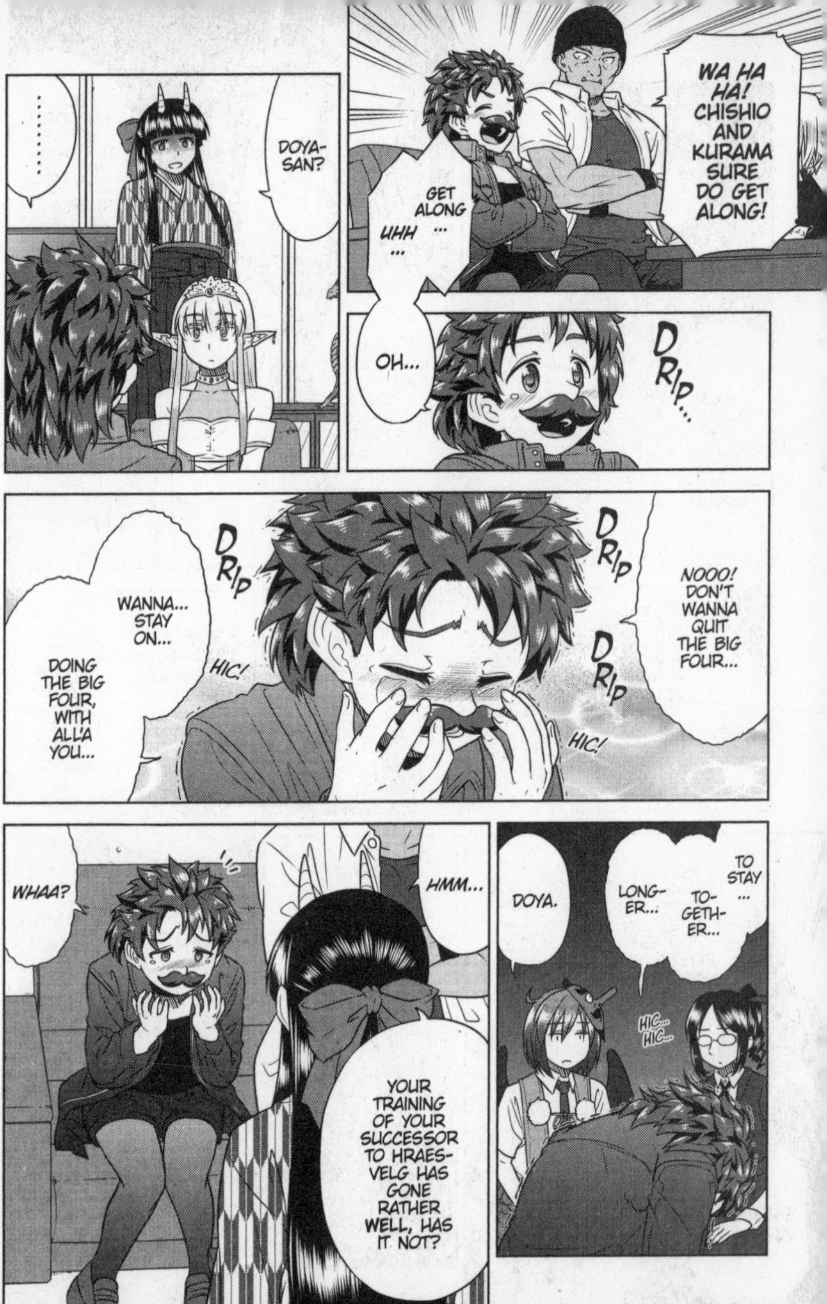

WA HA HA! CHISHIO AND KURAMA SURE DO GET ALONG!
GET ALONG...
UHH...
OH...
DRIP...
DOYA-SAN?
......
NOOO! DON'T WANNA QUIT THE BIG FOUR...
DRIP
DRIP
HIC!
WANNA... STAY ON...
DOING THE BIG FOUR, WITH ALL'A YOU...
DRIP
HIC!
TO STAY...
TO-GETH-ER...
LONG-ER...
DOYA.
HIC... HIC...
HMM...
YOUR TRAINING OF YOUR SUCCESSOR TO HRAES-VELG HAS GONE RATHER WELL, HAS IT NOT?
WHAA?

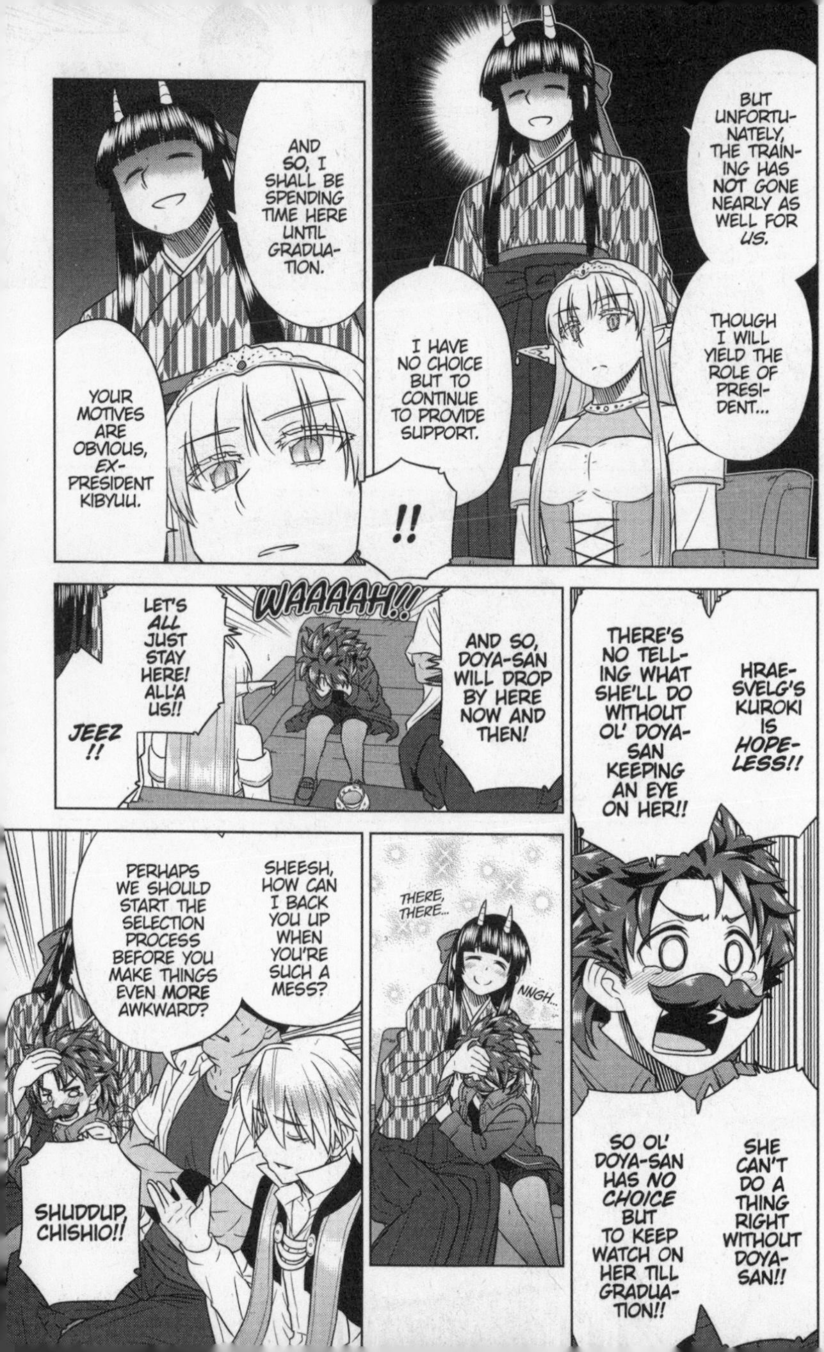

BUT UNFORTUNATELY, THE TRAINING HAS NOT GONE NEARLY AS WELL FOR *US.*
THOUGH I WILL YIELD THE ROLE OF PRESIDENT...
I HAVE NO CHOICE BUT TO CONTINUE TO PROVIDE SUPPORT.
!!
AND SO, I SHALL BE SPENDING TIME HERE UNTIL GRADUATION.
YOUR MOTIVES ARE OBVIOUS, *EX*-PRESIDENT KIBYUU.
HRAESVELG'S KUROKI IS *HOPELESS!!*
THERE'S NO TELLING WHAT SHE'LL DO WITHOUT OL' DOYA-SAN KEEPING AN EYE ON HER!!
SHE CAN'T DO A THING RIGHT WITHOUT DOYA-SAN!!
SO OL' DOYA-SAN HAS *NO CHOICE* BUT TO KEEP WATCH ON HER TILL GRADUATION!!
AND SO, DOYA-SAN WILL DROP BY HERE NOW AND THEN!
WAAAAH!!
LET'S *ALL* JUST STAY HERE! ALL'A US!!
JEEZ!!
THERE, THERE...
NNGH...
SHEESH, HOW CAN I BACK YOU UP WHEN YOU'RE SUCH A MESS?
PERHAPS WE SHOULD START THE SELECTION PROCESS BEFORE YOU MAKE THINGS EVEN MORE AWKWARD?
SHUDDUP, CHISHIO!!

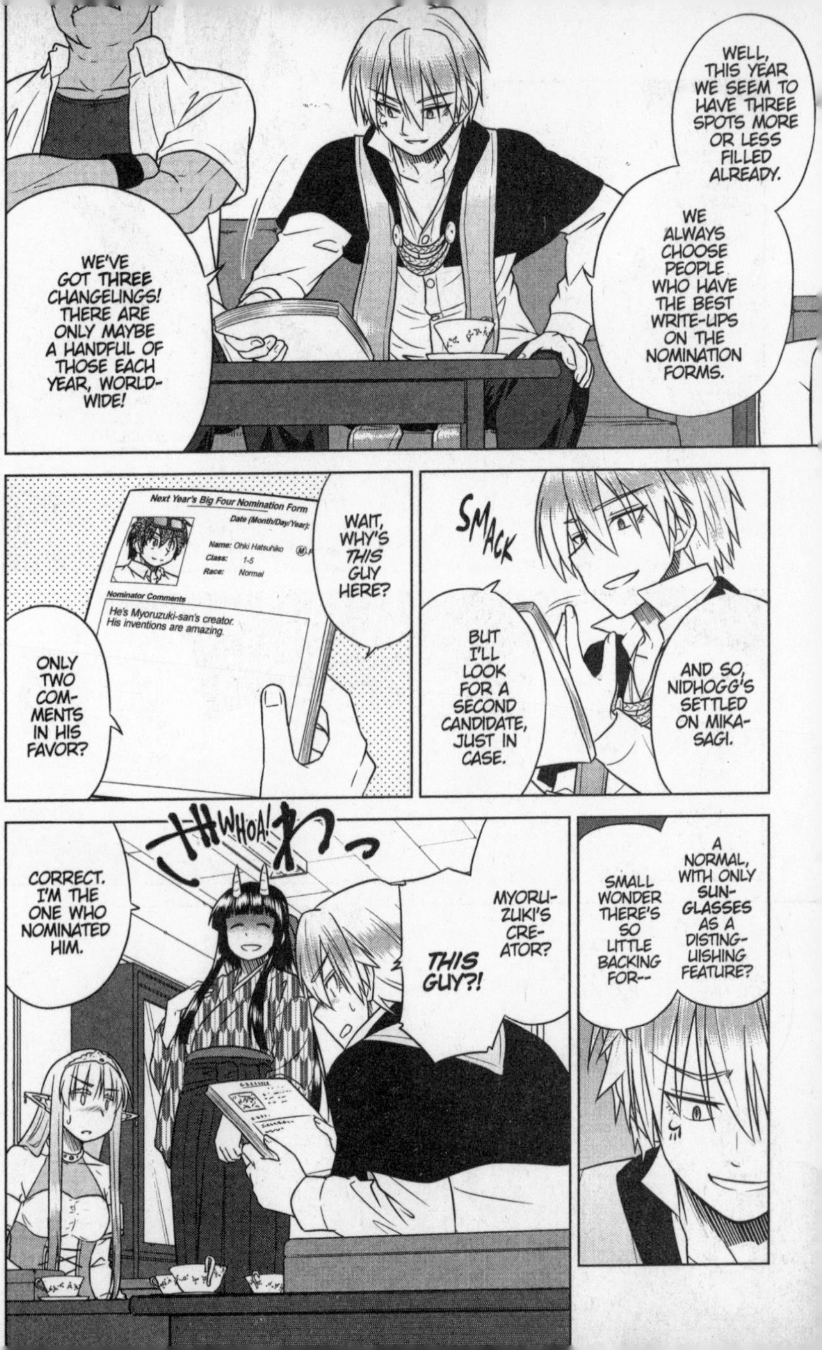
WELL, THIS YEAR WE SEEM TO HAVE THREE SPOTS MORE OR LESS FILLED ALREADY.
WE ALWAYS CHOOSE PEOPLE WHO HAVE THE BEST WRITE-UPS ON THE NOMINATION FORMS.
WE'VE GOT THREE CHANGELINGS! THERE ARE ONLY MAYBE A HANDFUL OF THOSE EACH YEAR, WORLD-WIDE!
SMACK
AND SO, NIDHOGG'S SETTLED ON MIKA-SAGI.
BUT I'LL LOOK FOR A SECOND CANDIDATE, JUST IN CASE.
Next Year's Big Four Nomination Form
Date (Month/Day/Year):
Name: Ohki Hatsuhiko
Class: 1-5
Race: Normal
Nominator Comments
He's Myoruzuki-san's creator. His inventions are amazing.
WAIT, WHY'S THIS GUY HERE?
ONLY TWO COM-MENTS IN HIS FAVOR?
A NORMAL, WITH ONLY SUN-GLASSES AS A DISTING-UISHING FEATURE?
SMALL WONDER THERE'S SO LITTLE BACKING FOR--
WHOA!
THIS GUY?!
MYORU-ZUKI'S CRE-ATOR?
CORRECT. I'M THE ONE WHO NOMINATED HIM.

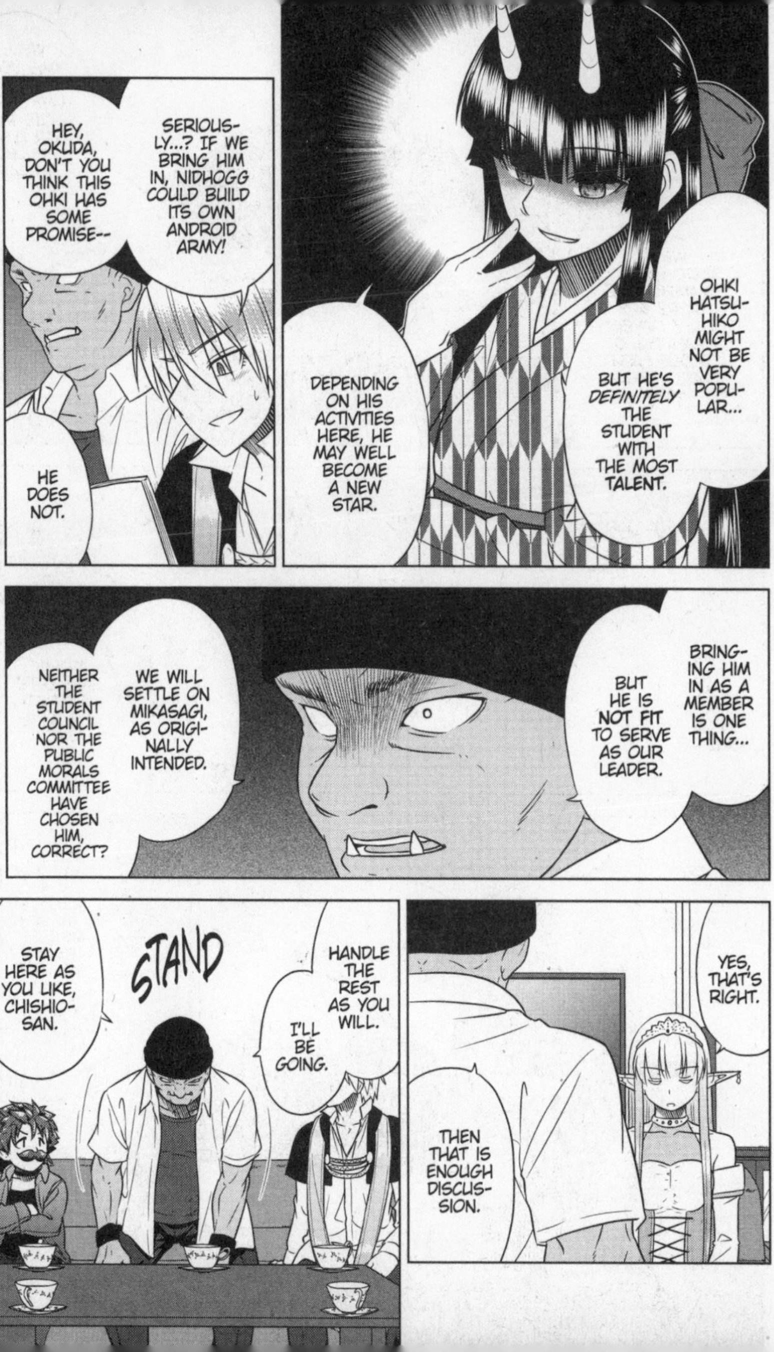
OHKI HATSUHIKO MIGHT NOT BE VERY POPULAR...
BUT HE'S *DEFINITELY* THE STUDENT WITH THE MOST TALENT.
DEPENDING ON HIS ACTIVITIES HERE, HE MAY WELL BECOME A NEW STAR.
SERIOUSLY...? IF WE BRING HIM IN, NIDHOGG COULD BUILD ITS OWN ANDROID ARMY!
HEY, OKUDA, DON'T YOU THINK THIS OHKI HAS SOME PROMISE--
HE DOES NOT.
BRINGING HIM IN AS A MEMBER IS ONE THING...
BUT HE IS NOT FIT TO SERVE AS OUR LEADER.
WE WILL SETTLE ON MIKASAGI, AS ORIGINALLY INTENDED.
NEITHER THE STUDENT COUNCIL NOR THE PUBLIC MORALS COMMITTEE HAVE CHOSEN HIM, CORRECT?
YES, THAT'S RIGHT.
THEN THAT IS ENOUGH DISCUSSION.
HANDLE THE REST AS YOU WILL.
I'LL BE GOING.
STAND
STAY HERE AS YOU LIKE, CHISHIO-SAN.

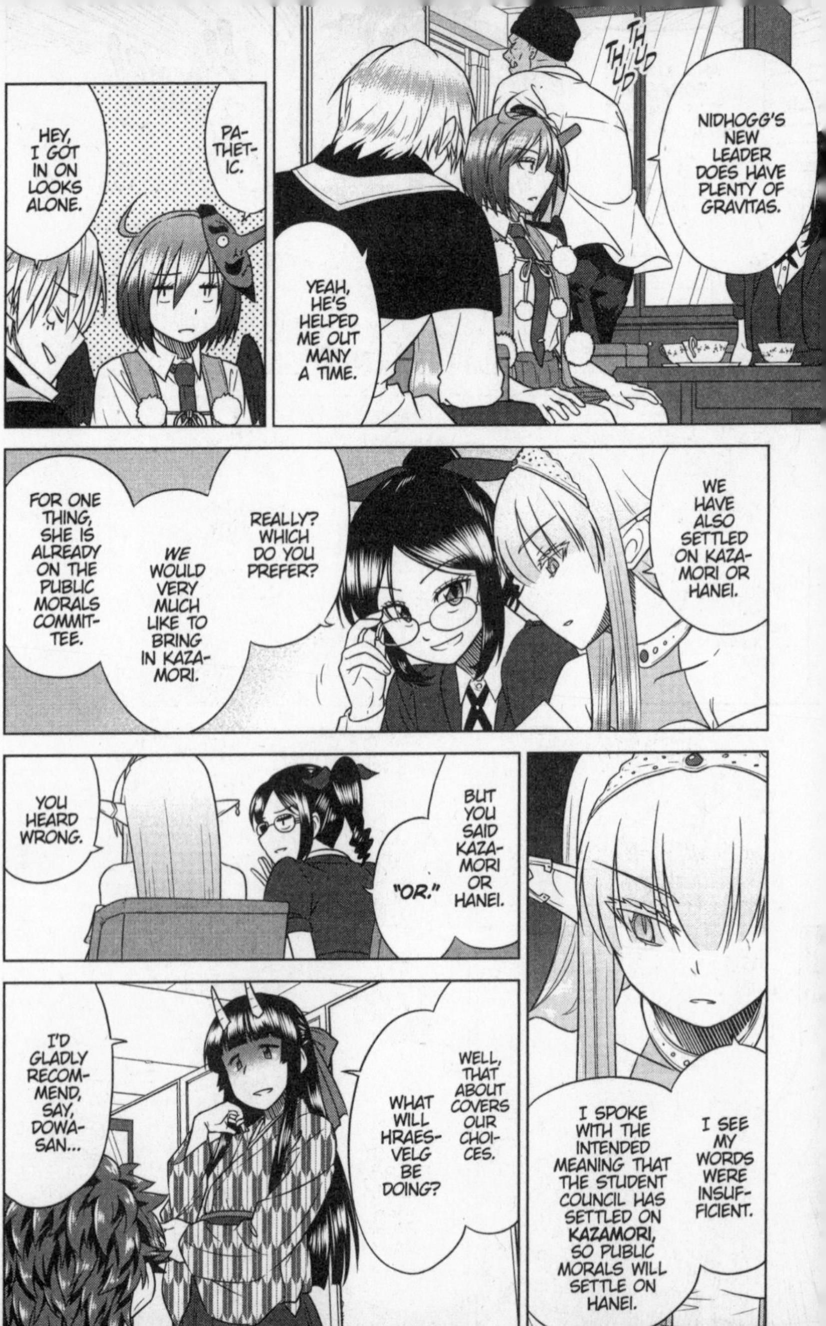
THUD THUD
NIDHOGG'S NEW LEADER DOES HAVE PLENTY OF GRAVITAS.
YEAH, HE'S HELPED ME OUT MANY A TIME.
PATHETIC.
HEY, I GOT IN ON LOOKS ALONE.
WE HAVE ALSO SETTLED ON KAZAMORI OR HANEI.
REALLY? WHICH DO YOU PREFER?
WE WOULD VERY MUCH LIKE TO BRING IN KAZAMORI.
FOR ONE THING, SHE IS ALREADY ON THE PUBLIC MORALS COMMITTEE.
I SEE MY WORDS WERE INSUFFICIENT.
I SPOKE WITH THE INTENDED MEANING THAT THE STUDENT COUNCIL HAS SETTLED ON KAZAMORI, SO PUBLIC MORALS WILL SETTLE ON HANEI.
BUT YOU SAID KAZAMORI OR HANEI.
"OR."
YOU HEARD WRONG.
WELL, THAT ABOUT COVERS OUR CHOICES.
WHAT WILL HRAESVELG BE DOING?
I'D GLADLY RECOMMEND, SAY, DOWA-SAN...

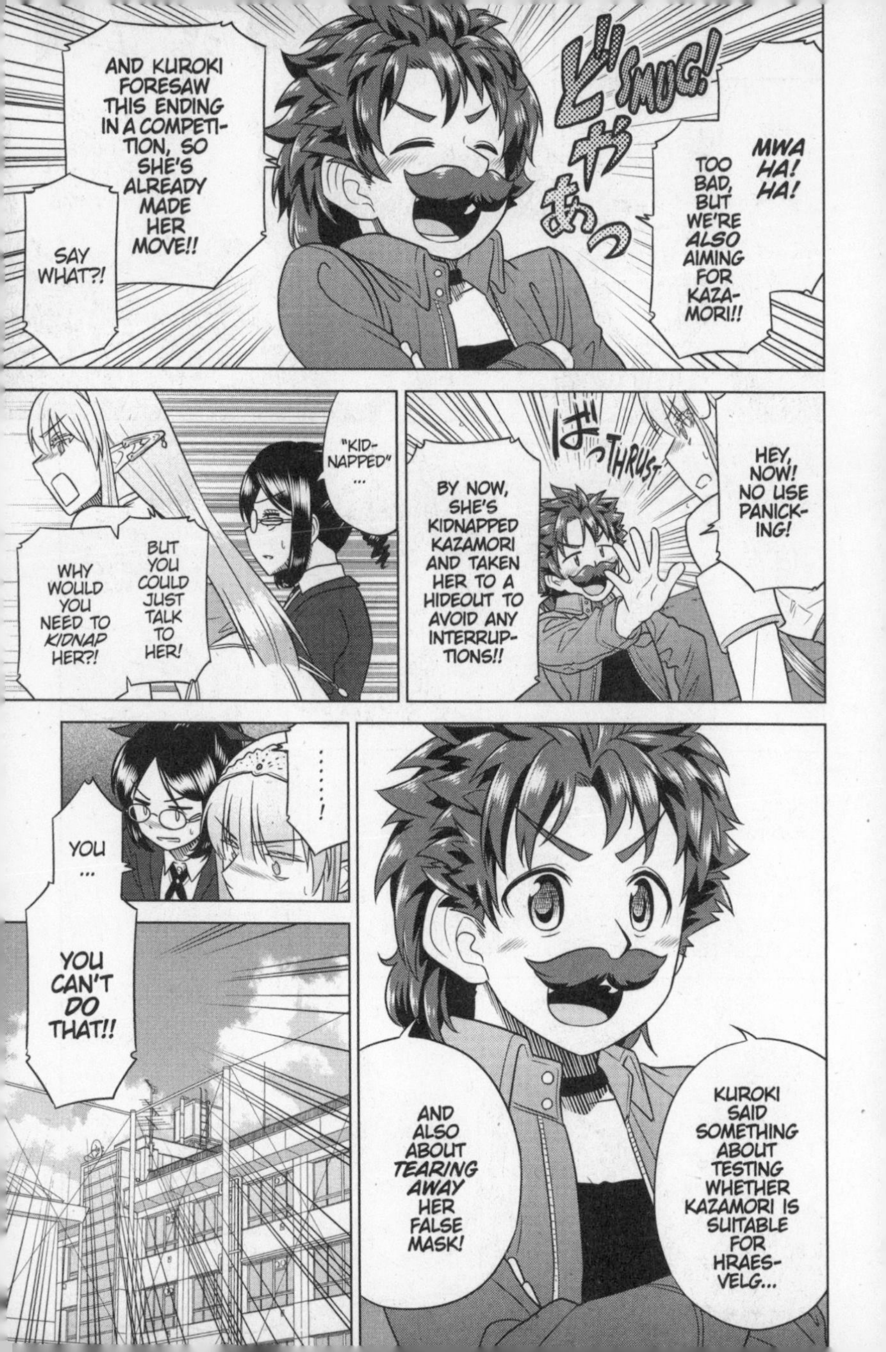
MWA HA! HA!
TOO BAD, BUT WE'RE *ALSO* AIMING FOR KAZAMORI!!
SMUG!
AND KUROKI FORESAW THIS ENDING IN A COMPETITION, SO SHE'S ALREADY MADE HER MOVE!!
SAY WHAT?!
HEY, NOW! NO USE PANICKING!
THRUST
BY NOW, SHE'S KIDNAPPED KAZAMORI AND TAKEN HER TO A HIDEOUT TO AVOID ANY INTERRUPTIONS!!
"KIDNAPPED" ...
BUT YOU COULD JUST TALK TO HER!
WHY WOULD YOU NEED TO *KIDNAP* HER?!
KUROKI SAID SOMETHING ABOUT TESTING WHETHER KAZAMORI IS SUITABLE FOR HRAESVELG...
AND ALSO ABOUT *TEARING AWAY* HER FALSE MASK!
......!
YOU ...
YOU CAN'T *DO* THAT!!

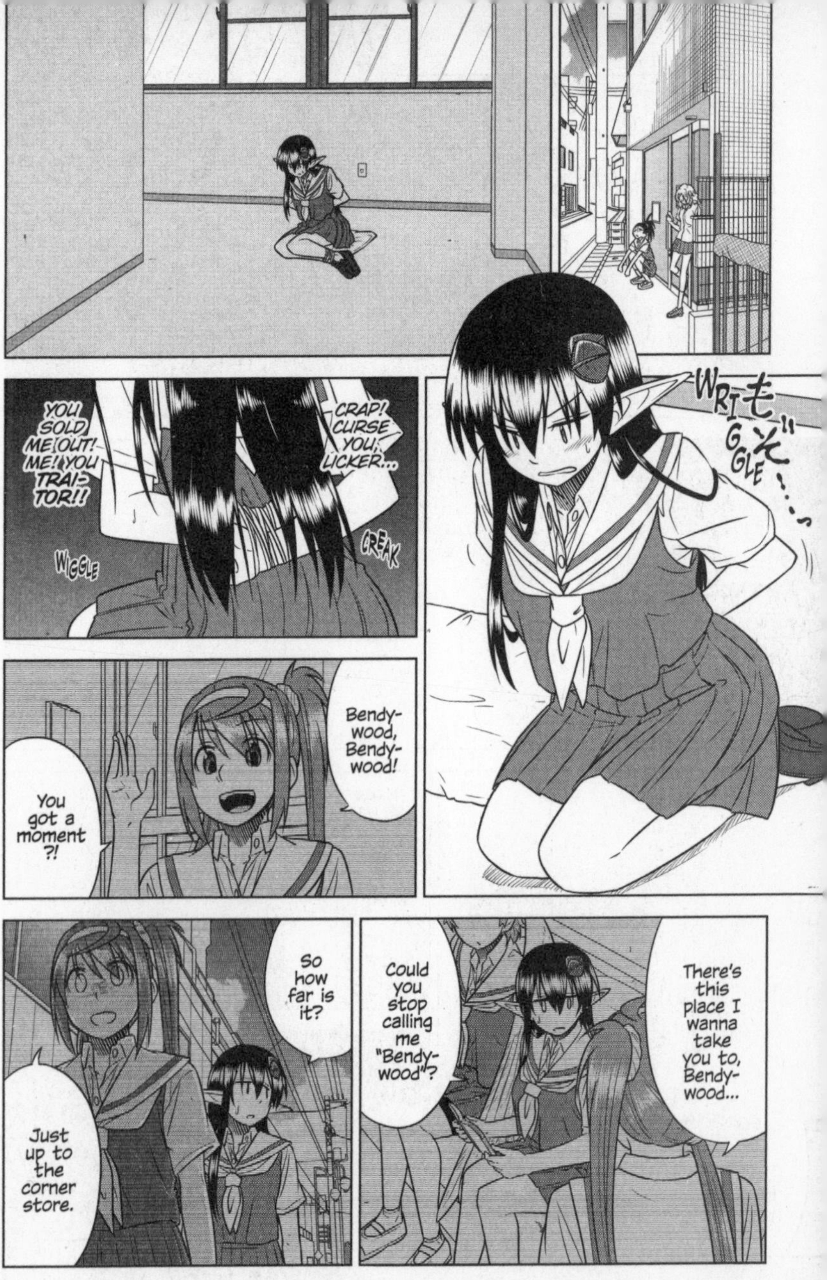
WRIGGLE
CRAP! CURSE YOU, LICKER...
YOU SOLD ME OUT! ME! YOU TRAITOR!!
CREAK
WIGGLE
Bendywood, Bendywood!
You got a moment?!
There's this place I wanna take you to, Bendywood...
Could you stop calling me "Bendywood"?
So how far is it?
Just up to the corner store.

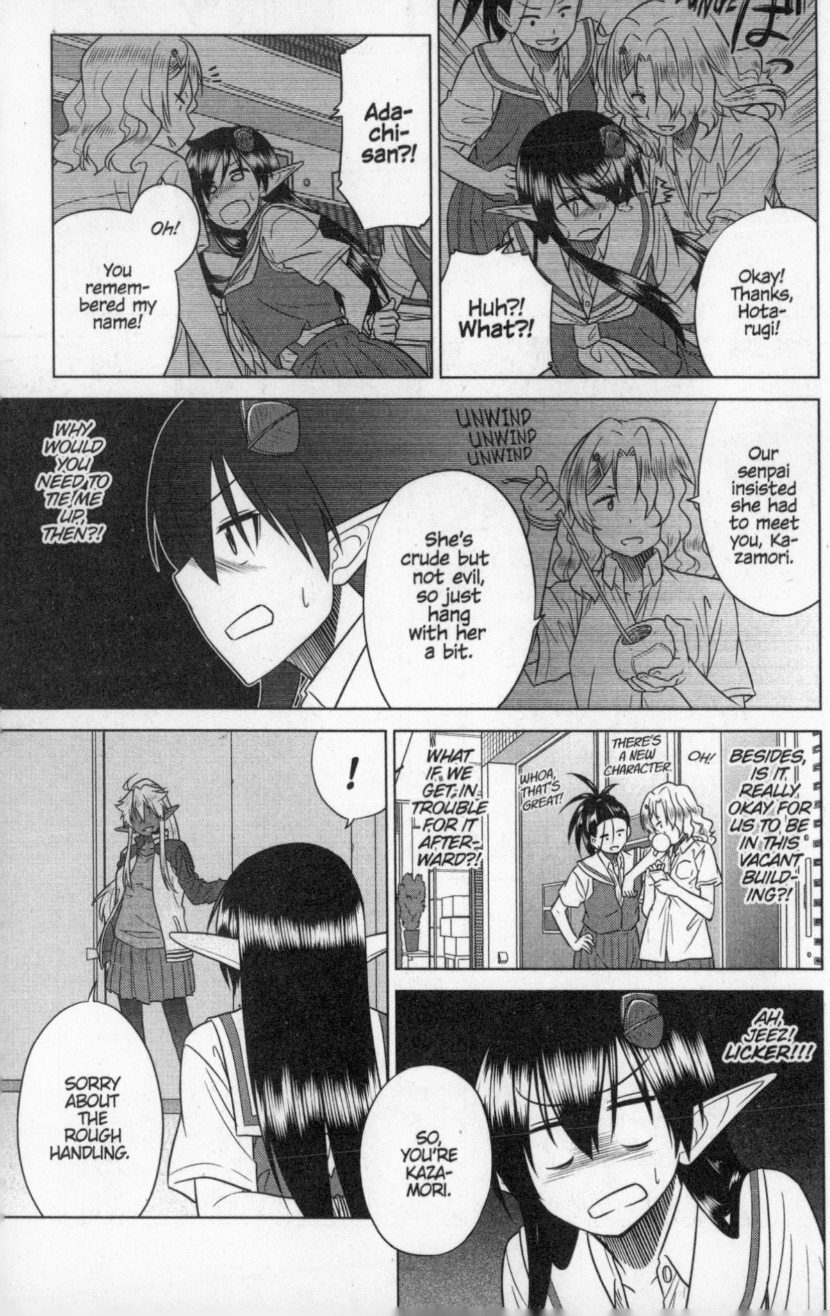
LUNGE
ばっ
Okay! Thanks, Hota-rugi!
Huh?! What?!
Ada-chi-san?!
Oh!
You remem-bered my name!
Our senpai insisted she had to meet you, Ka-zamori.
UNWIND UNWIND UNWIND
She's crude but not evil, so just hang with her a bit.
WHY WOULD YOU NEED TO TIE ME UP, THEN?!
BESIDES, IS IT REALLY OKAY FOR US TO BE IN THIS VACANT BUILD-ING?!
OH!
THERE'S A NEW CHARACTER.
WHOA, THAT'S GREAT!
WHAT IF WE GET IN TROUBLE FOR IT AFTER-WARD?!
AH, JEEZ! LICKER!!!
!
SO, YOU'RE KAZA-MORI.
SORRY ABOUT THE ROUGH HANDLING.

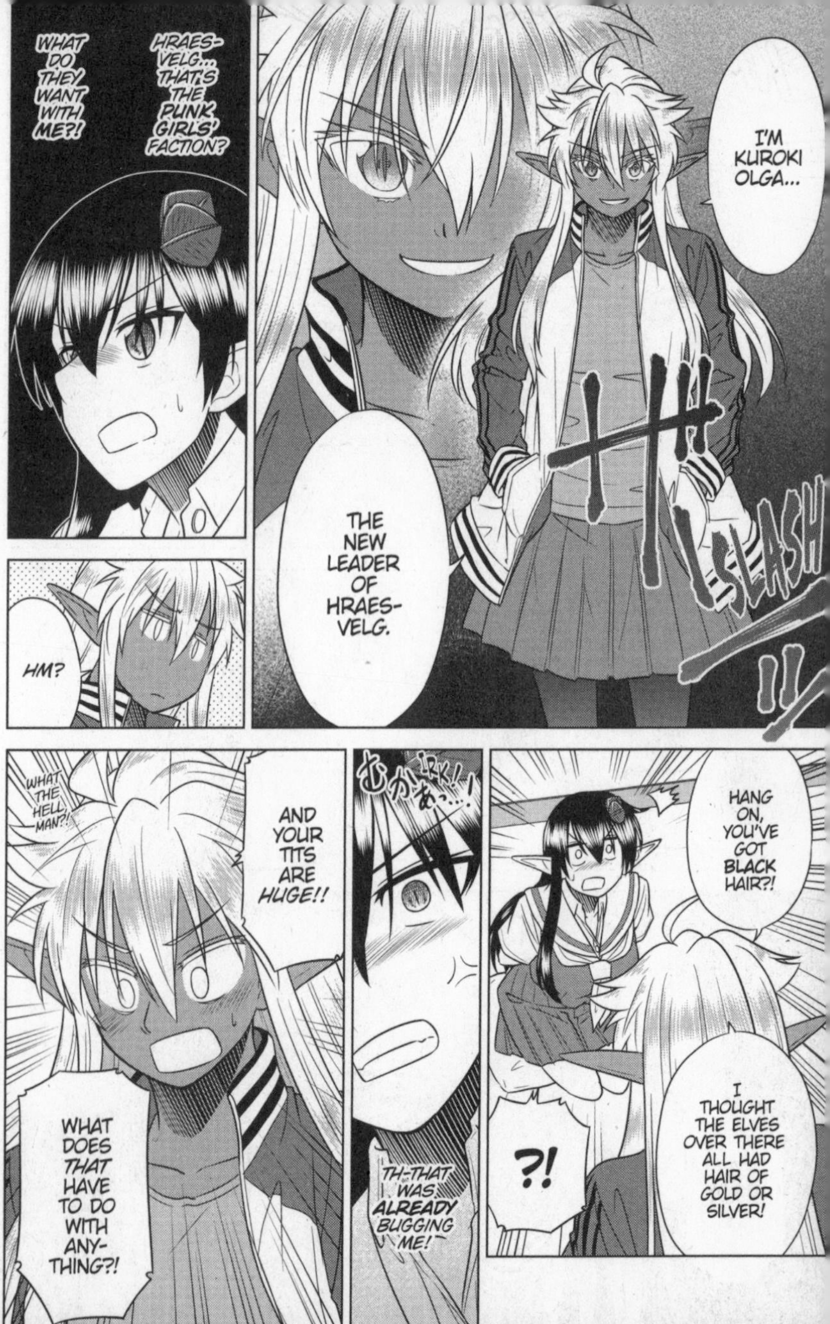
I'M KUROKI OLGA...
THE NEW LEADER OF HRAES-VELG.
SLASH
HRAES-VELG... THAT'S THE PUNK GIRLS' FACTION?
WHAT DO THEY WANT WITH ME?!
HM?
HANG ON, YOU'VE GOT BLACK HAIR?!
I THOUGHT THE ELVES OVER THERE ALL HAD HAIR OF GOLD OR SILVER!
?!
むかぁっ
IRK!
TH-THAT WAS ALREADY BUGGING ME!
AND YOUR TITS ARE HUGE!!
WHAT THE HELL, MAN?!
WHAT DOES THAT HAVE TO DO WITH ANY-THING?!

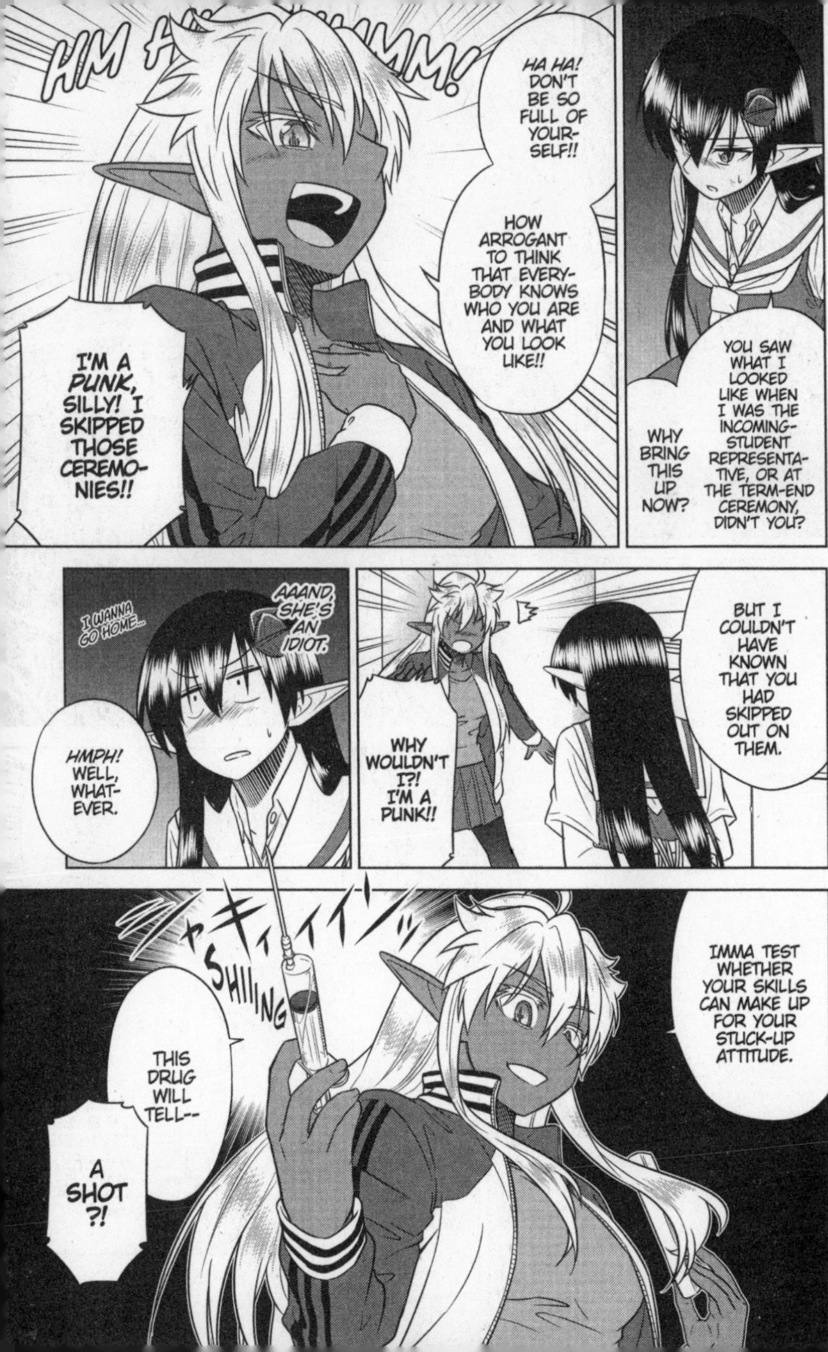
YOU SAW WHAT I LOOKED LIKE WHEN I WAS THE INCOMING-STUDENT REPRESENTATIVE, OR AT THE TERM-END CEREMONY, DIDN'T YOU?
WHY BRING THIS UP NOW?
HA HA! DON'T BE SO FULL OF YOURSELF!!
HOW ARROGANT TO THINK THAT EVERYBODY KNOWS WHO YOU ARE AND WHAT YOU LOOK LIKE!!
I'M A *PUNK*, SILLY! I SKIPPED THOSE CEREMONIES!!
BUT I COULDN'T HAVE KNOWN THAT YOU HAD SKIPPED OUT ON THEM.
WHY WOULDN'T I?! I'M A PUNK!!
AAAND, SHE'S AN IDIOT.
I WANNA GO HOME...
HMPH! WELL, WHATEVER.
IMMA TEST WHETHER YOUR SKILLS CAN MAKE UP FOR YOUR STUCK-UP ATTITUDE.
SHIIING
THIS DRUG WILL TELL--
A SHOT?!

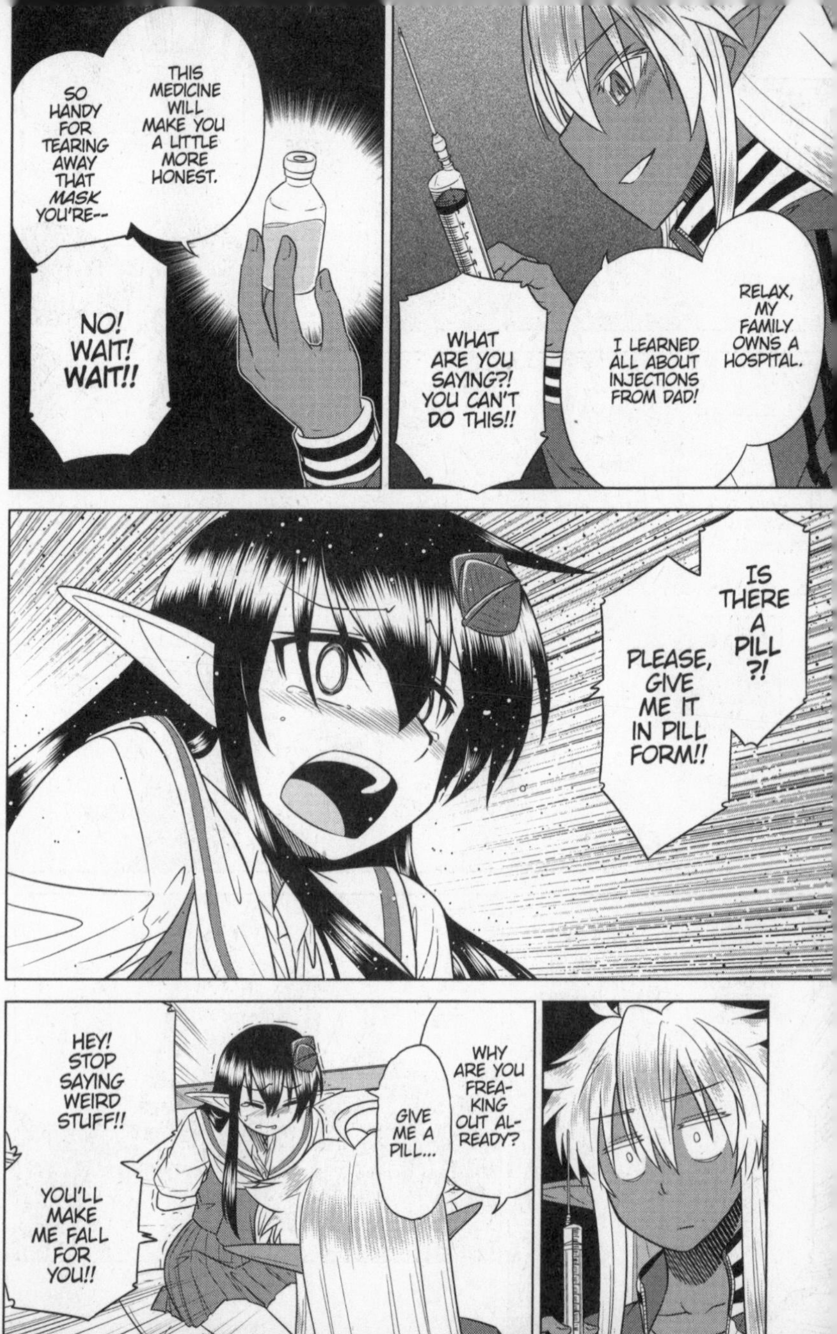
RELAX, MY FAMILY OWNS A HOSPITAL.
I LEARNED ALL ABOUT INJECTIONS FROM DAD!
WHAT ARE YOU SAYING?! YOU CAN'T DO THIS!!
THIS MEDICINE WILL MAKE YOU A LITTLE MORE HONEST.
SO HANDY FOR TEARING AWAY THAT *MASK* YOU'RE--
NO! WAIT! WAIT!!
IS THERE A PILL?!
PLEASE, GIVE ME IT IN PILL FORM!!
WHY ARE YOU FREA-KING OUT AL-READY?
GIVE ME A PILL...
HEY! STOP SAYING WEIRD STUFF!!
YOU'LL MAKE ME FALL FOR YOU!!

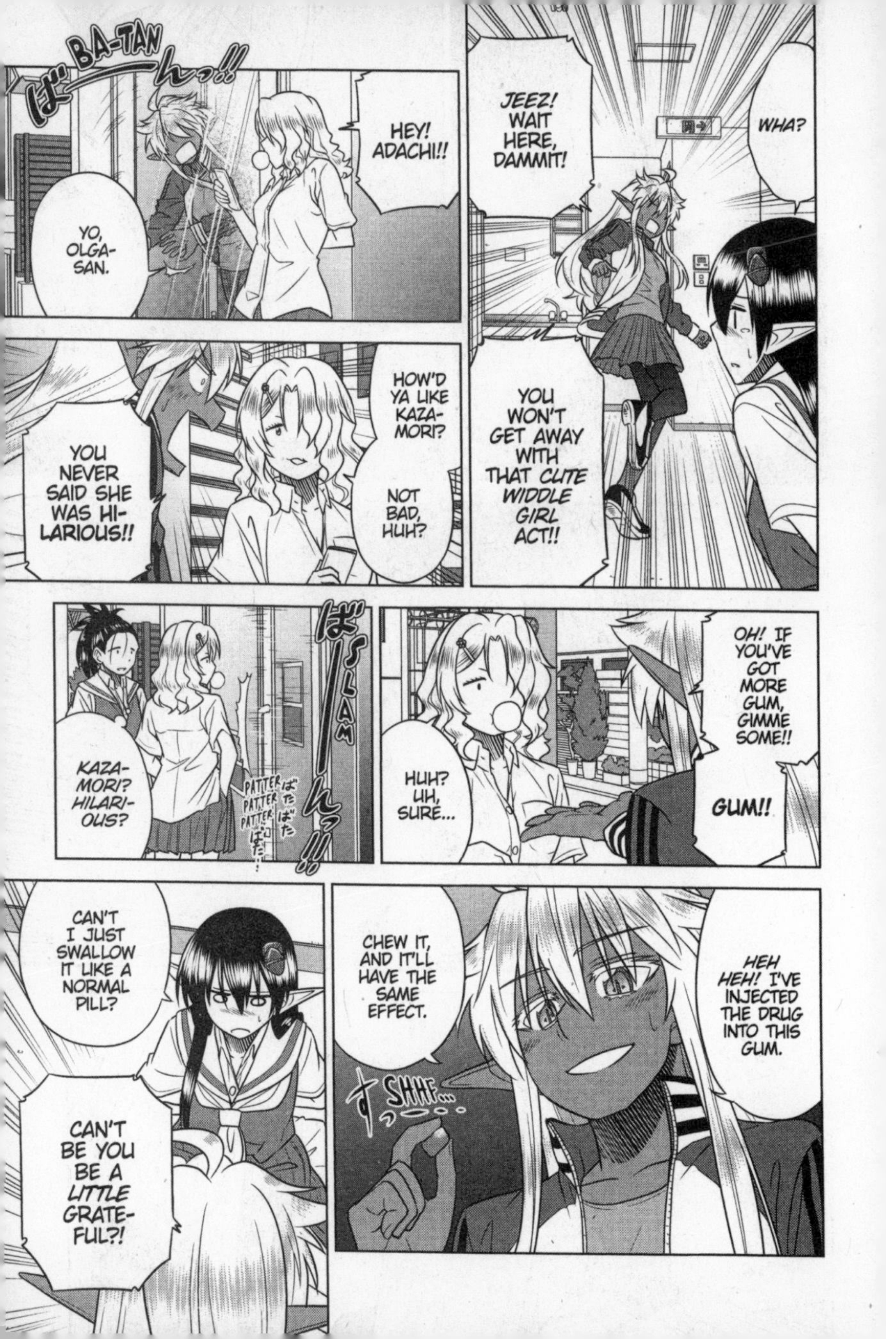
WHA?
JEEZ! WAIT HERE, DAMMIT!
YOU WON'T GET AWAY WITH THAT CUTE WIDDLE GIRL ACT!!
BA-TAN
HEY! ADACHI!!
YO, OLGA-SAN.
HOW'D YA LIKE KAZAMORI?
NOT BAD, HUH?
YOU NEVER SAID SHE WAS HILARIOUS!!
OH! IF YOU'VE GOT MORE GUM, GIMME SOME!!
GUM!!
HUH? UH, SURE...
SLAM
PATTER PATTER PATTER
KAZAMORI? HILARIOUS?
HEH HEH! I'VE INJECTED THE DRUG INTO THIS GUM.
CHEW IT, AND IT'LL HAVE THE SAME EFFECT.
SHHF...
CAN'T I JUST SWALLOW IT LIKE A NORMAL PILL?
CAN'T BE YOU BE A LITTLE GRATEFUL?!

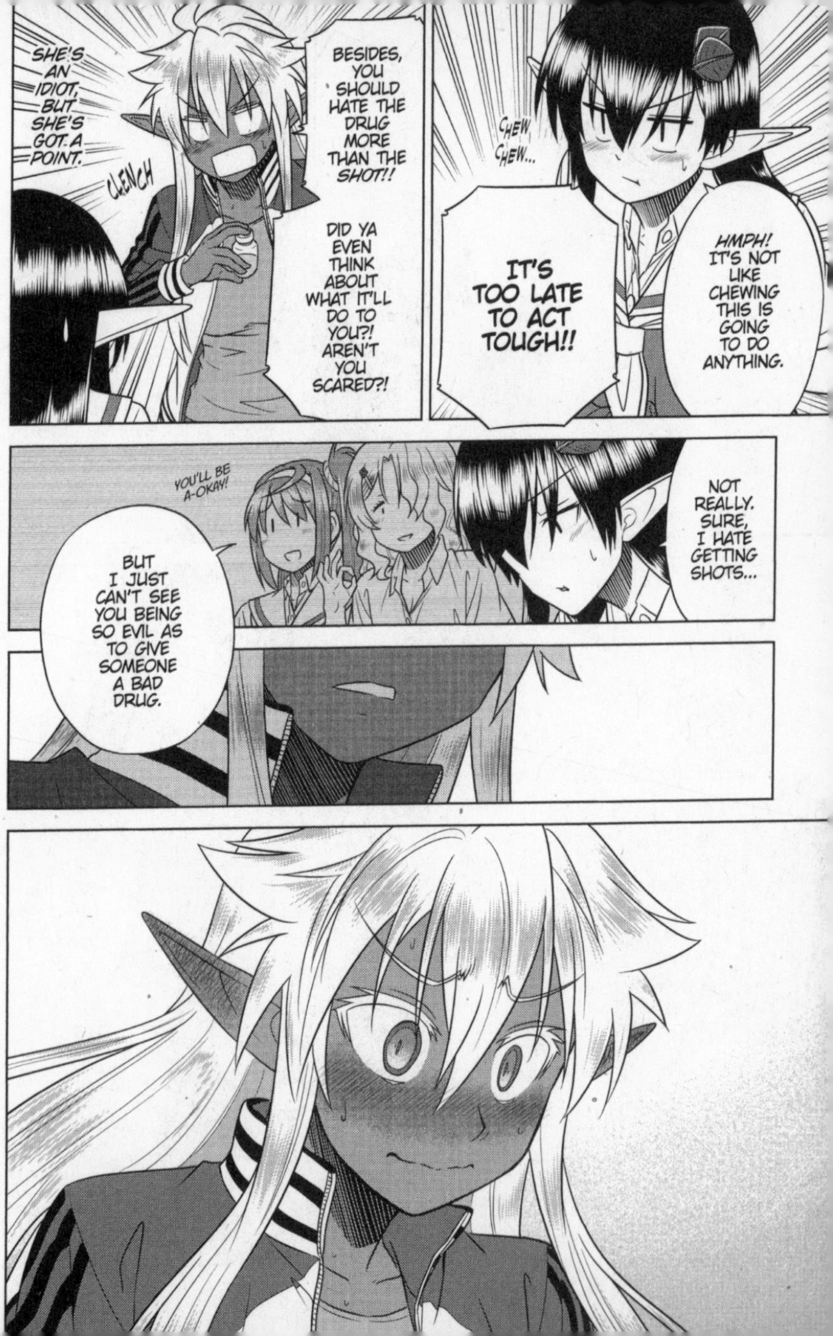
CHEW CHEW...
HMPH! IT'S NOT LIKE CHEWING THIS IS GOING TO DO ANYTHING.
IT'S TOO LATE TO ACT TOUGH!!
BESIDES, YOU SHOULD HATE THE DRUG MORE THAN THE SHOT!!
SHE'S AN IDIOT, BUT SHE'S GOT A POINT.
CLENCH
DID YA EVEN THINK ABOUT WHAT IT'LL DO TO YOU?! AREN'T YOU SCARED?!
NOT REALLY. SURE, I HATE GETTING SHOTS...
YOU'LL BE A-OKAY!
BUT I JUST CAN'T SEE YOU BEING SO EVIL AS TO GIVE SOMEONE A BAD DRUG.

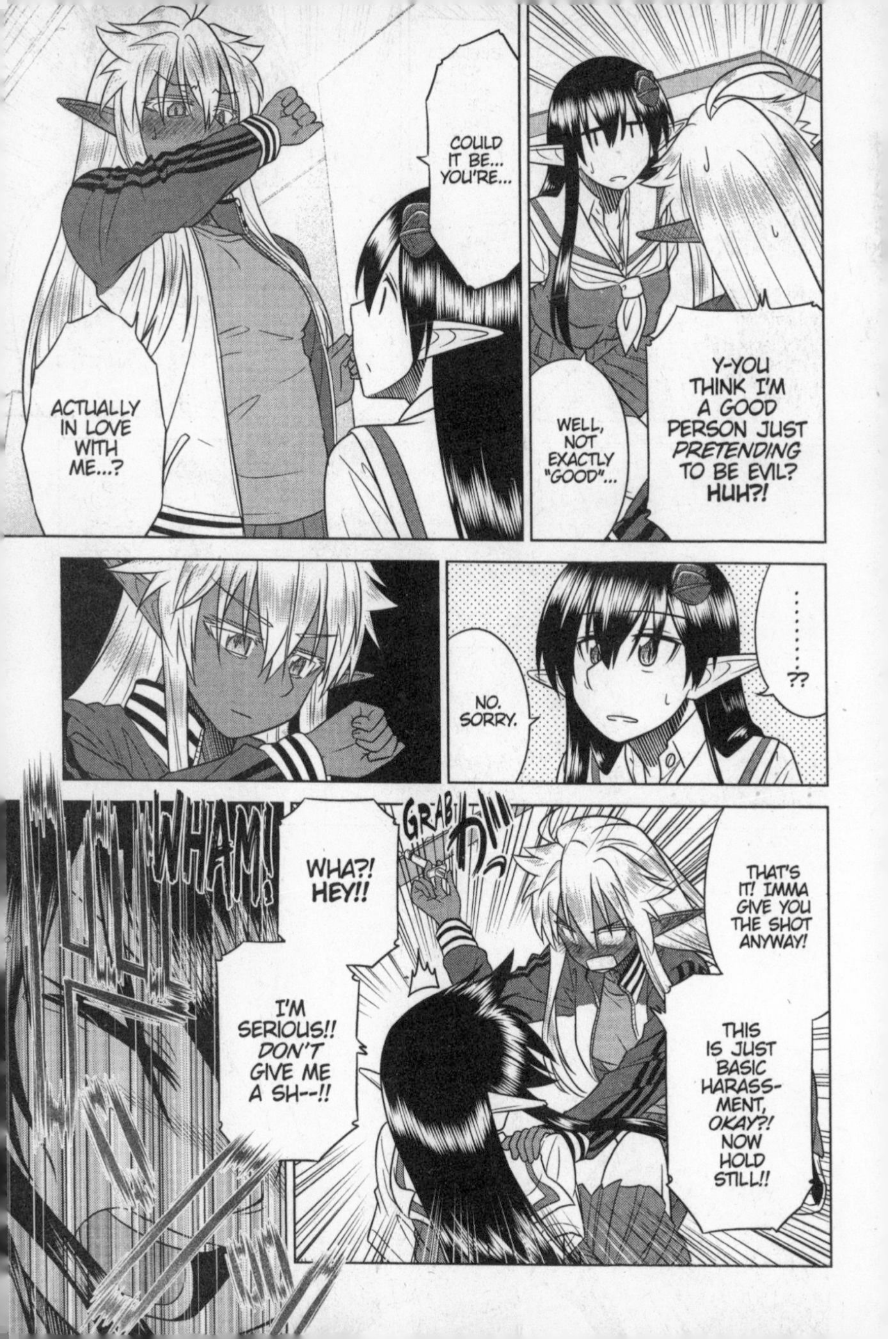
Y-YOU THINK I'M A GOOD PERSON JUST *PRETENDING* TO BE EVIL? **HUH?!**
WELL, NOT EXACTLY "GOOD"...
COULD IT BE... YOU'RE...
ACTUALLY IN LOVE WITH ME...?
......
??
NO. SORRY.
GRAB
THAT'S IT! IMMA GIVE YOU THE SHOT ANYWAY!
THIS IS JUST BASIC HARASS-MENT, *OKAY?!* NOW HOLD STILL!!
WHA?! HEY!!
I'M SERIOUS!! *DON'T* GIVE ME A SH--!!
WHAM!

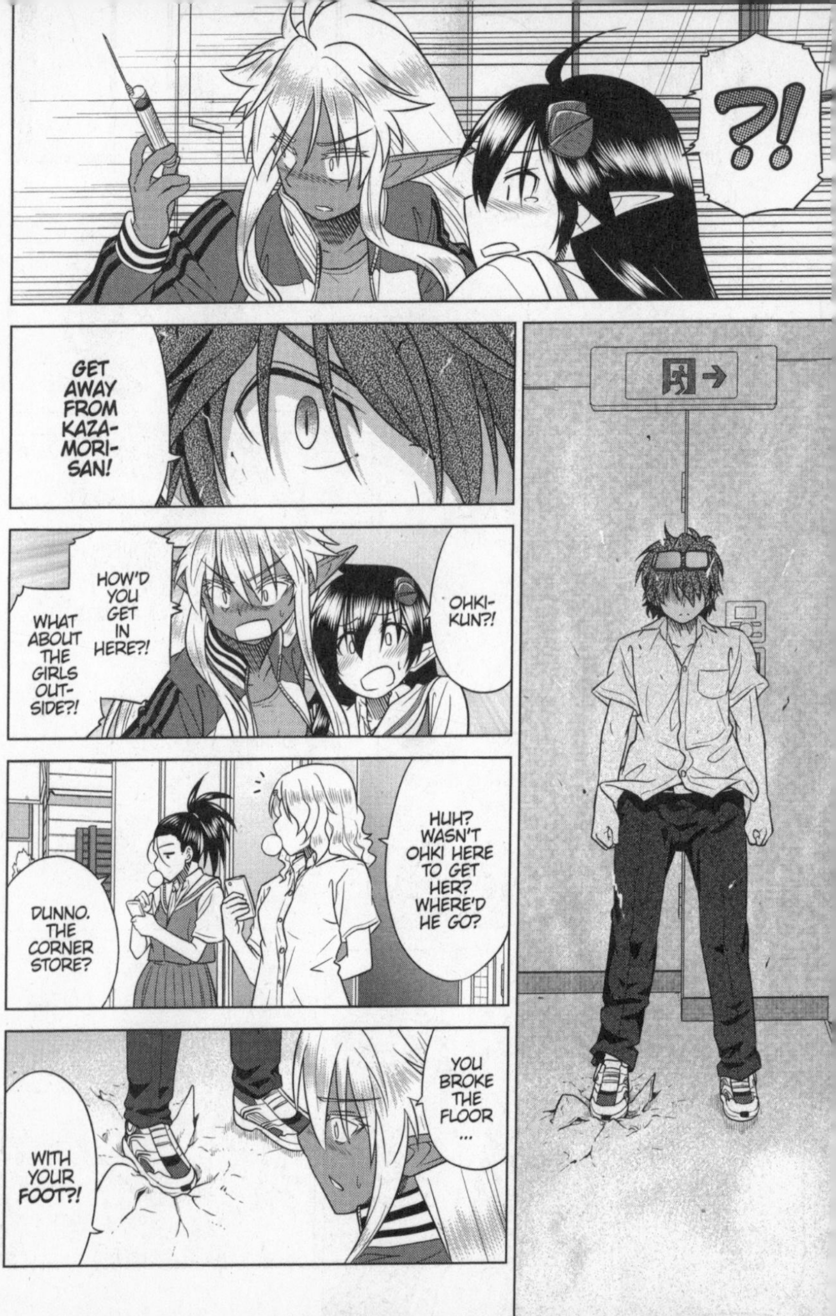
?!
GET AWAY FROM KAZA-MORI-SAN!
OHKI-KUN?!
HOW'D YOU GET IN HERE?!
WHAT ABOUT THE GIRLS OUT-SIDE?!
HUH? WASN'T OHKI HERE TO GET HER? WHERE'D HE GO?
DUNNO. THE CORNER STORE?
YOU BROKE THE FLOOR ...
WITH YOUR FOOT?!

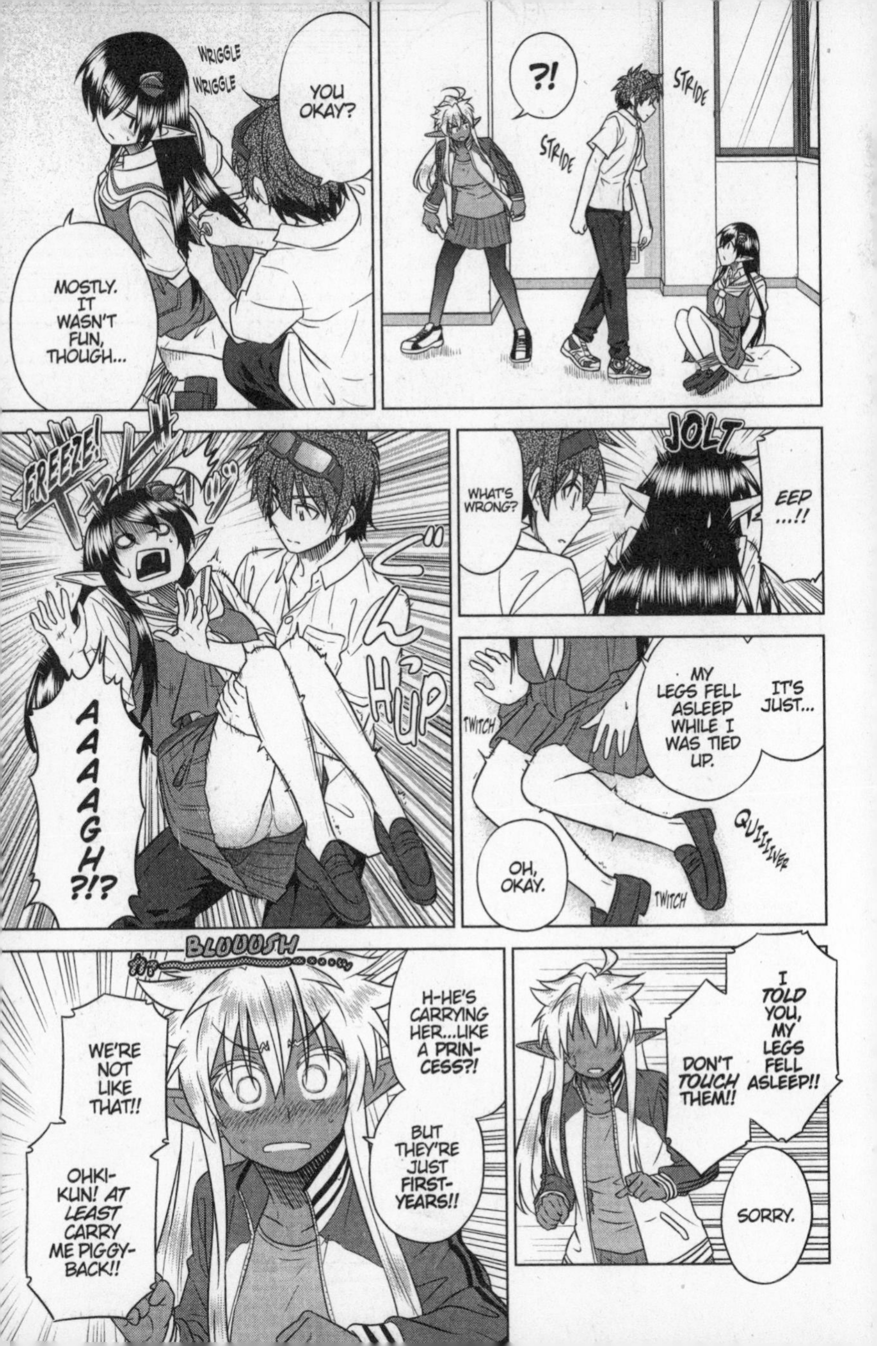
?!
STRIDE
STRIDE
WRIGGLE WRIGGLE
YOU OKAY?
MOSTLY. IT WASN'T FUN, THOUGH...
JOLT
EEP ...!!
WHAT'S WRONG?
IT'S JUST...
MY LEGS FELL ASLEEP WHILE I WAS TIED UP.
TWITCH
QUIIIIVER
OH, OKAY.
TWITCH
FREEZE!
HUP
AAAAAGH?!?
I *TOLD* YOU, MY LEGS FELL ASLEEP!!
DON'T *TOUCH* THEM!!
SORRY.
BLUUUSH
H-HE'S CARRYING HER...LIKE A PRINCESS?!
BUT THEY'RE JUST FIRST-YEARS!!
WE'RE NOT LIKE THAT!!
OHKI-KUN! *AT LEAST* CARRY ME PIGGY-BACK!!

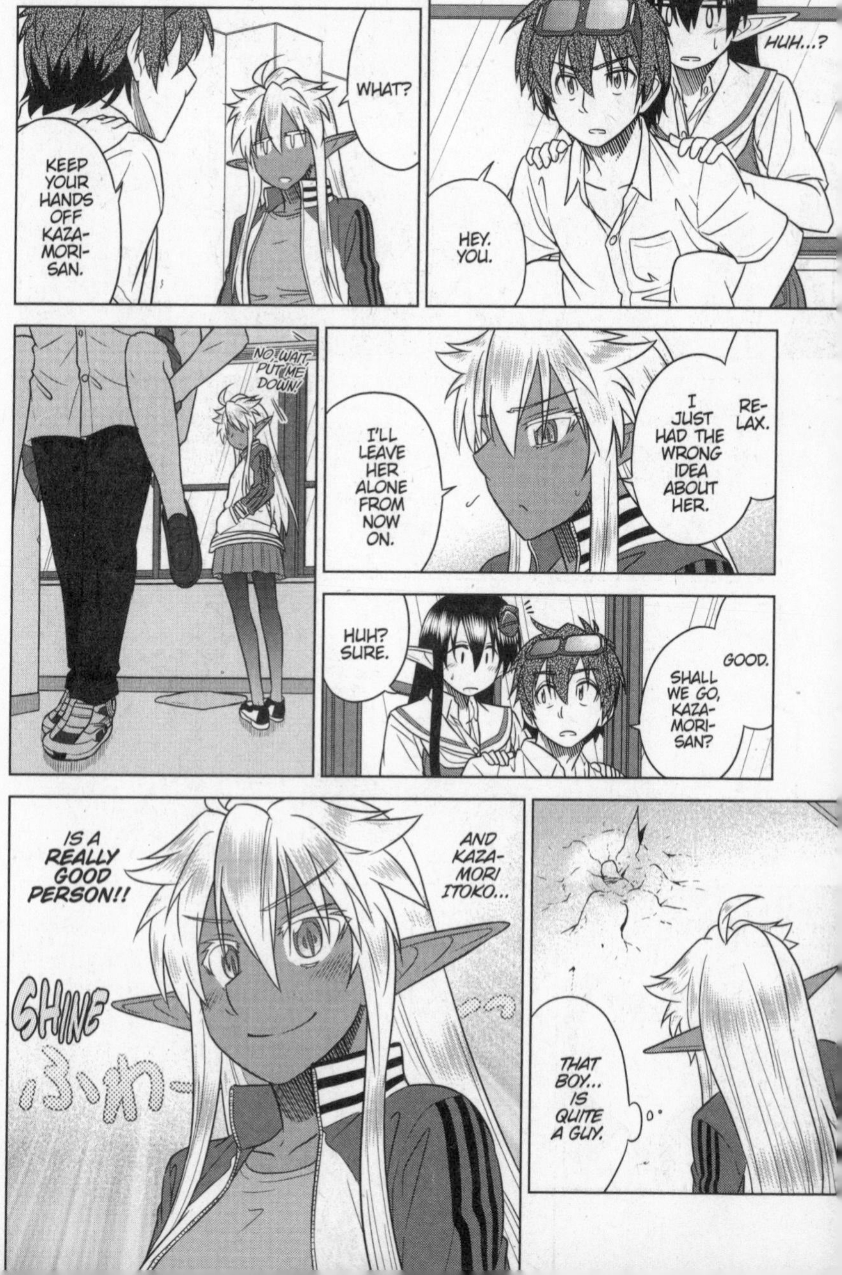
HUH...?
HEY. YOU.
WHAT?
KEEP YOUR HANDS OFF KAZA-MORI-SAN.
RE-LAX.
I JUST HAD THE WRONG IDEA ABOUT HER.
I'LL LEAVE HER ALONE FROM NOW ON.
GOOD.
SHALL WE GO, KAZA-MORI-SAN?
HUH? SURE.
NO, WAIT, PUT ME DOWN!
THAT BOY... IS QUITE A GUY.
AND KAZA-MORI ITOKO...
IS A REALLY GOOD PERSON!!
SHINE
ふわー

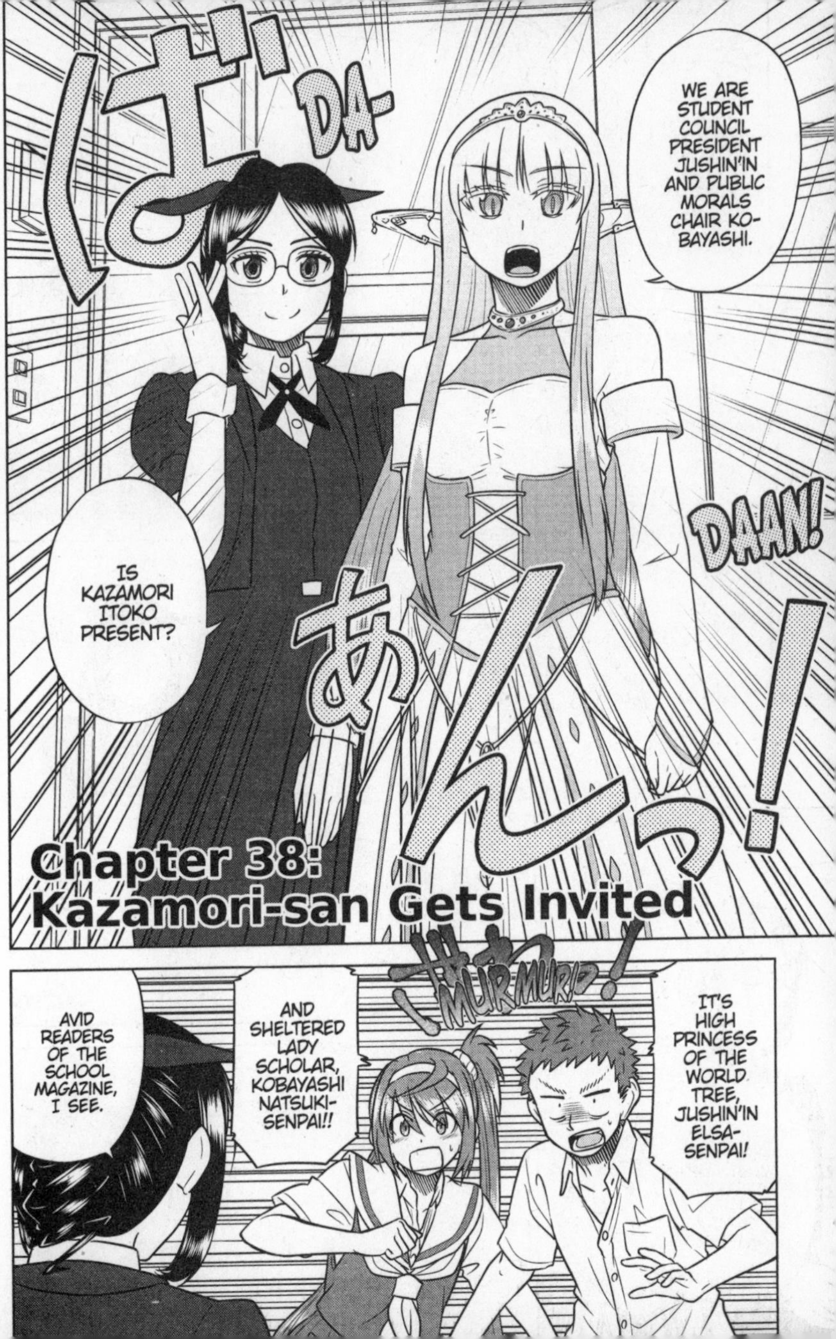
WE ARE STUDENT COUNCIL PRESIDENT JUSHIN'IN AND PUBLIC MORALS CHAIR KO-BAYASHI.
DA-DAAN!
IS KAZAMORI ITOKO PRESENT?
Chapter 38: Kazamori-san Gets Invited
MURMUR!
IT'S HIGH PRINCESS OF THE WORLD TREE, JUSHIN'IN ELSA-SENPAI!
AND SHELTERED LADY SCHOLAR, KOBAYASHI NATSUKI-SENPAI!!
AVID READERS OF THE SCHOOL MAGAZINE, I SEE.

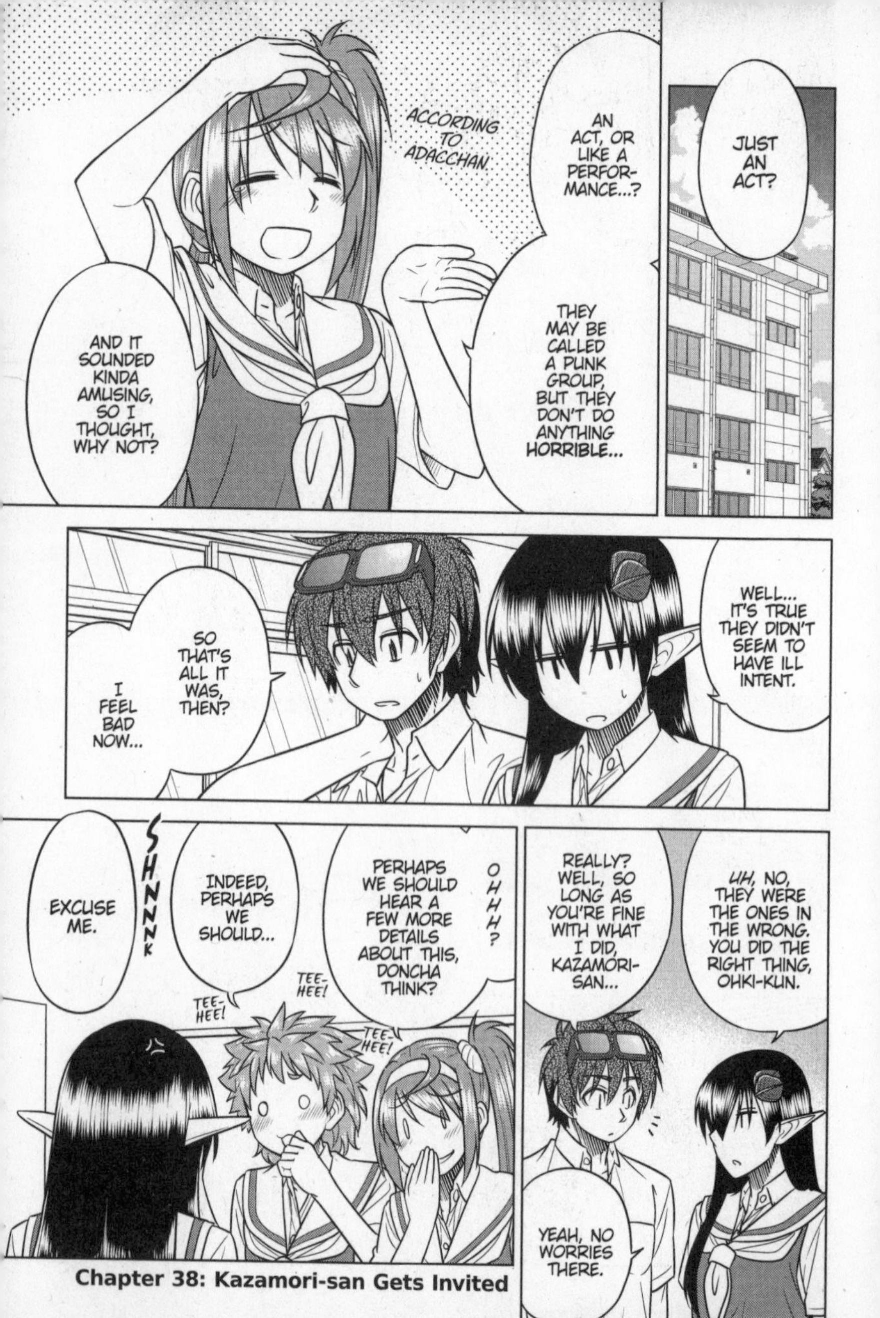
JUST AN ACT?
AN ACT, OR LIKE A PERFOR-MANCE...?
ACCORDING TO ADACCHAN.
THEY MAY BE CALLED A PUNK GROUP, BUT THEY DON'T DO ANYTHING HORRIBLE...
AND IT SOUNDED KINDA AMUSING, SO I THOUGHT, WHY NOT?
WELL... IT'S TRUE THEY DIDN'T SEEM TO HAVE ILL INTENT.
SO THAT'S ALL IT WAS, THEN?
I FEEL BAD NOW...
UH, NO, THEY WERE THE ONES IN THE WRONG. YOU DID THE RIGHT THING, OHKI-KUN.
REALLY? WELL, SO LONG AS YOU'RE FINE WITH WHAT I DID, KAZAMORI-SAN...
YEAH, NO WORRIES THERE.
OHHH?
PERHAPS WE SHOULD HEAR A FEW MORE DETAILS ABOUT THIS, DONCHA THINK?
TEE-HEE!
INDEED, PERHAPS WE SHOULD...
TEE-HEE!
TEE-HEE!
SHNNNK
EXCUSE ME.

Chapter 38: Kazamori-san Gets Invited

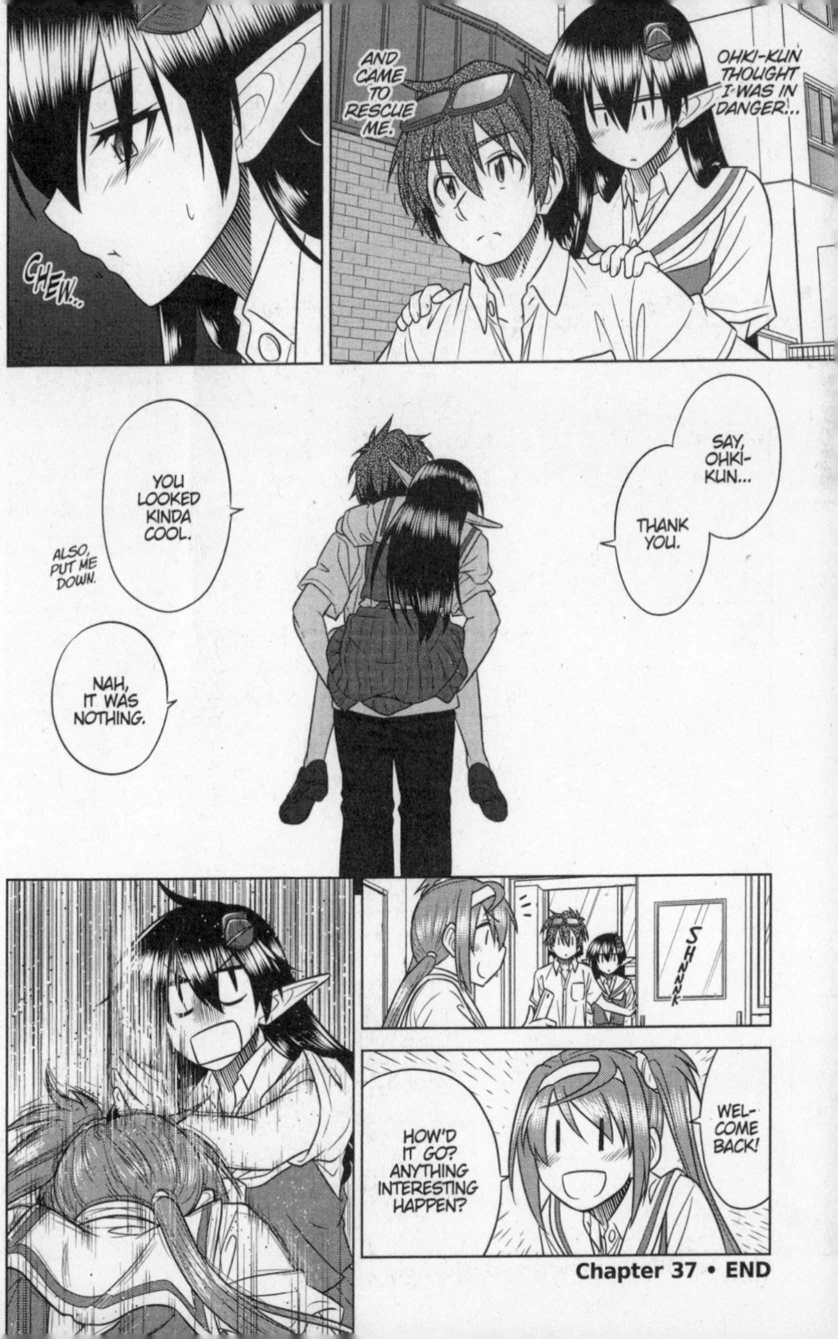
OHKI-KUN THOUGHT I-WAS IN DANGER...
AND CAME TO RESCUE ME.
CHEW...
SAY, OHKI-KUN...
THANK YOU.
YOU LOOKED KINDA COOL.
ALSO, PUT ME DOWN.
NAH, IT WAS NOTHING.
SHNNNK
WEL-COME BACK!
HOW'D IT GO? ANYTHING INTERESTING HAPPEN?

Chapter 37 • END

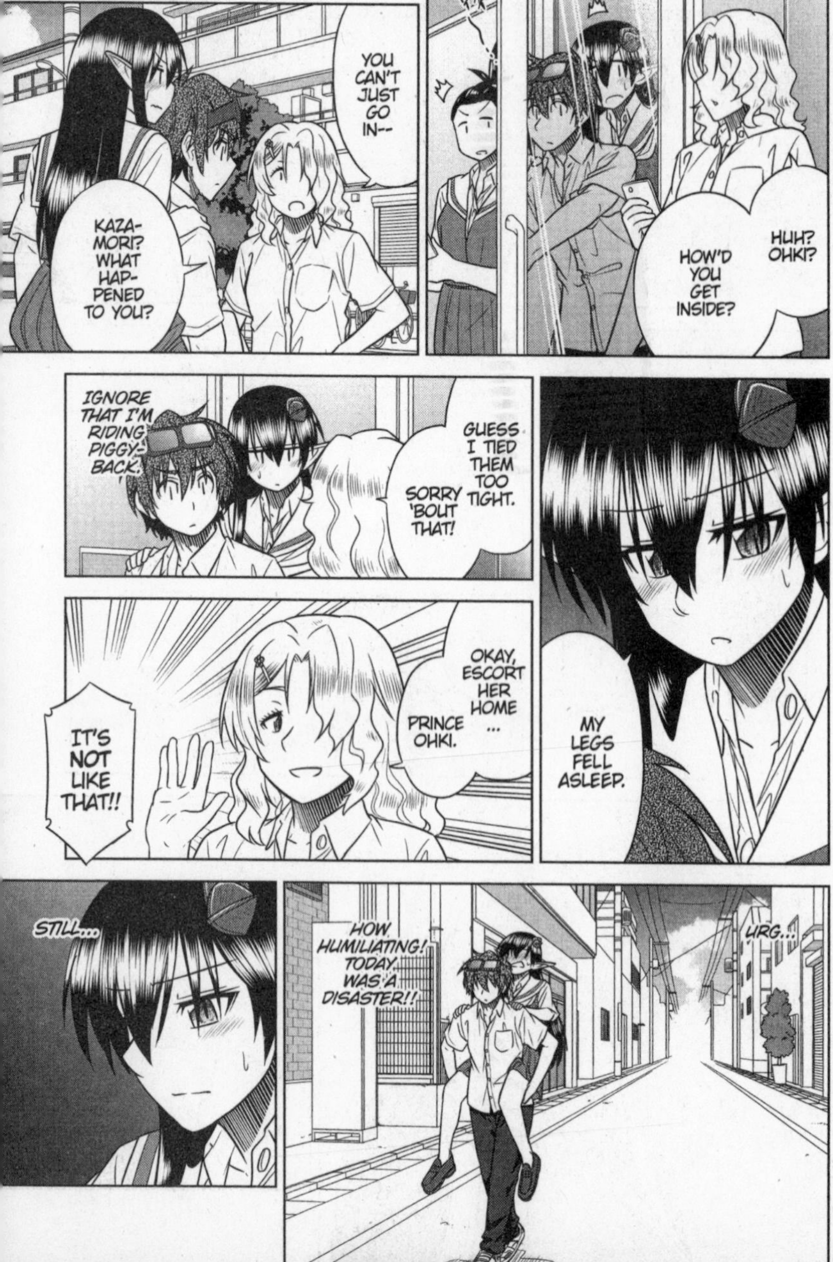
CREAK
HUH? OHKI?
HOW'D YOU GET INSIDE?
YOU CAN'T JUST GO IN--
KAZAMORI? WHAT HAPPENED TO YOU?
MY LEGS FELL ASLEEP.
GUESS I TIED THEM TOO TIGHT.
SORRY 'BOUT THAT!
IGNORE THAT I'M RIDING PIGGY-BACK.
OKAY, ESCORT HER HOME...
PRINCE OHKI.
IT'S NOT LIKE THAT!!
URG...
HOW HUMILIATING! TODAY WAS A DISASTER!!
STILL...

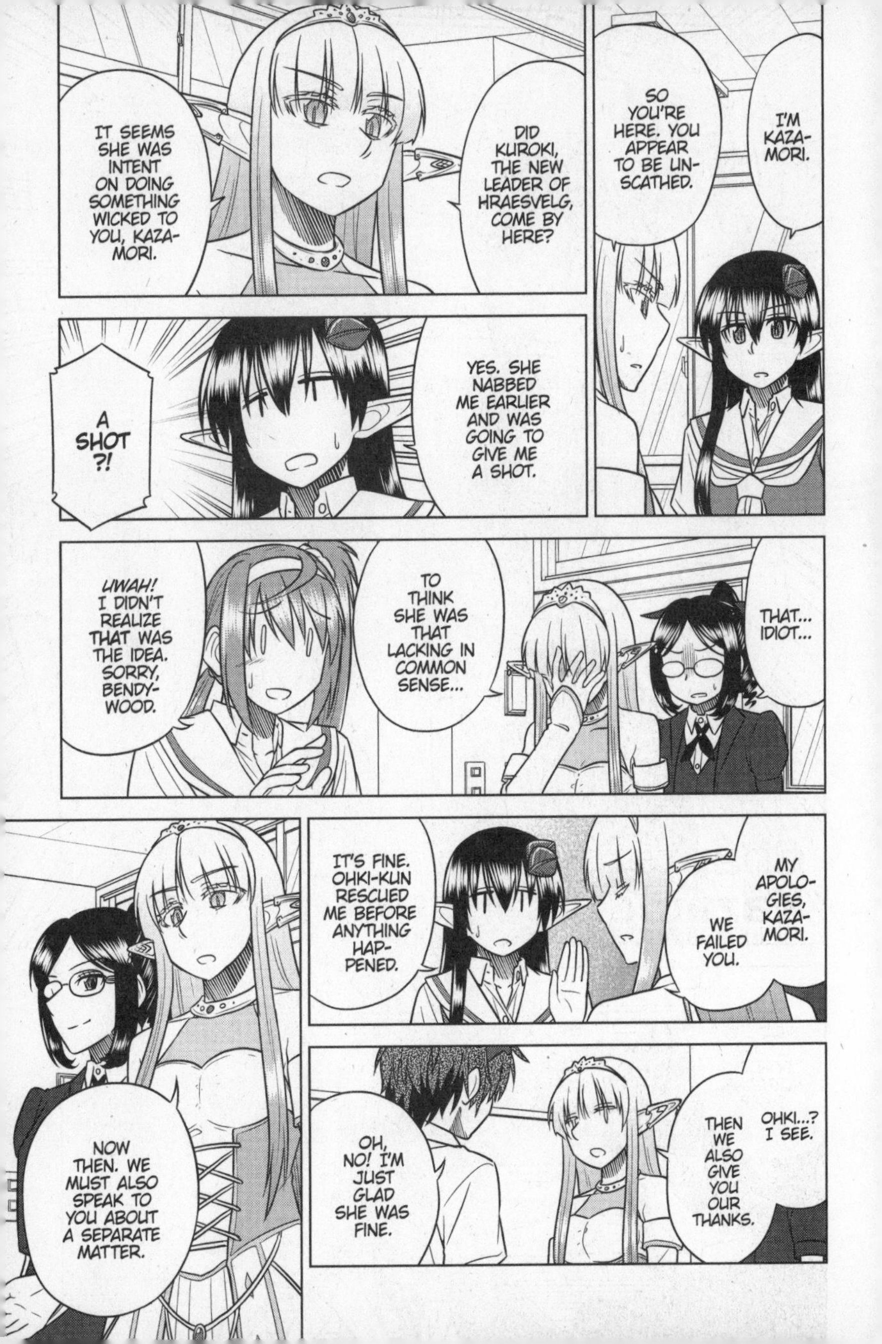
I'M KAZA-MORI.
SO YOU'RE HERE. YOU APPEAR TO BE UN-SCATHED.
DID KUROKI, THE NEW LEADER OF HRAESVELG, COME BY HERE?
IT SEEMS SHE WAS INTENT ON DOING SOMETHING WICKED TO YOU, KAZA-MORI.
YES. SHE NABBED ME EARLIER AND WAS GOING TO GIVE ME A SHOT.
A SHOT?!
THAT... IDIOT...
TO THINK SHE WAS THAT LACKING IN COMMON SENSE...
UWAH! I DIDN'T REALIZE THAT WAS THE IDEA. SORRY, BENDY-WOOD.
MY APOLO-GIES, KAZA-MORI.
WE FAILED YOU.
IT'S FINE. OHKI-KUN RESCUED ME BEFORE ANYTHING HAP-PENED.
OHKI...? I SEE.
THEN WE ALSO GIVE YOU OUR THANKS.
OH, NO! I'M JUST GLAD SHE WAS FINE.
NOW THEN. WE MUST ALSO SPEAK TO YOU ABOUT A SEPARATE MATTER.

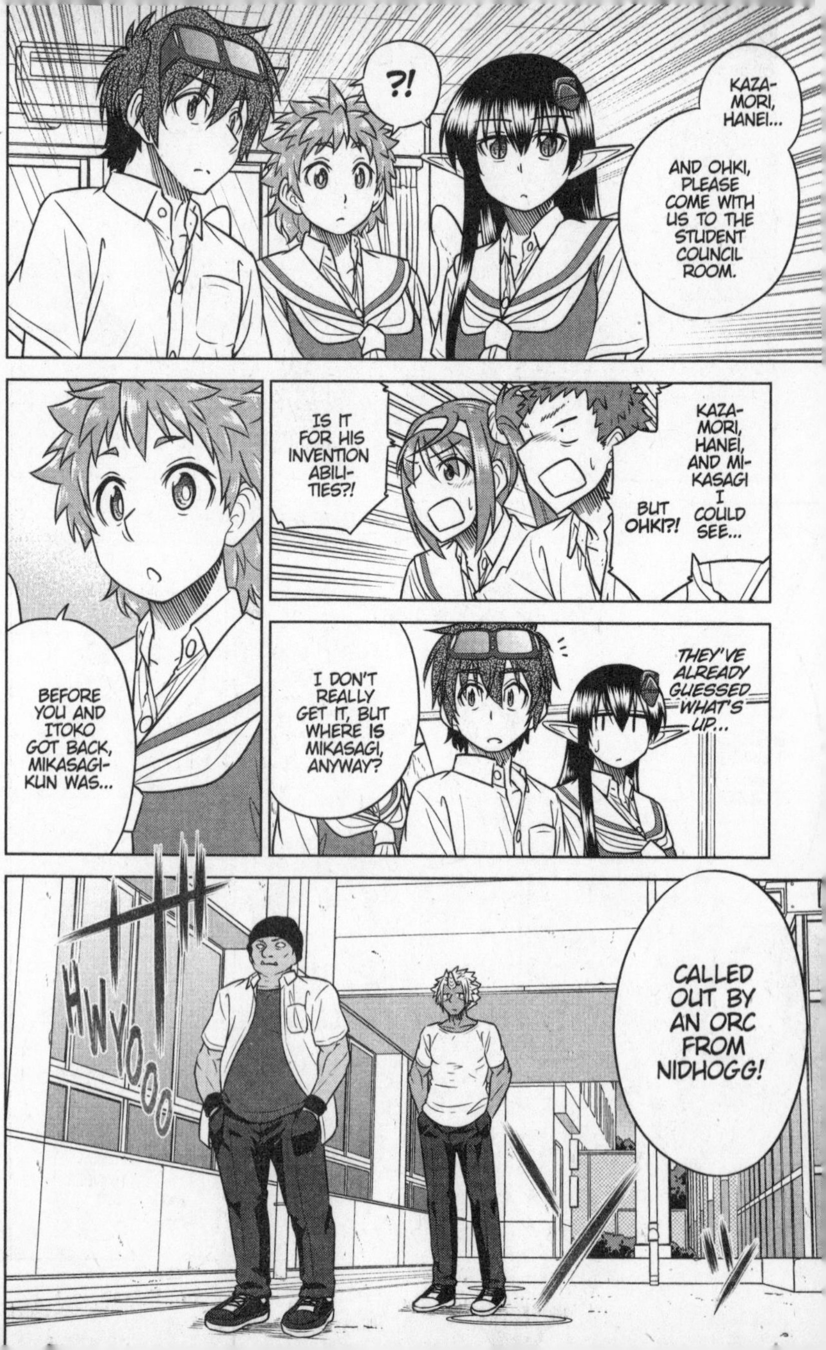
KAZAMORI, HANEI... AND OHKI, PLEASE COME WITH US TO THE STUDENT COUNCIL ROOM.
?!
KAZAMORI, HANEI, AND MIKASAGI I COULD SEE...
BUT OHKI?!
IS IT FOR HIS INVENTION ABILITIES?!
THEY'VE ALREADY GUESSED WHAT'S UP...
I DON'T REALLY GET IT, BUT WHERE IS MIKASAGI, ANYWAY?
BEFORE YOU AND ITOKO GOT BACK, MIKASAGI-KUN WAS...
CALLED OUT BY AN ORC FROM NIDHOGG!
HWYOOO

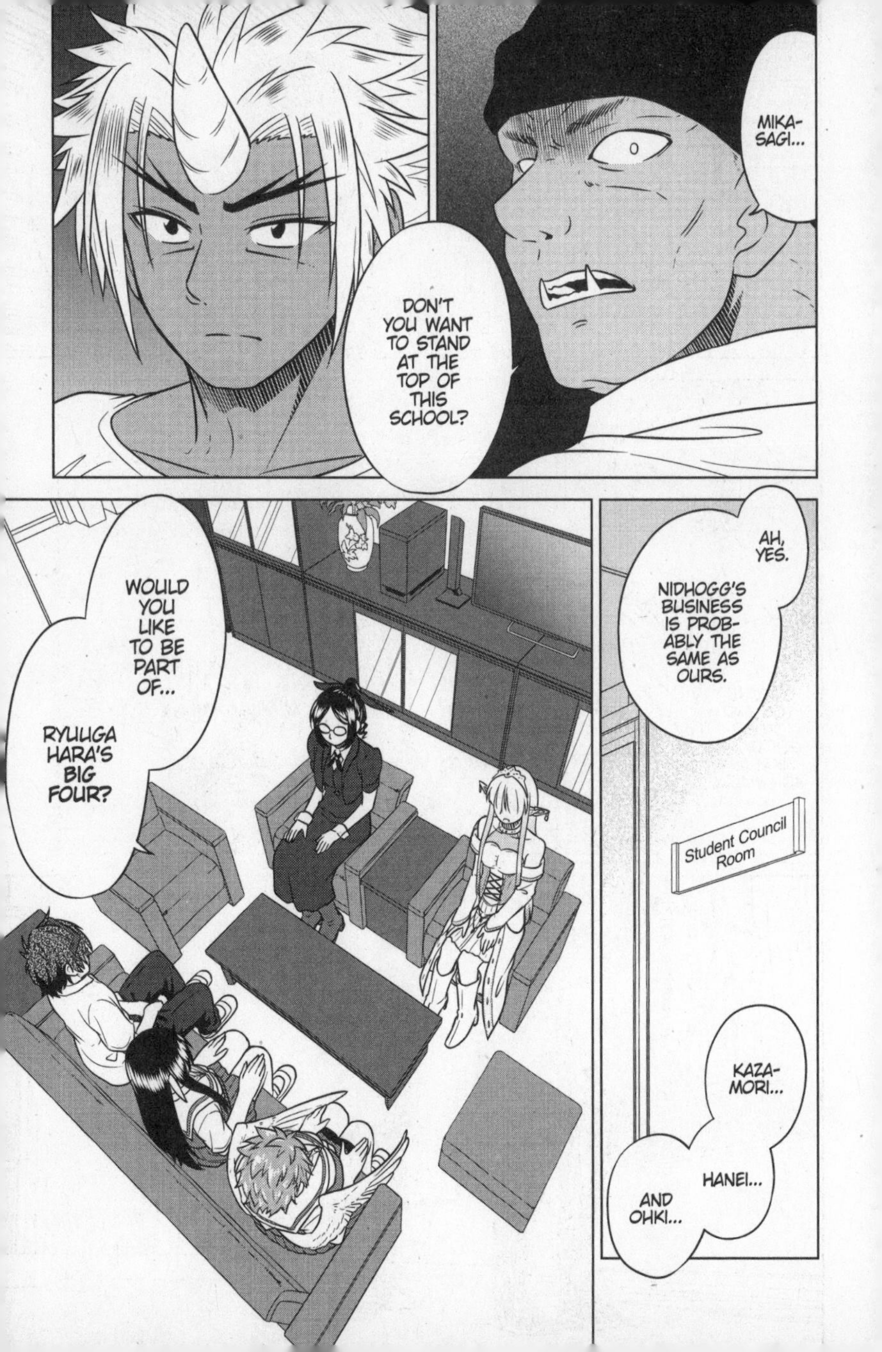
MIKA-SAGI...
DON'T YOU WANT TO STAND AT THE TOP OF THIS SCHOOL?
AH, YES.
NIDHOGG'S BUSINESS IS PROB-ABLY THE SAME AS OURS.
Student Council Room
KAZA-MORI...
HANEI...
AND OHKI...
WOULD YOU LIKE TO BE PART OF...
RYUUGA HARA'S BIG FOUR?

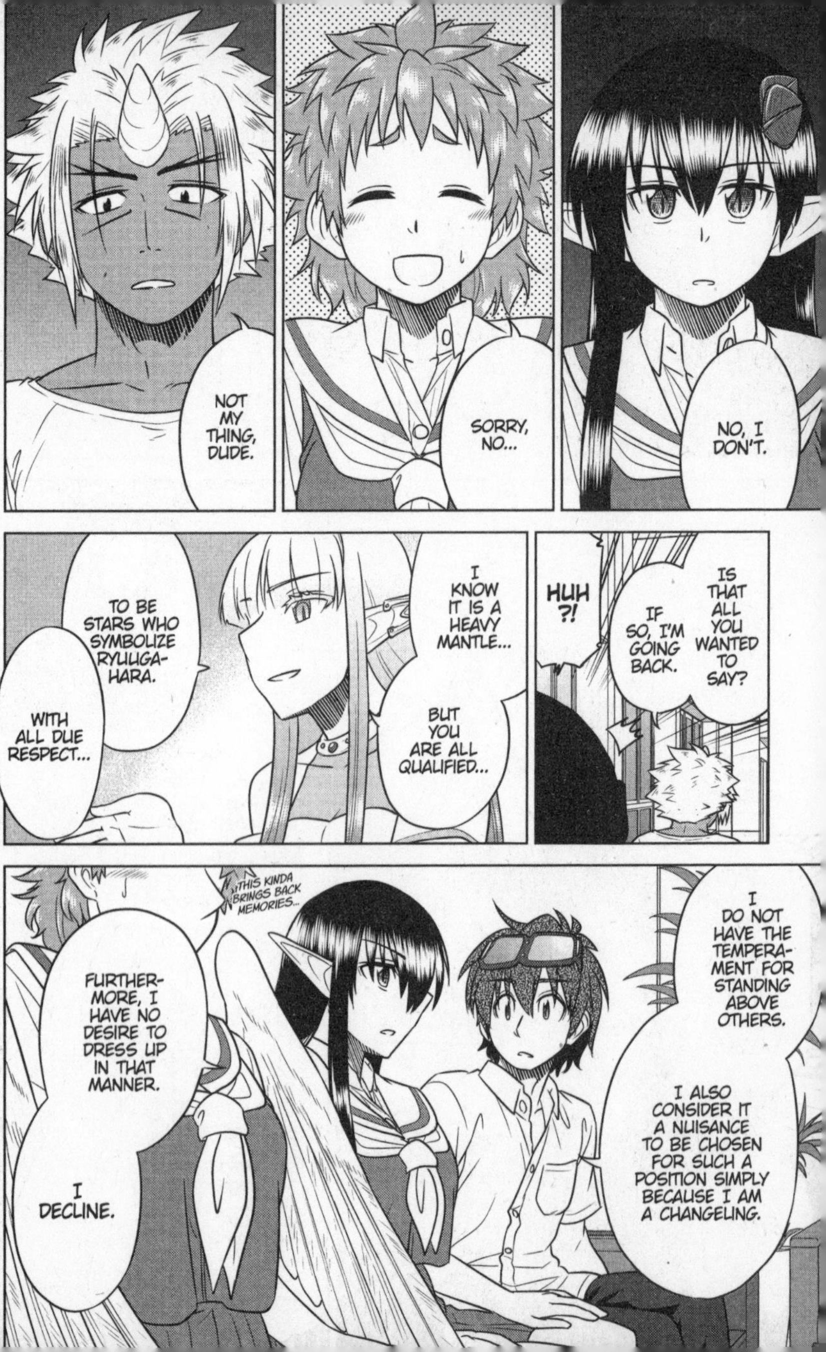
NO, I DON'T.
SORRY, NO...
NOT MY THING, DUDE.
IS THAT ALL YOU WANTED TO SAY?
IF SO, I'M GOING BACK.
HUH ?!
I KNOW IT IS A HEAVY MANTLE...
BUT YOU ARE ALL QUALIFIED...
TO BE STARS WHO SYMBOLIZE RYUUGA-HARA.
WITH ALL DUE RESPECT...
I DO NOT HAVE THE TEMPERA-MENT FOR STANDING ABOVE OTHERS.
I ALSO CONSIDER IT A NUISANCE TO BE CHOSEN FOR SUCH A POSITION SIMPLY BECAUSE I AM A CHANGELING.
THIS KINDA BRINGS BACK MEMORIES...
FURTHER-MORE, I HAVE NO DESIRE TO DRESS UP IN THAT MANNER.
I DECLINE.

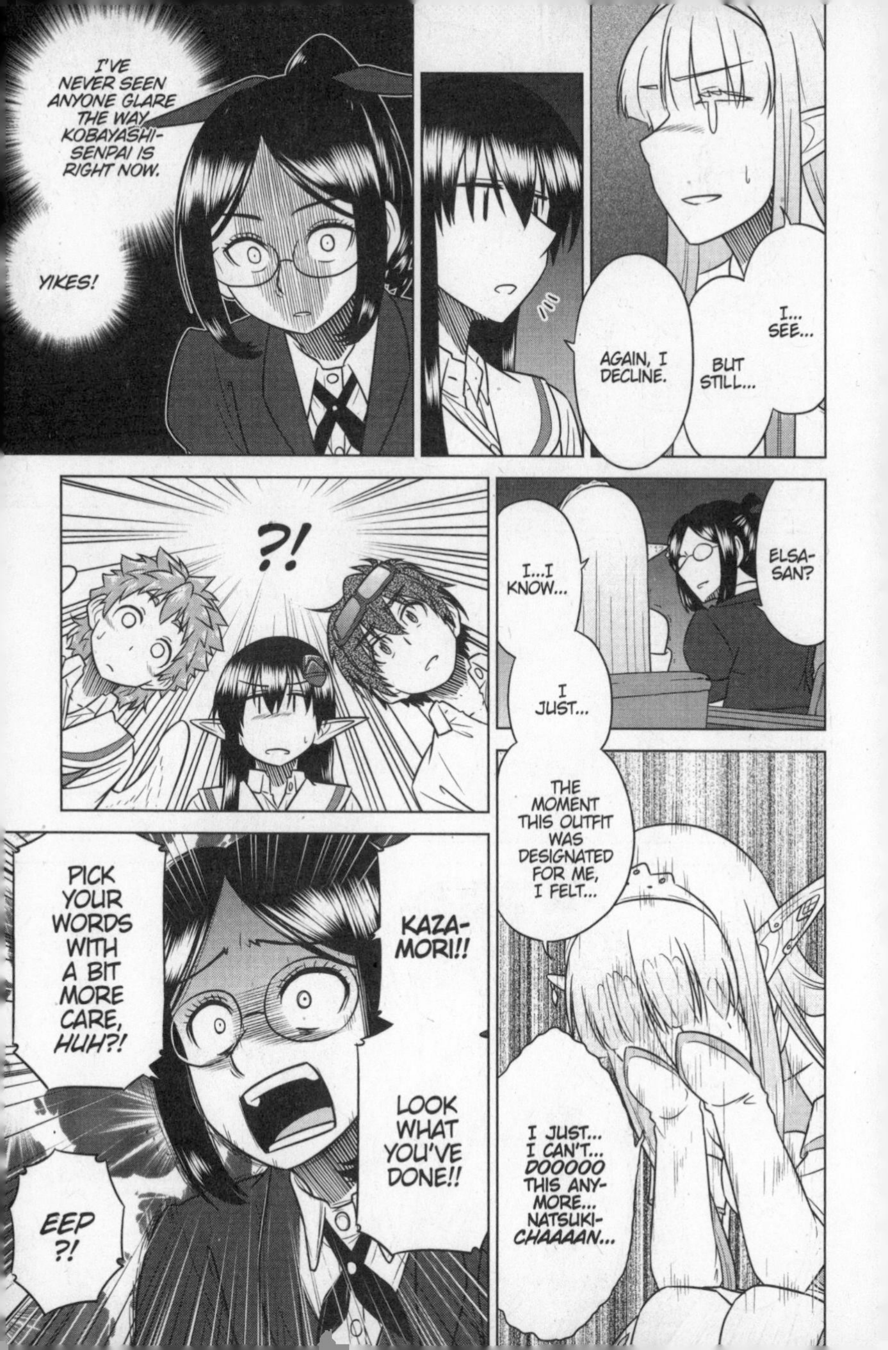

I... SEE...
BUT STILL...
AGAIN, I DECLINE.
I'VE NEVER SEEN ANYONE GLARE THE WAY KOBAYASHI-SENPAI IS RIGHT NOW.
YIKES!
ELSA-SAN?
I...I KNOW...
I JUST...
?!
THE MOMENT THIS OUTFIT WAS DESIGNATED FOR ME, I FELT...
I JUST... I CAN'T... DOOOOO THIS ANYMORE... NATSUKI-CHAAAAN...
KAZAMORI!!
PICK YOUR WORDS WITH A BIT MORE CARE, HUH?!
LOOK WHAT YOU'VE DONE!!
EEP?!

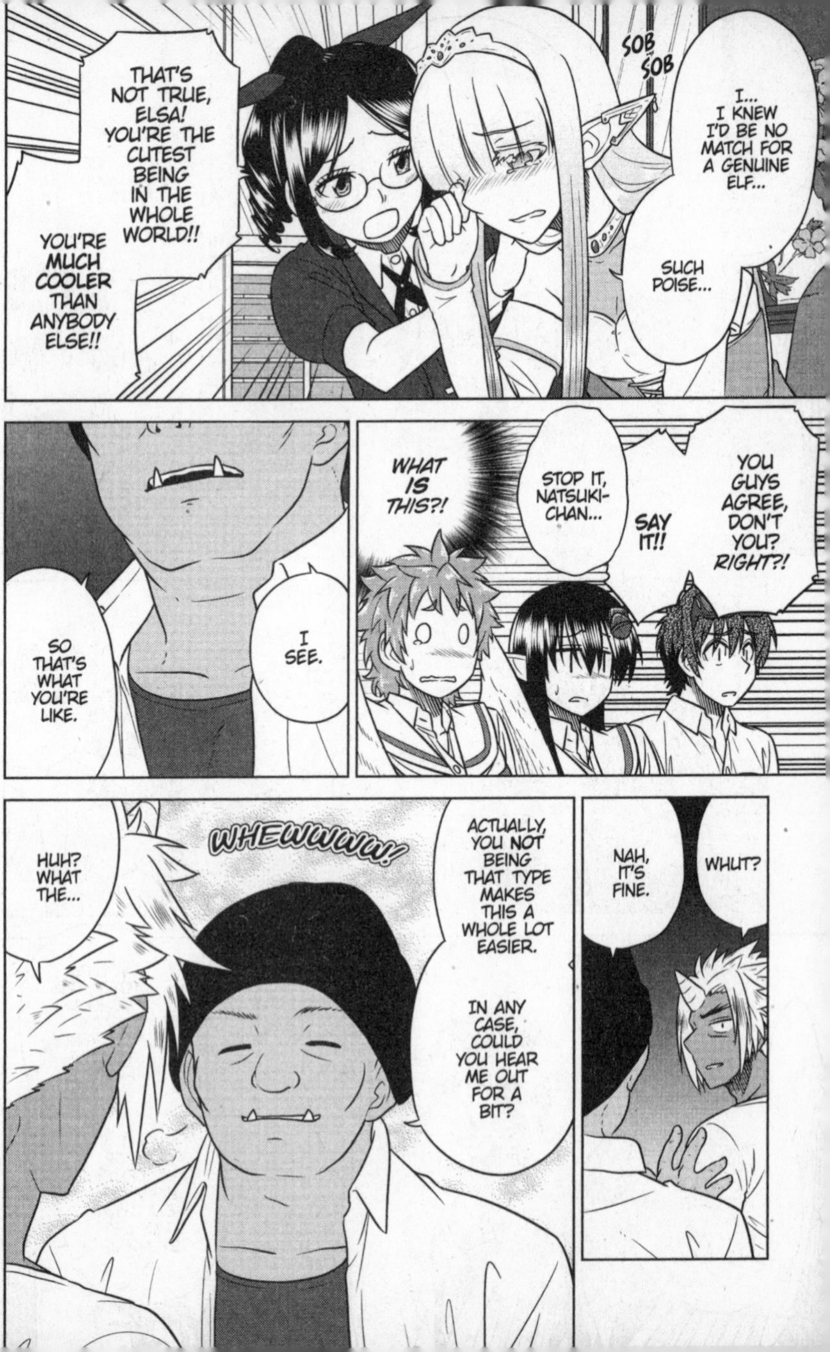
SOB SOB
I... I KNEW I'D BE NO MATCH FOR A GENUINE ELF...
SUCH POISE...
THAT'S NOT TRUE, ELSA! YOU'RE THE CUTEST BEING IN THE WHOLE WORLD!!
YOU'RE MUCH COOLER THAN ANYBODY ELSE!!
YOU GUYS AGREE, DON'T YOU? RIGHT?!
SAY IT!!
STOP IT, NATSUKI-CHAN...
WHAT IS THIS?!
I SEE.
SO THAT'S WHAT YOU'RE LIKE.
WHUT?
NAH, IT'S FINE.
ACTUALLY, YOU NOT BEING THAT TYPE MAKES THIS A WHOLE LOT EASIER.
IN ANY CASE, COULD YOU HEAR ME OUT FOR A BIT?
WHEWWWWW!
HUH? WHAT THE...

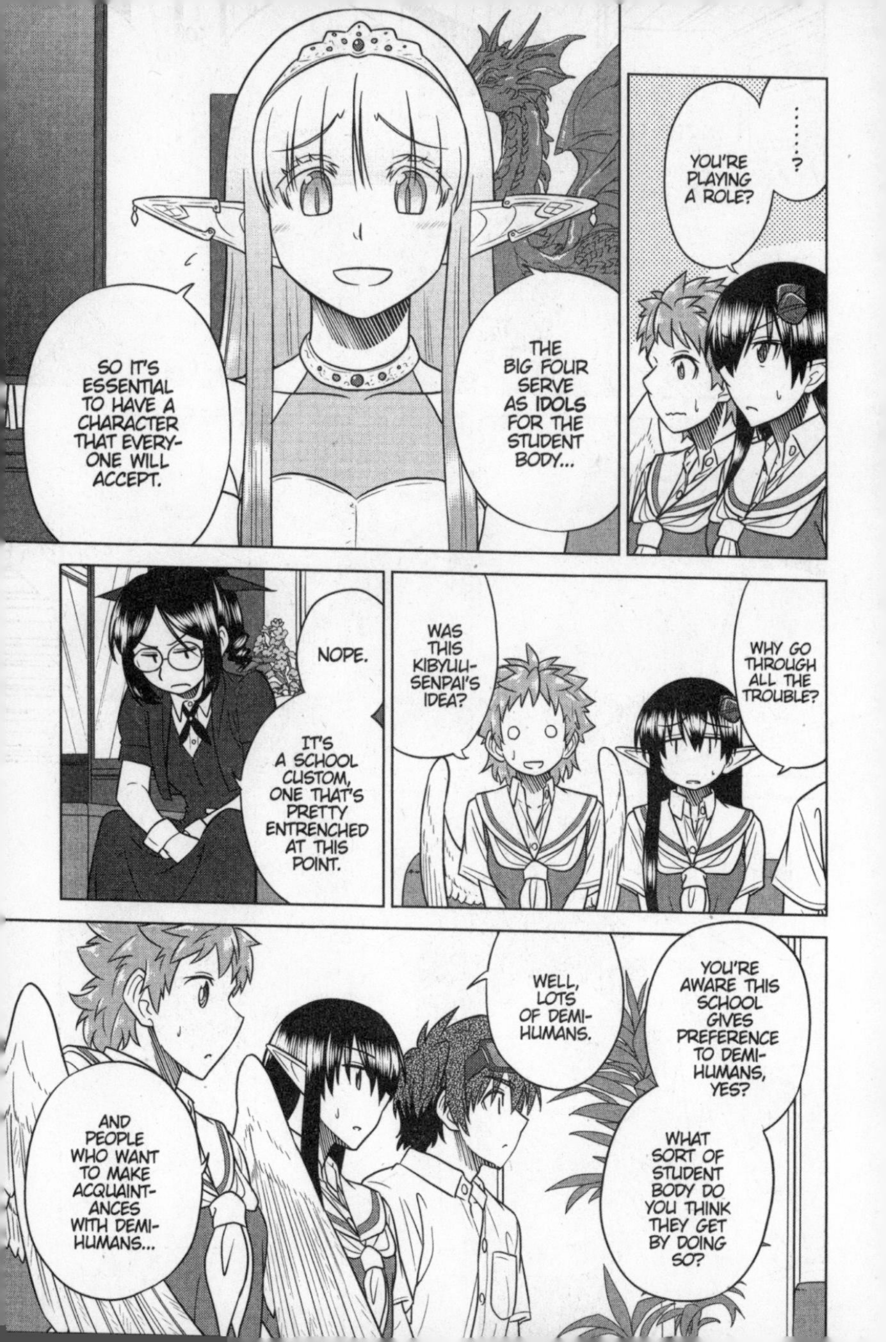
.....?
YOU'RE PLAYING A ROLE?
THE BIG FOUR SERVE AS IDOLS FOR THE STUDENT BODY...
SO IT'S ESSENTIAL TO HAVE A CHARACTER THAT EVERY-ONE WILL ACCEPT.
WHY GO THROUGH ALL THE TROUBLE?
WAS THIS KIBYUU-SENPAI'S IDEA?
NOPE.
IT'S A SCHOOL CUSTOM, ONE THAT'S PRETTY ENTRENCHED AT THIS POINT.
YOU'RE AWARE THIS SCHOOL GIVES PREFERENCE TO DEMI-HUMANS, YES?
WELL, LOTS OF DEMI-HUMANS.
WHAT SORT OF STUDENT BODY DO YOU THINK THEY GET BY DOING SO?
AND PEOPLE WHO WANT TO MAKE ACQUAINT-ANCES WITH DEMI-HUMANS...

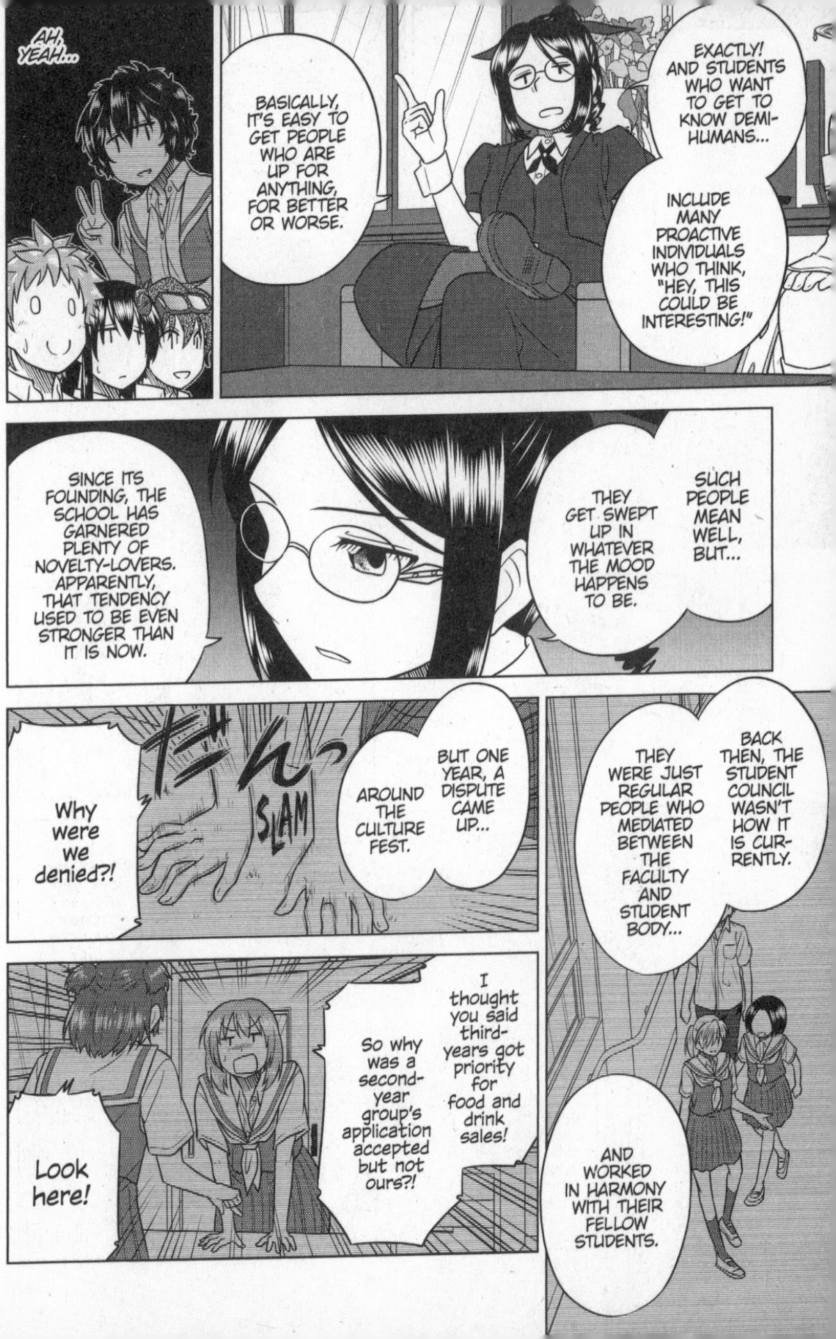
EXACTLY! AND STUDENTS WHO WANT TO GET TO KNOW DEMI-HUMANS...
INCLUDE MANY PROACTIVE INDIVIDUALS WHO THINK, "HEY, THIS COULD BE INTERESTING!"
BASICALLY, IT'S EASY TO GET PEOPLE WHO ARE UP FOR ANYTHING, FOR BETTER OR WORSE.
AH, YEAH...
SUCH PEOPLE MEAN WELL, BUT...
THEY GET SWEPT UP IN WHATEVER THE MOOD HAPPENS TO BE.
SINCE ITS FOUNDING, THE SCHOOL HAS GARNERED PLENTY OF NOVELTY-LOVERS. APPARENTLY, THAT TENDENCY USED TO BE EVEN STRONGER THAN IT IS NOW.
BACK THEN, THE STUDENT COUNCIL WASN'T HOW IT IS CUR-RENTLY.
THEY WERE JUST REGULAR PEOPLE WHO MEDIATED BETWEEN THE FACULTY AND STUDENT BODY...
AND WORKED IN HARMONY WITH THEIR FELLOW STUDENTS.
BUT ONE YEAR, A DISPUTE CAME UP...
AROUND THE CULTURE FEST.
SLAM
Why were we denied?!
I thought you said third-years got priority for food and drink sales!
So why was a second-year group's application accepted but not ours?!
Look here!

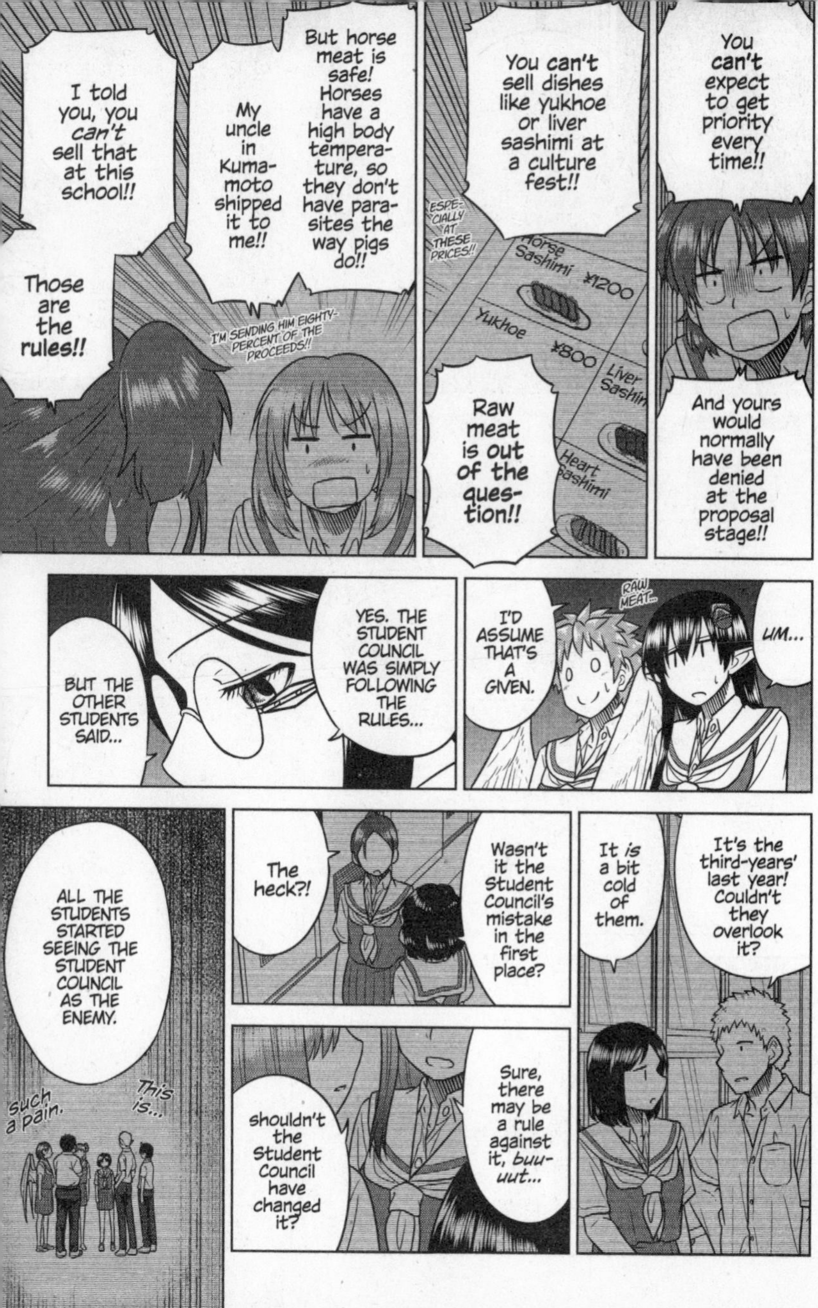
You *can't* expect to get priority every time!!
And yours would normally have been denied at the proposal stage!!
You can't sell dishes like yukhoe or liver sashimi at a culture fest!!
ESPECIALLY AT THESE PRICES!!
Horse Sashimi ¥1200
Yukhoe ¥800
Liver Sashimi
Heart Sashimi
Raw meat is out of the question!!
But horse meat is safe! Horses have a high body temperature, so they don't have parasites the way pigs do!!
My uncle in Kumamoto shipped it to me!!
I'M SENDING HIM EIGHTY-PERCENT OF THE PROCEEDS!!
I told you, you *can't* sell that at this school!!
Those are the rules!!
UM...
RAW MEAT...
I'D ASSUME THAT'S A GIVEN.
YES. THE STUDENT COUNCIL WAS SIMPLY FOLLOWING THE RULES...
BUT THE OTHER STUDENTS SAID...
It's the third-years' last year! Couldn't they overlook it?
It *is* a bit cold of them.
Wasn't it the Student Council's mistake in the first place?
The heck?!
Sure, there may be a rule against it, *buuuut*...
shouldn't the Student Council have changed it?
ALL THE STUDENTS STARTED SEEING THE STUDENT COUNCIL AS THE ENEMY.
This is...
such a pain.

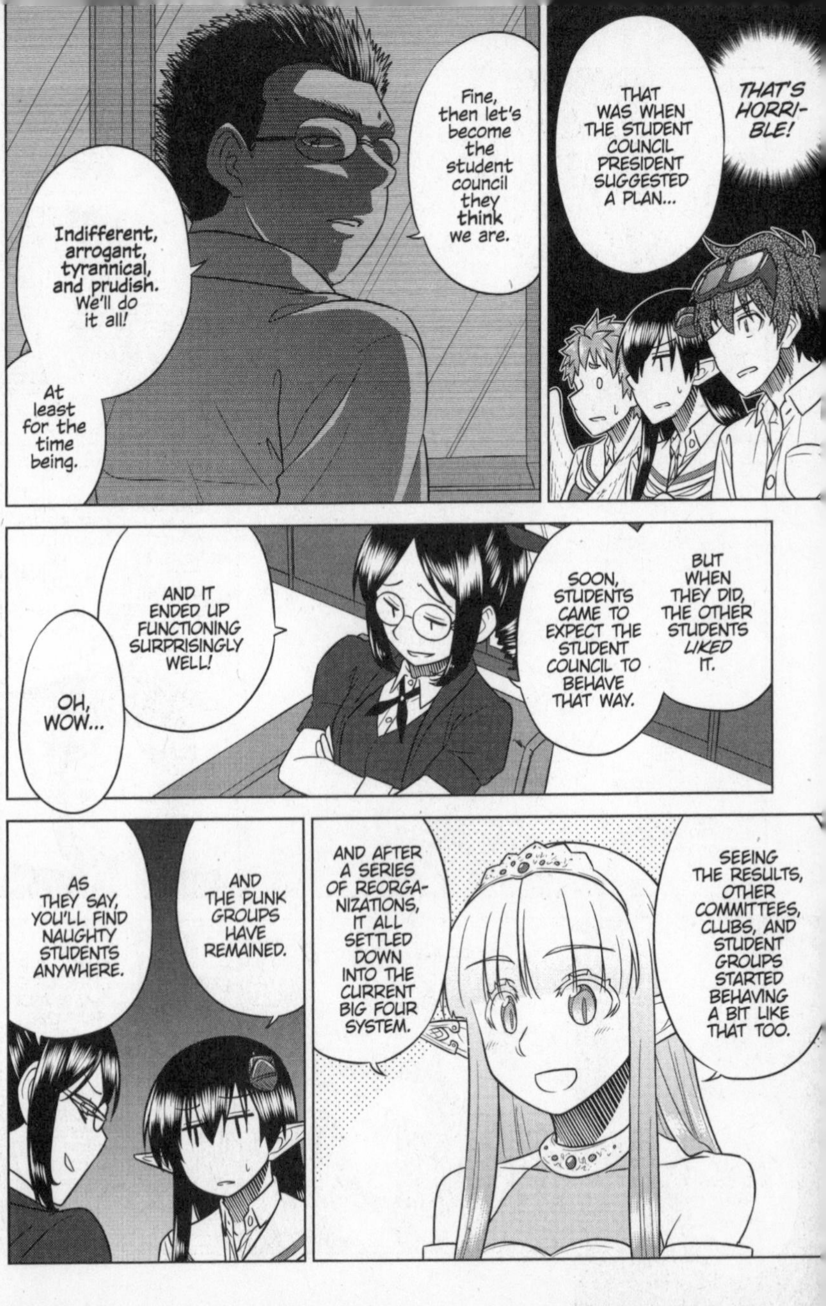
THAT'S HORRI-BLE!
THAT WAS WHEN THE STUDENT COUNCIL PRESIDENT SUGGESTED A PLAN...
Fine, then let's become the student council they think we are.
Indifferent, arrogant, tyrannical, and prudish. We'll do it all!
At least for the time being.
BUT WHEN THEY DID, THE OTHER STUDENTS *LIKED* IT.
SOON, STUDENTS CAME TO EXPECT THE STUDENT COUNCIL TO BEHAVE THAT WAY.
AND IT ENDED UP FUNCTIONING SURPRISINGLY WELL!
OH, WOW...
SEEING THE RESULTS, OTHER COMMITTEES, CLUBS, AND STUDENT GROUPS STARTED BEHAVING A BIT LIKE THAT TOO.
AND AFTER A SERIES OF REORGA-NIZATIONS, IT ALL SETTLED DOWN INTO THE CURRENT BIG FOUR SYSTEM.
AND THE PUNK GROUPS HAVE REMAINED.
AS THEY SAY, YOU'LL FIND NAUGHTY STUDENTS ANYWHERE.

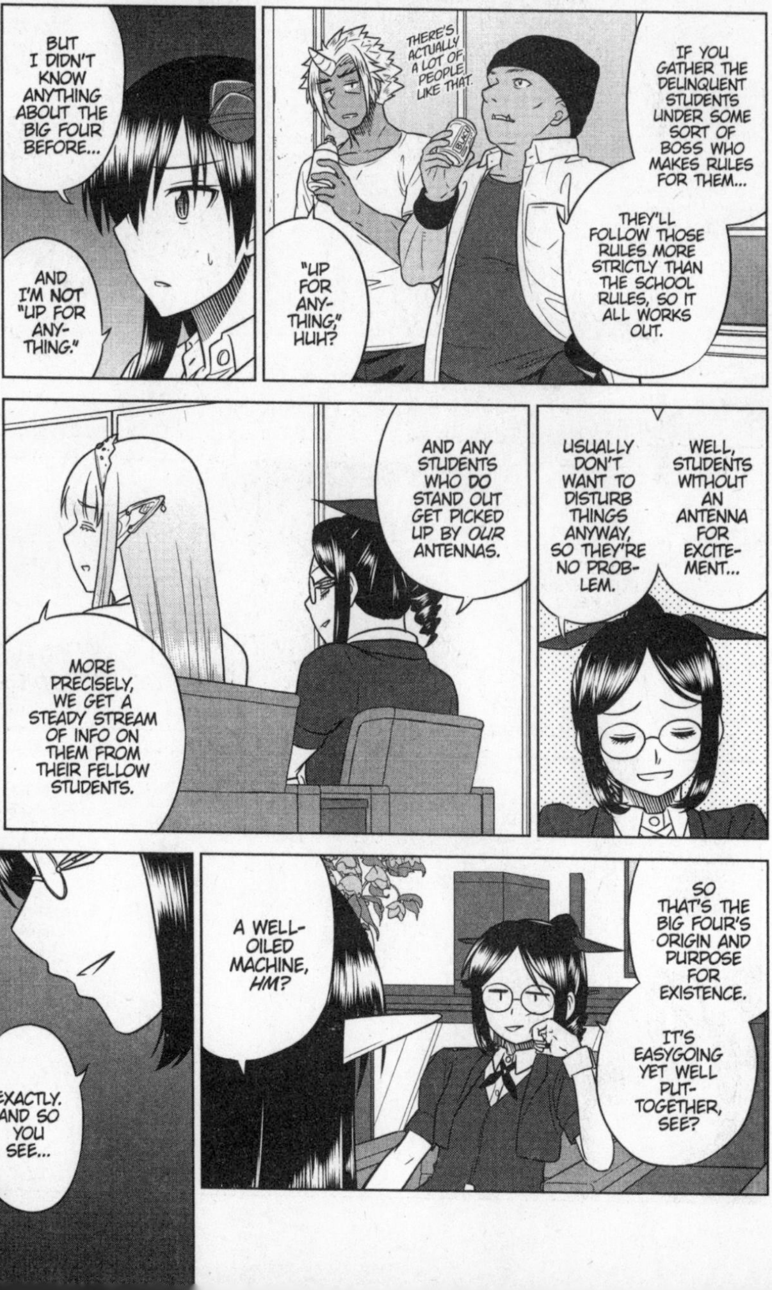
IF YOU GATHER THE DELINQUENT STUDENTS UNDER SOME SORT OF BOSS WHO MAKES RULES FOR THEM...
THEY'LL FOLLOW THOSE RULES MORE STRICTLY THAN THE SCHOOL RULES, SO IT ALL WORKS OUT.
THERE'S ACTUALLY A LOT OF PEOPLE LIKE THAT.
"UP FOR ANY-THING," HUH?
BUT I DIDN'T KNOW ANYTHING ABOUT THE BIG FOUR BEFORE...
AND I'M NOT "UP FOR ANY-THING."
WELL, STUDENTS WITHOUT AN ANTENNA FOR EXCITE-MENT...
USUALLY DON'T WANT TO DISTURB THINGS ANYWAY, SO THEY'RE NO PROB-LEM.
AND ANY STUDENTS WHO DO STAND OUT GET PICKED UP BY *OUR* ANTENNAS.
MORE PRECISELY, WE GET A STEADY STREAM OF INFO ON THEM FROM THEIR FELLOW STUDENTS.
SO THAT'S THE BIG FOUR'S ORIGIN AND PURPOSE FOR EXISTENCE.
IT'S EASYGOING YET WELL PUT-TOGETHER, SEE?
A WELL-OILED MACHINE, *HM*?
EXACTLY. AND SO YOU SEE...

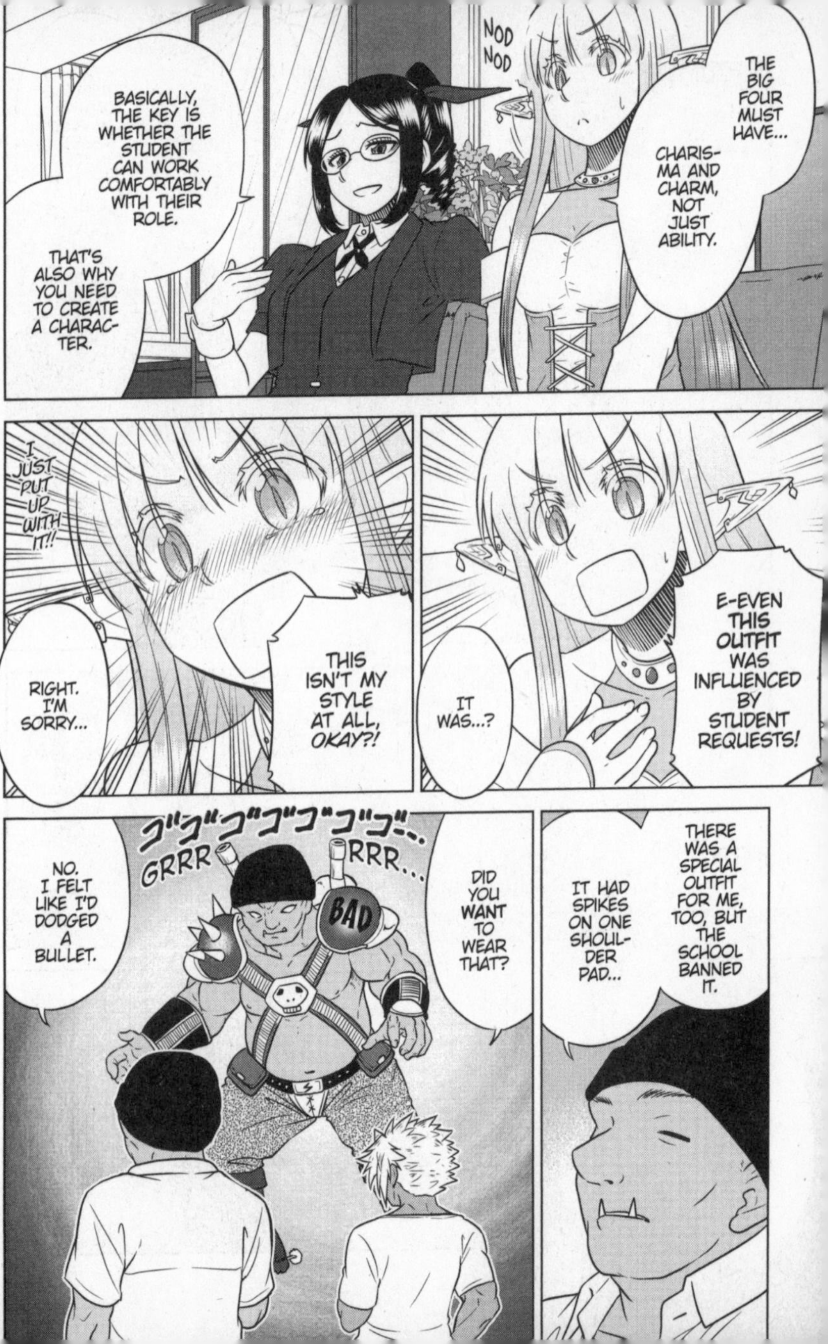
THE BIG FOUR MUST HAVE...
CHARISMA AND CHARM, NOT JUST ABILITY.
NOD NOD
BASICALLY, THE KEY IS WHETHER THE STUDENT CAN WORK COMFORTABLY WITH THEIR ROLE.
THAT'S ALSO WHY YOU NEED TO CREATE A CHARACTER.
E-EVEN THIS OUTFIT WAS INFLUENCED BY STUDENT REQUESTS!
IT WAS...?
I JUST PUT UP WITH IT!!
THIS ISN'T MY STYLE AT ALL, OKAY?!
RIGHT. I'M SORRY...
THERE WAS A SPECIAL OUTFIT FOR ME, TOO, BUT THE SCHOOL BANNED IT.
IT HAD SPIKES ON ONE SHOULDER PAD...
DID YOU WANT TO WEAR THAT?
ゴゴゴゴゴゴゴ...
GRRR RRR...
BAD
NO. I FELT LIKE I'D DODGED A BULLET.

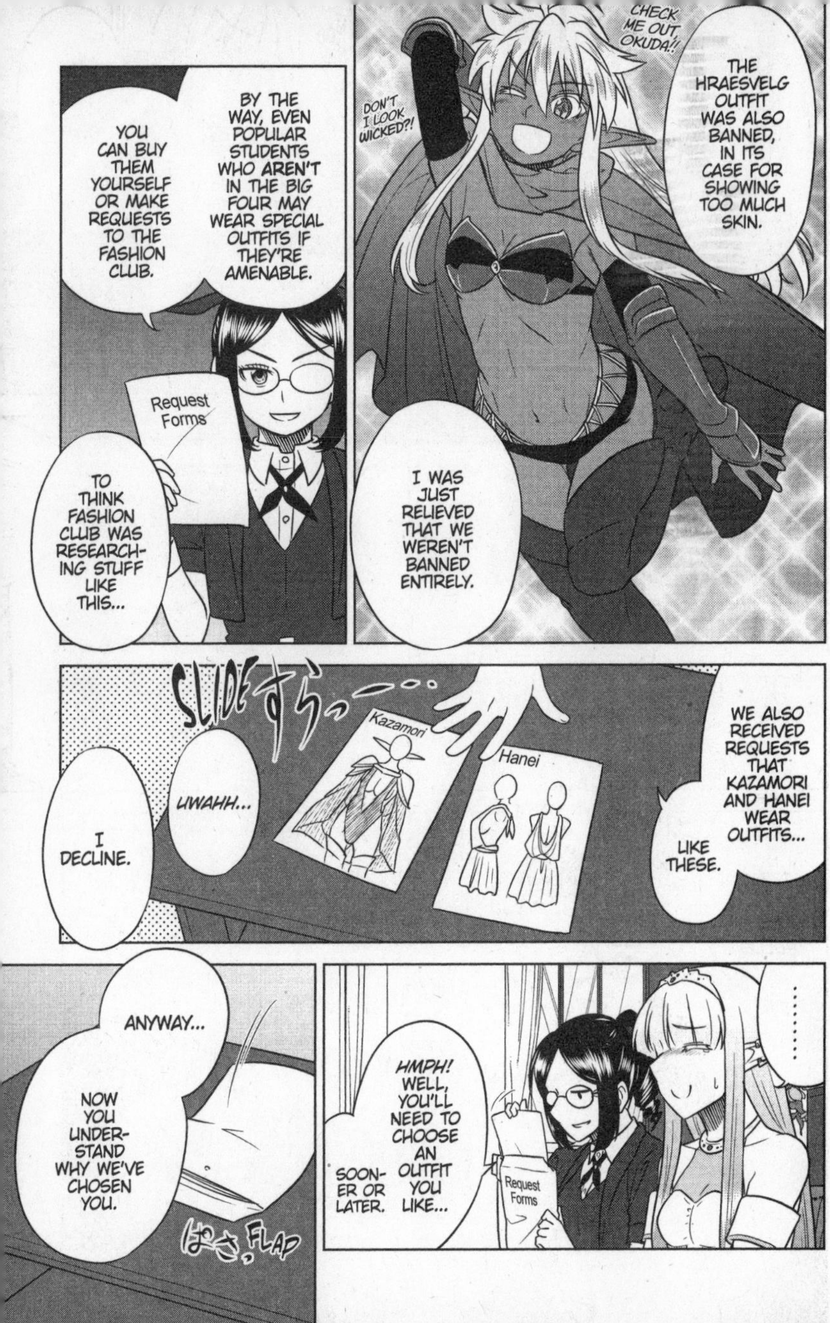
CHECK ME OUT, OKUDA!!
THE HRAESVELG OUTFIT WAS ALSO BANNED, IN ITS CASE FOR SHOWING TOO MUCH SKIN.
DON'T I LOOK WICKED?!
I WAS JUST RELIEVED THAT WE WEREN'T BANNED ENTIRELY.
BY THE WAY, EVEN POPULAR STUDENTS WHO AREN'T IN THE BIG FOUR MAY WEAR SPECIAL OUTFITS IF THEY'RE AMENABLE.
YOU CAN BUY THEM YOURSELF OR MAKE REQUESTS TO THE FASHION CLUB.
Request Forms
TO THINK FASHION CLUB WAS RESEARCHING STUFF LIKE THIS...
WE ALSO RECEIVED REQUESTS THAT KAZAMORI AND HANEI WEAR OUTFITS...
LIKE THESE.
SLIDE すらぁー
Kazamori
Hanei
UWAHH...
I DECLINE.
......
HMPH! WELL, YOU'LL NEED TO CHOOSE AN OUTFIT YOU LIKE...
SOONER OR LATER.
Request Forms
ANYWAY...
NOW YOU UNDERSTAND WHY WE'VE CHOSEN YOU.
ぱさ FLAP

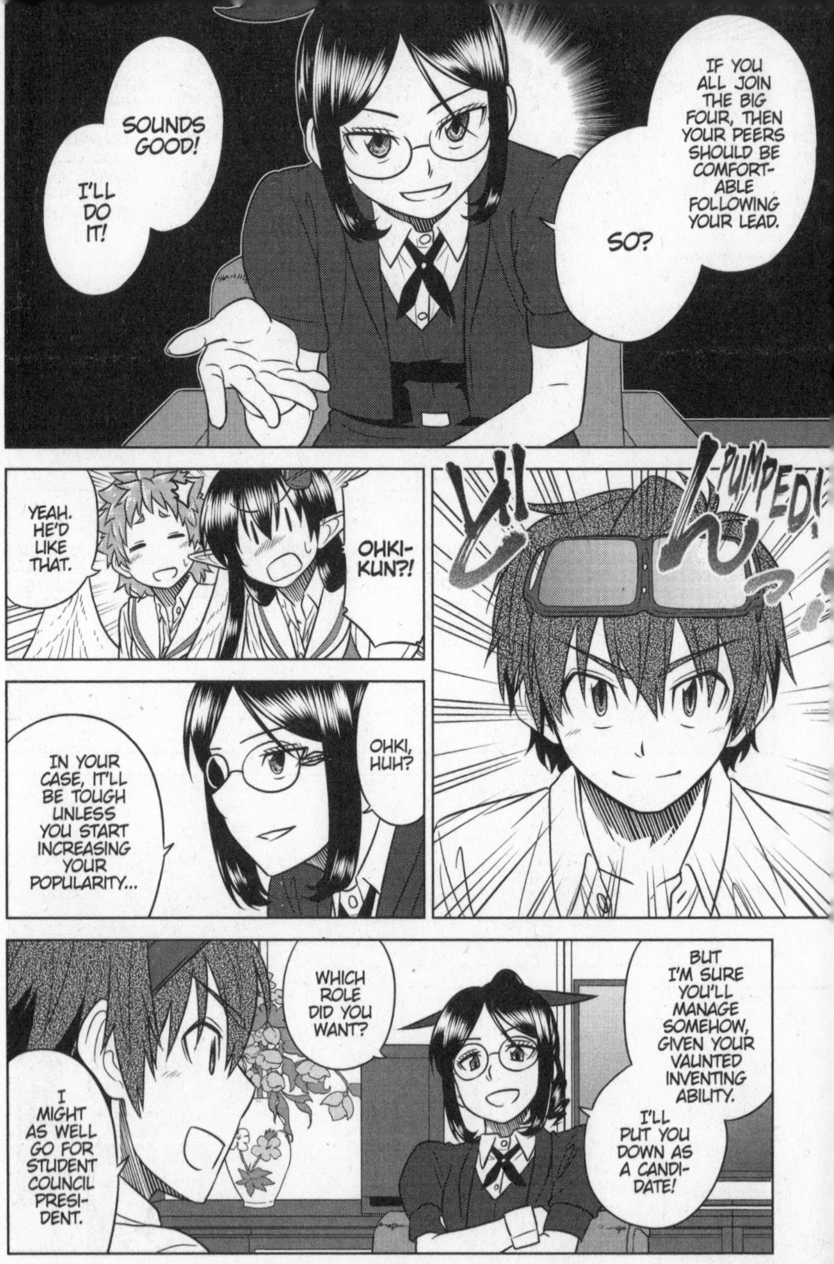
IF YOU ALL JOIN THE BIG FOUR, THEN YOUR PEERS SHOULD BE COMFORTABLE FOLLOWING YOUR LEAD.
SO?
SOUNDS GOOD!
I'LL DO IT!
PUMPED!
OHKI-KUN?!
YEAH. HE'D LIKE THAT.
OHKI, HUH?
IN YOUR CASE, IT'LL BE TOUGH UNLESS YOU START INCREASING YOUR POPULARITY...
BUT I'M SURE YOU'LL MANAGE SOMEHOW, GIVEN YOUR VAUNTED INVENTING ABILITY.
I'LL PUT YOU DOWN AS A CANDIDATE!
WHICH ROLE DID YOU WANT?
I MIGHT AS WELL GO FOR STUDENT COUNCIL PRESIDENT.

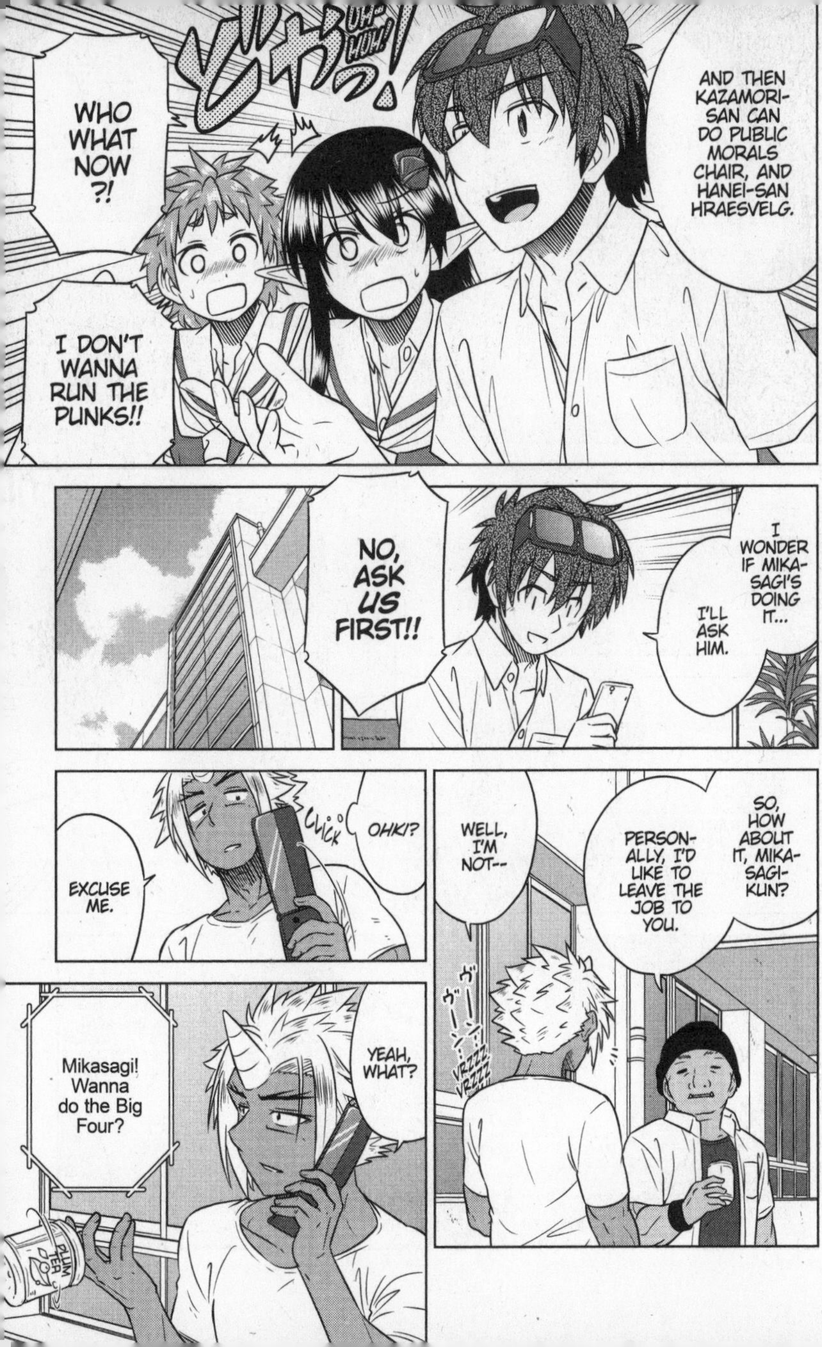
AND THEN KAZAMORI-SAN CAN DO PUBLIC MORALS CHAIR, AND HANEI-SAN HRAESVELG.
UH-WOH!
WHO WHAT NOW?!
I DON'T WANNA RUN THE PUNKS!!
I WONDER IF MIKASAGI'S DOING IT...
I'LL ASK HIM.
NO, ASK US FIRST!!
SO, HOW ABOUT IT, MIKA-SAGI-KUN?
PERSON-ALLY, I'D LIKE TO LEAVE THE JOB TO YOU.
WELL, I'M NOT--
VRZZZ VRZZZ
OHKI?
CLICK
EXCUSE ME.
YEAH, WHAT?
Mikasagi! Wanna do the Big Four?
PLUM TEA

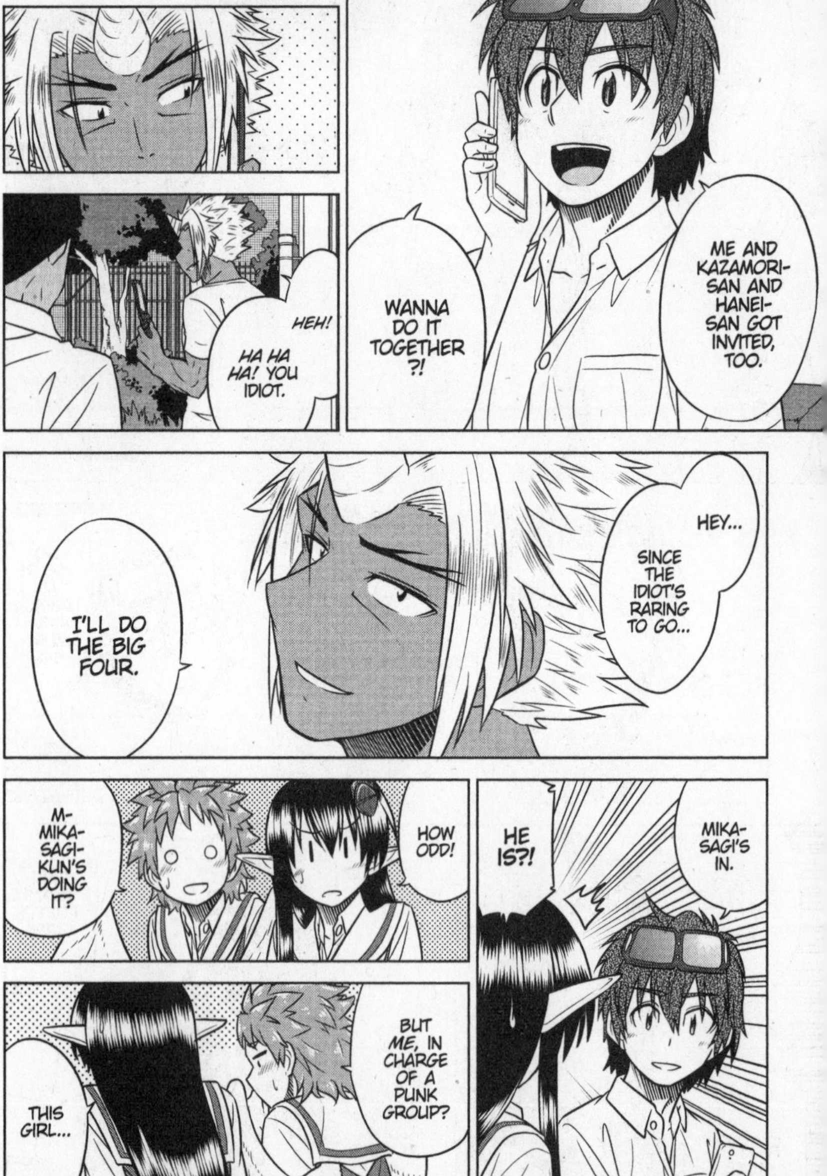
ME AND KAZAMORI-SAN AND HANEI-SAN GOT INVITED, TOO.
WANNA DO IT TOGETHER?!
HEH!
HA HA HA! YOU IDIOT.
HEY...
SINCE THE IDIOT'S RARING TO GO...
I'LL DO THE BIG FOUR.
MIKA-SAGI'S IN.
HE IS?!
HOW ODD!
M-MIKA-SAGI-KUN'S DOING IT?
BUT ME, IN CHARGE OF A PUNK GROUP?
THIS GIRL...

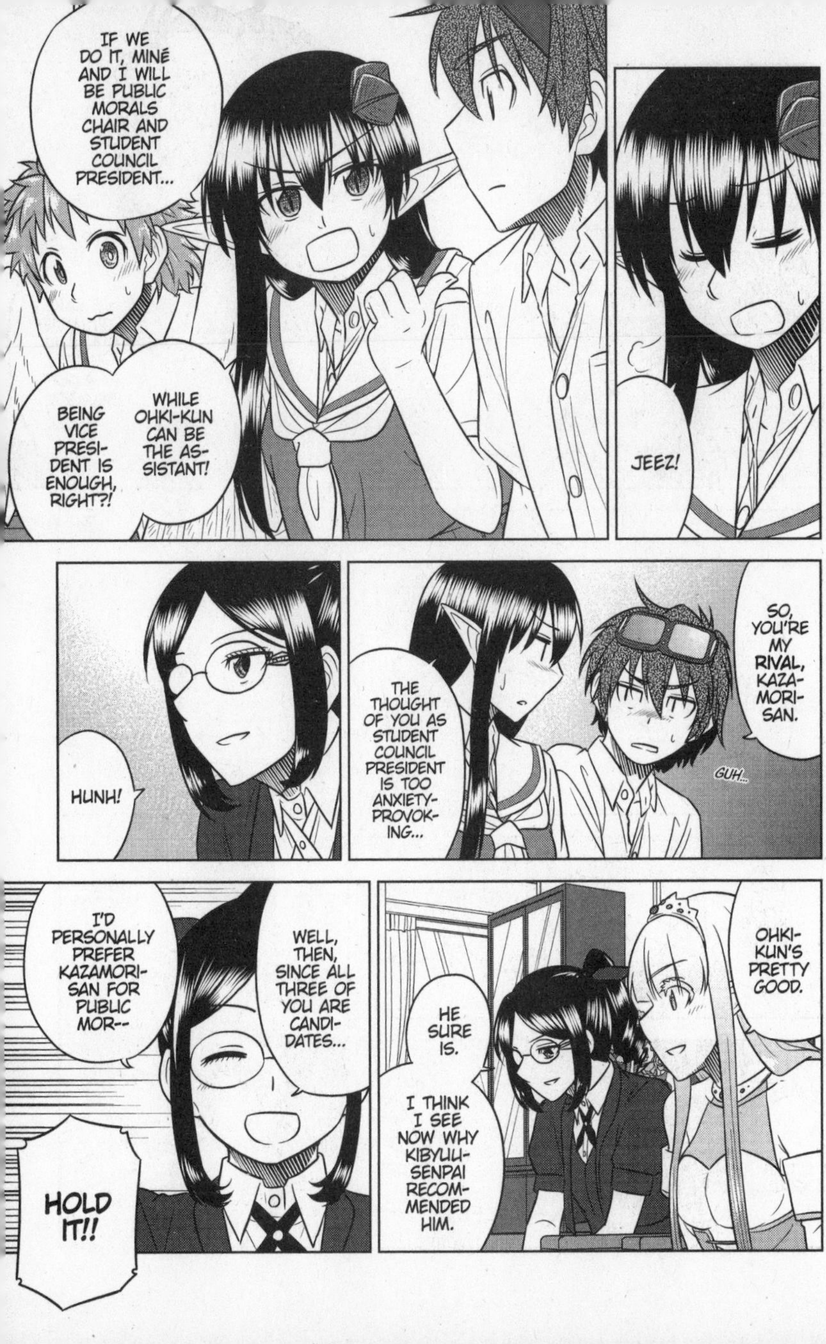
JEEZ!
IF WE DO IT, MINÉ AND I WILL BE PUBLIC MORALS CHAIR AND STUDENT COUNCIL PRESIDENT...
WHILE OHKI-KUN CAN BE THE AS-SISTANT!
BEING VICE PRESI-DENT IS ENOUGH, RIGHT?!
SO, YOU'RE MY RIVAL, KAZA-MORI-SAN.
GUH...
THE THOUGHT OF YOU AS STUDENT COUNCIL PRESIDENT IS TOO ANXIETY-PROVOK-ING...
HUNH!
OHKI-KUN'S PRETTY GOOD.
HE SURE IS.
I THINK I SEE NOW WHY KIBYUU-SENPAI RECOM-MENDED HIM.
WELL, THEN, SINCE ALL THREE OF YOU ARE CANDI-DATES...
I'D PERSONALLY PREFER KAZAMORI-SAN FOR PUBLIC MOR--
HOLD IT!!

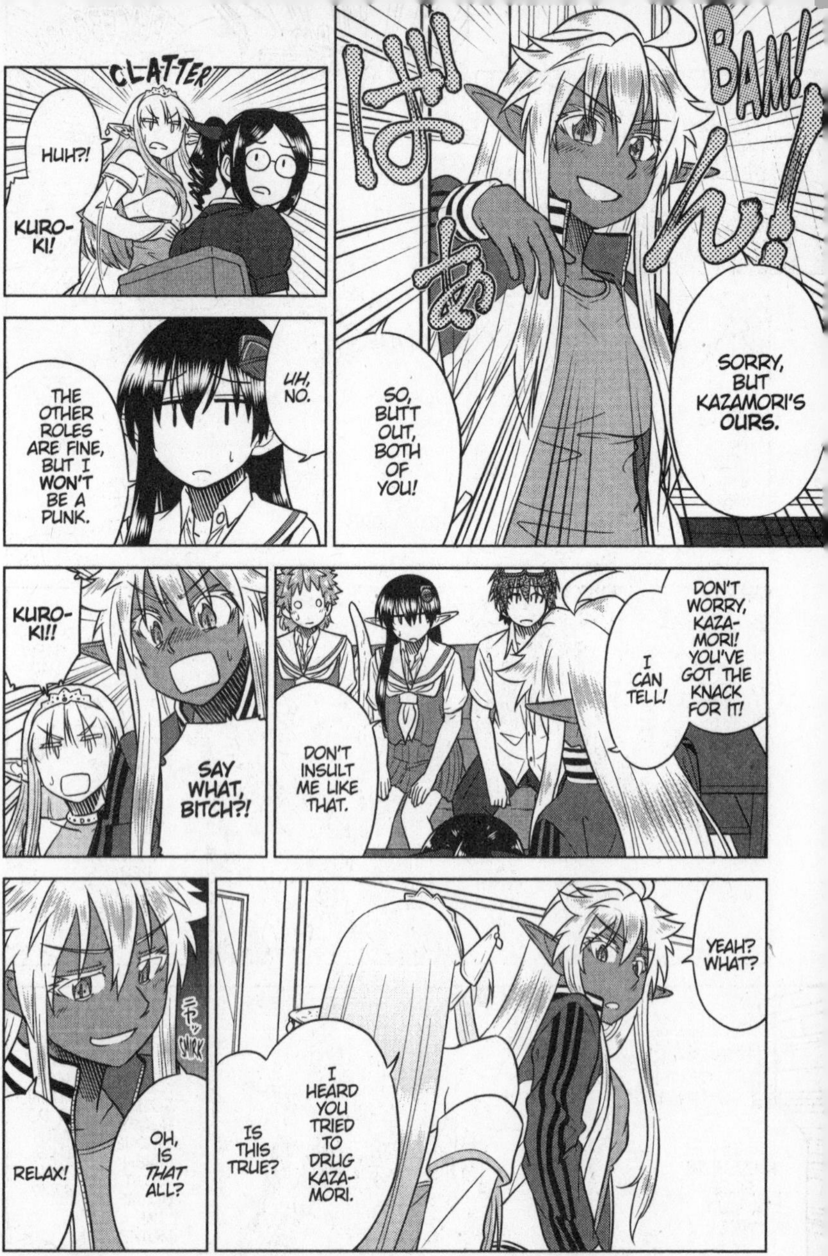
BAM!
ばぁん!
SORRY, BUT KAZAMORI'S OURS.
SO, BUTT OUT, BOTH OF YOU!
CLATTER
HUH?!
KURO-KI!
UH, NO.
THE OTHER ROLES ARE FINE, BUT I WON'T BE A PUNK.
DON'T WORRY, KAZA-MORI! YOU'VE GOT THE KNACK FOR IT!
I CAN TELL!
DON'T INSULT ME LIKE THAT.
KURO-KI!!
SAY WHAT, BITCH?!
YEAH? WHAT?
I HEARD YOU TRIED TO DRUG KAZA-MORI.
IS THIS TRUE?
OH, IS *THAT* ALL?
SMIRK
RELAX!

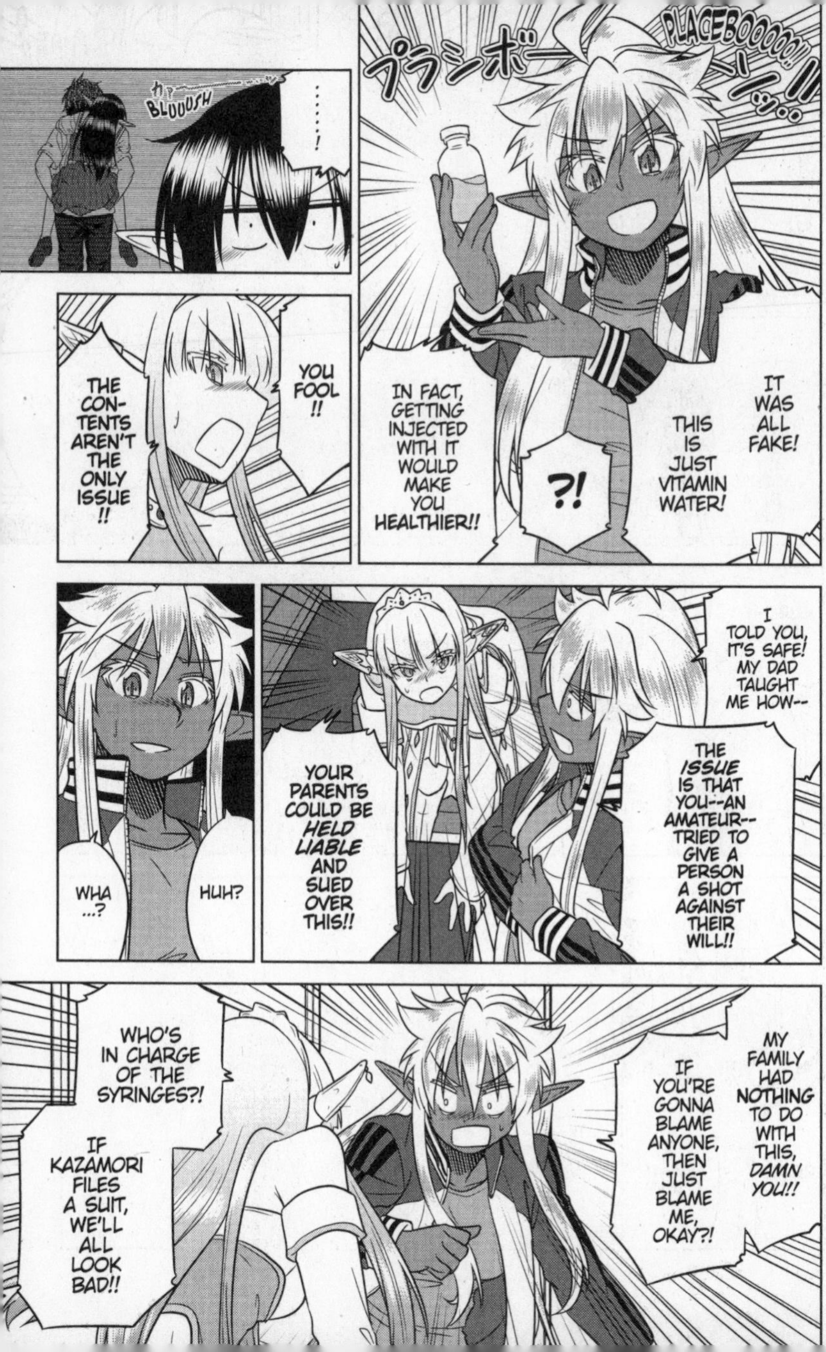
プラシボー
PLACEBOOOOO!!
IT WAS ALL FAKE!
THIS IS JUST VITAMIN WATER!
?!
IN FACT, GETTING INJECTED WITH IT WOULD MAKE YOU HEALTHIER!!
BLUUUSH
......!
YOU FOOL!!
THE CONTENTS AREN'T THE ONLY ISSUE!!
I TOLD YOU, IT'S SAFE! MY DAD TAUGHT ME HOW--
THE *ISSUE* IS THAT YOU--AN AMATEUR--TRIED TO GIVE A PERSON A SHOT AGAINST THEIR WILL!!
YOUR PARENTS COULD BE *HELD LIABLE* AND SUED OVER THIS!!
HUH?
WHA ...?
MY FAMILY HAD NOTHING TO DO WITH THIS, *DAMN YOU!!*
IF YOU'RE GONNA BLAME ANYONE, THEN JUST BLAME ME, OKAY?!
WHO'S IN CHARGE OF THE SYRINGES?!
IF KAZAMORI FILES A SUIT, WE'LL ALL LOOK BAD!!

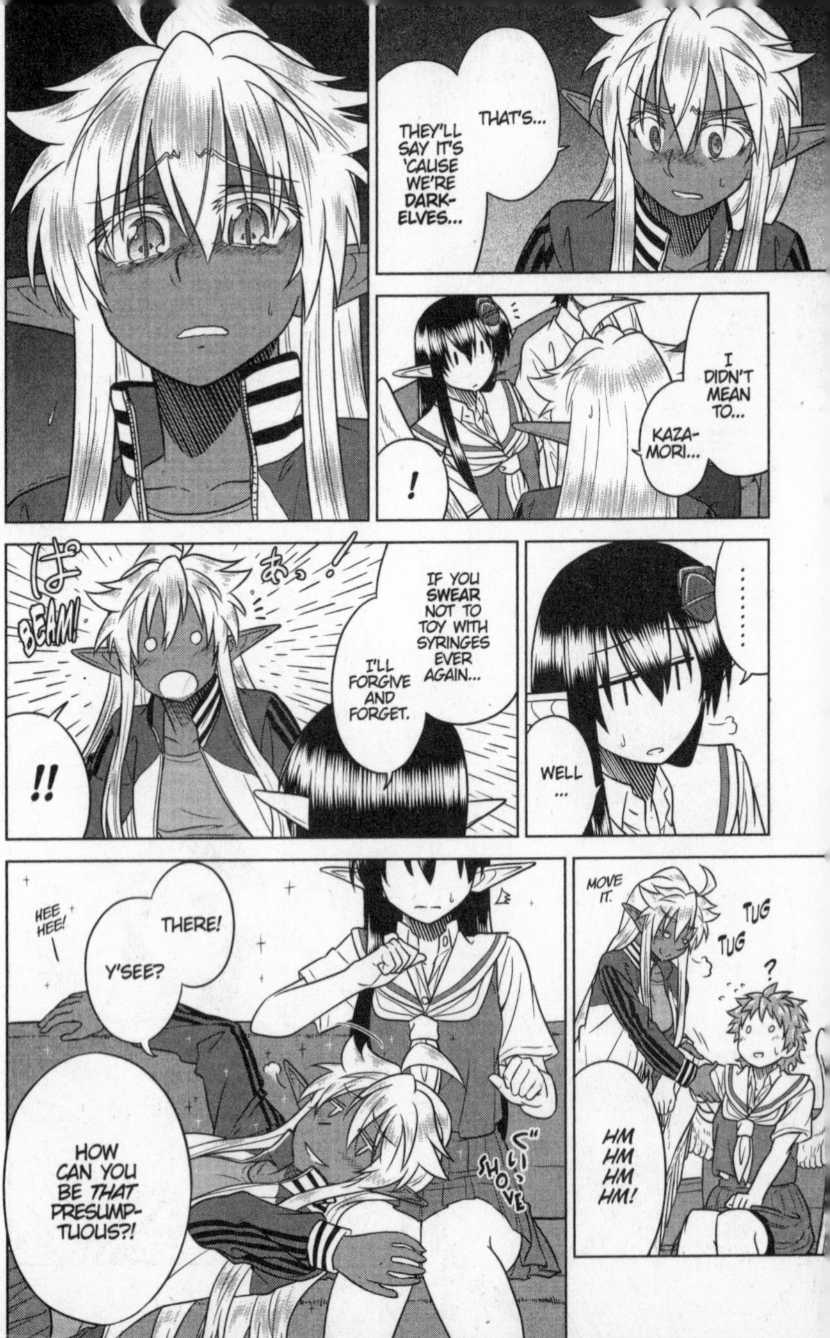

THAT'S...
THEY'LL SAY IT'S 'CAUSE WE'RE DARK-ELVES...
I DIDN'T MEAN TO...
KAZAMORI...
!
......
WELL ...
IF YOU SWEAR NOT TO TOY WITH SYRINGES EVER AGAIN...
I'LL FORGIVE AND FORGET.
あっ!
ぱ
BEAM!
!!
MOVE IT.
TUG
TUG
?
HM HM HM HM!
THERE!
Y'SEE?
HEE HEE!
HOW CAN YOU BE THAT PRESUMPTUOUS?!
ぐいっ
SHOVE

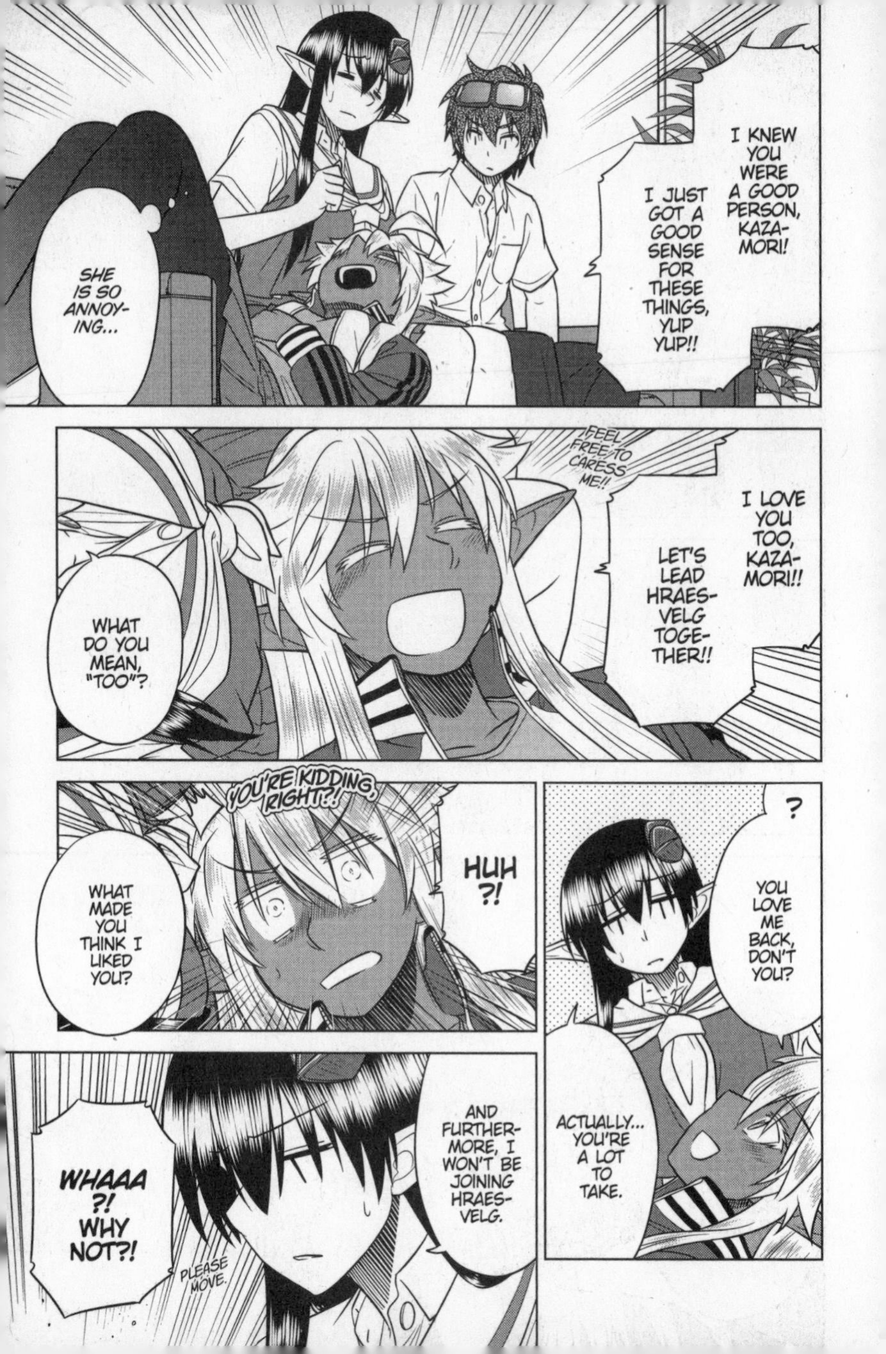
I KNEW YOU WERE A GOOD PERSON, KAZAMORI!
I JUST GOT A GOOD SENSE FOR THESE THINGS, YUP YUP!!
SHE IS SO ANNOYING...
I LOVE YOU TOO, KAZAMORI!!
LET'S LEAD HRAESVELG TOGETHER!!
FEEL FREE TO CARESS ME!!
WHAT DO YOU MEAN, "TOO"?
?
YOU LOVE ME BACK, DON'T YOU?
ACTUALLY... YOU'RE A LOT TO TAKE.
HUH ?!
YOU'RE KIDDING, RIGHT?!
WHAT MADE YOU THINK I LIKED YOU?
AND FURTHERMORE, I WON'T BE JOINING HRAESVELG.
WHAAA ?! WHY NOT?!
PLEASE MOVE.

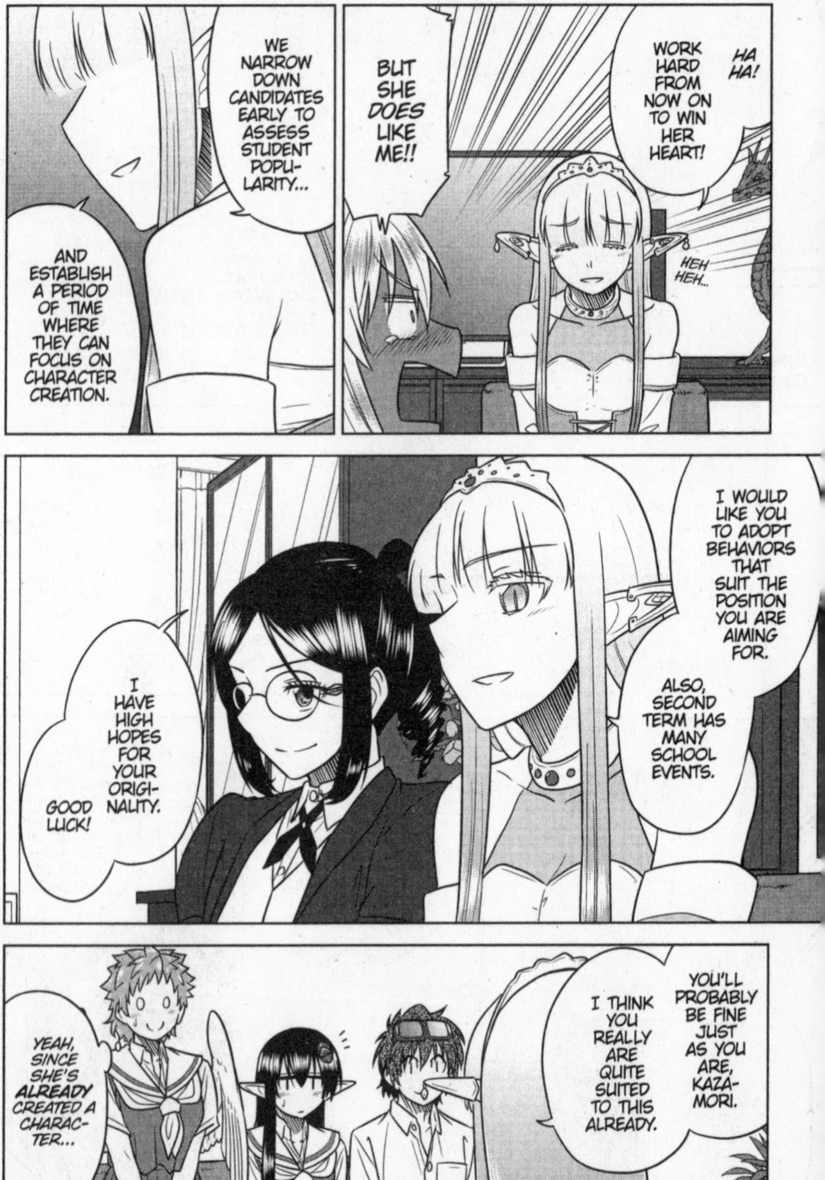
WORK HARD FROM NOW ON TO WIN HER HEART!
HA HA!
HEH HEH...
BUT SHE *DOES* LIKE ME!!
WE NARROW DOWN CANDIDATES EARLY TO ASSESS STUDENT POPULARITY...
AND ESTABLISH A PERIOD OF TIME WHERE THEY CAN FOCUS ON CHARACTER CREATION.
I WOULD LIKE YOU TO ADOPT BEHAVIORS THAT SUIT THE POSITION YOU ARE AIMING FOR.
ALSO, SECOND TERM HAS MANY SCHOOL EVENTS.
I HAVE HIGH HOPES FOR YOUR ORIGINALITY.
GOOD LUCK!
YOU'LL PROBABLY BE FINE JUST AS YOU ARE, KAZAMORI.
I THINK YOU REALLY ARE QUITE SUITED TO THIS ALREADY.
YEAH, SINCE SHE'S **ALREADY** CREATED A CHARACTER...

Chapter 38 • END

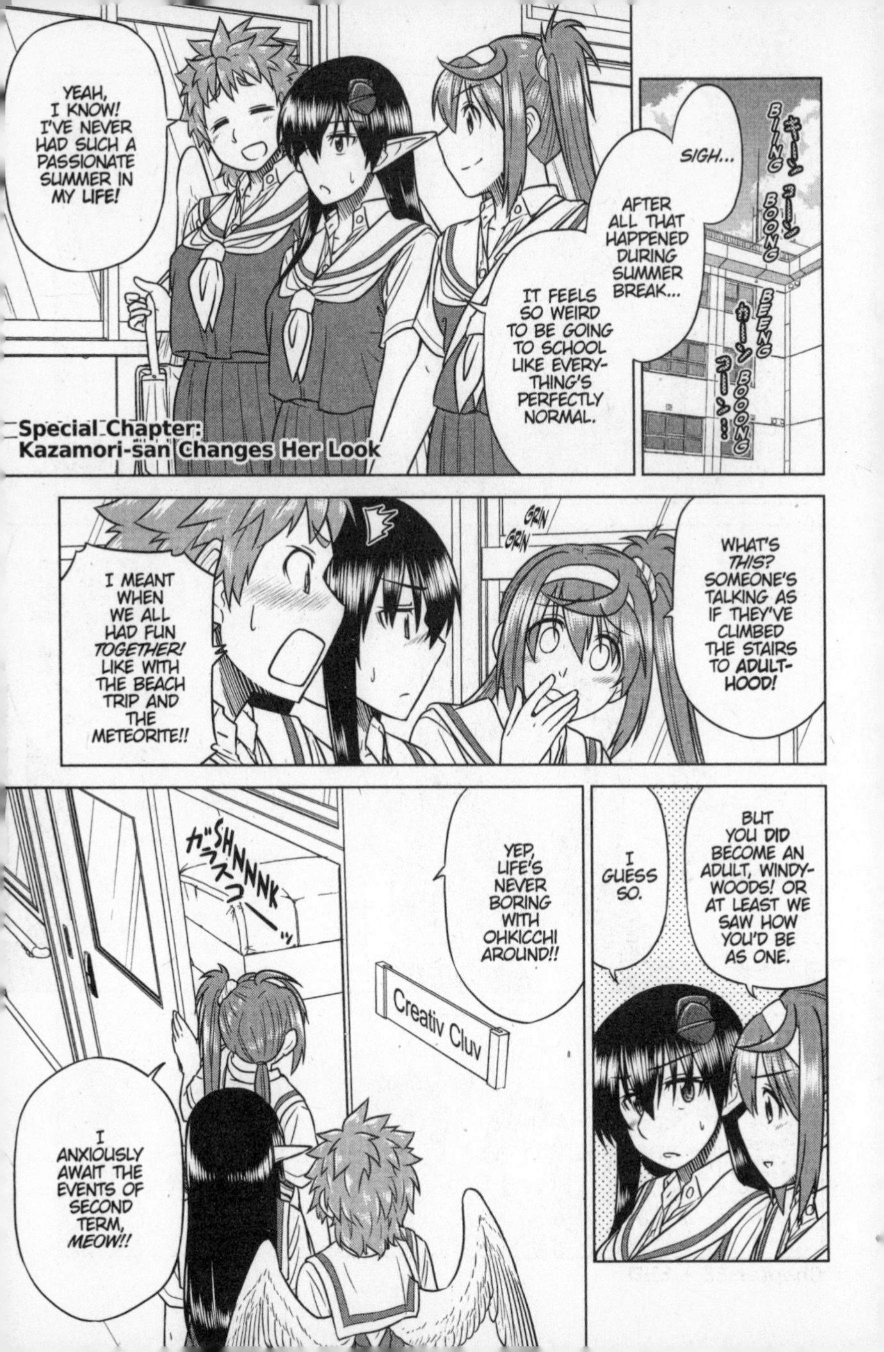
BIING BOONG
BEENG BOOONG...
SIGH...
AFTER ALL THAT HAPPENED DURING SUMMER BREAK...
IT FEELS SO WEIRD TO BE GOING TO SCHOOL LIKE EVERYTHING'S PERFECTLY NORMAL.
YEAH, I KNOW! I'VE NEVER HAD SUCH A PASSIONATE SUMMER IN MY LIFE!
Special Chapter: Kazamori-san Changes Her Look
GRIN GRIN
WHAT'S THIS? SOMEONE'S TALKING AS IF THEY'VE CLIMBED THE STAIRS TO ADULTHOOD!
I MEANT WHEN WE ALL HAD FUN TOGETHER! LIKE WITH THE BEACH TRIP AND THE METEORITE!!
BUT YOU DID BECOME AN ADULT, WINDYWOODS! OR AT LEAST WE SAW HOW YOU'D BE AS ONE.
I GUESS SO.
YEP, LIFE'S NEVER BORING WITH OHKICCHI AROUND!!
SHNNNNK
Creativ Cluv
I ANXIOUSLY AWAIT THE EVENTS OF SECOND TERM, MEOW!!

Special Chapter: Kazamori-san Changes Her Look

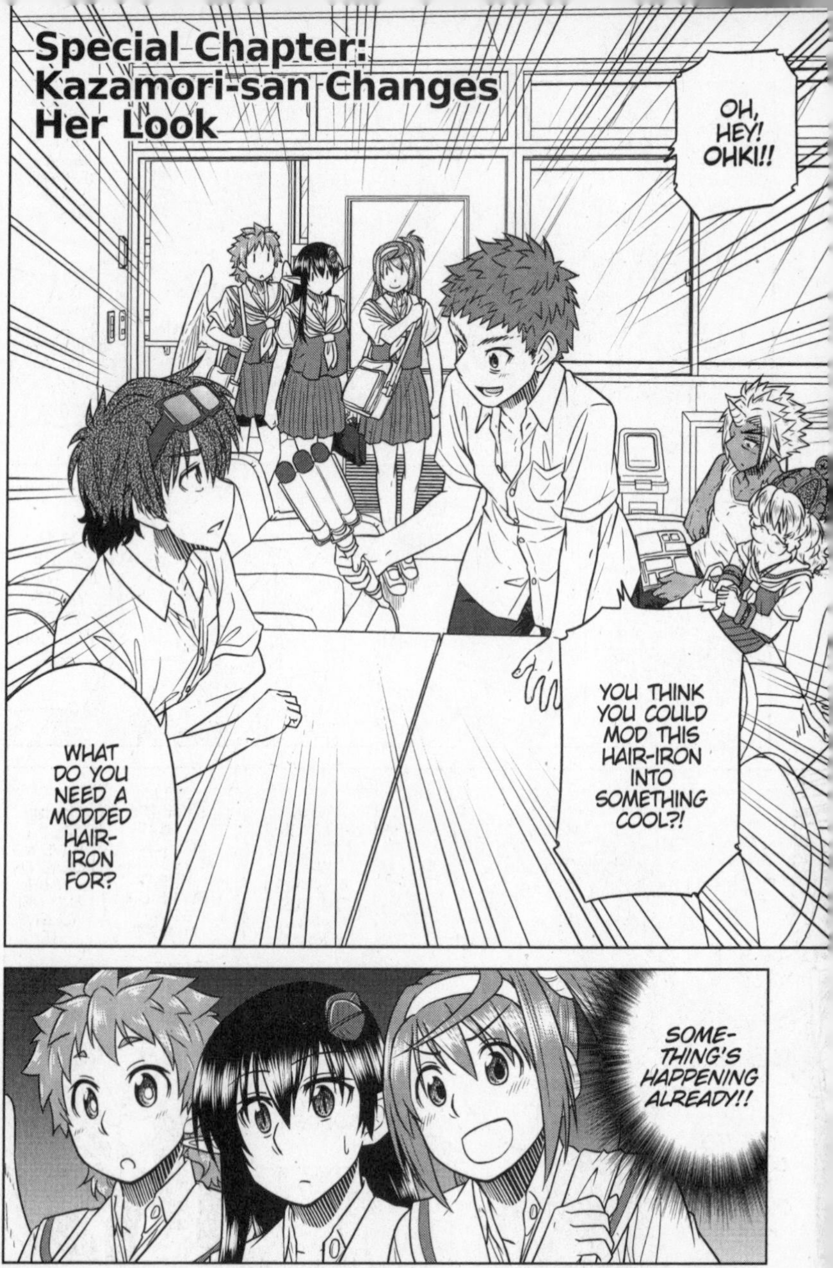
OH, HEY! OHKI!!
YOU THINK YOU COULD MOD THIS HAIR-IRON INTO SOMETHING COOL?!
WHAT DO YOU NEED A MODDED HAIR-IRON FOR?
SOME-THING'S HAPPENING ALREADY!!

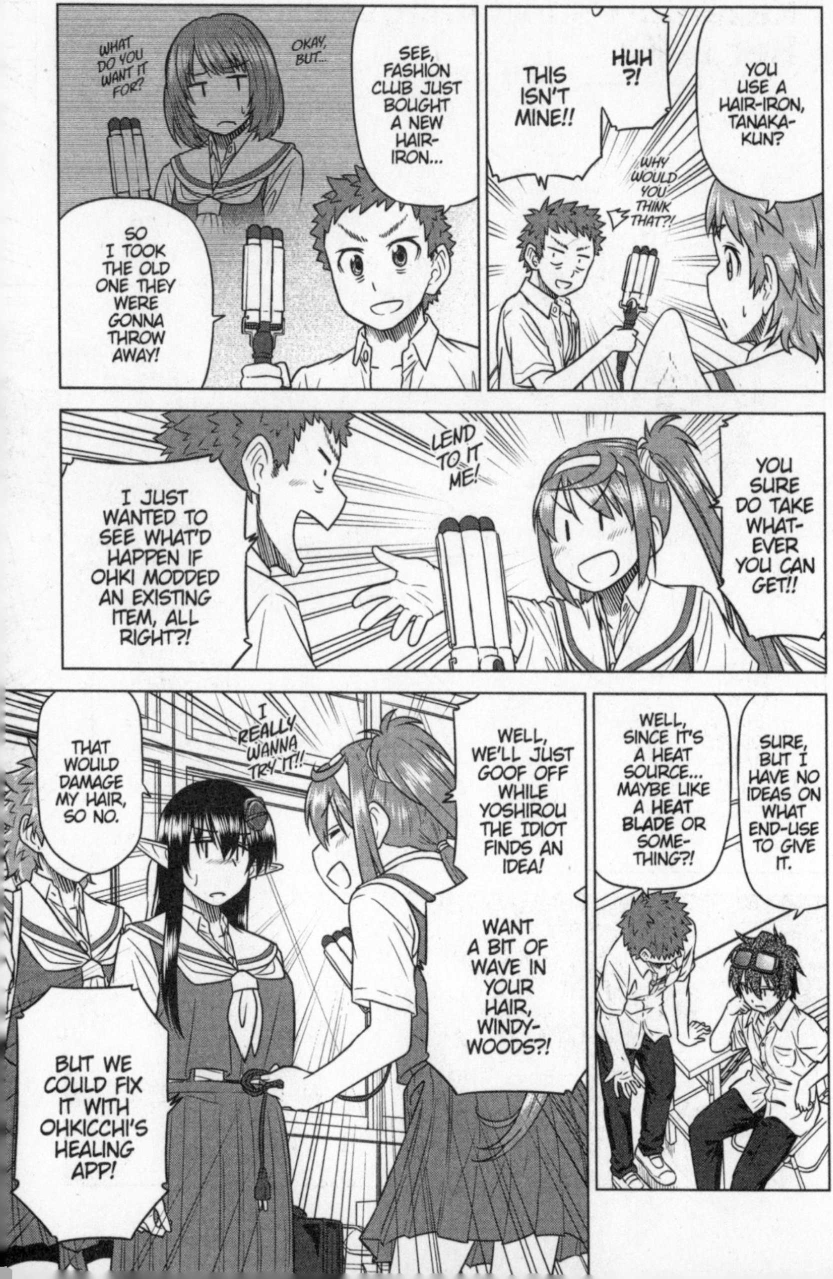

YOU USE A HAIR-IRON, TANAKA-KUN?
HUH ?!
THIS ISN'T MINE!!
WHY WOULD YOU THINK THAT?!
SEE, FASHION CLUB JUST BOUGHT A NEW HAIR-IRON...
OKAY, BUT...
WHAT DO YOU WANT IT FOR?
SO I TOOK THE OLD ONE THEY WERE GONNA THROW AWAY!
YOU SURE DO TAKE WHAT-EVER YOU CAN GET!!
LEND IT TO ME!
I JUST WANTED TO SEE WHAT'D HAPPEN IF OHKI MODDED AN EXISTING ITEM, ALL RIGHT?!
SURE, BUT I HAVE NO IDEAS ON WHAT END-USE TO GIVE IT.
WELL, SINCE IT'S A HEAT SOURCE... MAYBE LIKE A HEAT BLADE OR SOME-THING?!
WELL, WE'LL JUST GOOF OFF WHILE YOSHIROU THE IDIOT FINDS AN IDEA!
I REALLY WANNA TRY IT!!
WANT A BIT OF WAVE IN YOUR HAIR, WINDY-WOODS?!
THAT WOULD DAMAGE MY HAIR, SO NO.
BUT WE COULD FIX IT WITH OHKICCHI'S HEALING APP!

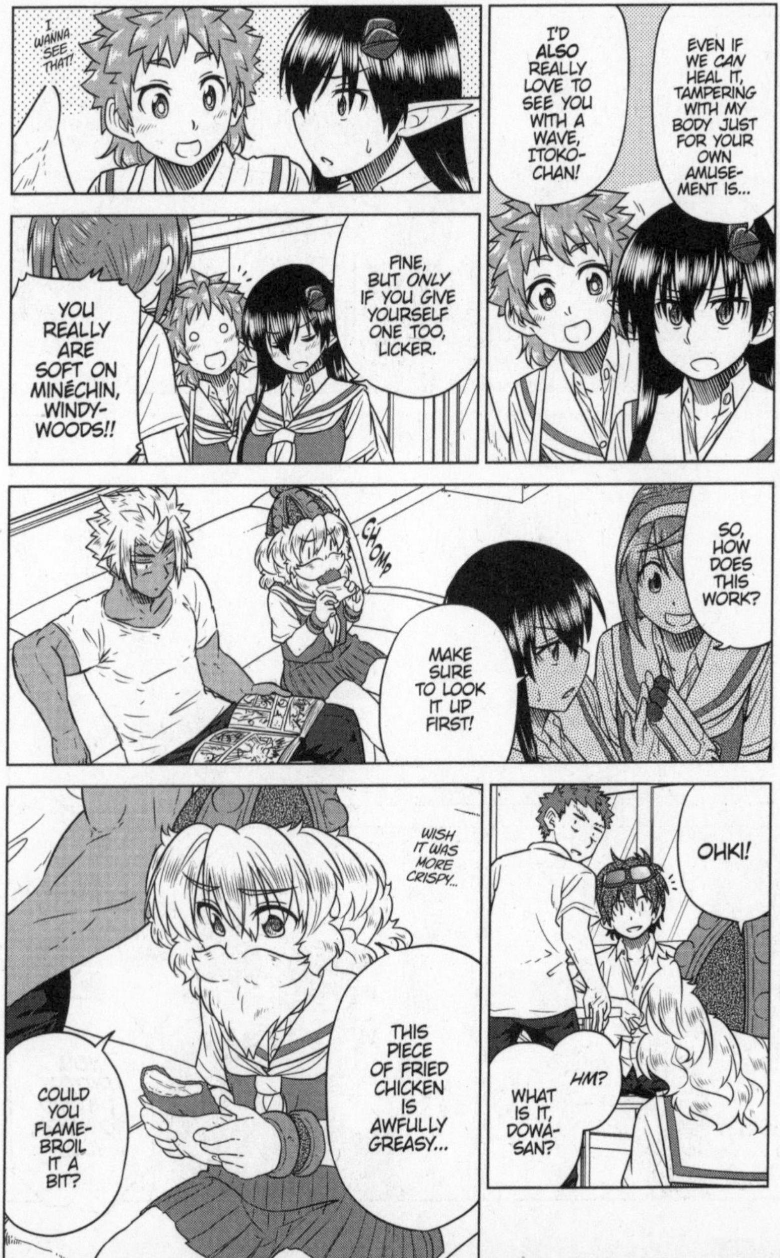
EVEN IF WE CAN HEAL IT, TAMPERING WITH MY BODY JUST FOR YOUR OWN AMUSEMENT IS...
I'D ALSO REALLY LOVE TO SEE YOU WITH A WAVE, ITOKO-CHAN!
I WANNA SEE THAT!
FINE, BUT ONLY IF YOU GIVE YOURSELF ONE TOO, LICKER.
YOU REALLY ARE SOFT ON MINÉCHIN, WINDY-WOODS!!
SO, HOW DOES THIS WORK?
MAKE SURE TO LOOK IT UP FIRST!
CHOMP
OHKI!
HM?
WHAT IS IT, DOWA-SAN?
WISH IT WAS MORE CRISPY...
THIS PIECE OF FRIED CHICKEN IS AWFULLY GREASY...
COULD YOU FLAME-BROIL IT A BIT?

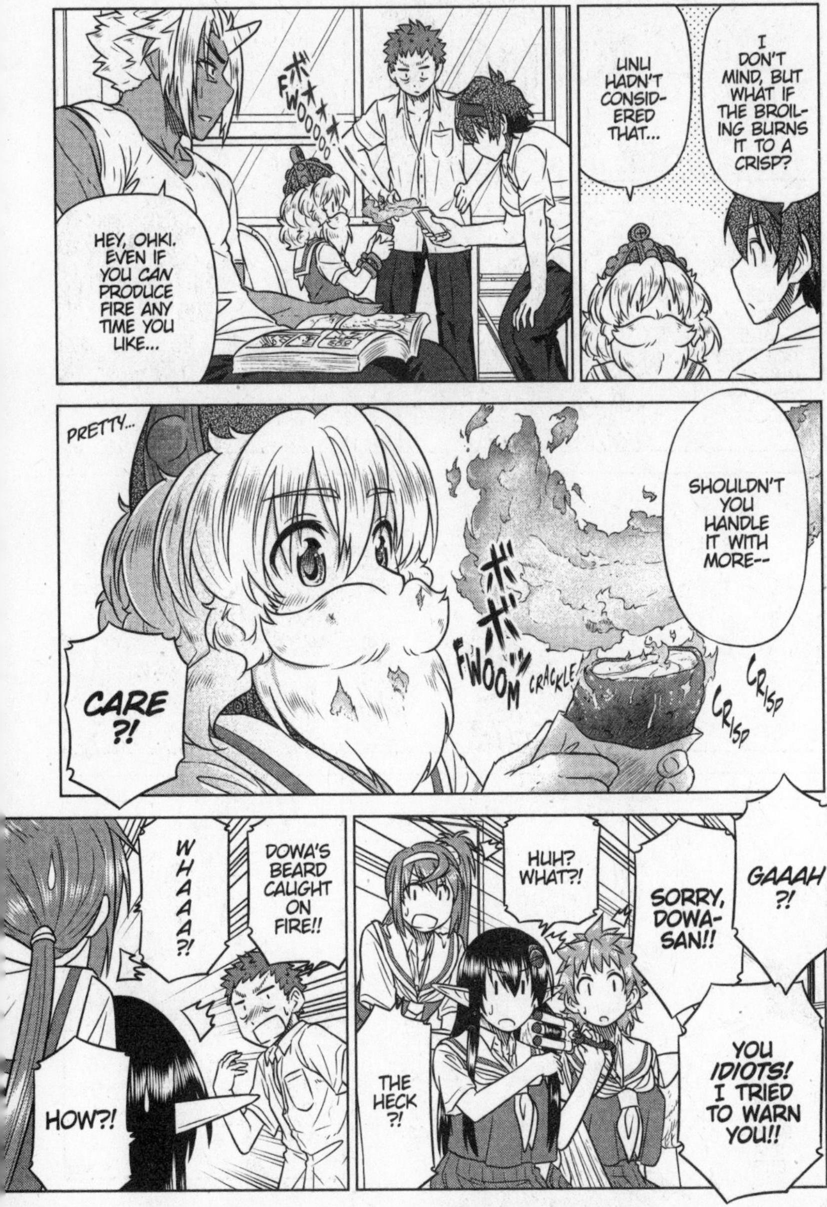

I DON'T MIND, BUT WHAT IF THE BROILING BURNS IT TO A CRISP?
UNU HADN'T CONSIDERED THAT...
FWOOOOOO
HEY, OHKI. EVEN IF YOU CAN PRODUCE FIRE ANY TIME YOU LIKE...
SHOULDN'T YOU HANDLE IT WITH MORE--
CRISP
CRISP
CRACKLE
FWOOM
PRETTY...
CARE?!
GAAAH?!
SORRY, DOWA-SAN!!
HUH? WHAT?!
YOU IDIOTS! I TRIED TO WARN YOU!!
THE HECK?!
DOWA'S BEARD CAUGHT ON FIRE!!
WHAAAA?!
HOW?!

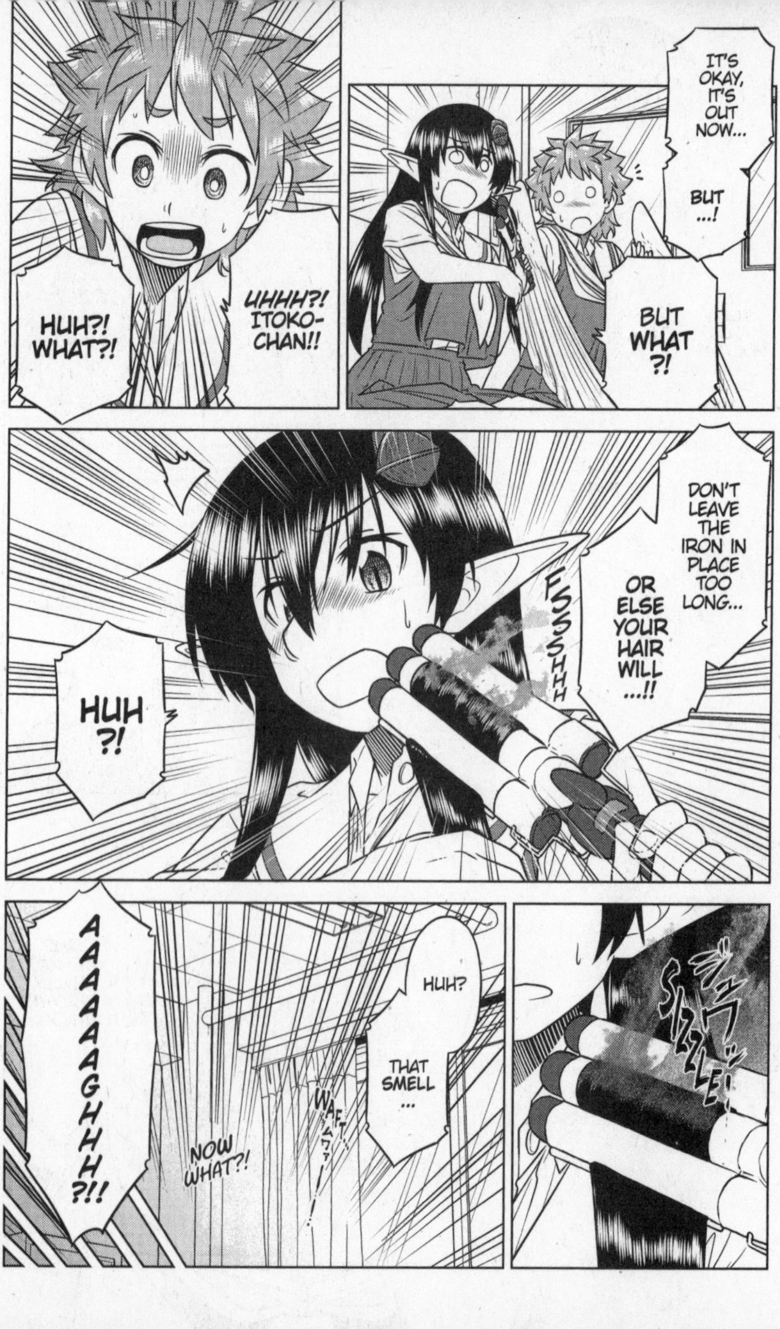
IT'S OKAY, IT'S OUT NOW...
BUT ...!
BUT WHAT ?!
UHHH?! ITOKO-CHAN!!
HUH?! WHAT?!
DON'T LEAVE THE IRON IN PLACE TOO LONG...
OR ELSE YOUR HAIR WILL ...!!
FSSSHHH
HUH ?!
SIZZLE!
HUH?
THAT SMELL ...
WAFT...
NOW WHAT?!
AAAAAAAGHHHH ?!!

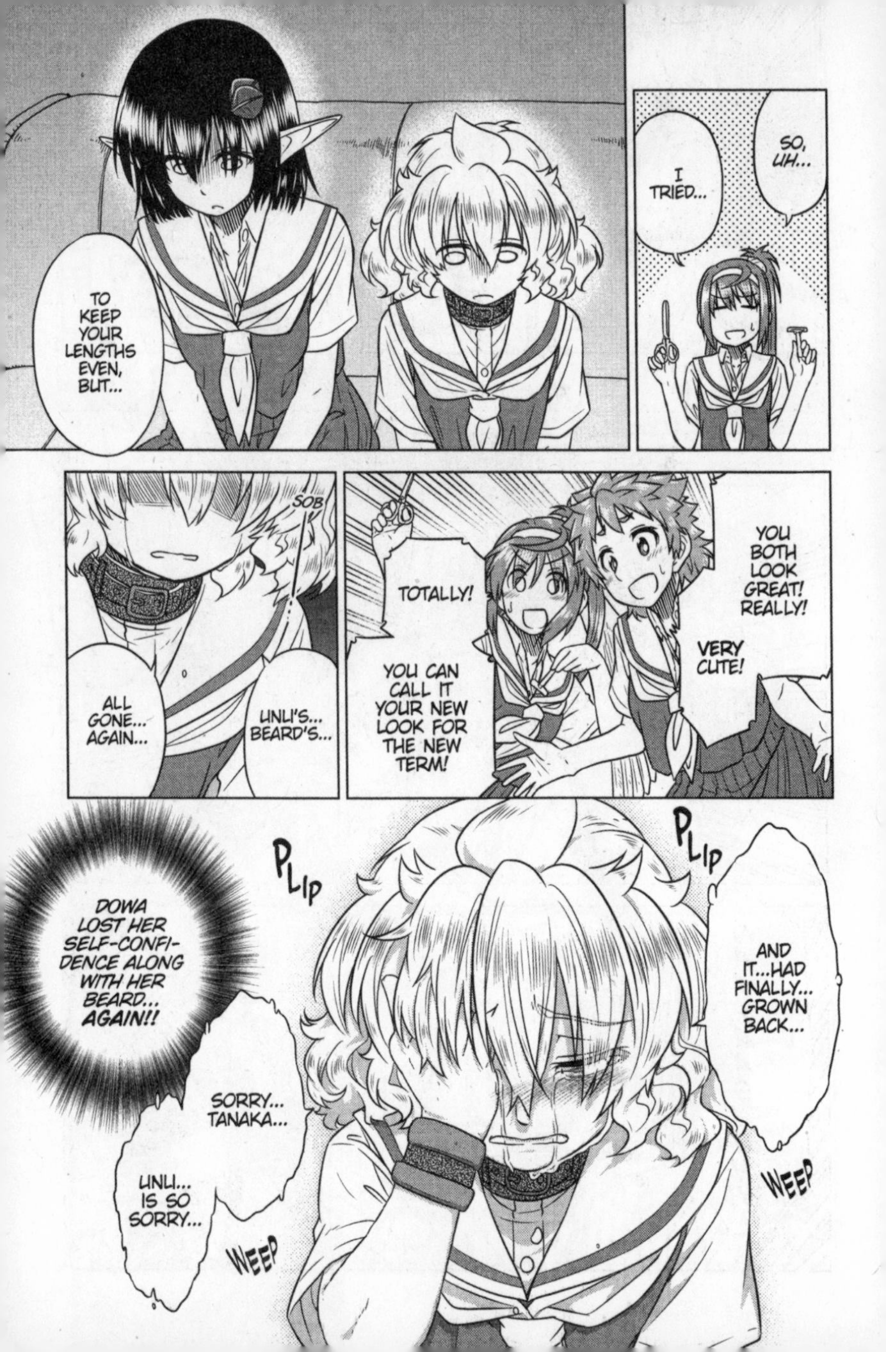
SO, UH...
I TRIED...
TO KEEP YOUR LENGTHS EVEN, BUT...
YOU BOTH LOOK GREAT! REALLY!
VERY CUTE!
TOTALLY!
YOU CAN CALL IT YOUR NEW LOOK FOR THE NEW TERM!
SOB
UNLI'S... BEARD'S...
ALL GONE... AGAIN...
PLIP
AND IT...HAD FINALLY... GROWN BACK...
PLIP
DOWA LOST HER SELF-CONFIDENCE ALONG WITH HER BEARD... AGAIN!!
WEEP
SORRY... TANAKA...
UNLI... IS SO SORRY...
WEEP

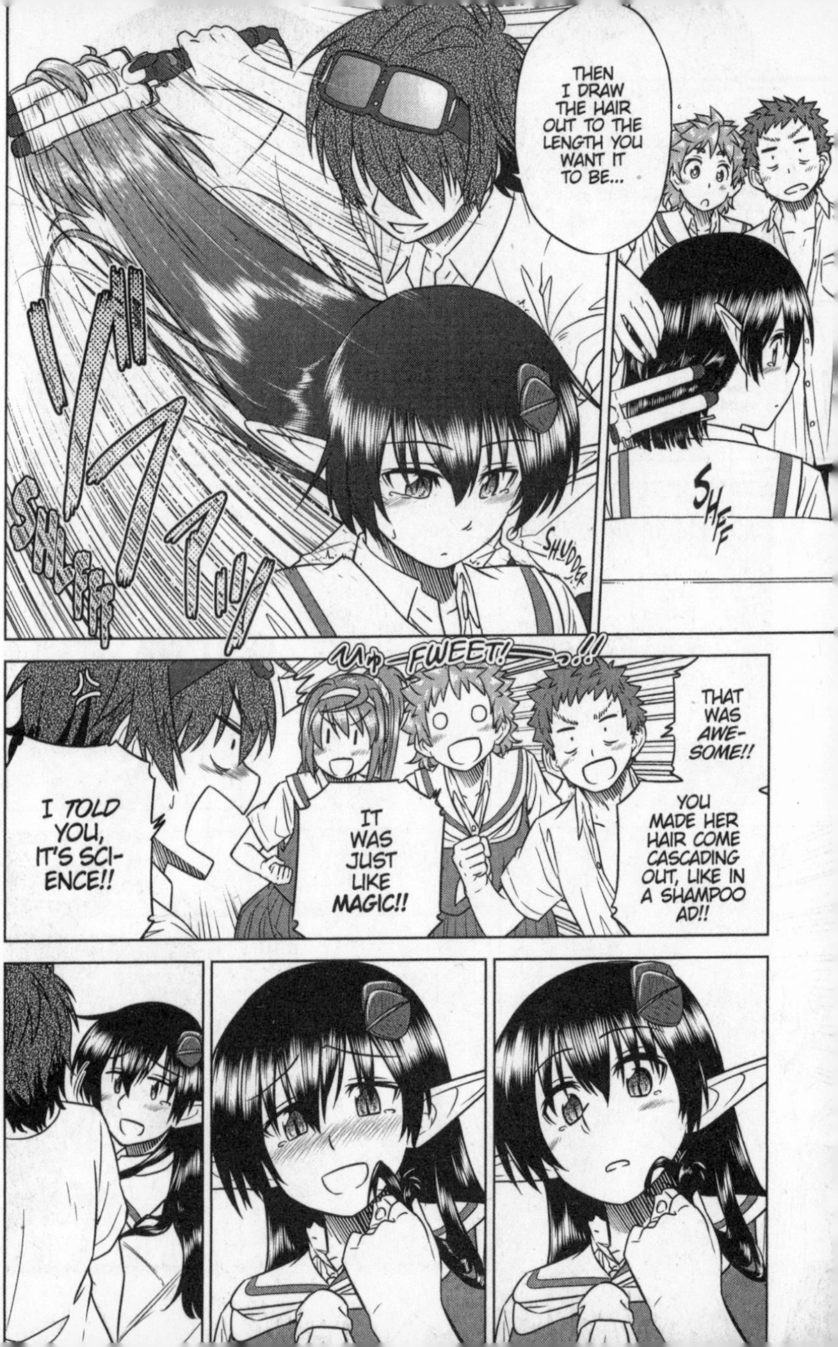
THEN I DRAW THE HAIR OUT TO THE LENGTH YOU WANT IT TO BE...
SHFF
SHUDDER
SHLFFF
FWEET!!
THAT WAS AWE-SOME!!
YOU MADE HER HAIR COME CASCADING OUT, LIKE IN A SHAMPOO AD!!
IT WAS JUST LIKE MAGIC!!
I TOLD YOU, IT'S SCI-ENCE!!

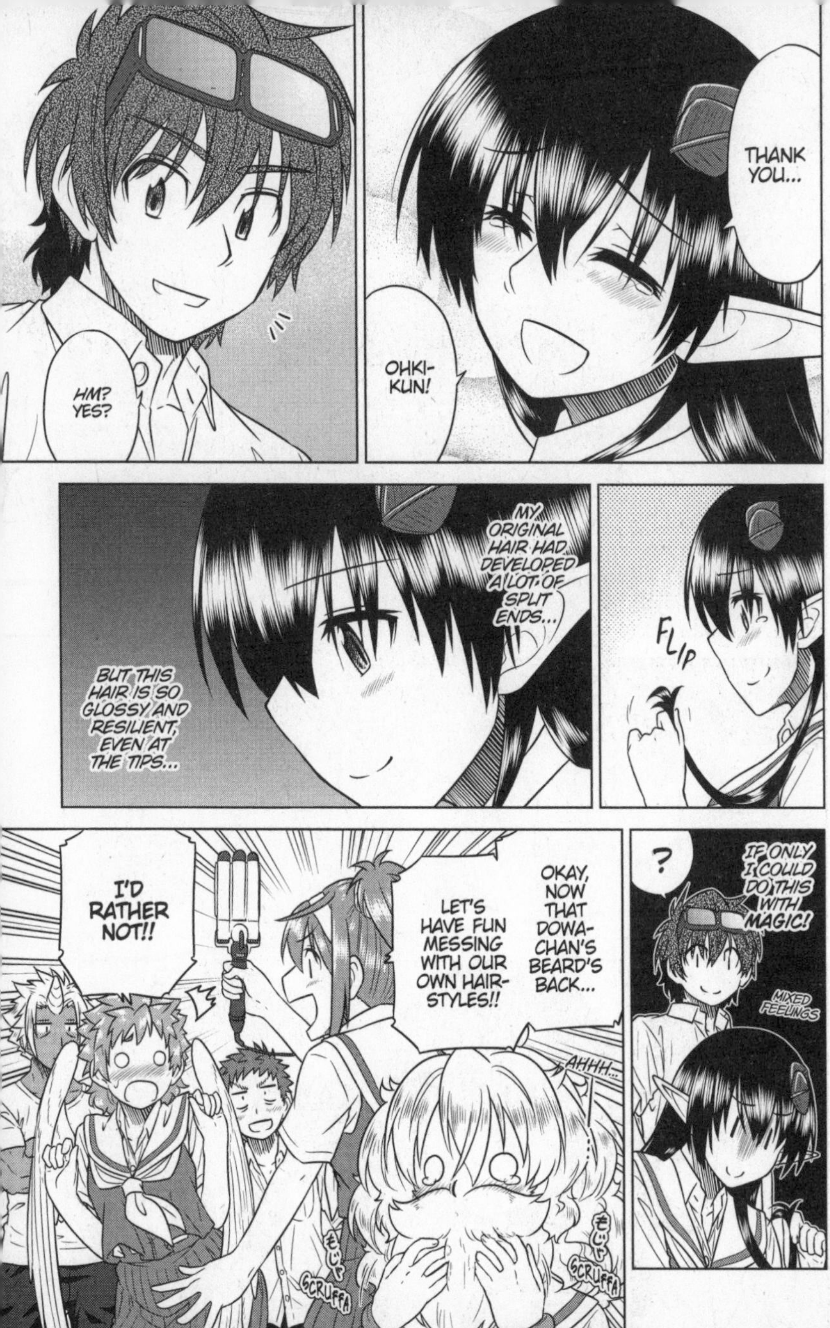
THANK YOU...
OHKI-KUN!
HM? YES?
FLIP
MY ORIGINAL HAIR HAD DEVELOPED A LOT OF SPLIT ENDS...
BUT THIS HAIR IS SO GLOSSY AND RESILIENT, EVEN AT THE TIPS...
?
IF ONLY I COULD DO THIS WITH MAGIC!
MIXED FEELINGS
OKAY, NOW THAT DOWA-CHAN'S BEARD'S BACK...
LET'S HAVE FUN MESSING WITH OUR OWN HAIR-STYLES!!
I'D RATHER NOT!!
AHHH...
もじゃ
SCRUFFA
もじゃ
SCRUFFA

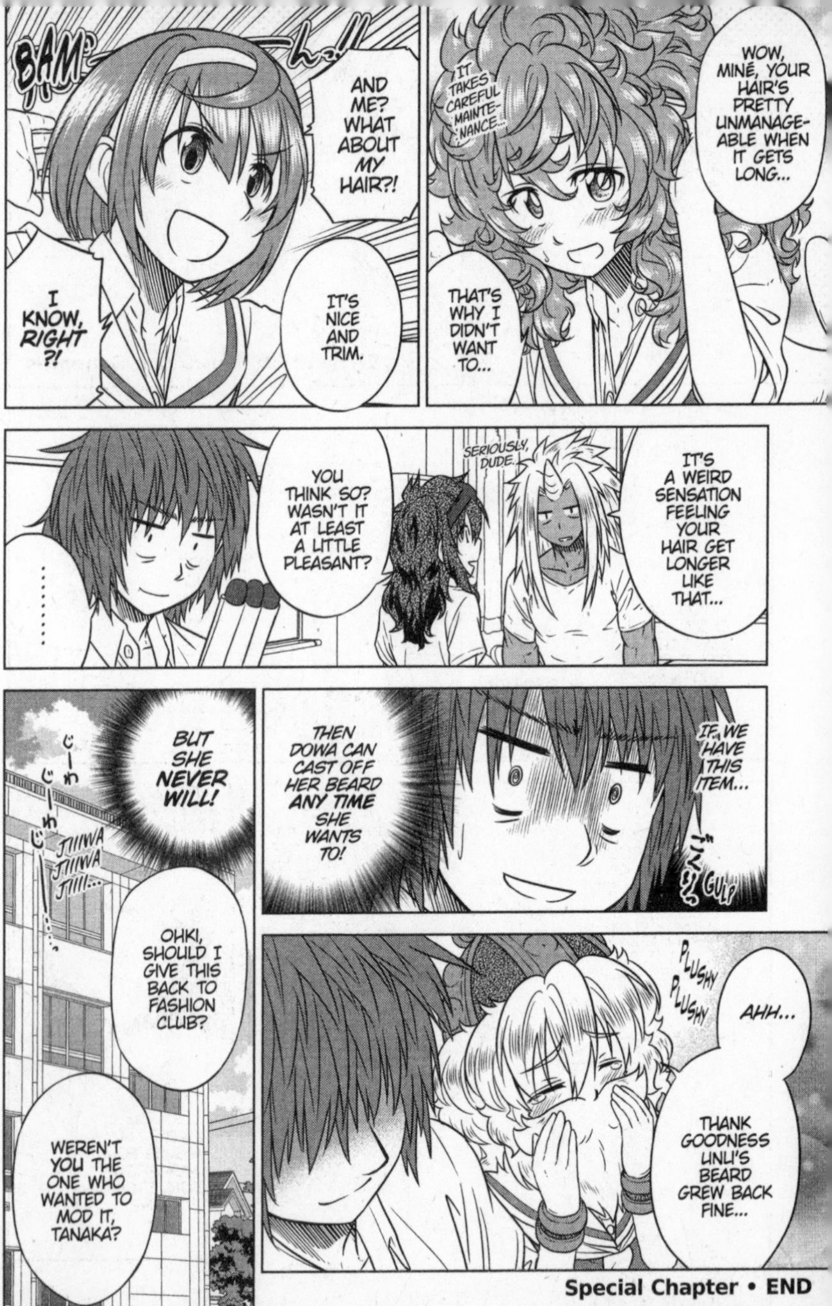
WOW, MINÉ, YOUR HAIR'S PRETTY UNMANAGEABLE WHEN IT GETS LONG...
IT TAKES CAREFUL MAINTENANCE...
THAT'S WHY I DIDN'T WANT TO...
BAM
AND ME? WHAT ABOUT MY HAIR?!
IT'S NICE AND TRIM.
I KNOW, RIGHT?!
IT'S A WEIRD SENSATION FEELING YOUR HAIR GET LONGER LIKE THAT...
SERIOUSLY, DUDE.
YOU THINK SO? WASN'T IT AT LEAST A LITTLE PLEASANT?
......
IF WE HAVE THIS ITEM...
GULP
THEN DOWA CAN CAST OFF HER BEARD ANY TIME SHE WANTS TO!
BUT SHE NEVER WILL!
PLUSHY PLUSHY
AHH...
THANK GOODNESS UNLI'S BEARD GREW BACK FINE...
JIIWA JIIWA JIIII...
OHKI, SHOULD I GIVE THIS BACK TO FASHION CLUB?
WEREN'T YOU THE ONE WHO WANTED TO MOD IT, TANAKA?

Special Chapter • END

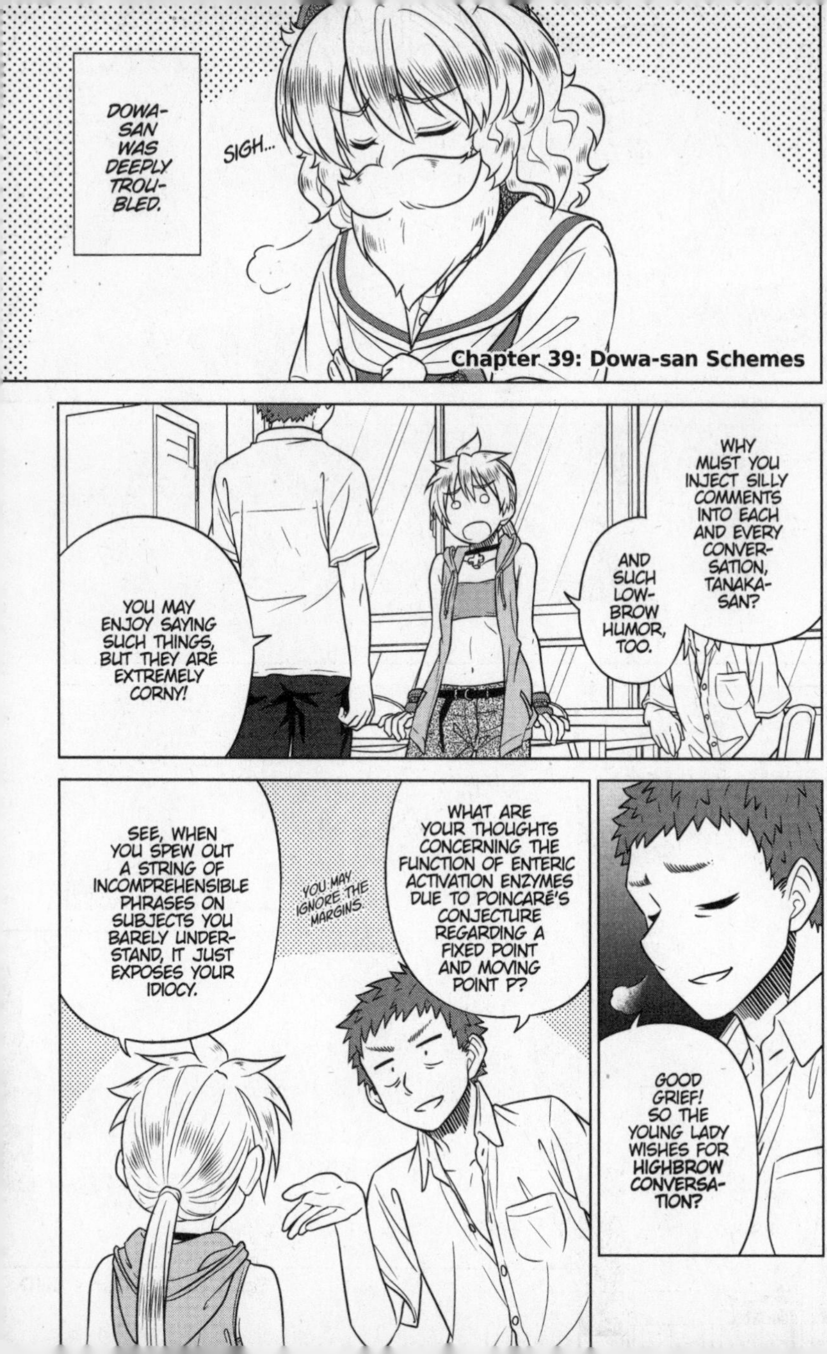
SIGH...
DOWA-SAN WAS DEEPLY TROUBLED.
Chapter 39: Dowa-san Schemes
WHY MUST YOU INJECT SILLY COMMENTS INTO EACH AND EVERY CONVERSATION, TANAKA-SAN?
AND SUCH LOW-BROW HUMOR, TOO.
YOU MAY ENJOY SAYING SUCH THINGS, BUT THEY ARE EXTREMELY CORNY!
GOOD GRIEF! SO THE YOUNG LADY WISHES FOR HIGHBROW CONVERSATION?
WHAT ARE YOUR THOUGHTS CONCERNING THE FUNCTION OF ENTERIC ACTIVATION ENZYMES DUE TO POINCARÉ'S CONJECTURE REGARDING A FIXED POINT AND MOVING POINT P?
YOU MAY IGNORE THE MARGINS.
SEE, WHEN YOU SPEW OUT A STRING OF INCOMPREHENSIBLE PHRASES ON SUBJECTS YOU BARELY UNDERSTAND, IT JUST EXPOSES YOUR IDIOCY.

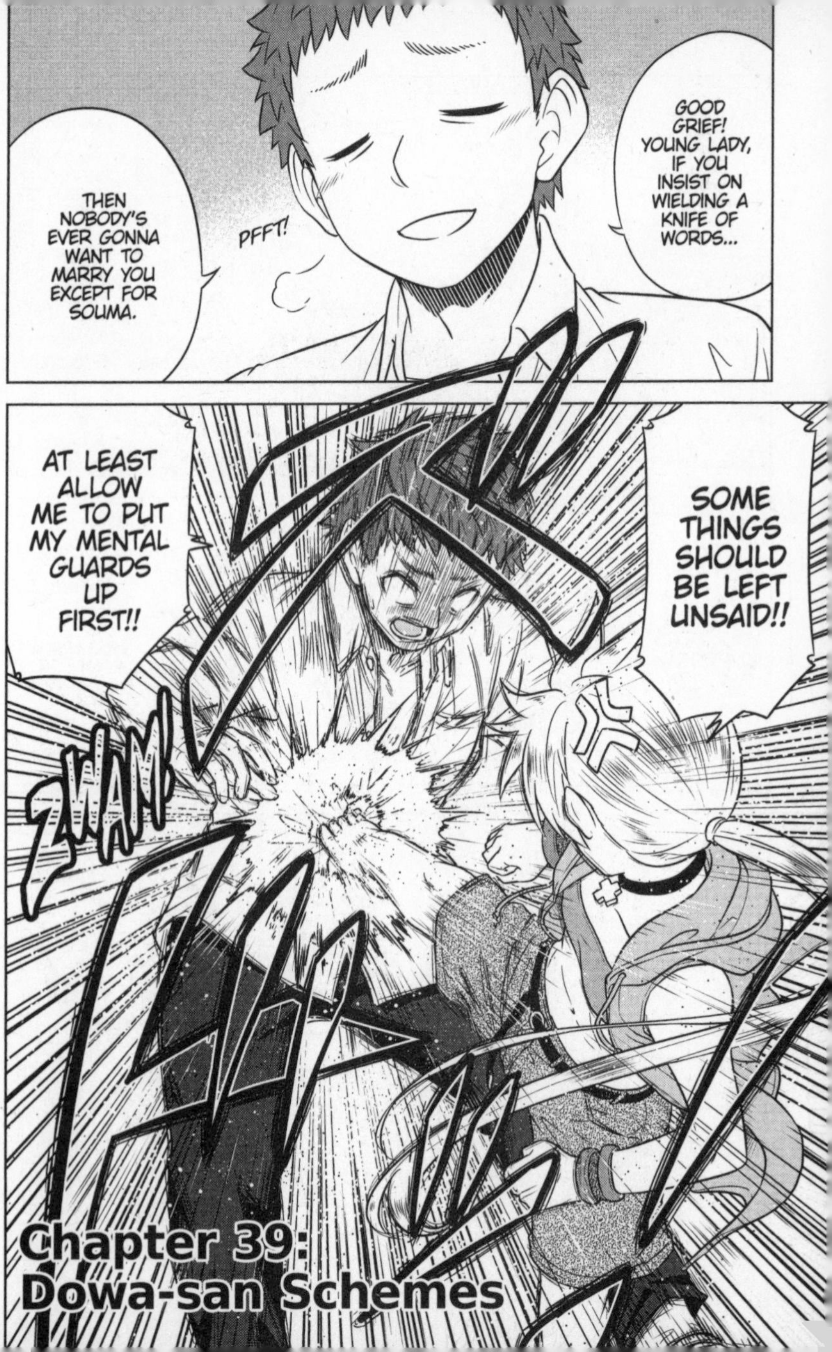
GOOD GRIEF! YOUNG LADY, IF YOU INSIST ON WIELDING A KNIFE OF WORDS...
PFFT!
THEN NOBODY'S EVER GONNA WANT TO MARRY YOU EXCEPT FOR SOUMA.
SOME THINGS SHOULD BE LEFT UNSAID!!
AT LEAST ALLOW ME TO PUT MY MENTAL GUARDS UP FIRST!!
ZWAM
Chapter 39:
Dowa-san Schemes

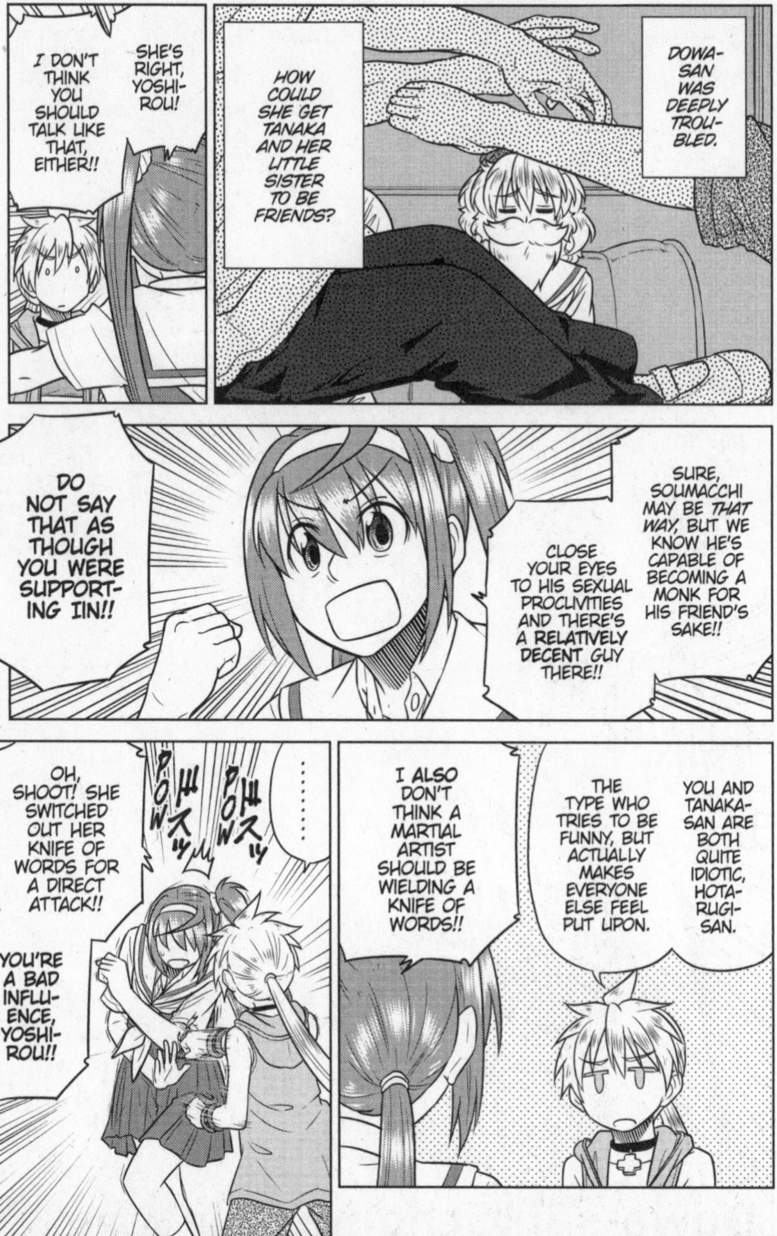
DOWA-SAN WAS DEEPLY TROUBLED.
HOW COULD SHE GET TANAKA AND HER LITTLE SISTER TO BE FRIENDS?
SHE'S RIGHT, YOSHIROU!
I DON'T THINK YOU SHOULD TALK LIKE THAT, EITHER!!
SURE, SOUMACCHI MAY BE *THAT WAY*, BUT WE KNOW HE'S CAPABLE OF BECOMING A MONK FOR HIS FRIEND'S SAKE!!
CLOSE YOUR EYES TO HIS SEXUAL PROCLIVITIES AND THERE'S A RELATIVELY DECENT GUY THERE!!
DO NOT SAY THAT AS THOUGH YOU WERE SUPPORTING IIN!!
YOU AND TANAKA-SAN ARE BOTH QUITE IDIOTIC, HOTARUGI-SAN.
THE TYPE WHO TRIES TO BE FUNNY, BUT ACTUALLY MAKES EVERYONE ELSE FEEL PUT UPON.
I ALSO DON'T THINK A MARTIAL ARTIST SHOULD BE WIELDING A KNIFE OF WORDS!!
......
POW
POW
OH, SHOOT! SHE SWITCHED OUT HER KNIFE OF WORDS FOR A DIRECT ATTACK!!
YOU'RE A BAD INFLUENCE, YOSHIROU!!

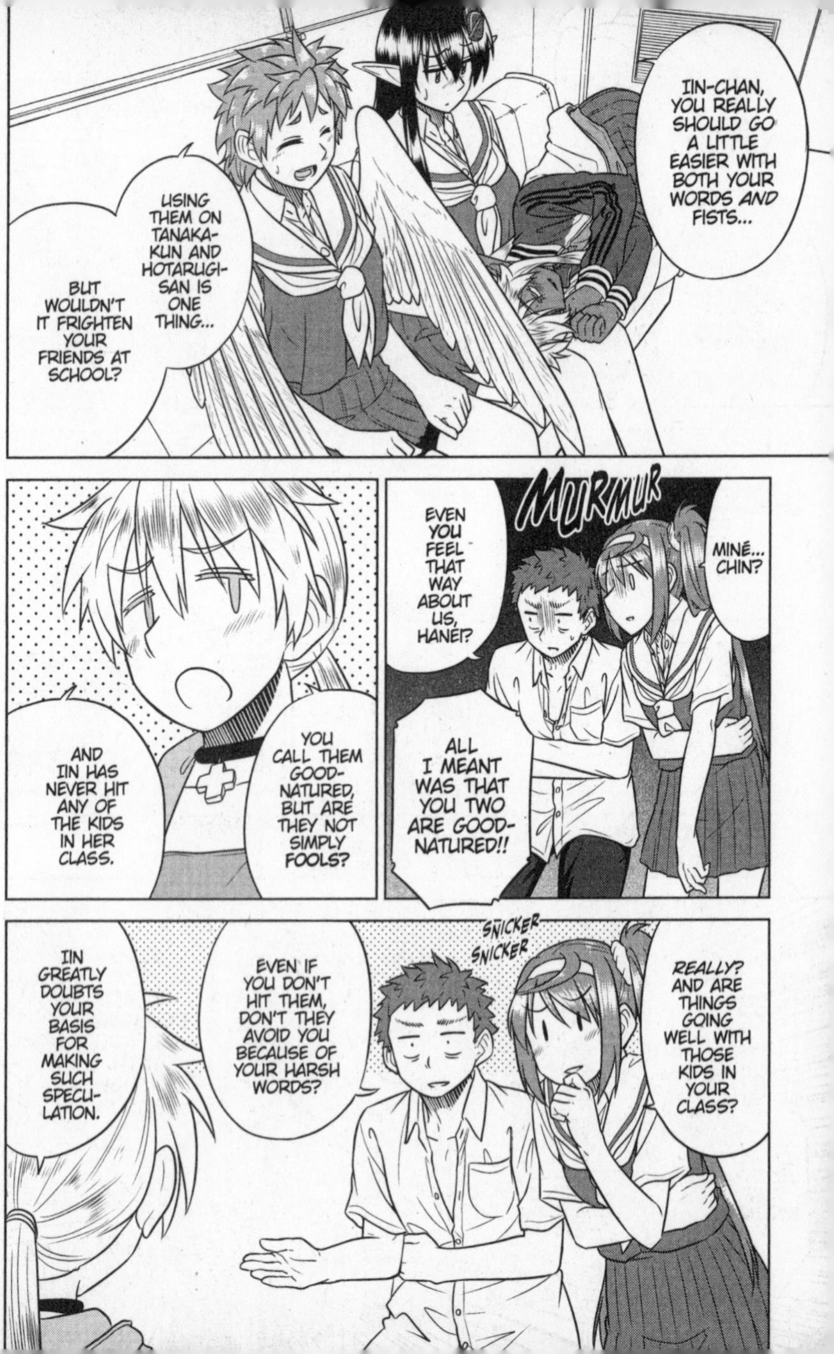
IIN-CHAN, YOU REALLY SHOULD GO A LITTLE EASIER WITH BOTH YOUR WORDS AND FISTS...
USING THEM ON TANAKA-KUN AND HOTARUGI-SAN IS ONE THING...
BUT WOULDN'T IT FRIGHTEN YOUR FRIENDS AT SCHOOL?
MINE... CHIN?
MURMUR
EVEN YOU FEEL THAT WAY ABOUT US, HANE!?
ALL I MEANT WAS THAT YOU TWO ARE GOOD-NATURED!!
YOU CALL THEM GOOD-NATURED, BUT ARE THEY NOT SIMPLY FOOLS?
AND IIN HAS NEVER HIT ANY OF THE KIDS IN HER CLASS.
REALLY? AND ARE THINGS GOING WELL WITH THOSE KIDS IN YOUR CLASS?
SNICKER SNICKER
EVEN IF YOU DON'T HIT THEM, DON'T THEY AVOID YOU BECAUSE OF YOUR HARSH WORDS?
IIN GREATLY DOUBTS YOUR BASIS FOR MAKING SUCH SPECULATION.

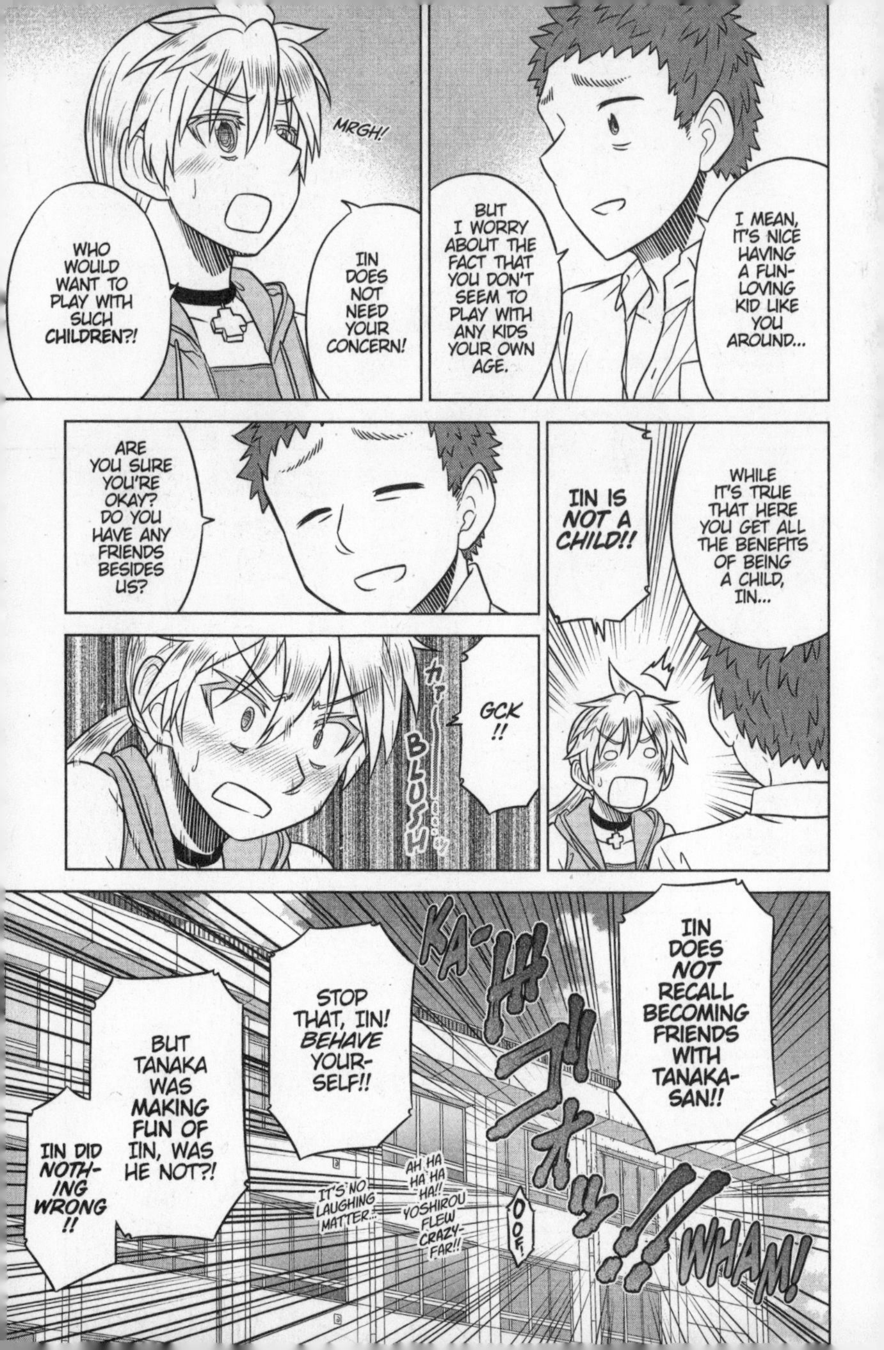
I MEAN, IT'S NICE HAVING A FUN-LOVING KID LIKE YOU AROUND...
BUT I WORRY ABOUT THE FACT THAT YOU DON'T SEEM TO PLAY WITH ANY KIDS YOUR OWN AGE.
MRGH!
IIN DOES NOT NEED YOUR CONCERN!
WHO WOULD WANT TO PLAY WITH SUCH CHILDREN?!
WHILE IT'S TRUE THAT HERE YOU GET ALL THE BENEFITS OF BEING A CHILD, IIN...
IIN IS NOT A CHILD!!
ARE YOU SURE YOU'RE OKAY? DO YOU HAVE ANY FRIENDS BESIDES US?
GCK!!
BLUSH
IIN DOES NOT RECALL BECOMING FRIENDS WITH TANAKA-SAN!!
KA-H
WHAM!
OOF!
AH HA HA HA!! YOSHIROU FLEW CRAZY-FAR!!
IT'S NO LAUGHING MATTER...
STOP THAT, IIN! BEHAVE YOURSELF!!
BUT TANAKA WAS MAKING FUN OF IIN, WAS HE NOT?!
IIN DID NOTHING WRONG!!

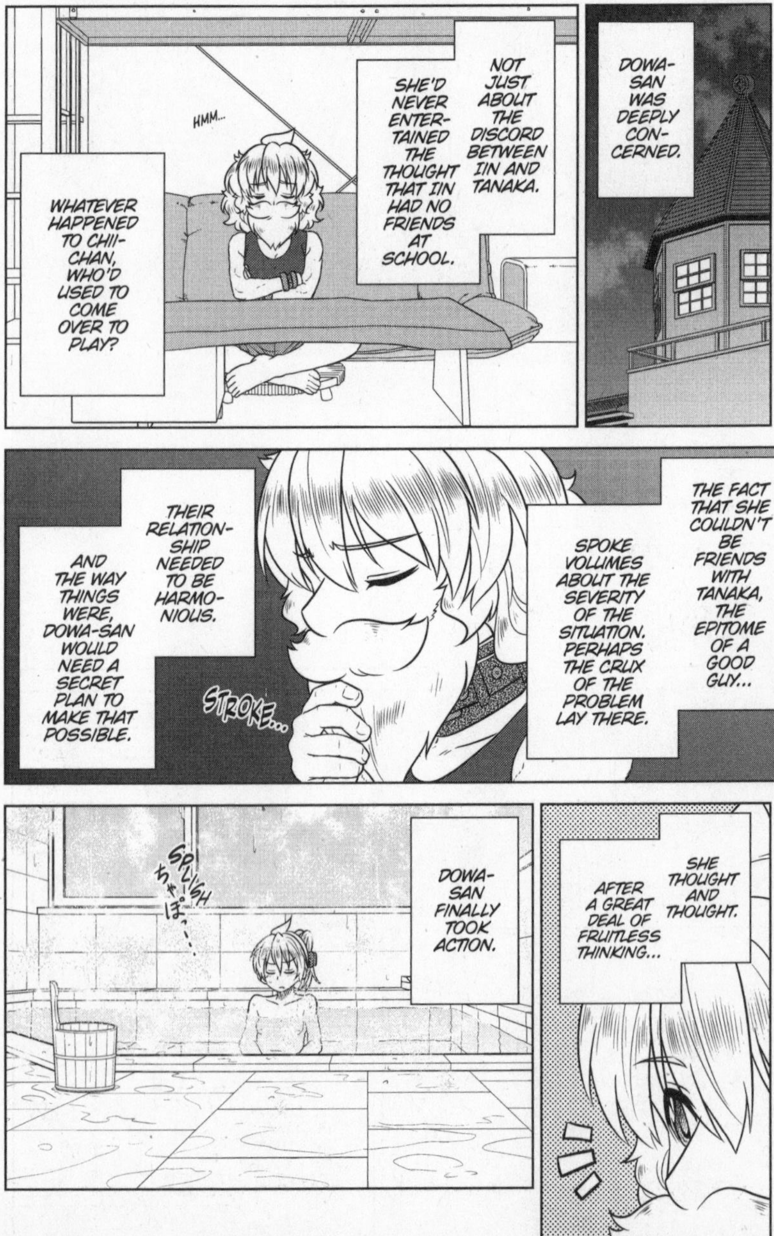
DOWA-SAN WAS DEEPLY CONCERNED.
NOT JUST ABOUT THE DISCORD BETWEEN IIN AND TANAKA.
SHE'D NEVER ENTERTAINED THE THOUGHT THAT IIN HAD NO FRIENDS AT SCHOOL.
HMM...
WHATEVER HAPPENED TO CHII-CHAN, WHO'D USED TO COME OVER TO PLAY?
THE FACT THAT SHE COULDN'T BE FRIENDS WITH TANAKA, THE EPITOME OF A GOOD GUY...
SPOKE VOLUMES ABOUT THE SEVERITY OF THE SITUATION. PERHAPS THE CRUX OF THE PROBLEM LAY THERE.
STROKE...
THEIR RELATIONSHIP NEEDED TO BE HARMONIOUS.
AND THE WAY THINGS WERE, DOWA-SAN WOULD NEED A SECRET PLAN TO MAKE THAT POSSIBLE.
SHE THOUGHT AND THOUGHT.
AFTER A GREAT DEAL OF FRUITLESS THINKING...
DOWA-SAN FINALLY TOOK ACTION.
SPLISH
ちゃぽ…

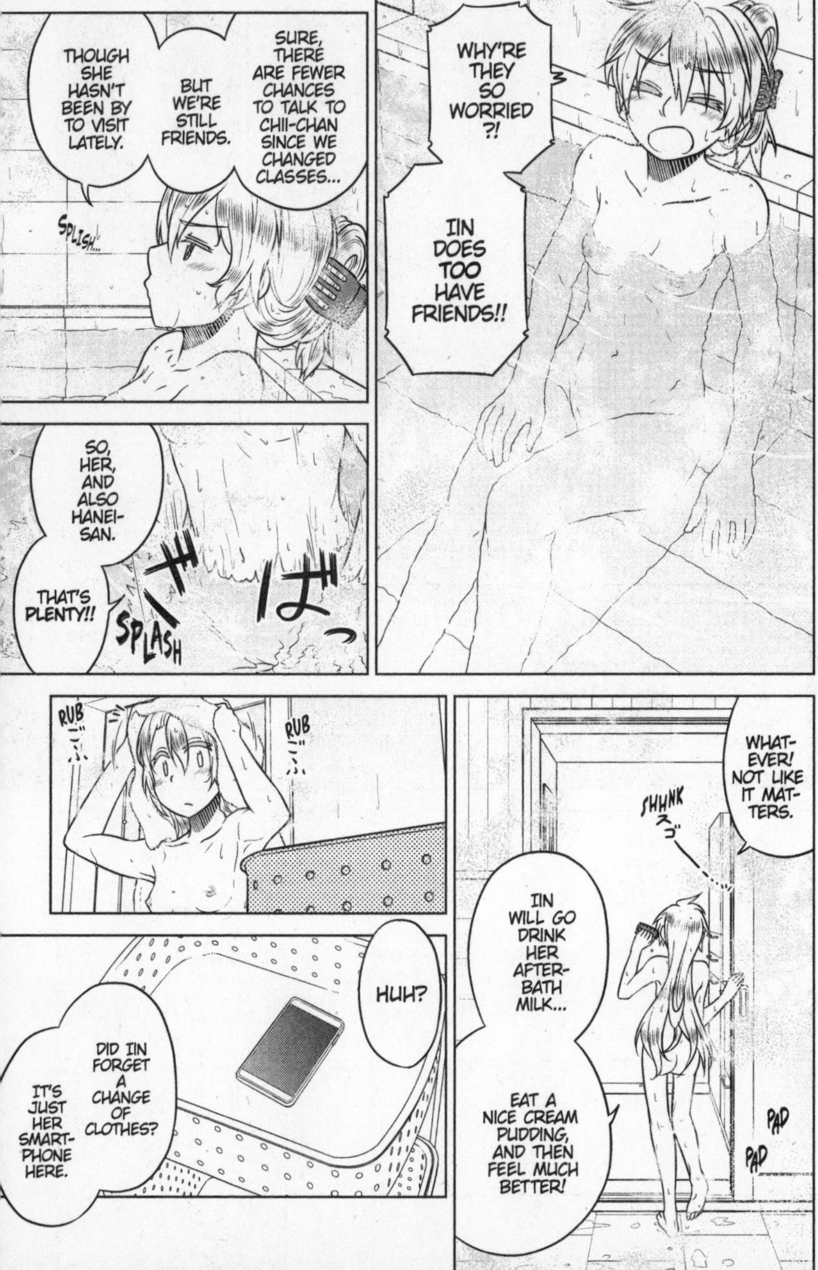
WHY'RE THEY SO WORRIED ?!
IIN DOES TOO HAVE FRIENDS!!
SURE, THERE ARE FEWER CHANCES TO TALK TO CHII-CHAN SINCE WE CHANGED CLASSES...
BUT WE'RE STILL FRIENDS.
THOUGH SHE HASN'T BEEN BY TO VISIT LATELY.
SPLISH...
SO, HER, AND ALSO HANEI-SAN.
THAT'S PLENTY!!
SPLASH
WHAT-EVER! NOT LIKE IT MAT-TERS.
SHHNK
IIN WILL GO DRINK HER AFTER-BATH MILK...
EAT A NICE CREAM PUDDING, AND THEN FEEL MUCH BETTER!
PAD
PAD
RUB
RUB
HUH?
DID IIN FORGET A CHANGE OF CLOTHES?
IT'S JUST HER SMART-PHONE HERE.

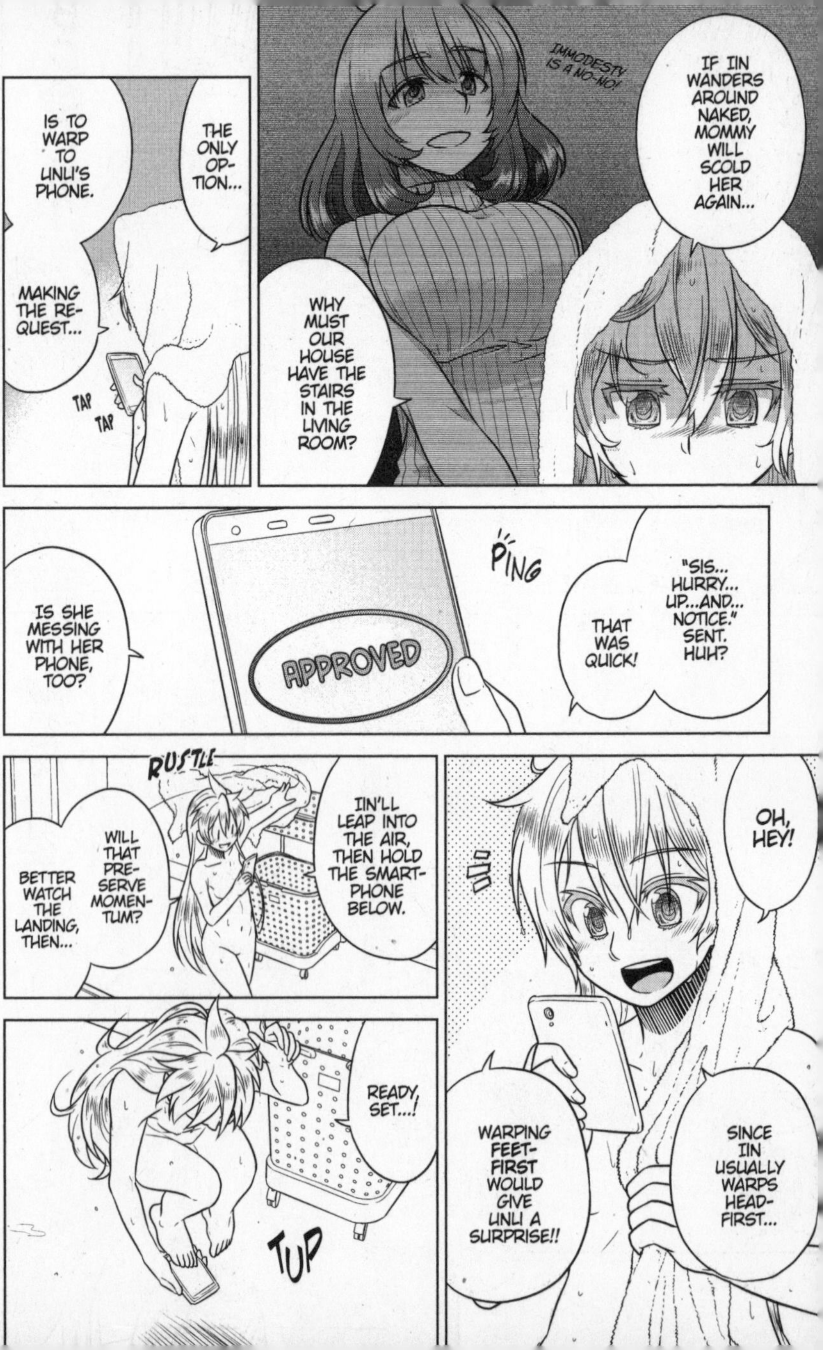
IMMODESTY IS A NO-NO!
IF IIN WANDERS AROUND NAKED, MOMMY WILL SCOLD HER AGAIN...
WHY MUST OUR HOUSE HAVE THE STAIRS IN THE LIVING ROOM?
THE ONLY OPTION...
IS TO WARP TO UNLI'S PHONE.
MAKING THE REQUEST...
TAP TAP
PING
"SIS... HURRY... UP...AND... NOTICE." SENT. HUH?
THAT WAS QUICK!
APPROVED
IS SHE MESSING WITH HER PHONE, TOO?
OH, HEY!
SINCE IIN USUALLY WARPS HEAD-FIRST...
WARPING FEET-FIRST WOULD GIVE UNLI A SURPRISE!!
RUSTLE
IIN'LL LEAP INTO THE AIR, THEN HOLD THE SMARTPHONE BELOW.
WILL THAT PRESERVE MOMENTUM?
BETTER WATCH THE LANDING, THEN...
READY, SET...!
TUP

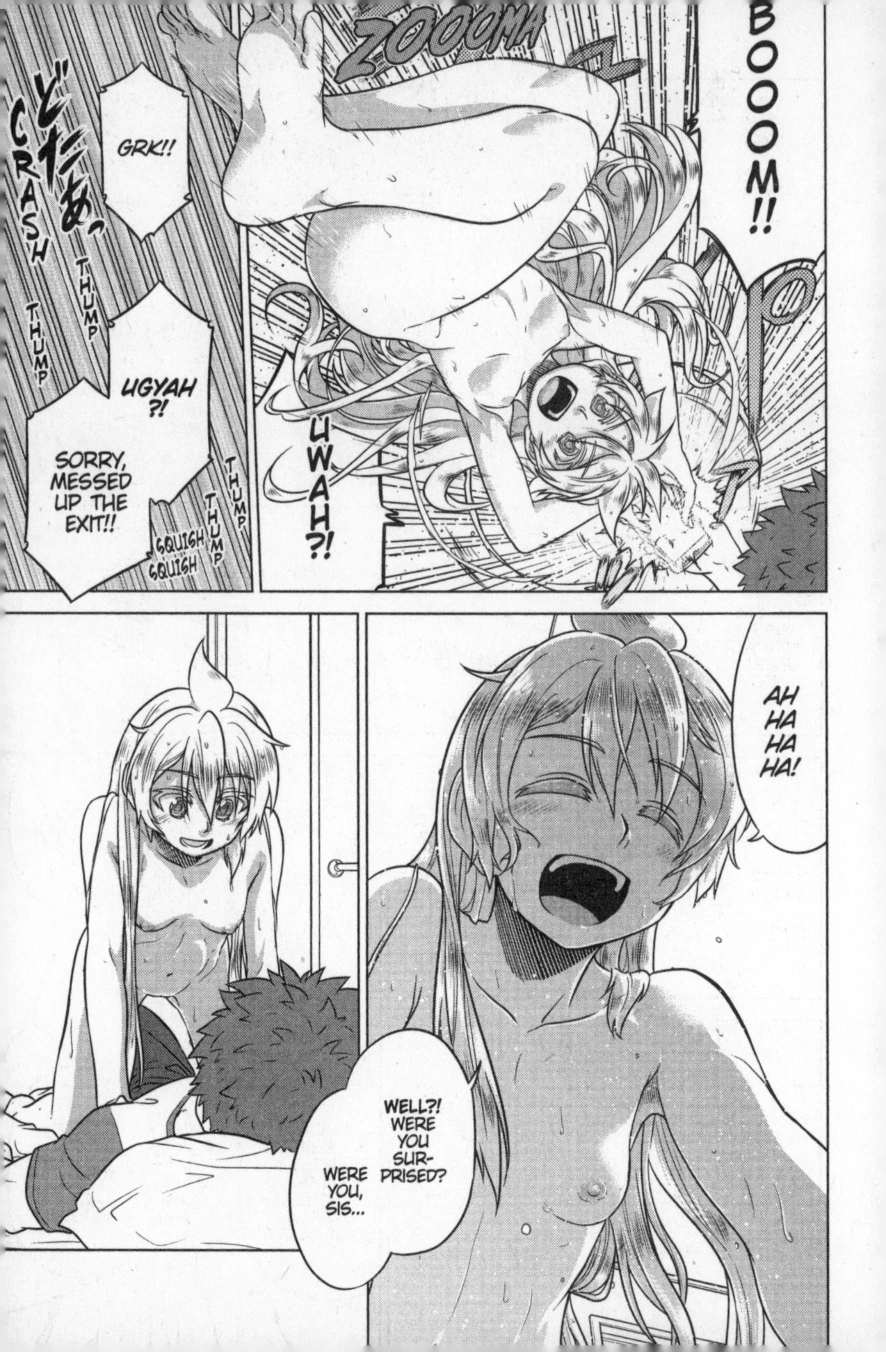
BOOOOM!!
ZOOOMM
UWAH?!
GRK!!
CRASH
THUMP
THUMP
UGYAH?!
SORRY, MESSED UP THE EXIT!!
THUMP
THUMP
SQUISH SQUISH
AH HA HA HA HA!
WELL?! WERE YOU SUR-PRISED?
WERE YOU, SIS...

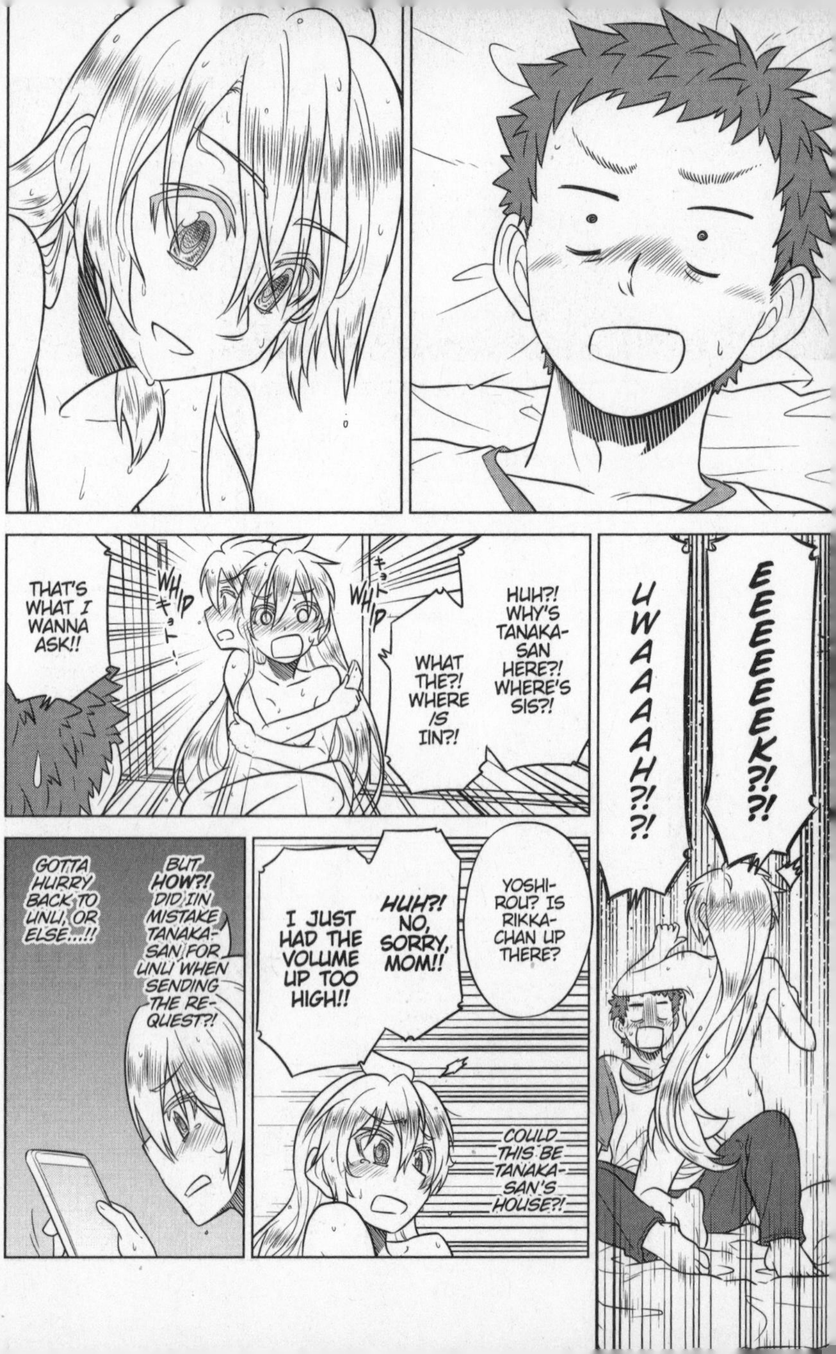
EEEEEEEK?!?!
UWAAAAAH?!?!
HUH?! WHY'S TANAKA-SAN HERE?! WHERE'S SIS?!
WHAT THE?! WHERE IS IIN?!
WHIP
WHIP
THAT'S WHAT I WANNA ASK!!
YOSHIROU? IS RIKKA-CHAN UP THERE?
HUH?! NO, SORRY, MOM!!
I JUST HAD THE VOLUME UP TOO HIGH!!
COULD THIS BE TANAKA-SAN'S HOUSE?!
BUT HOW?! DID IIN MISTAKE TANAKA-SAN FOR UNLI WHEN SENDING THE REQUEST?!
GOTTA HURRY BACK TO UNLI, OR ELSE...!!

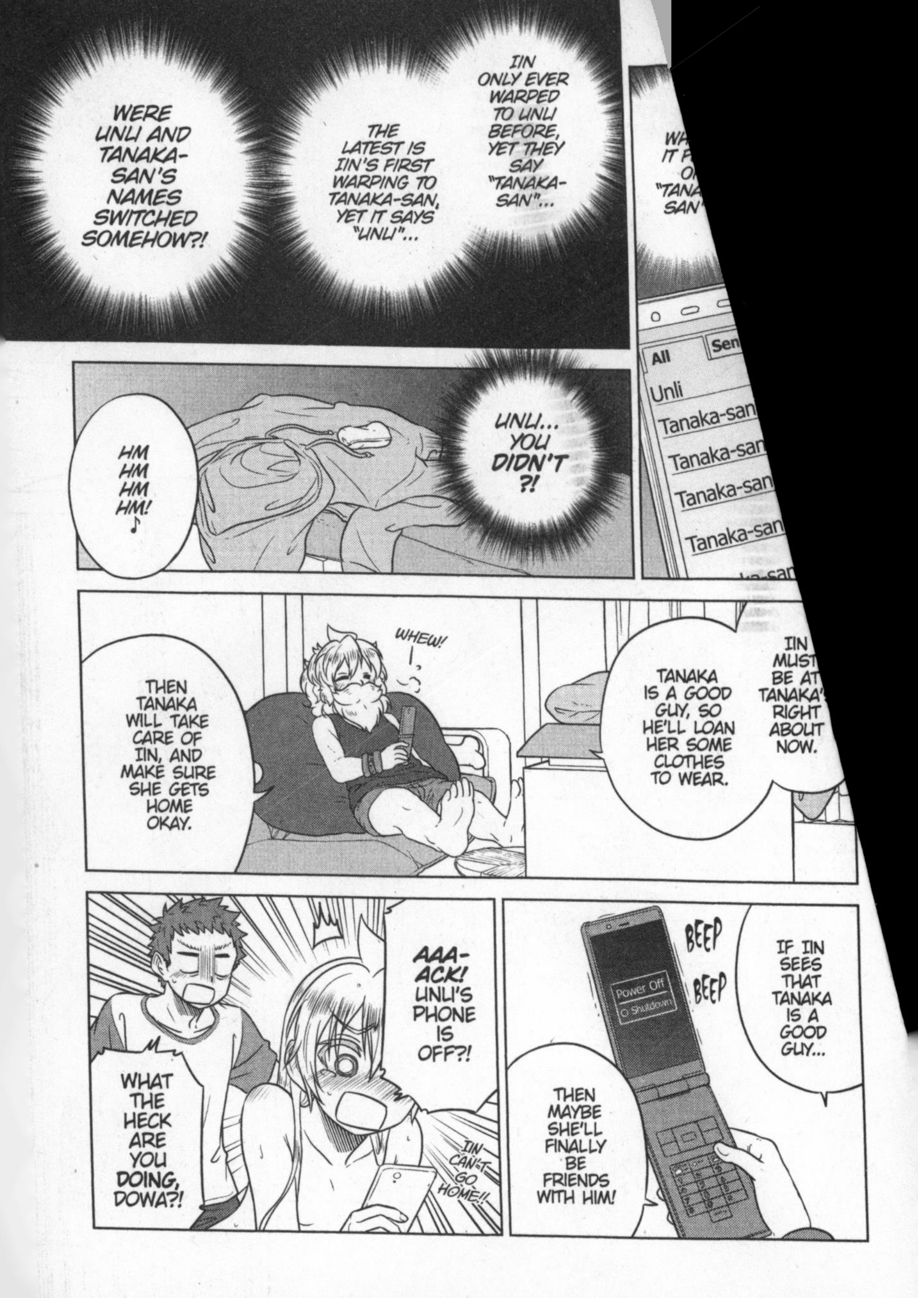
IIN ONLY EVER WARPED TO UNLI BEFORE, YET THEY SAY "TANAKA-SAN"...
THE LATEST IS IIN'S FIRST WARPING TO TANAKA-SAN, YET IT SAYS "UNLI"...
WERE UNLI AND TANAKA-SAN'S NAMES SWITCHED SOMEHOW?!
All
Unli
Tanaka-san
Tanaka-san
Tanaka-san
Tanaka-san
UNLI... YOU DIDN'T ?!
HM HM HM HM! ♪
IIN MUST BE AT TANAKA'S RIGHT ABOUT NOW.
TANAKA IS A GOOD GUY, SO HE'LL LOAN HER SOME CLOTHES TO WEAR.
WHEW!
THEN TANAKA WILL TAKE CARE OF IIN, AND MAKE SURE SHE GETS HOME OKAY.
IF IIN SEES THAT TANAKA IS A GOOD GUY...
BEEP
BEEP
Power Off
Shutdown
THEN MAYBE SHE'LL FINALLY BE FRIENDS WITH HIM!
AAA-ACK! UNLI'S PHONE IS OFF?!
IIN CAN'T GO HOME!!
WHAT THE HECK ARE YOU DOING, DOWA?!

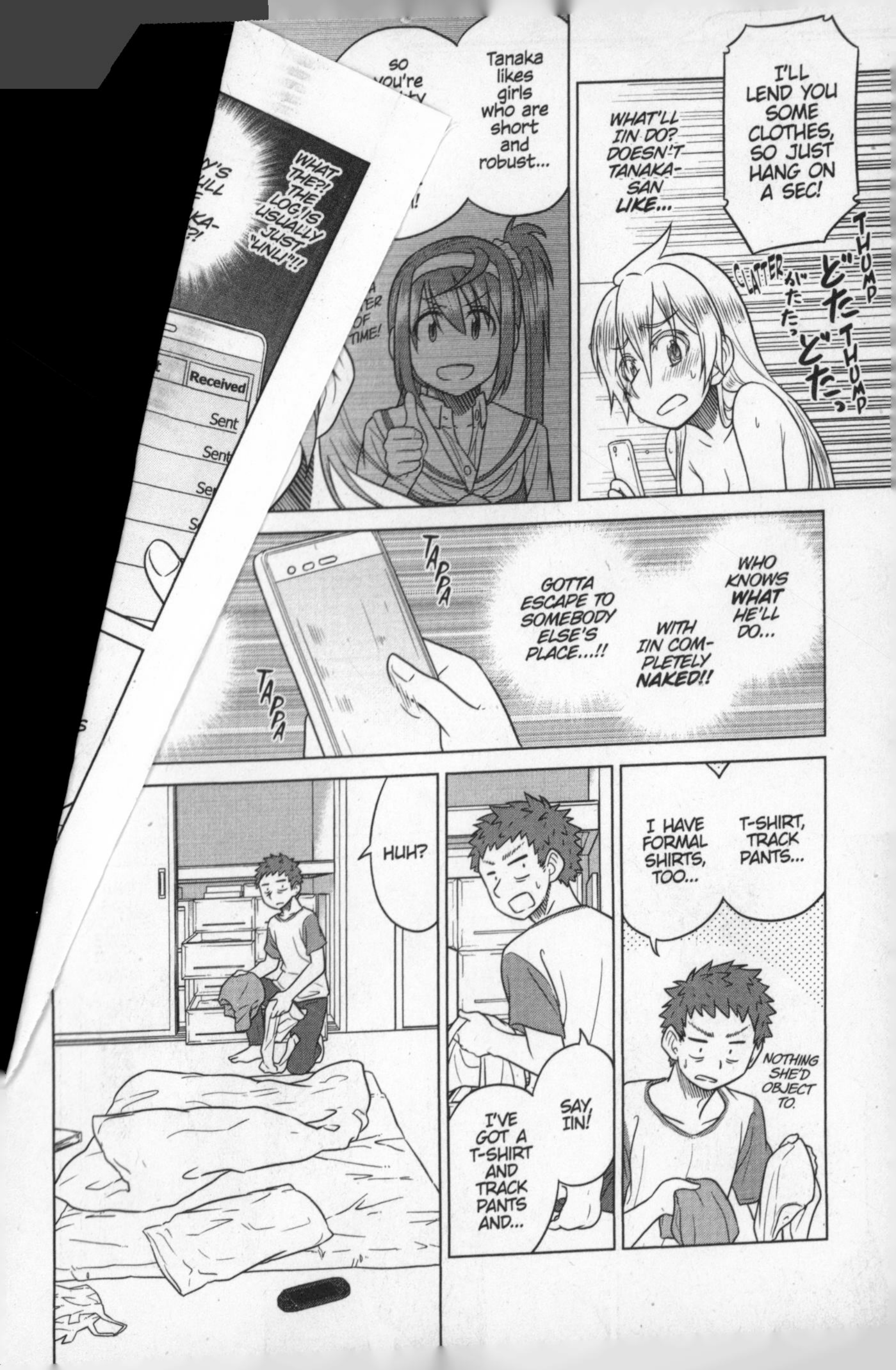

I'LL LEND YOU SOME CLOTHES, SO JUST HANG ON A SEC!
WHAT'LL IIN DO? DOESN'T TANAKA-SAN LIKE...
THUMP
THUMP
CLATTER
Tanaka likes girls who are short and robust...
WHAT THE?! THE LOG IS USUALLY JUST "UNU"!!
Received
Sent
Sent
TAPPA
TAPPA
WHO KNOWS WHAT HE'LL DO...
WITH IIN COMPLETELY NAKED!!
GOTTA ESCAPE TO SOMEBODY ELSE'S PLACE...!!
T-SHIRT, TRACK PANTS...
I HAVE FORMAL SHIRTS, TOO...
NOTHING SHE'D OBJECT TO.
SAY, IIN!
I'VE GOT A T-SHIRT AND TRACK PANTS AND...
HUH?

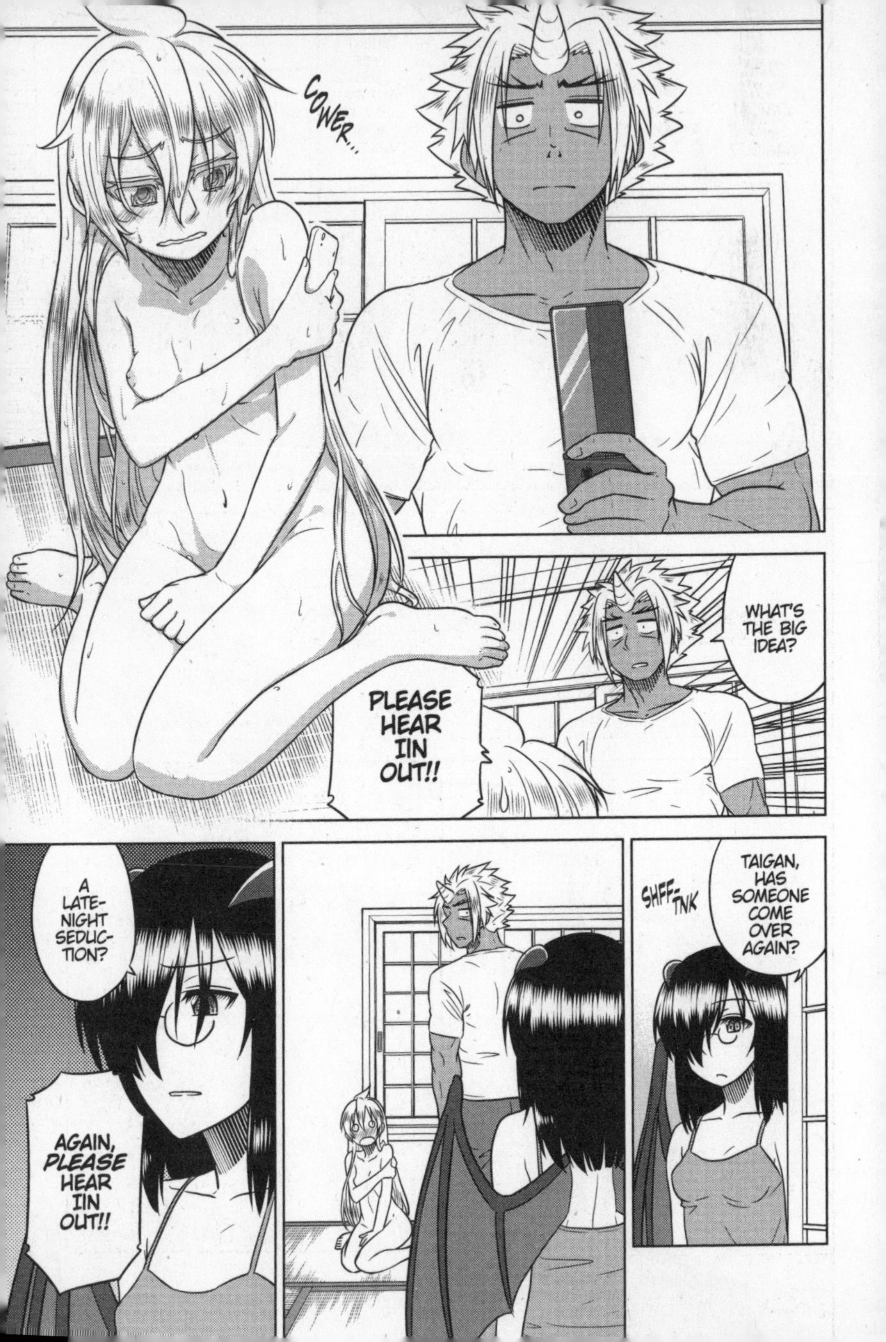
COWER...
WHAT'S THE BIG IDEA?
PLEASE HEAR IIN OUT!!
TAIGAN, HAS SOMEONE COME OVER AGAIN?
SHFF-TNK
A LATE-NIGHT SEDUC-TION?
AGAIN, PLEASE HEAR IIN OUT!!

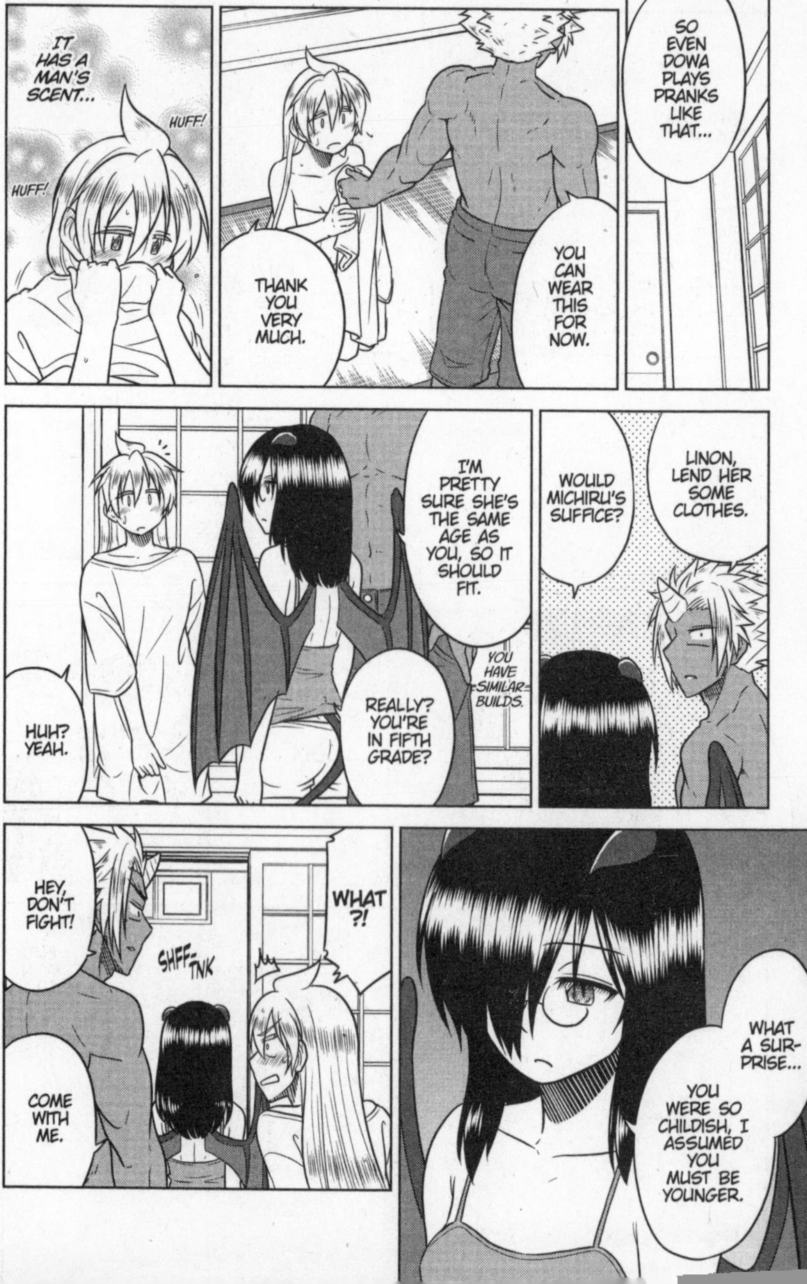
SO EVEN DOWA PLAYS PRANKS LIKE THAT...
YOU CAN WEAR THIS FOR NOW.
THANK YOU VERY MUCH.
IT HAS A MAN'S SCENT...
HUFF!
HUFF!
LINON, LEND HER SOME CLOTHES.
WOULD MICHIRU'S SUFFICE?
I'M PRETTY SURE SHE'S THE SAME AGE AS YOU, SO IT SHOULD FIT.
YOU HAVE SIMILAR BUILDS.
REALLY? YOU'RE IN FIFTH GRADE?
HUH? YEAH.
WHAT A SURPRISE... YOU WERE SO CHILDISH, I ASSUMED YOU MUST BE YOUNGER.
WHAT?!
SHFF-TNK
HEY, DON'T FIGHT!
COME WITH ME.

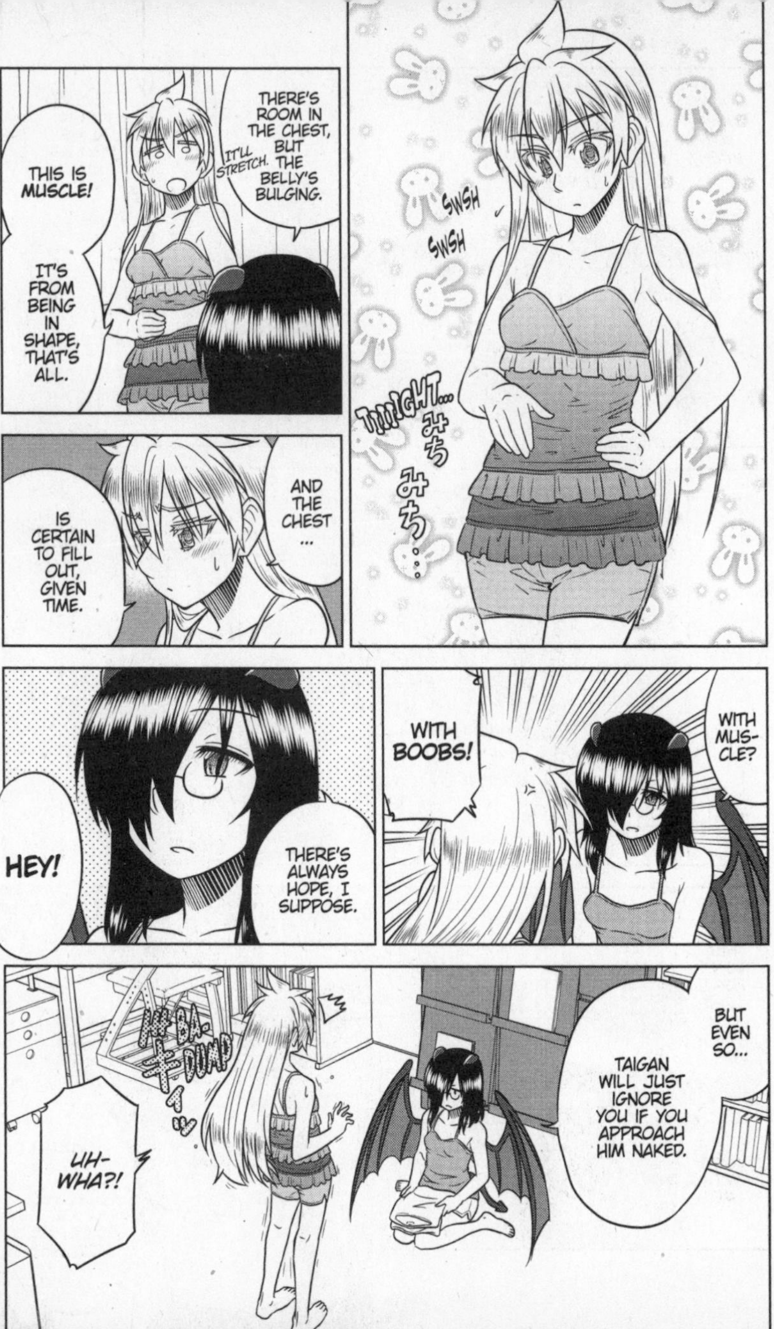
SWSH
SWSH
TIIIIGHT...
みち
みち...
THERE'S ROOM IN THE CHEST, BUT THE BELLY'S BULGING.
IT'LL STRETCH.
THIS IS MUSCLE!
IT'S FROM BEING IN SHAPE, THAT'S ALL.
AND THE CHEST...
IS CERTAIN TO FILL OUT, GIVEN TIME.
WITH MUS-CLE?
WITH BOOBS!
THERE'S ALWAYS HOPE, I SUPPOSE.
HEY!
BUT EVEN SO...
TAIGAN WILL JUST IGNORE YOU IF YOU APPROACH HIM NAKED.
KA-BA-DUMP
キイッ
UH-WHA?!

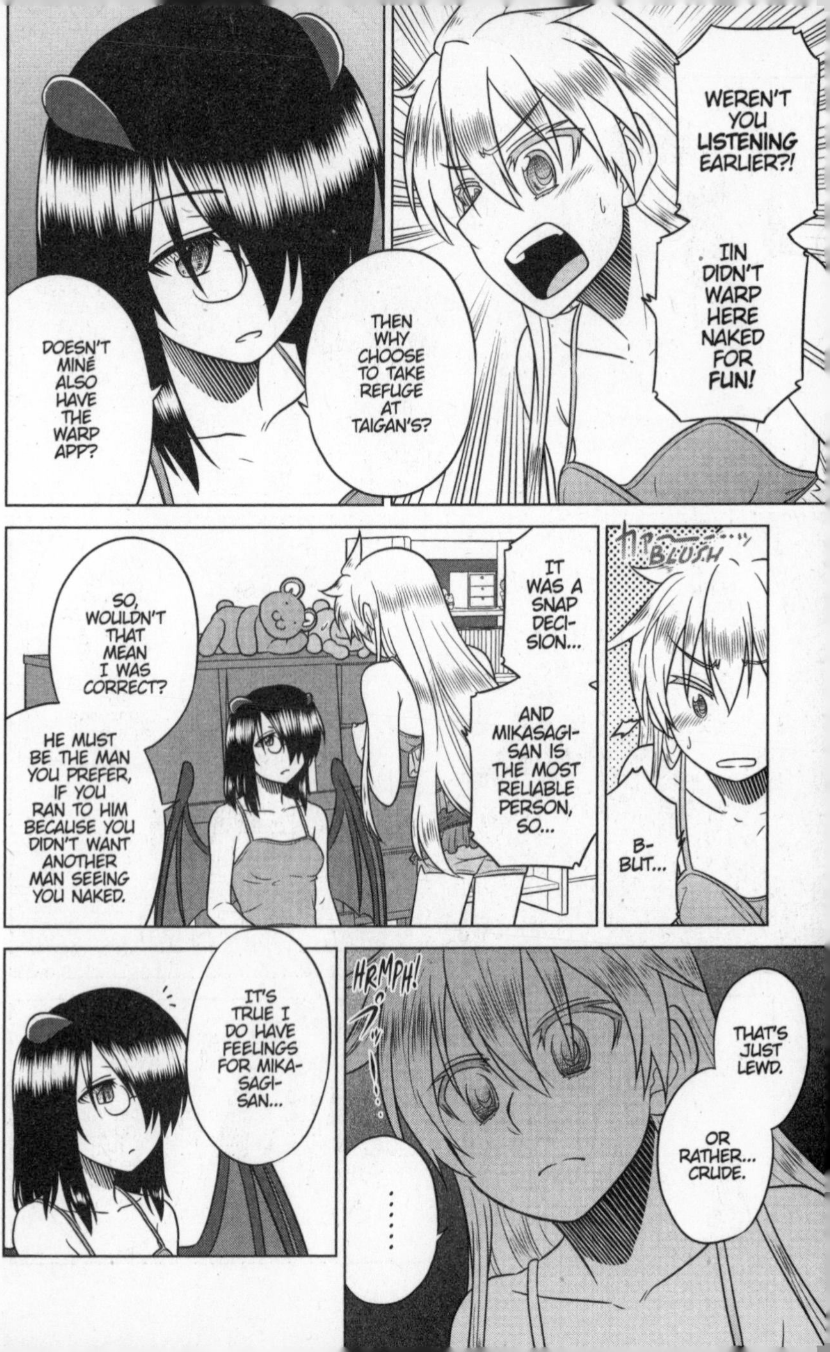

WEREN'T YOU LISTENING EARLIER?!
IIN DIDN'T WARP HERE NAKED FOR FUN!
DOESN'T MINÉ ALSO HAVE THE WARP APP?
THEN WHY CHOOSE TO TAKE REFUGE AT TAIGAN'S?
BLUSH
B-BUT...
IT WAS A SNAP DECISION...
AND MIKASAGI-SAN IS THE MOST RELIABLE PERSON, SO...
SO, WOULDN'T THAT MEAN I WAS CORRECT?
HE MUST BE THE MAN YOU PREFER, IF YOU RAN TO HIM BECAUSE YOU DIDN'T WANT ANOTHER MAN SEEING YOU NAKED.
HRMPH!
THAT'S JUST LEWD.
OR RATHER... CRUDE.
......
IT'S TRUE I DO HAVE FEELINGS FOR MIKASAGI-SAN...

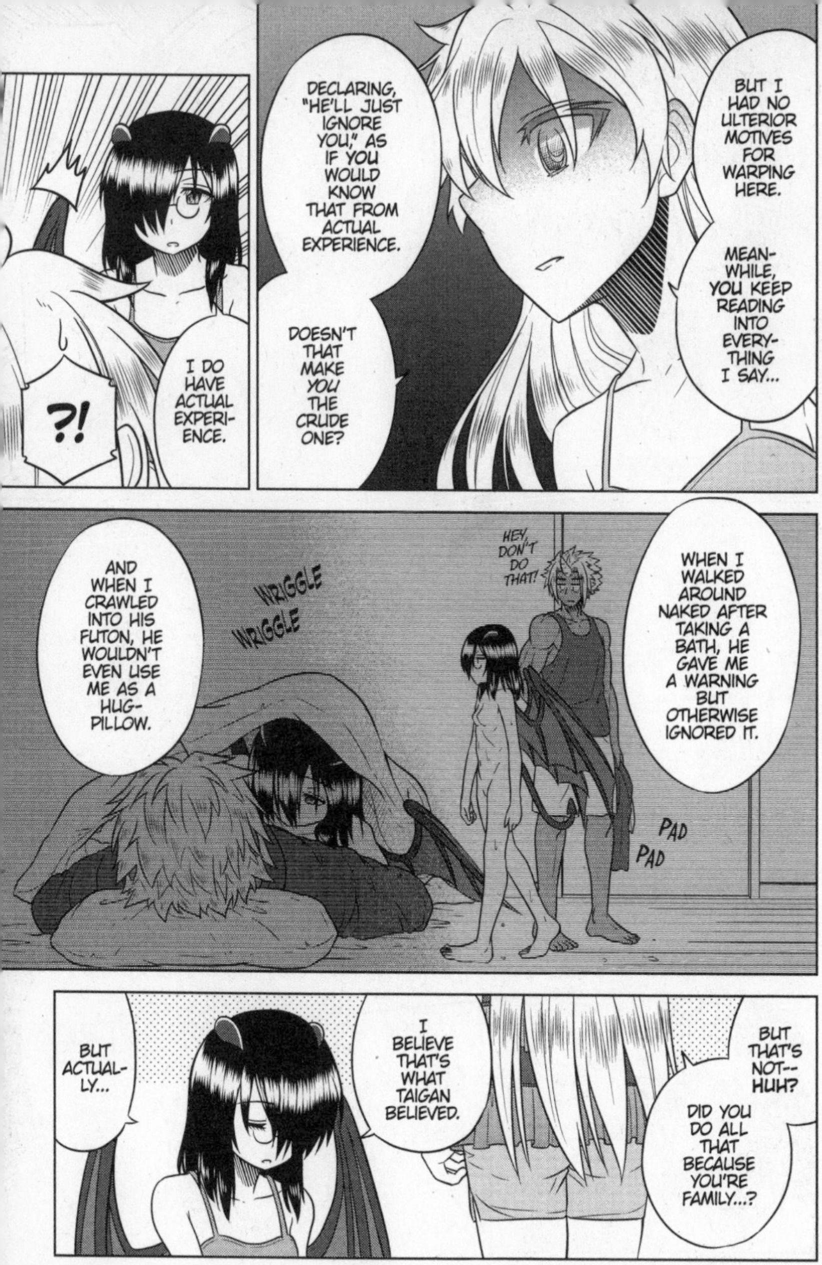
BUT I HAD NO ULTERIOR MOTIVES FOR WARPING HERE.
MEAN-WHILE, YOU KEEP READING INTO EVERY-THING I SAY...
DECLARING, "HE'LL JUST IGNORE YOU," AS IF YOU WOULD KNOW THAT FROM ACTUAL EXPERIENCE.
DOESN'T THAT MAKE YOU THE CRUDE ONE?
I DO HAVE ACTUAL EXPERI-ENCE.
?!
WHEN I WALKED AROUND NAKED AFTER TAKING A BATH, HE GAVE ME A WARNING BUT OTHERWISE IGNORED IT.
HEY, DON'T DO THAT!
PAD PAD
WRIGGLE WRIGGLE
AND WHEN I CRAWLED INTO HIS FUTON, HE WOULDN'T EVEN USE ME AS A HUG-PILLOW.
BUT THAT'S NOT-- HUH?
DID YOU DO ALL THAT BECAUSE YOU'RE FAMILY...?
I BELIEVE THAT'S WHAT TAIGAN BELIEVED.
BUT ACTUAL-LY...

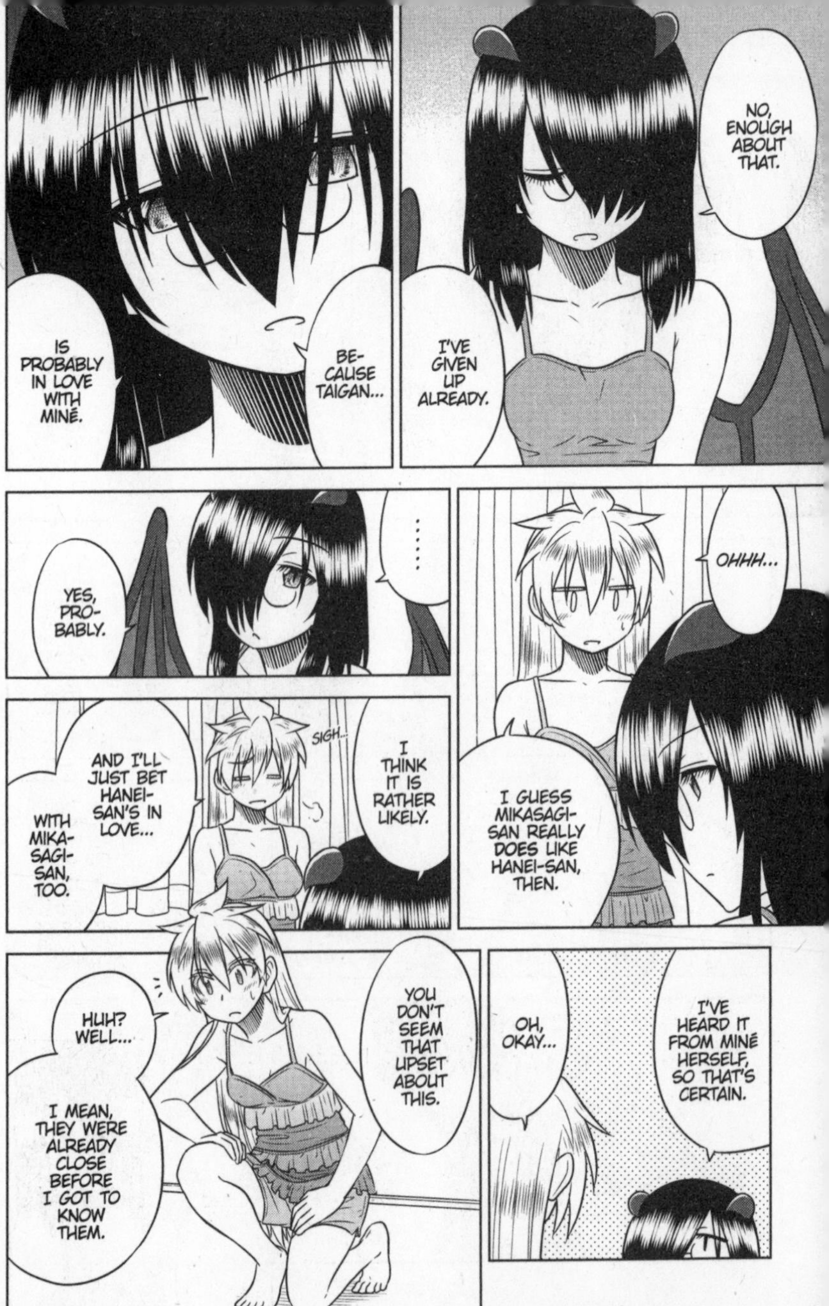
NO, ENOUGH ABOUT THAT.
I'VE GIVEN UP ALREADY.
BE-CAUSE TAIGAN...
IS PROBABLY IN LOVE WITH MINÉ.
OHHH...
......
YES, PRO-BABLY.
I GUESS MIKASAGI-SAN REALLY DOES LIKE HANEI-SAN, THEN.
I THINK IT IS RATHER LIKELY.
SIGH...
AND I'LL JUST BET HANEI-SAN'S IN LOVE...
WITH MIKA-SAGI-SAN, TOO.
I'VE HEARD IT FROM MINÉ HERSELF, SO THAT'S CERTAIN.
OH, OKAY...
YOU DON'T SEEM THAT UPSET ABOUT THIS.
HUH? WELL...
I MEAN, THEY WERE ALREADY CLOSE BEFORE I GOT TO KNOW THEM.

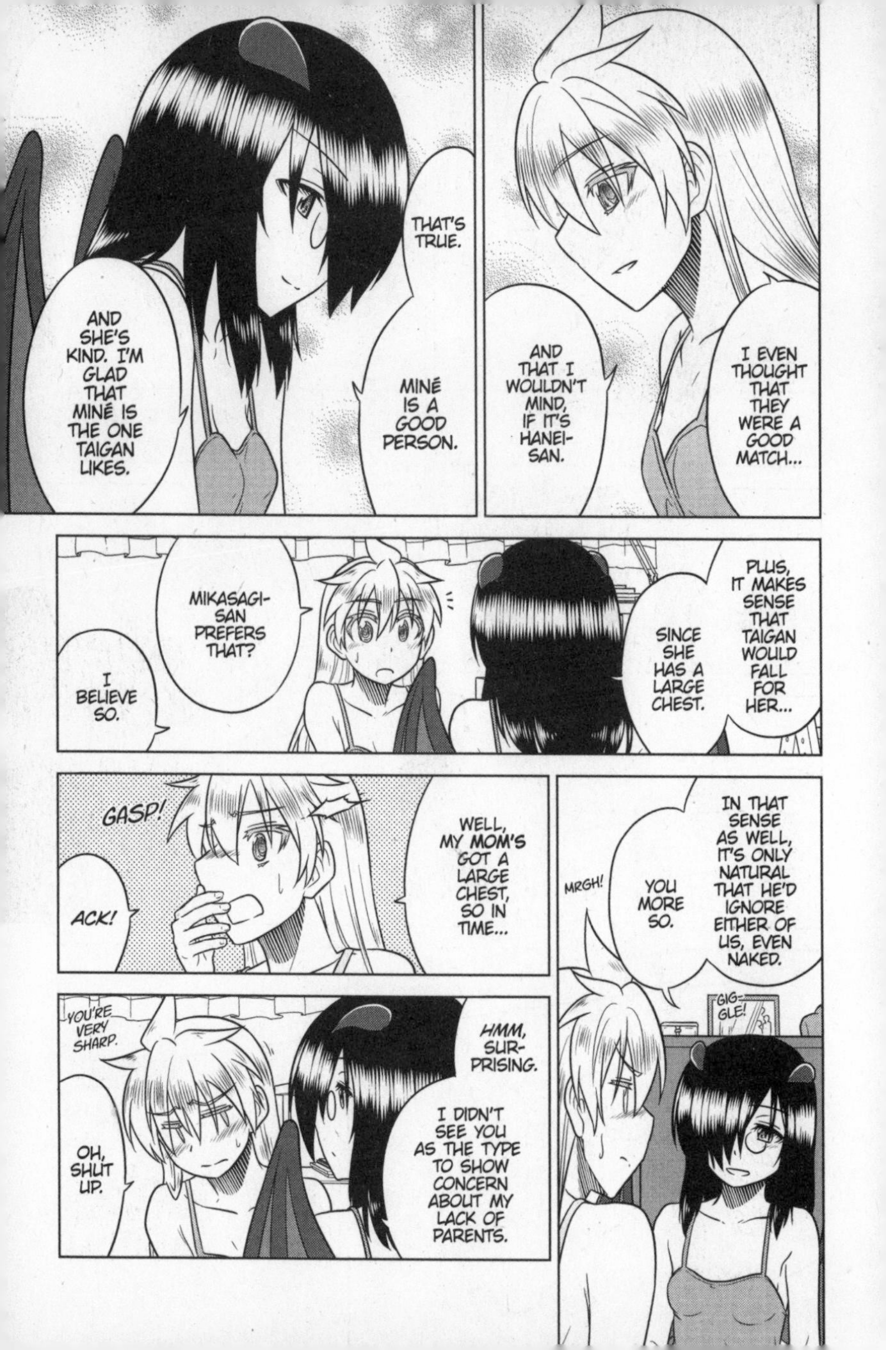
I EVEN THOUGHT THAT THEY WERE A GOOD MATCH...
AND THAT I WOULDN'T MIND, IF IT'S HANEI-SAN.
THAT'S TRUE.
MINÉ IS A GOOD PERSON.
AND SHE'S KIND. I'M GLAD THAT MINÉ IS THE ONE TAIGAN LIKES.
PLUS, IT MAKES SENSE THAT TAIGAN WOULD FALL FOR HER...
SINCE SHE HAS A LARGE CHEST.
MIKASAGI-SAN PREFERS THAT?
I BELIEVE SO.
IN THAT SENSE AS WELL, IT'S ONLY NATURAL THAT HE'D IGNORE EITHER OF US, EVEN NAKED.
YOU MORE SO.
MRGH!
GIG-GLE!
WELL, MY MOM'S GOT A LARGE CHEST, SO IN TIME...
GASP!
ACK!
HMM, SUR-PRISING.
I DIDN'T SEE YOU AS THE TYPE TO SHOW CONCERN ABOUT MY LACK OF PARENTS.
YOU'RE VERY SHARP.
OH, SHUT UP.

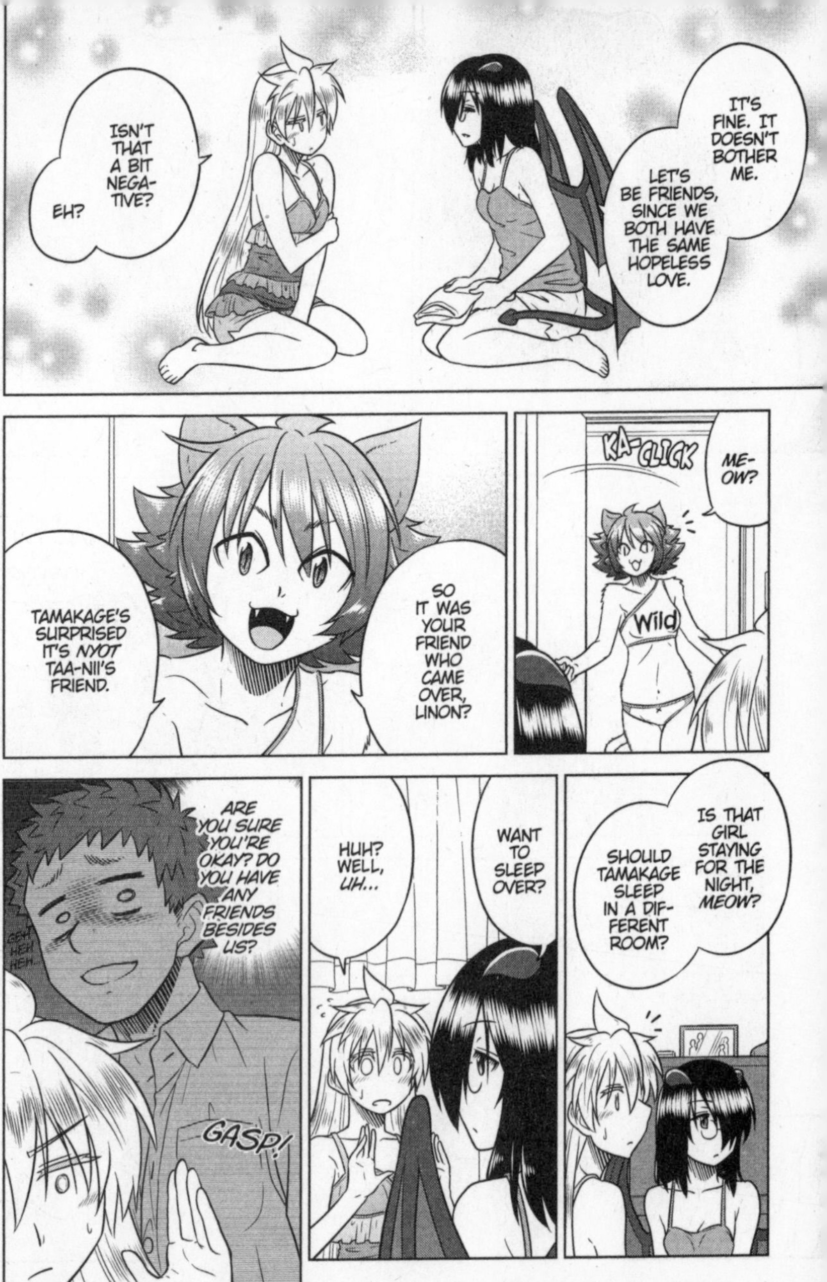
IT'S FINE. IT DOESN'T BOTHER ME.
LET'S BE FRIENDS, SINCE WE BOTH HAVE THE SAME HOPELESS LOVE.
ISN'T THAT A BIT NEGA-TIVE?
EH?
KA-CLICK
ME-OW?
SO IT WAS YOUR FRIEND WHO CAME OVER, LINON?
TAMAKAGE'S SURPRISED IT'S *NYOT* TAA-NII'S FRIEND.
IS THAT GIRL STAYING FOR THE NIGHT, *MEOW*?
SHOULD TAMAKAGE SLEEP IN A DIF-FERENT ROOM?
WANT TO SLEEP OVER?
HUH? WELL, UH...
ARE YOU SURE YOU'RE OKAY? DO YOU HAVE ANY FRIENDS BESIDES US?
GEH HEH HEH
GASP!

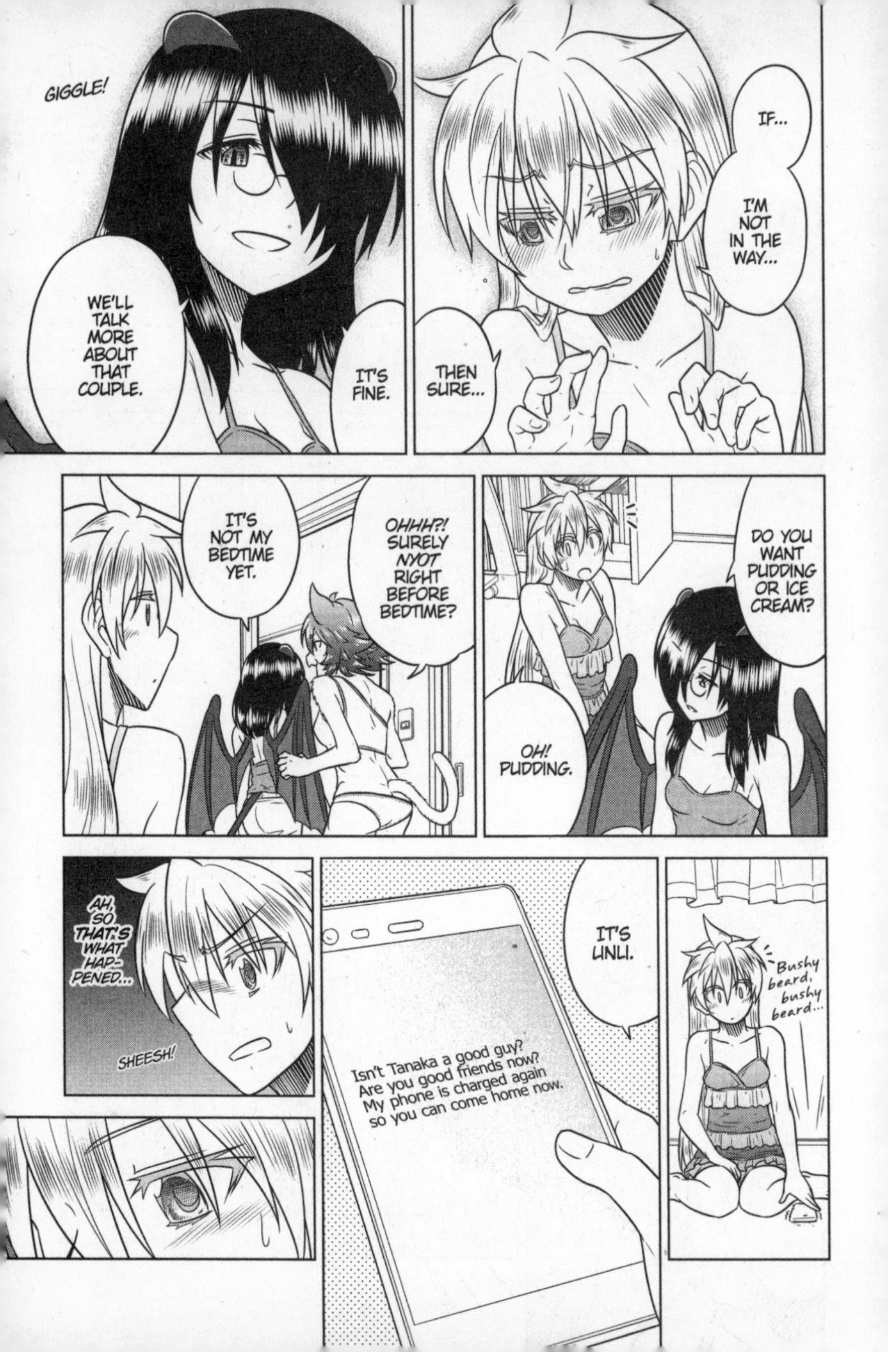
IF...
I'M NOT IN THE WAY...
THEN SURE...
IT'S FINE.
GIGGLE!
WE'LL TALK MORE ABOUT THAT COUPLE.
DO YOU WANT PUDDING OR ICE CREAM?
OH! PUDDING.
OHHH?! SURELY NYOT RIGHT BEFORE BEDTIME?
IT'S NOT MY BEDTIME YET.
Bushy beard, bushy beard...
IT'S UNLI.
Isn't Tanaka a good guy?
Are you good friends now?
My phone is charged again
so you can come home now.
AH, SO THAT'S WHAT HAP-PENED...
SHEESH!

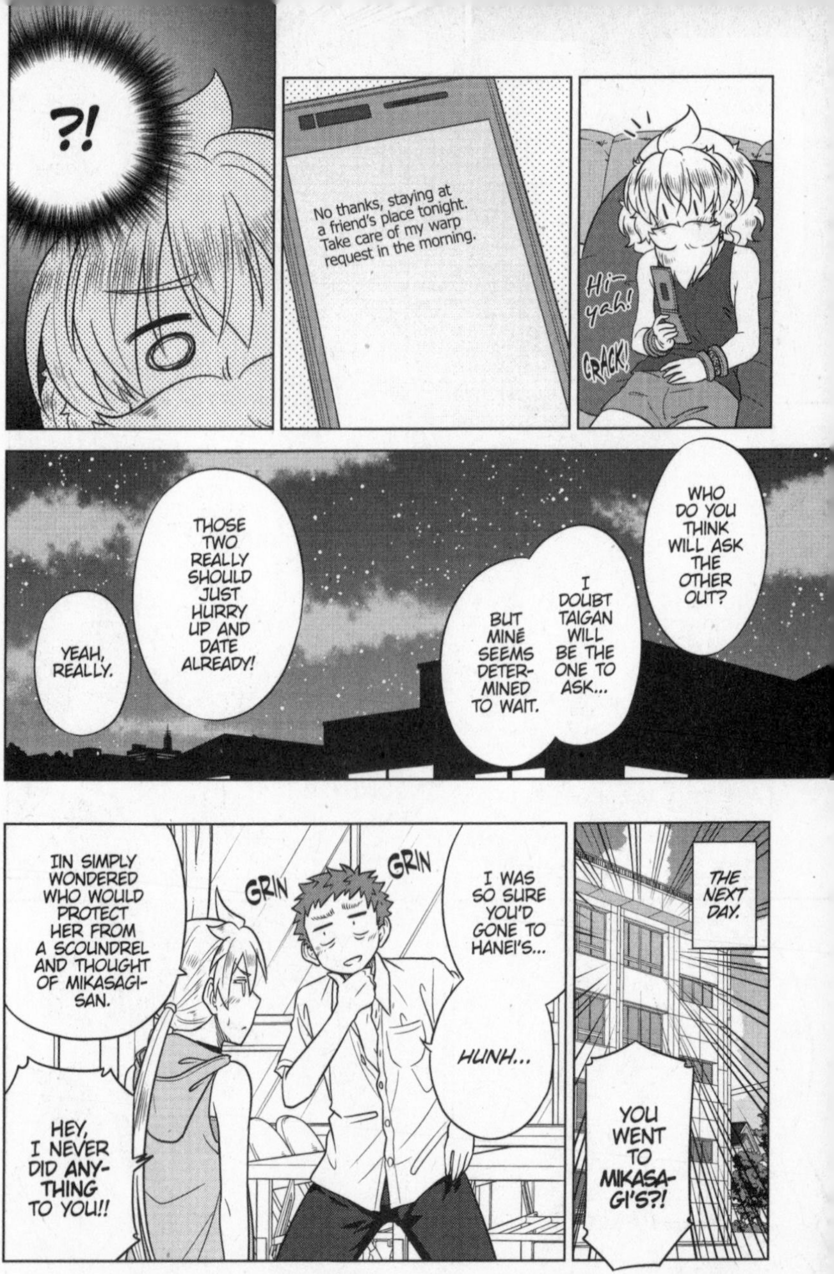
Hi-yah!
CRACK!
No thanks, staying at a friend's place tonight. Take care of my warp request in the morning.
?!
WHO DO YOU THINK WILL ASK THE OTHER OUT?
I DOUBT TAIGAN WILL BE THE ONE TO ASK...
BUT MINÉ SEEMS DETER-MINED TO WAIT.
THOSE TWO REALLY SHOULD JUST HURRY UP AND DATE ALREADY!
YEAH, REALLY.
THE NEXT DAY.
YOU WENT TO MIKASA-GI'S?!
I WAS SO SURE YOU'D GONE TO HANEI'S...
GRIN
GRIN
HUNH...
IIN SIMPLY WONDERED WHO WOULD PROTECT HER FROM A SCOUNDREL AND THOUGHT OF MIKASAGI-SAN.
HEY, I NEVER DID ANY-THING TO YOU!!

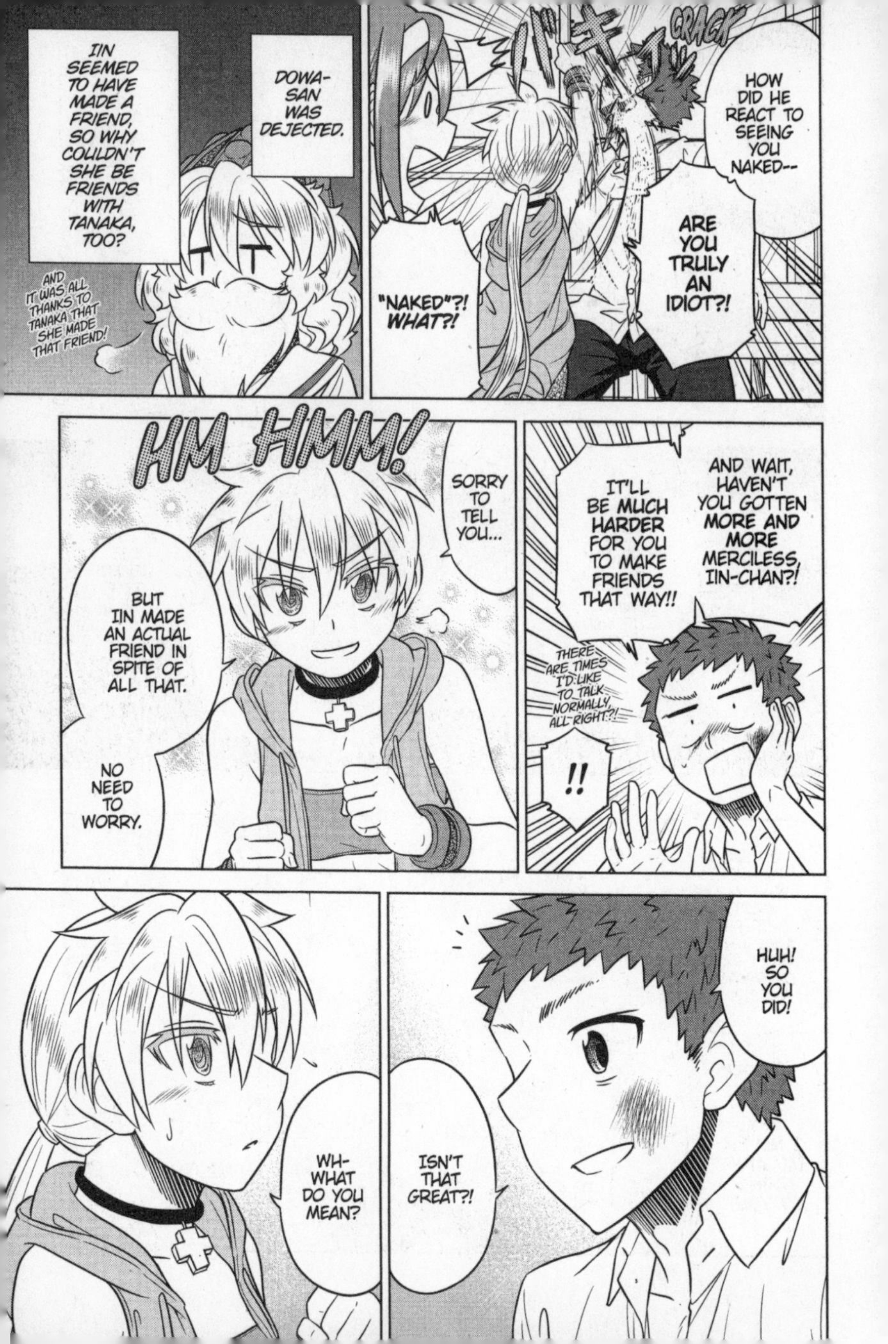
CRACK
HOW DID HE REACT TO SEEING YOU NAKED--
ARE YOU TRULY AN IDIOT?!
"NAKED"?! WHAT?!
DOWA-SAN WAS DEJECTED.
IIN SEEMED TO HAVE MADE A FRIEND, SO WHY COULDN'T SHE BE FRIENDS WITH TANAKA, TOO?
AND IT WAS ALL THANKS TO TANAKA THAT SHE MADE THAT FRIEND!
AND WAIT, HAVEN'T YOU GOTTEN MORE AND MORE MERCILESS, IIN-CHAN?!
IT'LL BE MUCH HARDER FOR YOU TO MAKE FRIENDS THAT WAY!!
THERE ARE TIMES I'D LIKE TO TALK NORMALLY, ALL RIGHT?!
!!
SORRY TO TELL YOU...
HM HMM!
BUT IIN MADE AN ACTUAL FRIEND IN SPITE OF ALL THAT.
NO NEED TO WORRY.
HUH! SO YOU DID!
ISN'T THAT GREAT?!
WH-WHAT DO YOU MEAN?

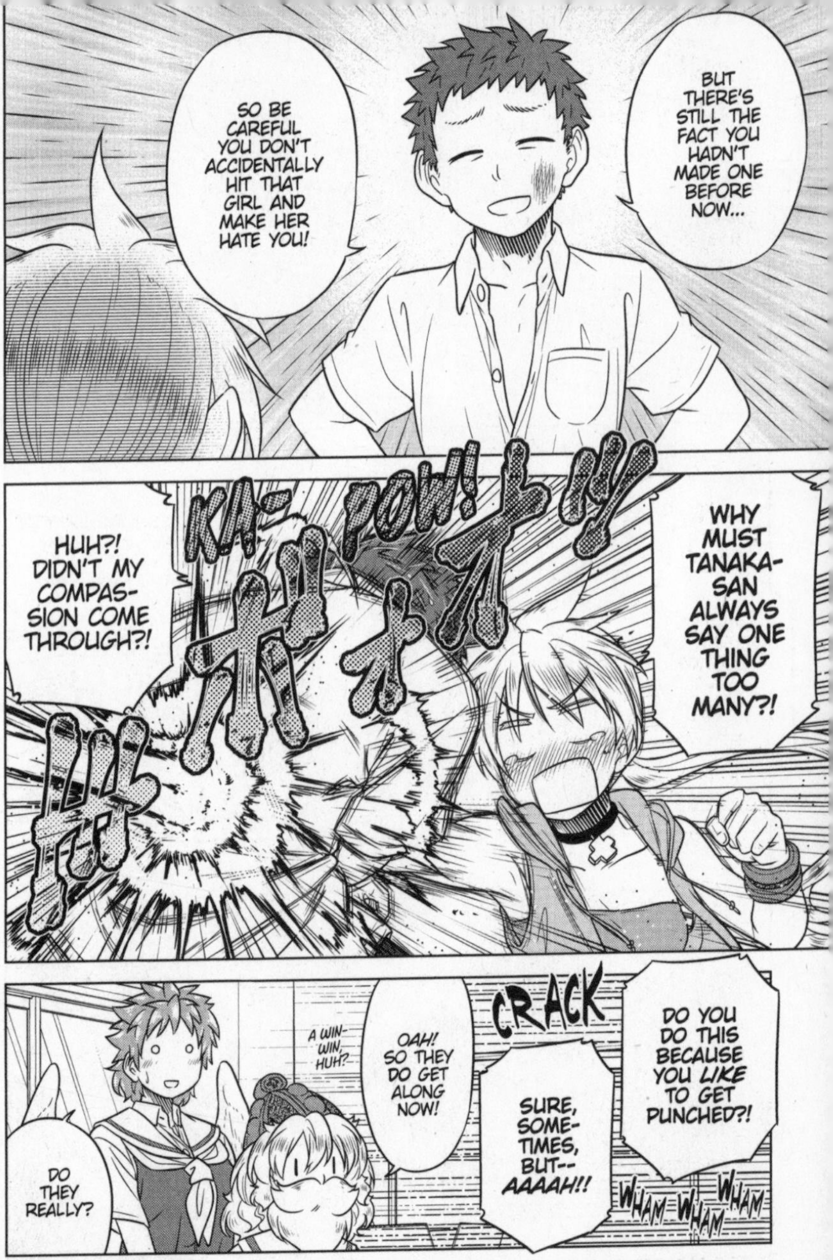
BUT THERE'S STILL THE FACT YOU HADN'T MADE ONE BEFORE NOW...
SO BE CAREFUL YOU DON'T ACCIDENTALLY HIT THAT GIRL AND MAKE HER HATE YOU!
WHY MUST TANAKA-SAN ALWAYS SAY ONE THING TOO MANY?!
KA-POW!
HUH?! DIDN'T MY COMPASSION COME THROUGH?!
DO YOU DO THIS BECAUSE YOU *LIKE* TO GET PUNCHED?!
CRACK
SURE, SOMETIMES, BUT-- AAAAH!!
WHAM WHAM WHAM
OAH! SO THEY DO GET ALONG NOW!
A WIN-WIN, HUH?
DO THEY REALLY?

Chapter 39 • END

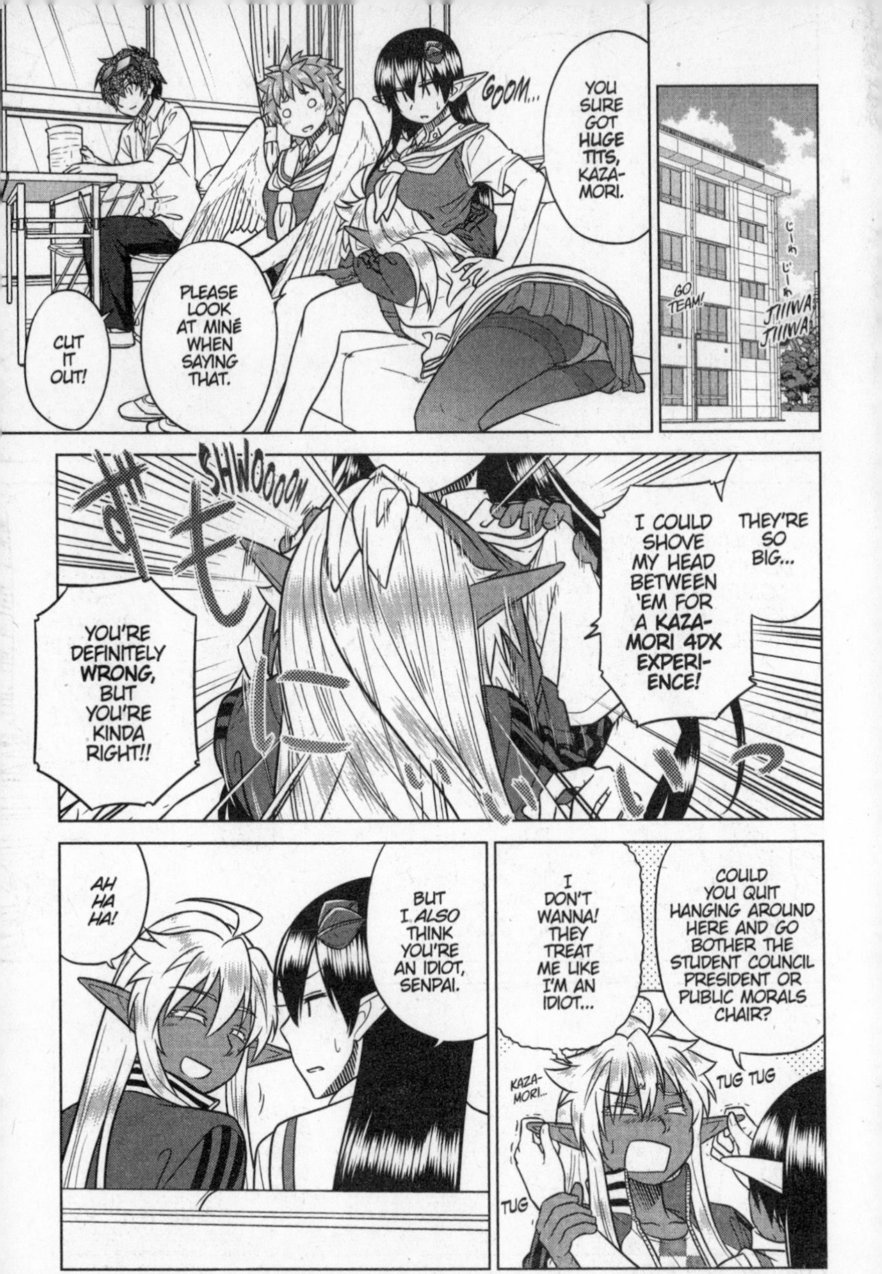
GO TEAM!
JIIIWA JIIIWA
GOOM...
YOU SURE GOT HUGE TITS, KAZAMORI.
PLEASE LOOK AT MINE WHEN SAYING THAT.
CUT IT OUT!
SHWOOOOM
THEY'RE SO BIG...
I COULD SHOVE MY HEAD BETWEEN 'EM FOR A KAZAMORI 4DX EXPERIENCE!
YOU'RE DEFINITELY WRONG, BUT YOU'RE KINDA RIGHT!!
COULD YOU QUIT HANGING AROUND HERE AND GO BOTHER THE STUDENT COUNCIL PRESIDENT OR PUBLIC MORALS CHAIR?
I DON'T WANNA! THEY TREAT ME LIKE I'M AN IDIOT...
TUG TUG
KAZAMORI...
TUG
BUT I *ALSO* THINK YOU'RE AN IDIOT, SENPAI.
AH HA HA!

Chapter 40: Kuroki-san Wants to Tell

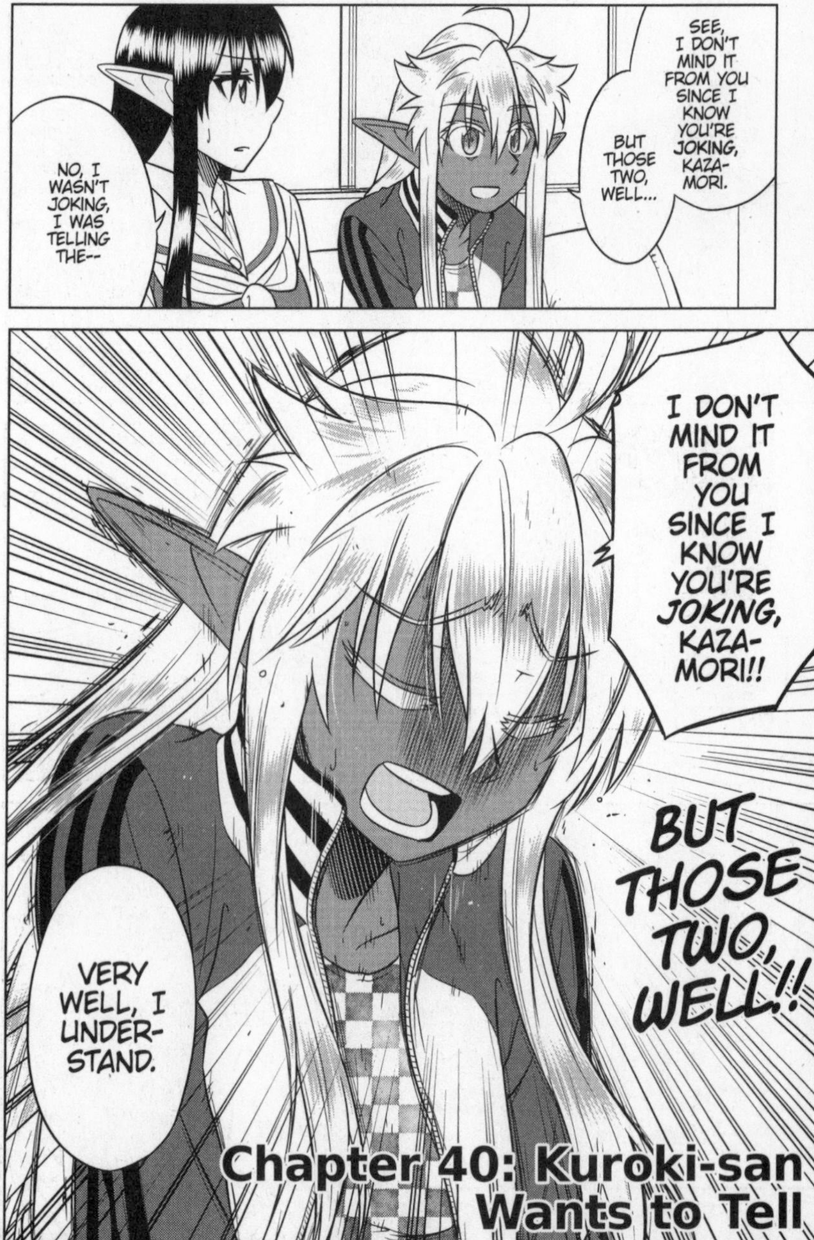
SEE, I DON'T MIND IT FROM YOU SINCE I KNOW YOU'RE JOKING, KAZAMORI.
BUT THOSE TWO, WELL...
NO, I WASN'T JOKING, I WAS TELLING THE--
I DON'T MIND IT FROM YOU SINCE I KNOW YOU'RE JOKING, KAZAMORI!!
BUT THOSE TWO, WELL!!
VERY WELL, I UNDERSTAND.

Chapter 40: Kuroki-san Wants to Tell

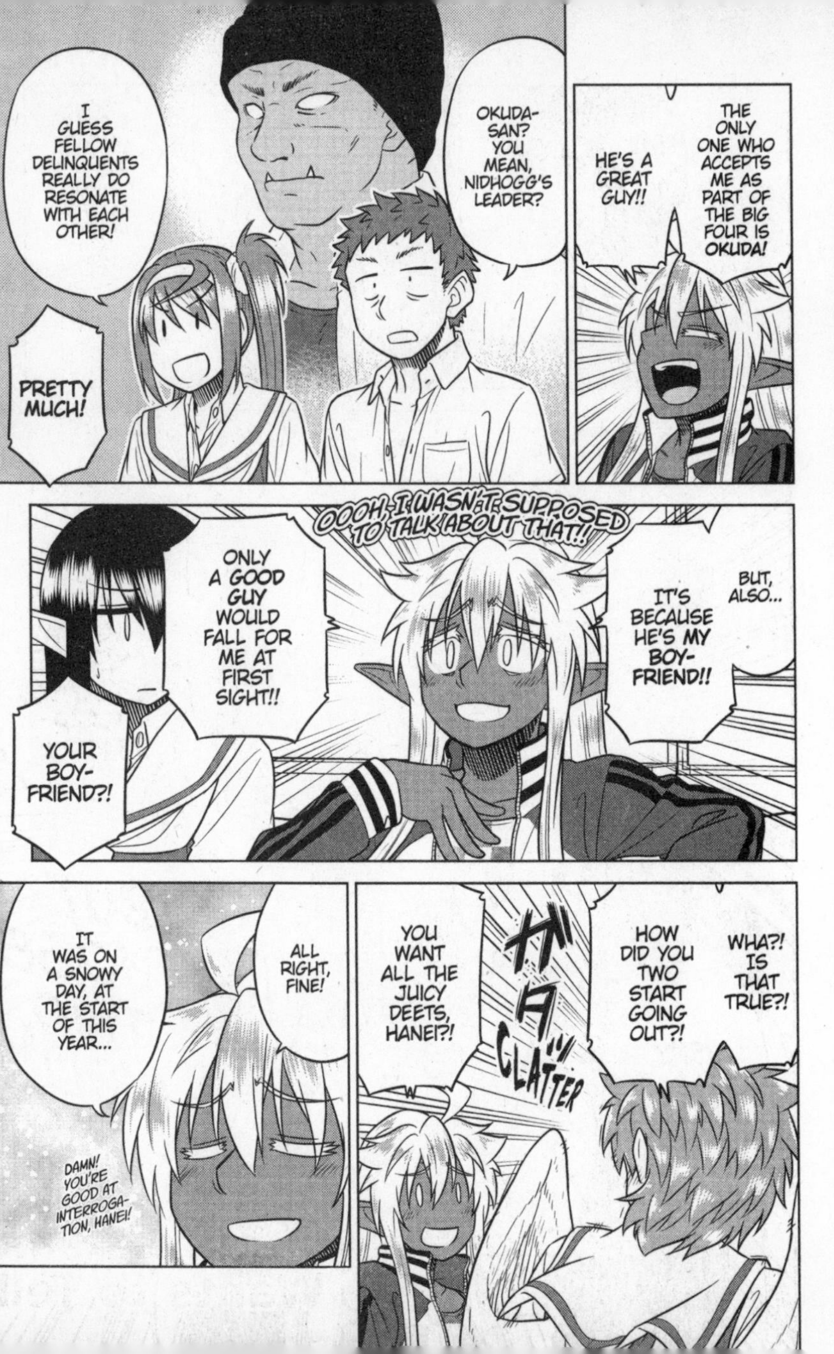
THE ONLY ONE WHO ACCEPTS ME AS PART OF THE BIG FOUR IS OKUDA!
HE'S A GREAT GUY!!
OKUDA-SAN? YOU MEAN, NIDHOGG'S LEADER?
I GUESS FELLOW DELINQUENTS REALLY DO RESONATE WITH EACH OTHER!
PRETTY MUCH!
OOOH, I WASN'T SUPPOSED TO TALK ABOUT THAT!!
BUT, ALSO...
IT'S BECAUSE HE'S MY BOYFRIEND!!
ONLY A GOOD GUY WOULD FALL FOR ME AT FIRST SIGHT!!
YOUR BOYFRIEND?!
WHA?! IS THAT TRUE?!
HOW DID YOU TWO START GOING OUT?!
CLATTER
YOU WANT ALL THE JUICY DEETS, HANEI?!
ALL RIGHT, FINE!
IT WAS ON A SNOWY DAY, AT THE START OF THIS YEAR...
DAMN! YOU'RE GOOD AT INTERROGATION, HANEI!

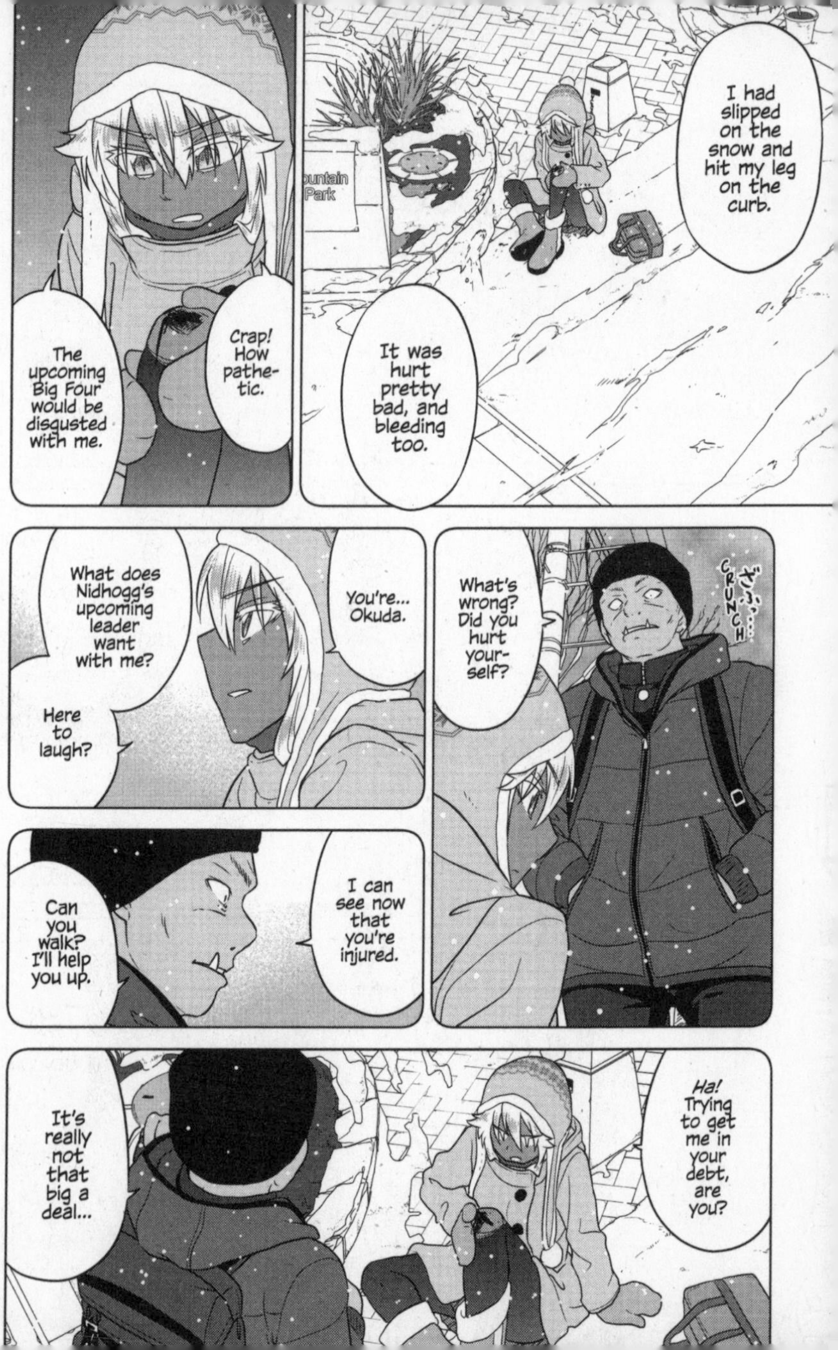
I had slipped on the snow and hit my leg on the curb.
It was hurt pretty bad, and bleeding too.
Crap! How pathetic.
The upcoming Big Four would be disgusted with me.
What's wrong? Did you hurt yourself?
CRUNCH
You're... Okuda.
What does Nidhogg's upcoming leader want with me?
Here to laugh?
I can see now that you're injured.
Can you walk? I'll help you up.
Ha! Trying to get me in your debt, are you?
It's really not that big a deal...

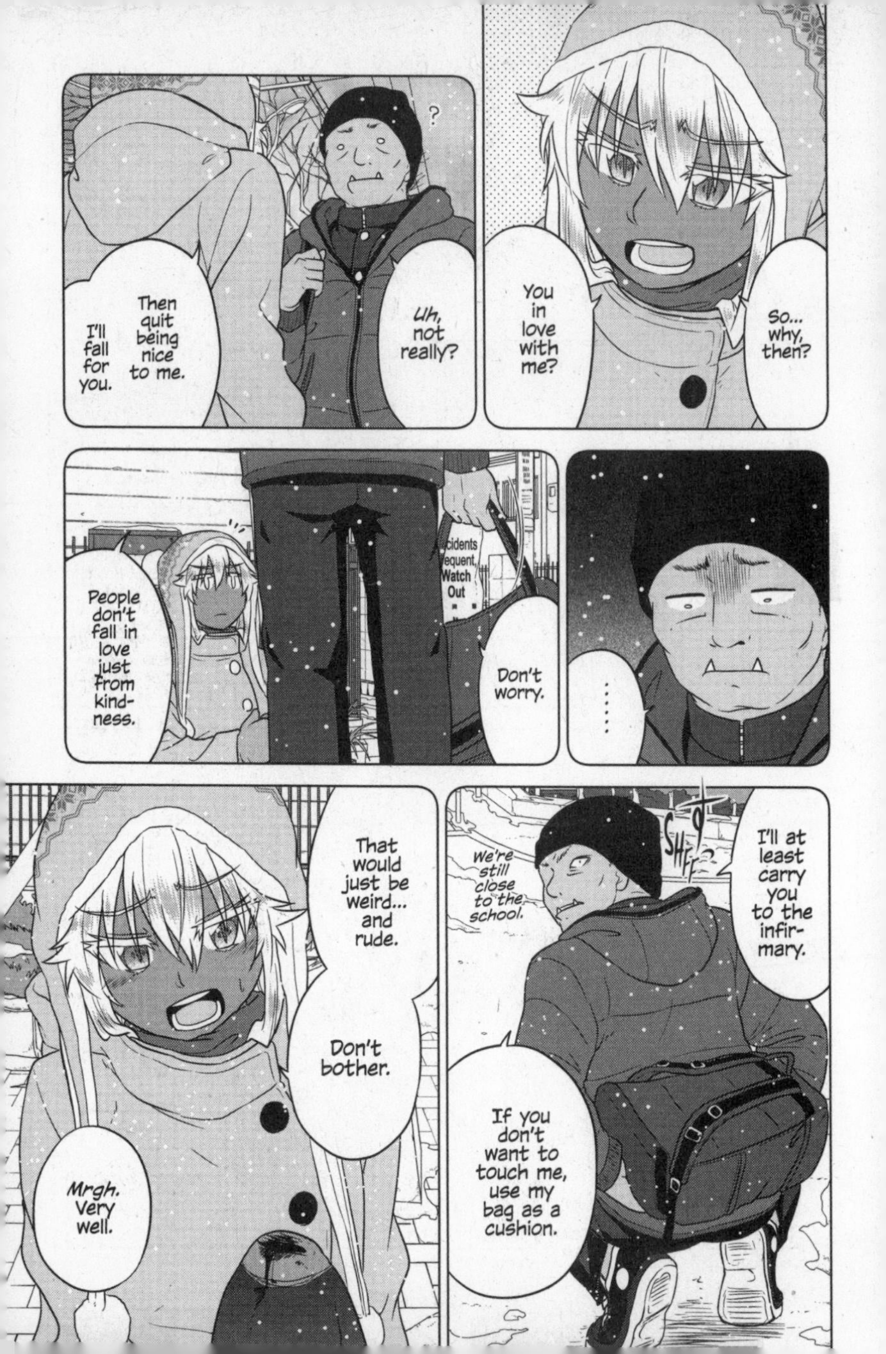

So... why, then?
You in love with me?
?
Uh, not really?
Then quit being nice to me.
I'll fall for you.
......
Don't worry.
Watch Out
People don't fall in love just from kindness.
I'll at least carry you to the infirmary.
SHFF
We're still close to the school.
If you don't want to touch me, use my bag as a cushion.
That would just be weird... and rude.
Don't bother.
Mrgh. Very well.

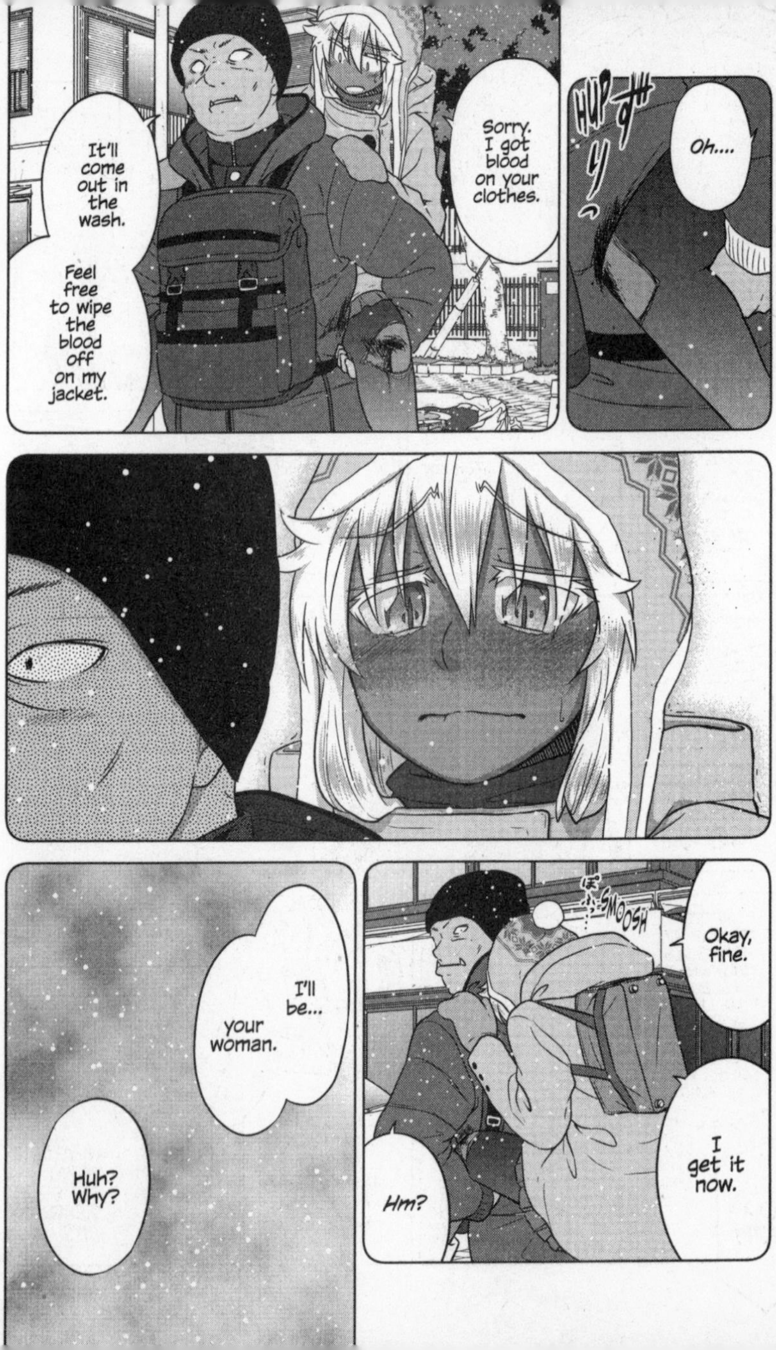
HUP
ずりっ
Oh....
Sorry. I got blood on your clothes.
It'll come out in the wash.
Feel free to wipe the blood off on my jacket.
Okay, fine.
SMOOSH
I get it now.
Hm?
I'll be... your woman.
Huh? Why?

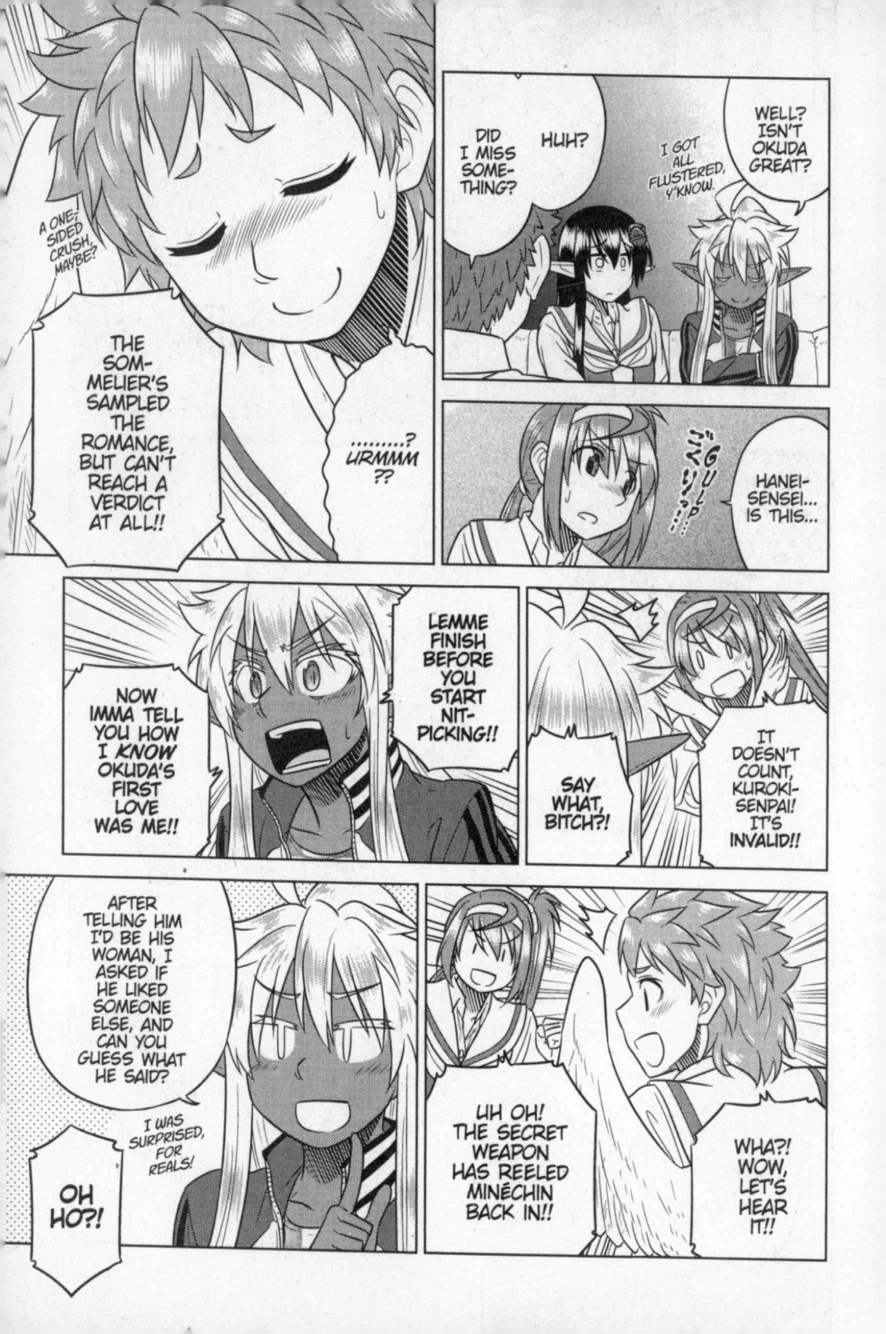
WELL? ISN'T OKUDA GREAT?
I GOT ALL FLUSTERED, Y'KNOW.
HUH?
DID I MISS SOME-THING?
HANEI-SENSEI... IS THIS...
GULP...
A ONE-SIDED CRUSH, MAYBE?
........? URMMM ??
THE SOM-MELIER'S SAMPLED THE ROMANCE, BUT CAN'T REACH A VERDICT AT ALL!!
IT DOESN'T COUNT, KUROKI-SENPAI! IT'S INVALID!!
SAY WHAT, BITCH?!
LEMME FINISH BEFORE YOU START NIT-PICKING!!
NOW IMMA TELL YOU HOW I KNOW OKUDA'S FIRST LOVE WAS ME!!
WHA?! WOW, LET'S HEAR IT!!
UH OH! THE SECRET WEAPON HAS REELED MINÉCHIN BACK IN!!
AFTER TELLING HIM I'D BE HIS WOMAN, I ASKED IF HE LIKED SOMEONE ELSE, AND CAN YOU GUESS WHAT HE SAID?
I WAS SURPRISED, FOR REALS!
OH HO?!

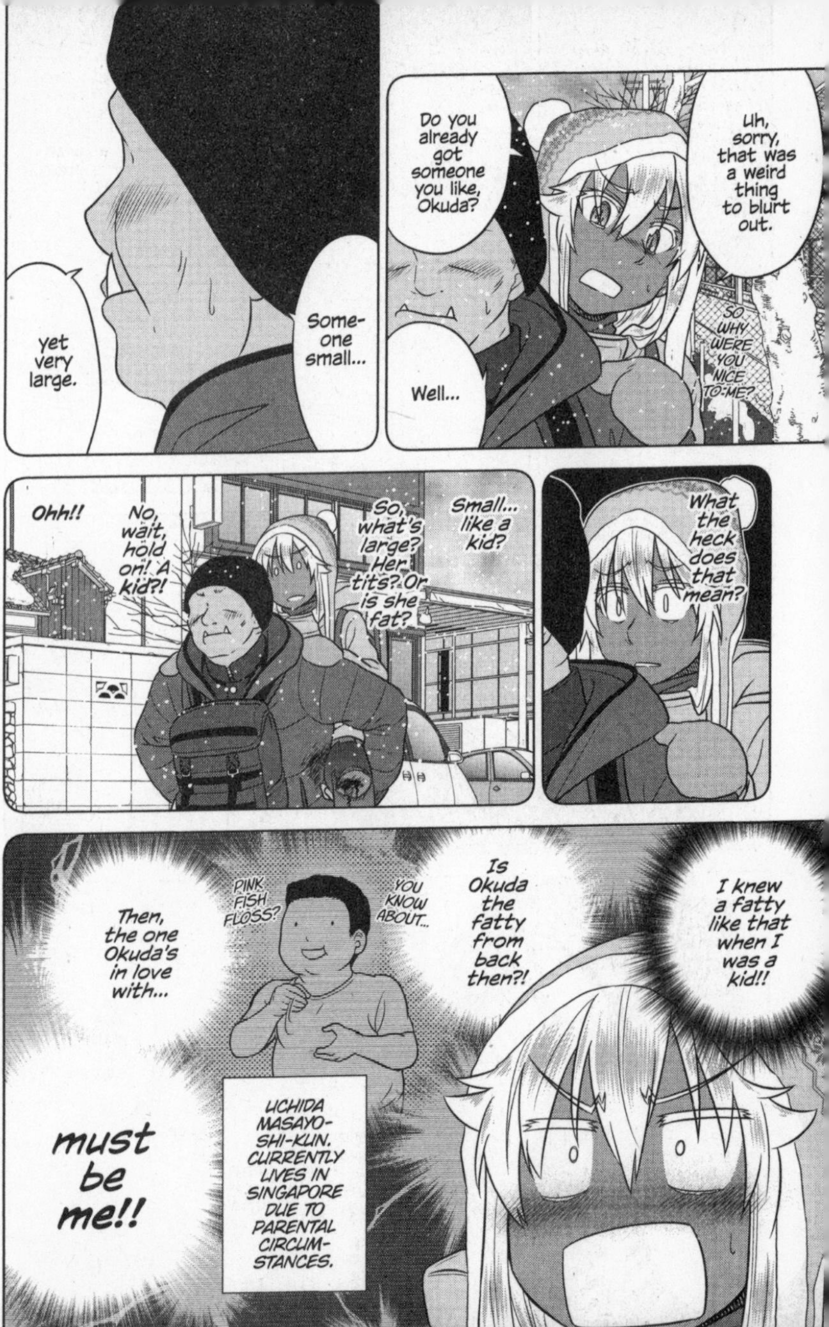
Uh, sorry, that was a weird thing to blurt out.
Do you already got someone you like, Okuda?
SO WHY WERE YOU NICE TO ME?
Well...
Some-one small...
yet very large.
What the heck does that mean?
Small... like a kid?
So, what's large? Her tits? Or is she fat?
No, wait, hold on! A kid?!
Ohh!!
I knew a fatty like that when I was a kid!!
Is Okuda the fatty from back then?!
YOU KNOW ABOUT...
PINK FISH FLOSS?
Then, the one Okuda's in love with...
UCHIDA MASAYO-SHI-KUN. CURRENTLY LIVES IN SINGAPORE DUE TO PARENTAL CIRCUM-STANCES.
must be me!!

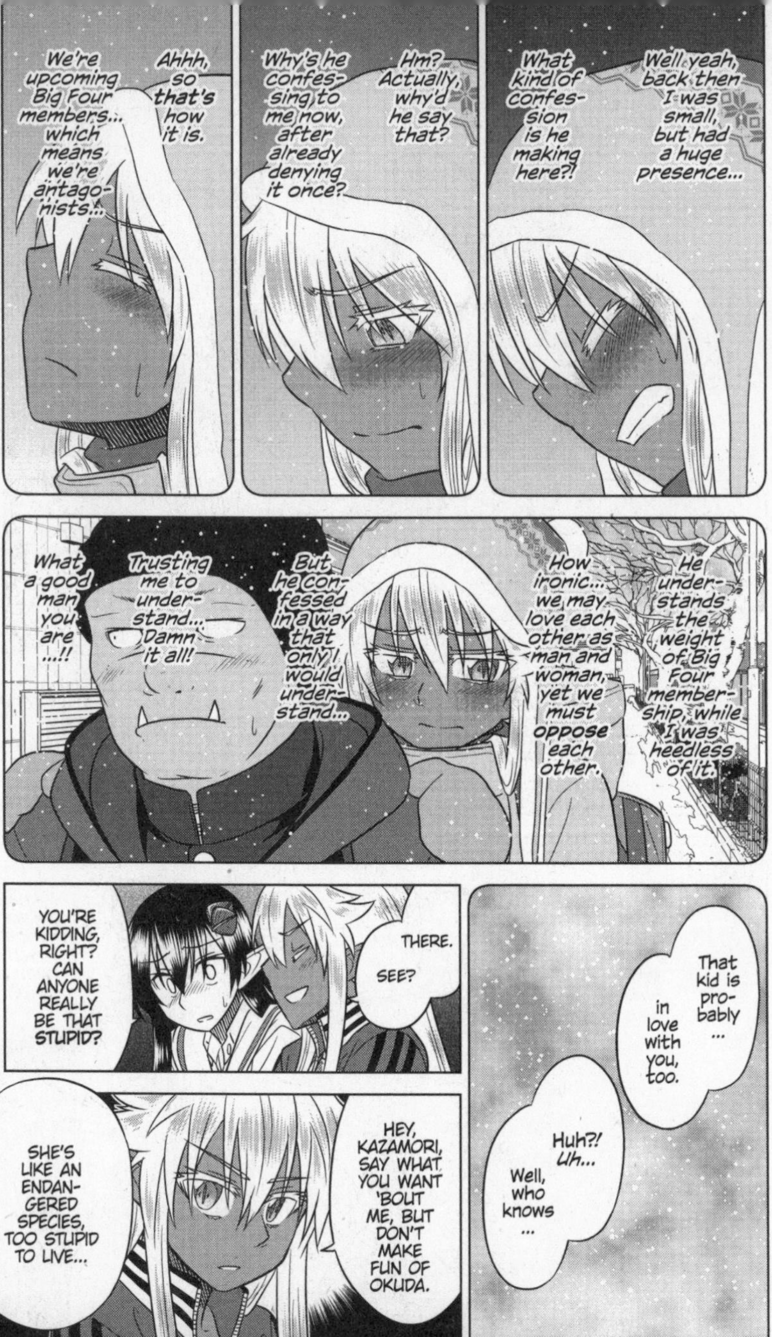
Well yeah, back then I was small, but had a huge presence...
What kind of confession is he making here?!
Hm? Actually, why'd he say that?
Why's he confessing to me now, after already denying it once?
Ahhh, so that's how it is.
We're upcoming Big Four members... which means we're antagonists...
He understands the weight of Big Four membership, while I was heedless of it.
How ironic... we may love each other as man and woman, yet we must oppose each other.
But he confessed in a way that only I would understand...
Trusting me to understand... Damn it all!
What a good man you are...!!
That kid is probably... in love with you, too.
Huh?! Uh...
Well, who knows...
THERE.
SEE?
YOU'RE KIDDING, RIGHT? CAN ANYONE REALLY BE THAT STUPID?
HEY, KAZAMORI, SAY WHAT YOU WANT 'BOUT ME, BUT DON'T MAKE FUN OF OKUDA.
SHE'S LIKE AN ENDANGERED SPECIES, TOO STUPID TO LIVE...

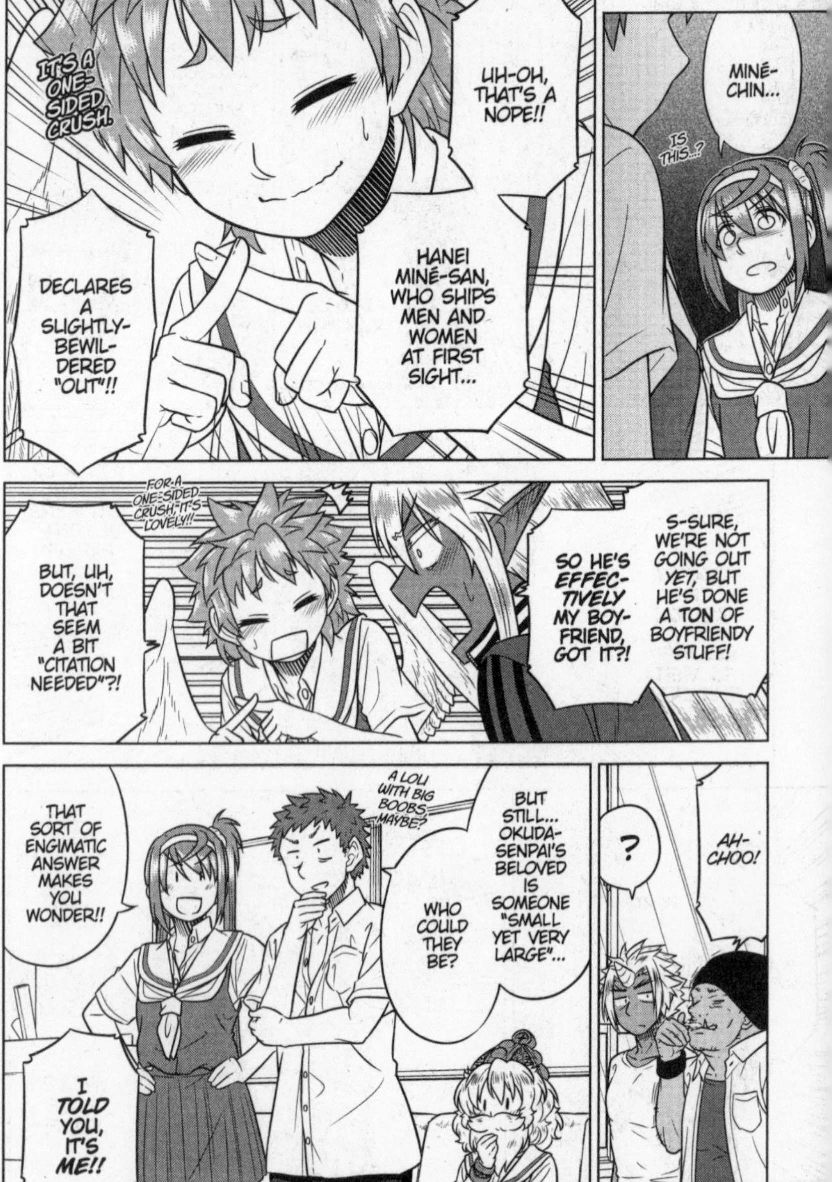
MINÉ-CHIN...
IS THIS...?
UH-OH, THAT'S A NOPE!!
IT'S A ONE-SIDED CRUSH.
HANEI MINÉ-SAN, WHO SHIPS MEN AND WOMEN AT FIRST SIGHT...
DECLARES A SLIGHTLY-BEWILDERED "OUT"!!
S-SURE, WE'RE NOT GOING OUT *YET*, BUT HE'S DONE A TON OF BOYFRIENDY STUFF!
SO HE'S *EFFECTIVELY* MY BOYFRIEND, GOT IT?!
FOR A ONE-SIDED CRUSH, IT'S LOVELY!!
BUT, UH, DOESN'T THAT SEEM A BIT "CITATION NEEDED"?!
AH-CHOO!
?
BUT STILL... OKUDA-SENPAI'S BELOVED IS SOMEONE "SMALL YET VERY LARGE"...
A LOLI WITH BIG BOOBS, MAYBE?
WHO COULD THEY BE?
THAT SORT OF ENGIMATIC ANSWER MAKES YOU WONDER!!
I *TOLD* YOU, IT'S *ME*!!

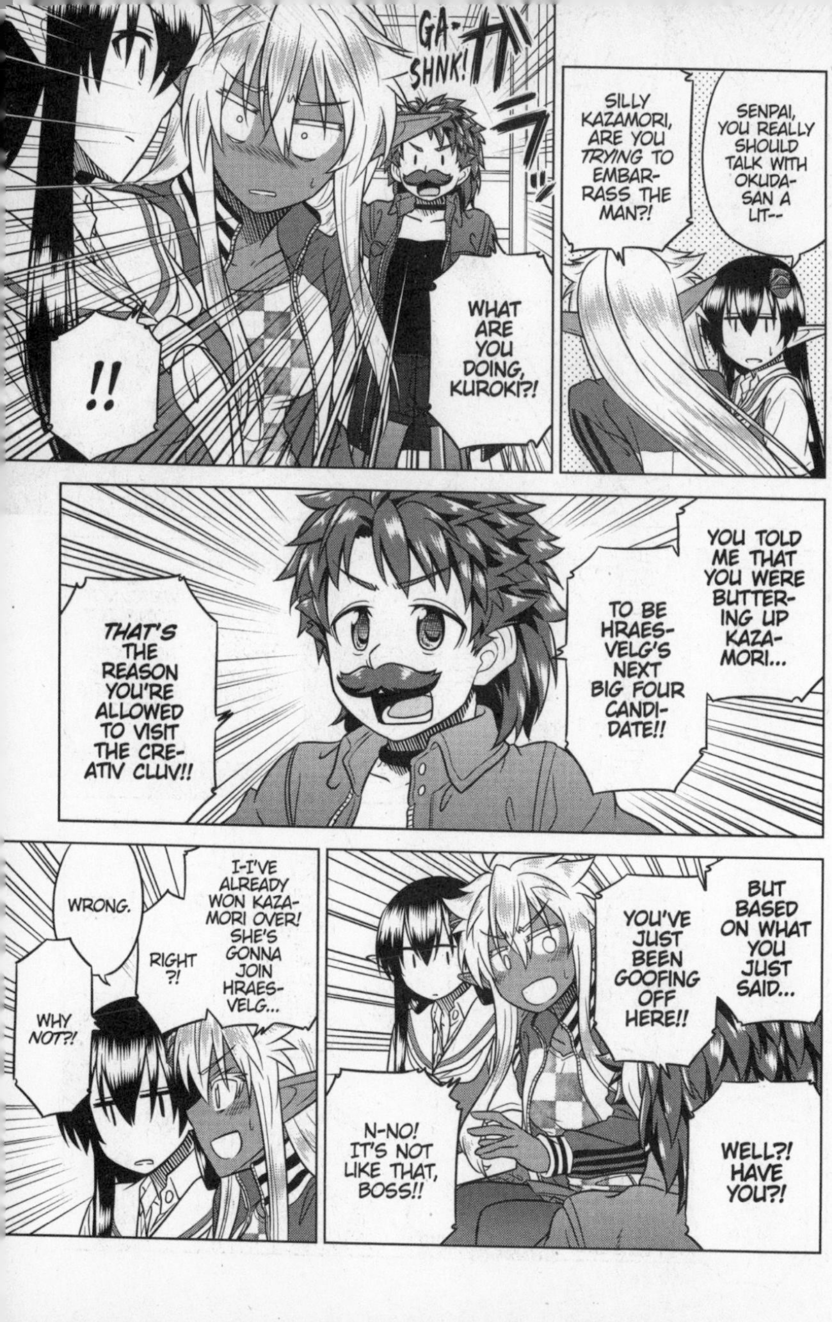
SENPAI, YOU REALLY SHOULD TALK WITH OKUDA-SAN A LIT--
SILLY KAZAMORI, ARE YOU *TRYING* TO EMBARRASS THE MAN?!
GA-SHNK!
WHAT ARE YOU DOING, KUROKI?!
!!
YOU TOLD ME THAT YOU WERE BUTTERING UP KAZAMORI...
TO BE HRAESVELG'S NEXT BIG FOUR CANDIDATE!!
THAT'S THE REASON YOU'RE ALLOWED TO VISIT THE CREATIV CLUV!!
BUT BASED ON WHAT YOU JUST SAID...
YOU'VE JUST BEEN GOOFING OFF HERE!!
WELL?! HAVE YOU?!
N-NO! IT'S NOT LIKE THAT, BOSS!!
I-I'VE ALREADY WON KAZAMORI OVER! SHE'S GONNA JOIN HRAESVELG...
RIGHT?!
WRONG.
WHY *NOT*?!

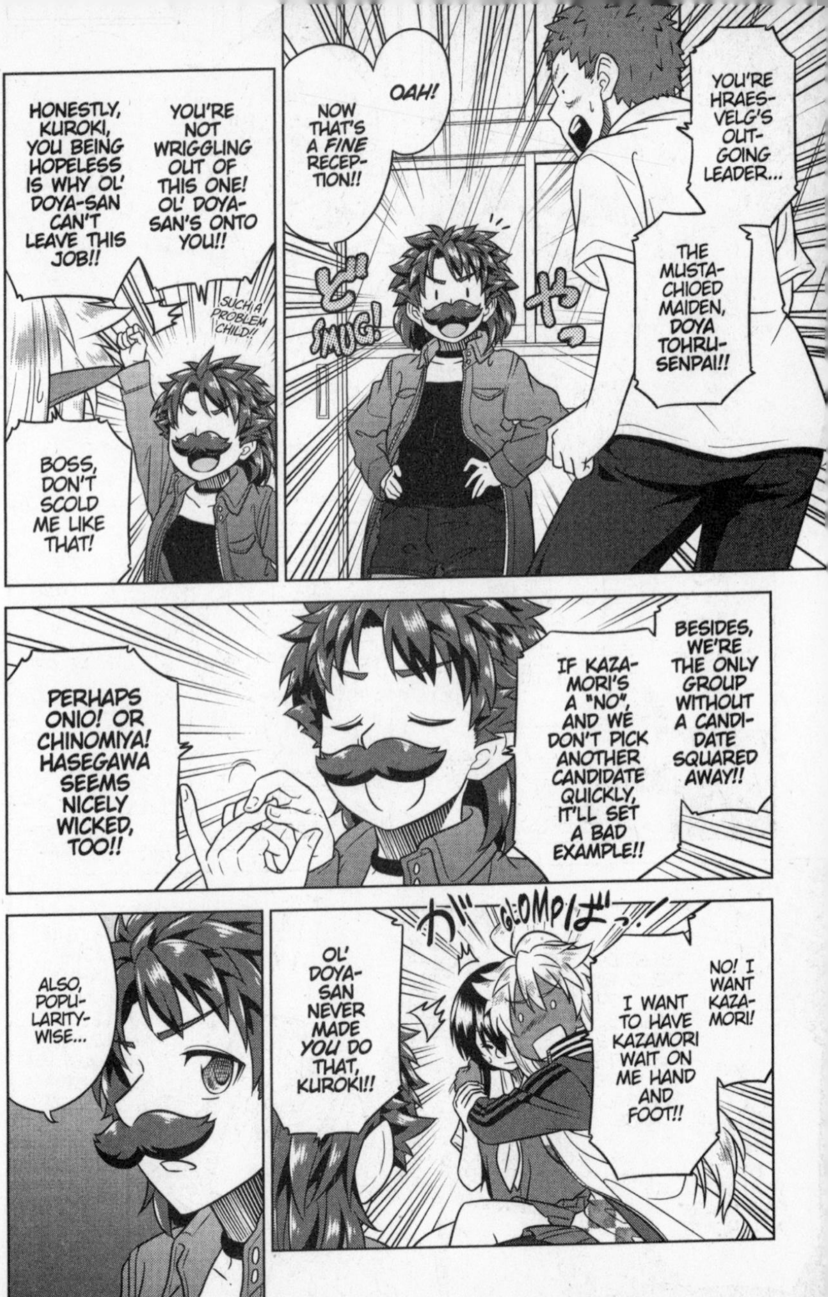
YOU'RE HRAESVELG'S OUTGOING LEADER...
THE MUSTACHIOED MAIDEN, DOYA TOHRU-SENPAI!!
OAH!
NOW THAT'S A *FINE* RECEPTION!!
SMUG!
YOU'RE NOT WRIGGLING OUT OF THIS ONE! OL' DOYA-SAN'S ONTO YOU!!
HONESTLY, KUROKI, YOU BEING HOPELESS IS WHY OL' DOYA-SAN CAN'T LEAVE THIS JOB!!
SUCH A PROBLEM CHILD!!
BOSS, DON'T SCOLD ME LIKE THAT!
BESIDES, WE'RE THE ONLY GROUP WITHOUT A CANDIDATE SQUARED AWAY!!
IF KAZAMORI'S A "NO", AND WE DON'T PICK ANOTHER CANDIDATE QUICKLY, IT'LL SET A BAD EXAMPLE!!
PERHAPS ONIO! OR CHINOMIYA! HASEGAWA SEEMS NICELY WICKED, TOO!!
GLOMP
NO! I WANT KAZAMORI!
I WANT TO HAVE KAZAMORI WAIT ON ME HAND AND FOOT!!
OL' DOYA-SAN NEVER MADE *YOU* DO THAT, KUROKI!!
ALSO, POPULARITY-WISE...

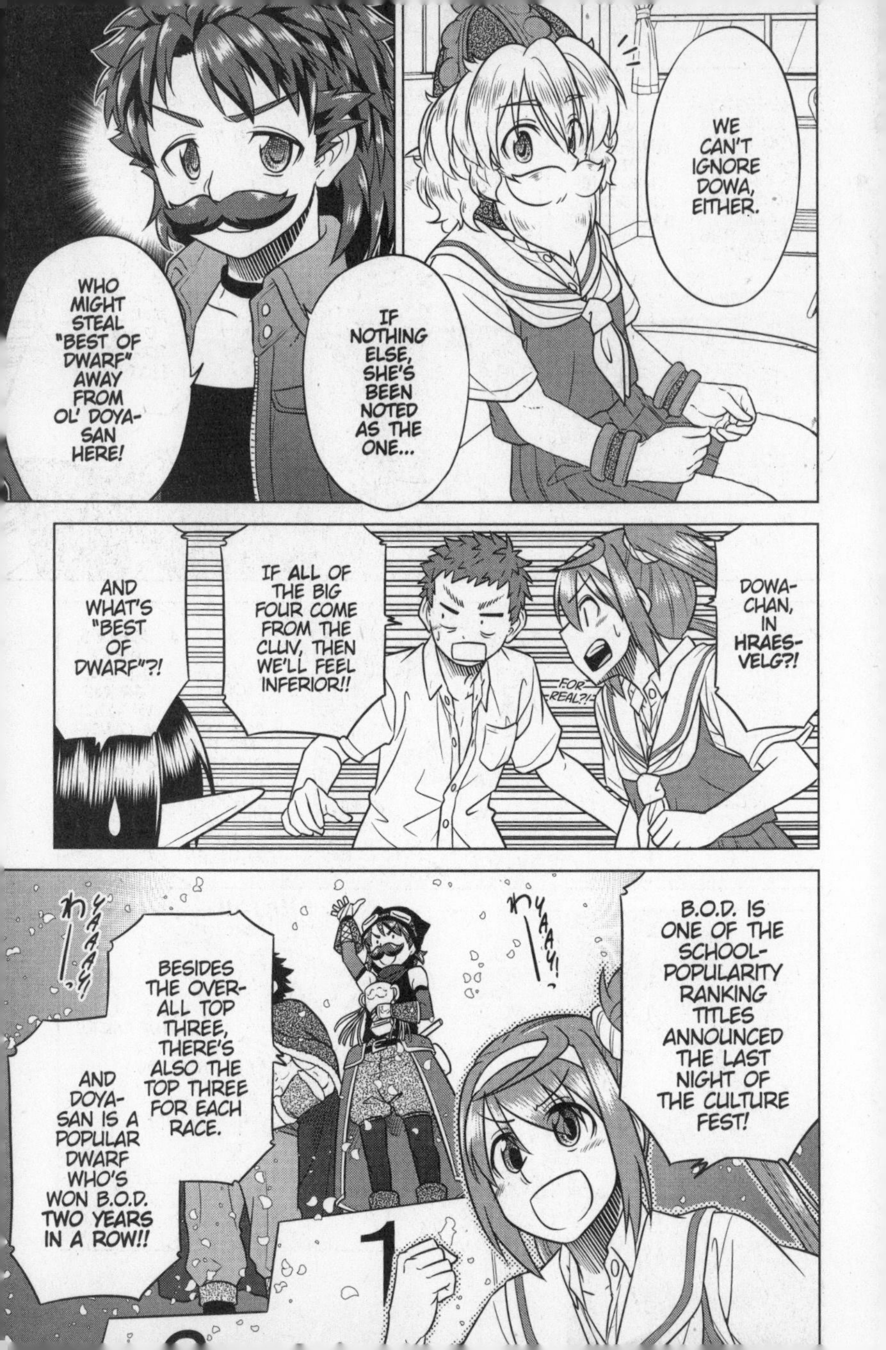
WE CAN'T IGNORE DOWA, EITHER.
IF NOTHING ELSE, SHE'S BEEN NOTED AS THE ONE...
WHO MIGHT STEAL "BEST OF DWARF" AWAY FROM OL' DOYA-SAN HERE!
DOWA-CHAN, IN HRAES-VELG?!
FOR REAL?!
IF ALL OF THE BIG FOUR COME FROM THE CLUV, THEN WE'LL FEEL INFERIOR!!
AND WHAT'S "BEST OF DWARF"?!
B.O.D. IS ONE OF THE SCHOOL-POPULARITY RANKING TITLES ANNOUNCED THE LAST NIGHT OF THE CULTURE FEST!
わーYAAAY!
BESIDES THE OVER-ALL TOP THREE, THERE'S ALSO THE TOP THREE FOR EACH RACE.
AND DOYA-SAN IS A POPULAR DWARF WHO'S WON B.O.D. TWO YEARS IN A ROW!!
わーYAAAY!
1

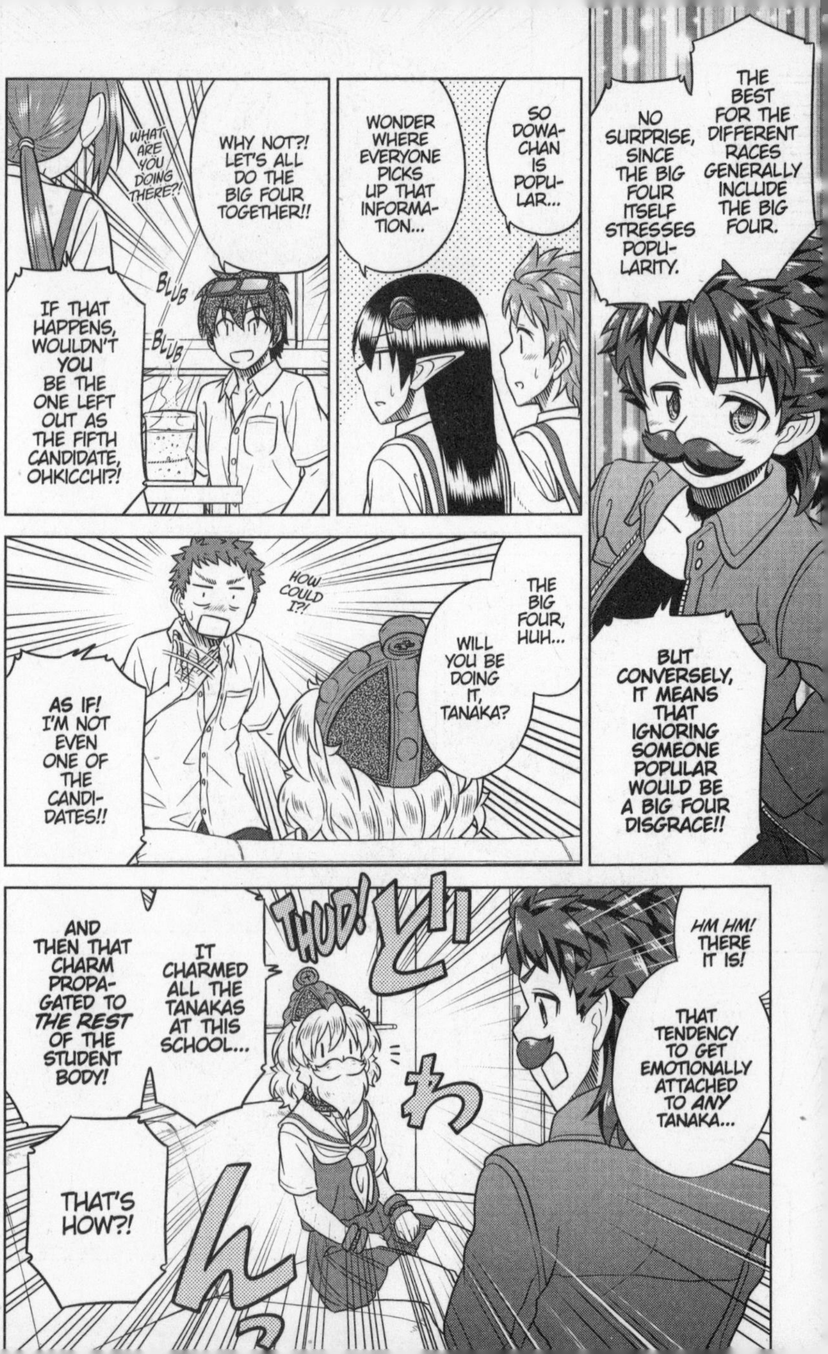
THE BEST FOR THE DIFFERENT RACES GENERALLY INCLUDE THE BIG FOUR.
NO SURPRISE, SINCE THE BIG FOUR ITSELF STRESSES POPULARITY.
BUT CONVERSELY, IT MEANS THAT IGNORING SOMEONE POPULAR WOULD BE A BIG FOUR DISGRACE!!
SO DOWA-CHAN IS POPULAR...
WONDER WHERE EVERYONE PICKS UP THAT INFORMATION...
WHY NOT?! LET'S ALL DO THE BIG FOUR TOGETHER!!
WHAT ARE YOU DOING THERE?!
BLUB
BLUB
IF THAT HAPPENS, WOULDN'T YOU BE THE ONE LEFT OUT AS THE FIFTH CANDIDATE, OHKICCHI?!
THE BIG FOUR, HUH...
WILL YOU BE DOING IT, TANAKA?
HOW COULD I?!
AS IF! I'M NOT EVEN ONE OF THE CANDIDATES!!
HM HM! THERE IT IS!
THAT TENDENCY TO GET EMOTIONALLY ATTACHED TO *ANY* TANAKA...
THUD!
ど
わ
ん
IT CHARMED ALL THE TANAKAS AT THIS SCHOOL...
AND THEN THAT CHARM PROPAGATED TO *THE REST* OF THE STUDENT BODY!
THAT'S HOW?!

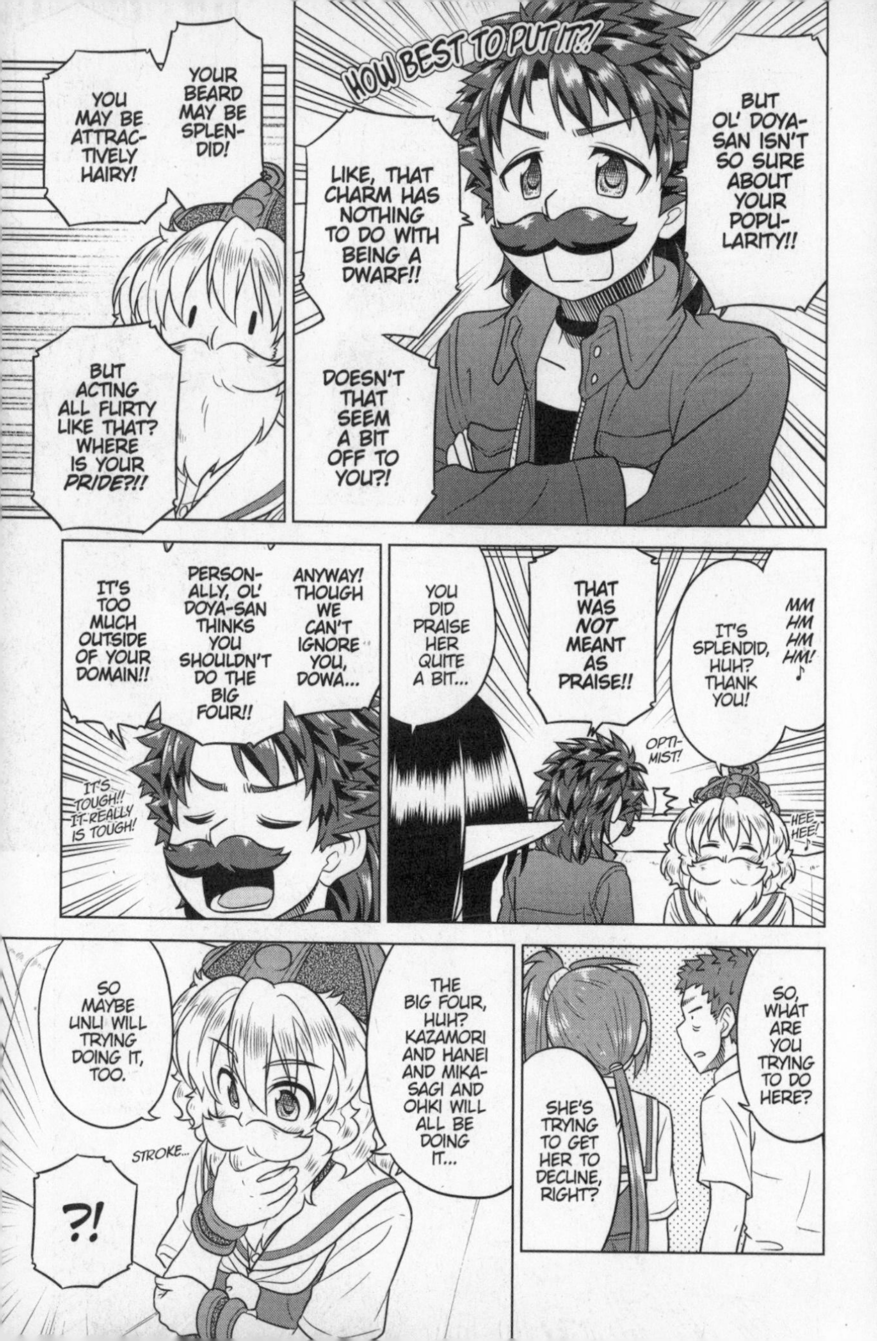
HOW BEST TO PUT IT?!
BUT OL' DOYA-SAN ISN'T SO SURE ABOUT YOUR POPU-LARITY!!
LIKE, THAT CHARM HAS NOTHING TO DO WITH BEING A DWARF!!
DOESN'T THAT SEEM A BIT OFF TO YOU?!
YOUR BEARD MAY BE SPLEN-DID!
YOU MAY BE ATTRAC-TIVELY HAIRY!
BUT ACTING ALL FLIRTY LIKE THAT? WHERE IS YOUR *PRIDE?!!*
MM HM HM HM! ♪
IT'S SPLENDID, HUH? THANK YOU!
THAT WAS *NOT* MEANT AS PRAISE!!
YOU DID PRAISE HER QUITE A BIT...
OPTI-MIST!
HEE, HEE! ♪
ANYWAY! THOUGH WE CAN'T IGNORE YOU, DOWA...
PERSON-ALLY, OL' DOYA-SAN THINKS YOU SHOULDN'T DO THE BIG FOUR!!
IT'S TOO MUCH OUTSIDE OF YOUR DOMAIN!!
IT'S TOUGH!! IT REALLY IS TOUGH!
SO, WHAT ARE YOU TRYING TO DO HERE?
SHE'S TRYING TO GET HER TO DECLINE, RIGHT?
THE BIG FOUR, HUH? KAZAMORI AND HANEI AND MIKA-SAGI AND OHKI WILL ALL BE DOING IT...
SO MAYBE UNLI WILL TRYING DOING IT, TOO.
STROKE...
?!

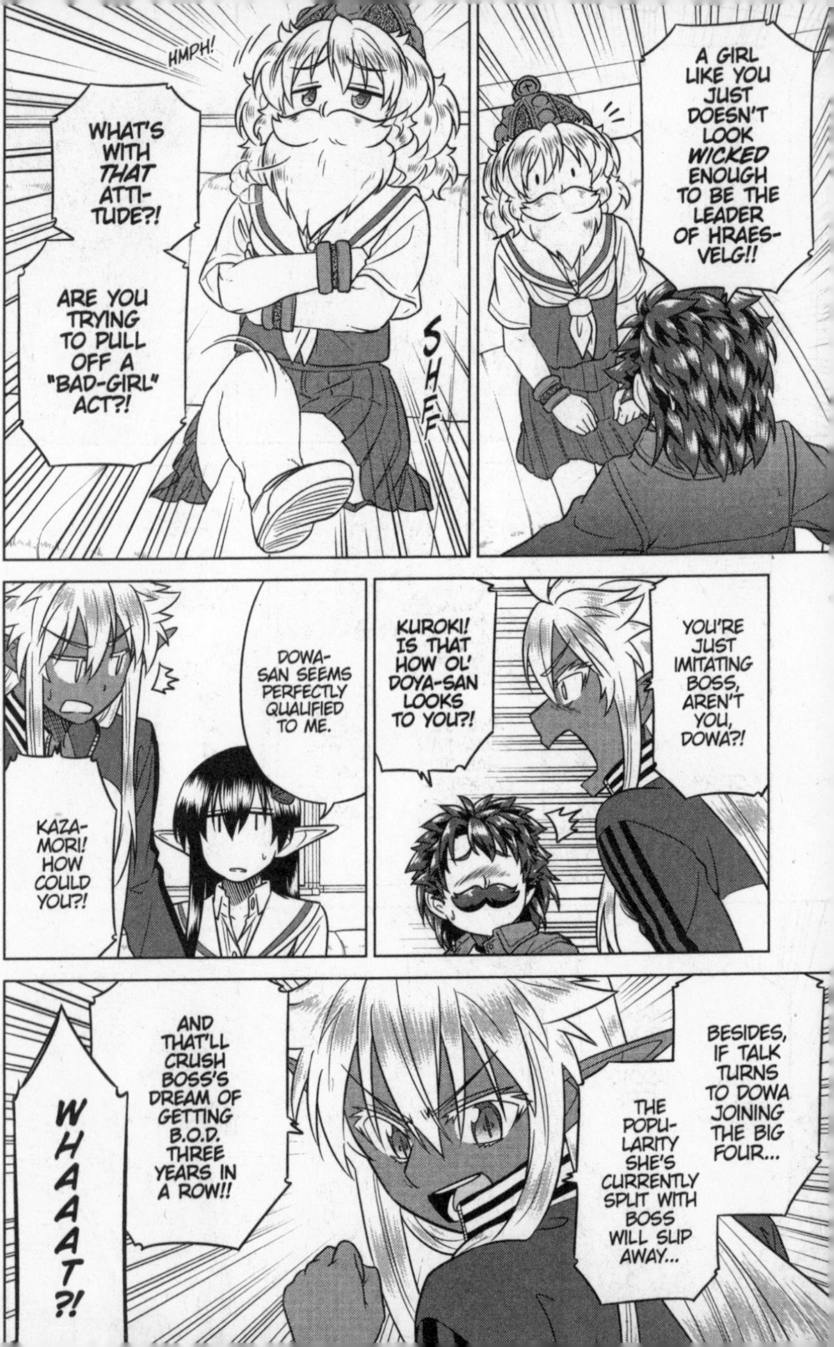
A GIRL LIKE YOU JUST DOESN'T LOOK *WICKED* ENOUGH TO BE THE LEADER OF HRAES-VELG!!
HMPH!
WHAT'S WITH *THAT* ATTI-TUDE?!
ARE YOU TRYING TO PULL OFF A "BAD-GIRL" ACT?!
SHFF
YOU'RE JUST IMITATING BOSS, AREN'T YOU, DOWA?!
KUROKI! IS THAT HOW OL' DOYA-SAN LOOKS TO YOU?!
DOWA-SAN SEEMS PERFECTLY QUALIFIED TO ME.
KAZA-MORI! HOW COULD YOU?!
BESIDES, IF TALK TURNS TO DOWA JOINING THE BIG FOUR...
THE POPU-LARITY SHE'S CURRENTLY SPLIT WITH BOSS WILL SLIP AWAY...
AND THAT'LL CRUSH BOSS'S DREAM OF GETTING B.O.D. THREE YEARS IN A ROW!!
WHAAAAT?!

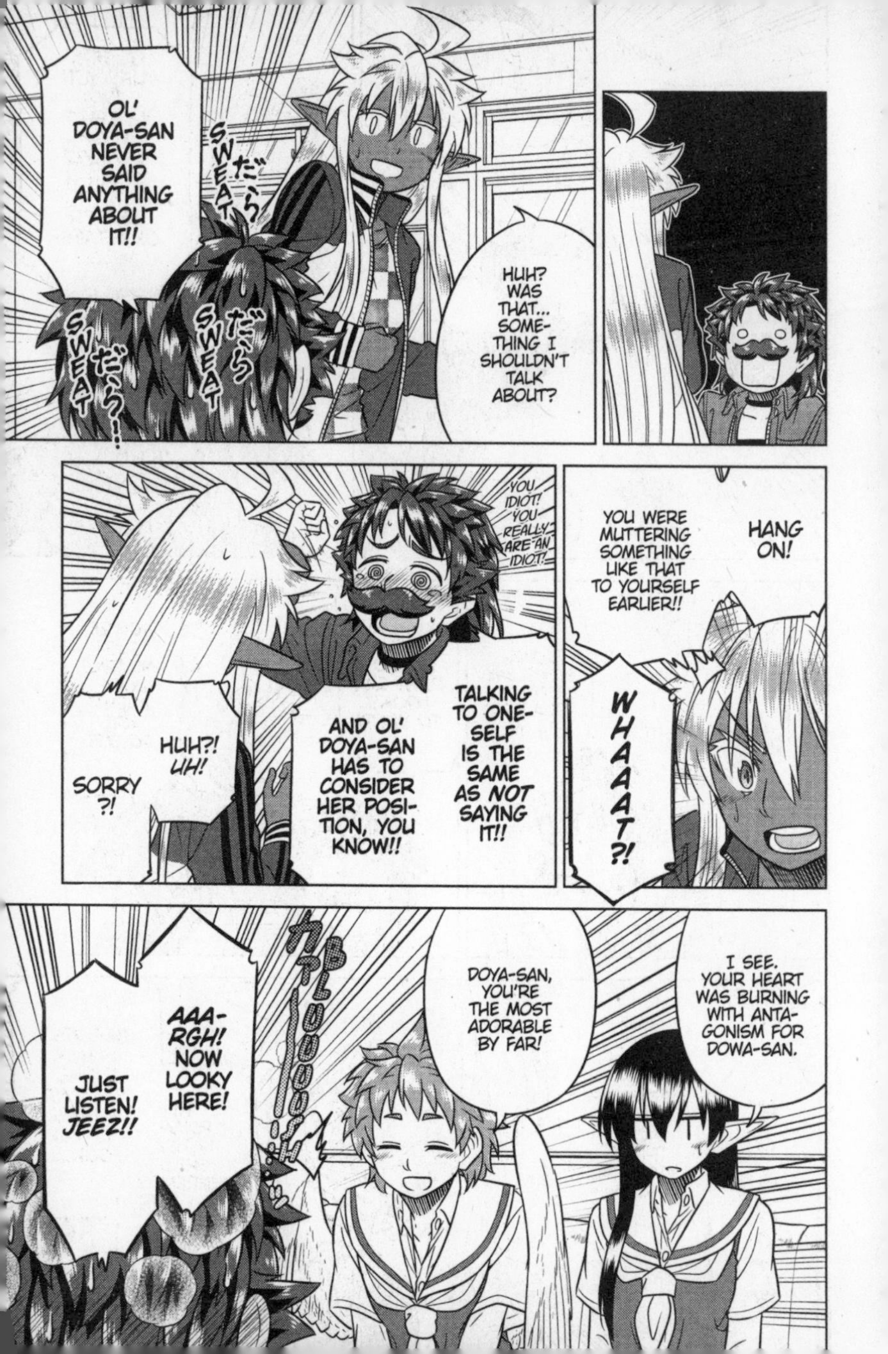
HUH? WAS THAT... SOME-THING I SHOULDN'T TALK ABOUT?
SWEAT
SWEAT
SWEAT
OL' DOYA-SAN NEVER SAID ANYTHING ABOUT IT!!
HANG ON!
YOU WERE MUTTERING SOMETHING LIKE THAT TO YOURSELF EARLIER!!
WHAAAAT?!
YOU IDIOT! YOU REALLY ARE AN IDIOT!
TALKING TO ONE-SELF IS THE SAME AS NOT SAYING IT!!
AND OL' DOYA-SAN HAS TO CONSIDER HER POSI-TION, YOU KNOW!!
HUH?! UH!
SORRY?!
I SEE. YOUR HEART WAS BURNING WITH ANTA-GONISM FOR DOWA-SAN.
DOYA-SAN, YOU'RE THE MOST ADORABLE BY FAR!
AAA-RGH! NOW LOOKY HERE!
JUST LISTEN! JEEZ!!

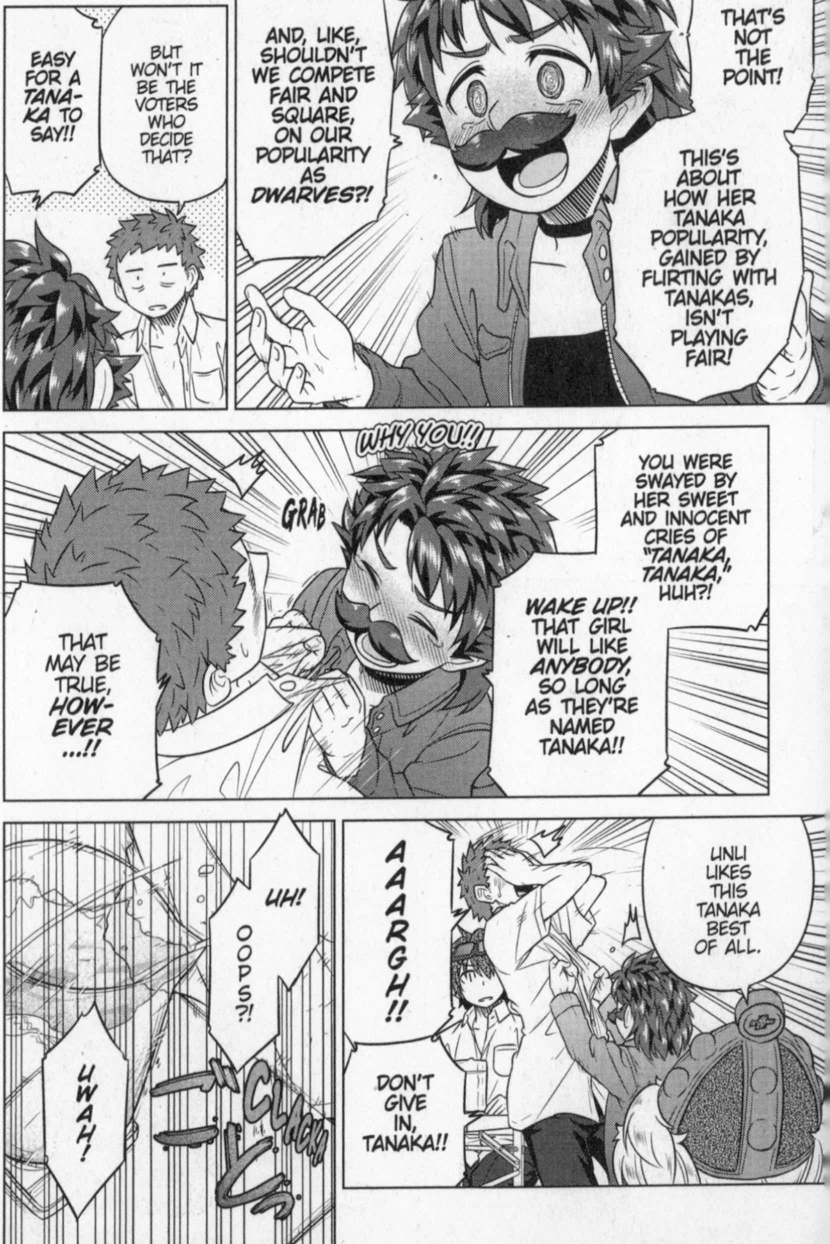
THAT'S NOT THE POINT!
THIS'S ABOUT HOW HER TANAKA POPULARITY, GAINED BY FLIRTING WITH TANAKAS, ISN'T PLAYING FAIR!
AND, LIKE, SHOULDN'T WE COMPETE FAIR AND SQUARE, ON OUR POPULARITY AS *DWARVES?!*
BUT WON'T IT BE THE VOTERS WHO DECIDE THAT?
EASY FOR A *TANAKA* TO SAY!!
WHY YOU!!
YOU WERE SWAYED BY HER SWEET AND INNOCENT CRIES OF *"TANAKA, TANAKA,"* HUH?!
WAKE UP!! THAT GIRL WILL LIKE *ANYBODY,* SO LONG AS THEY'RE NAMED TANAKA!!
GRAB
THAT MAY BE TRUE, *HOWEVER...!!*
UNLI LIKES THIS TANAKA BEST OF ALL.
AAAARGH!!
DON'T GIVE IN, TANAKA!!
UH!
OOPS?!
UWAH!
CLACK!!

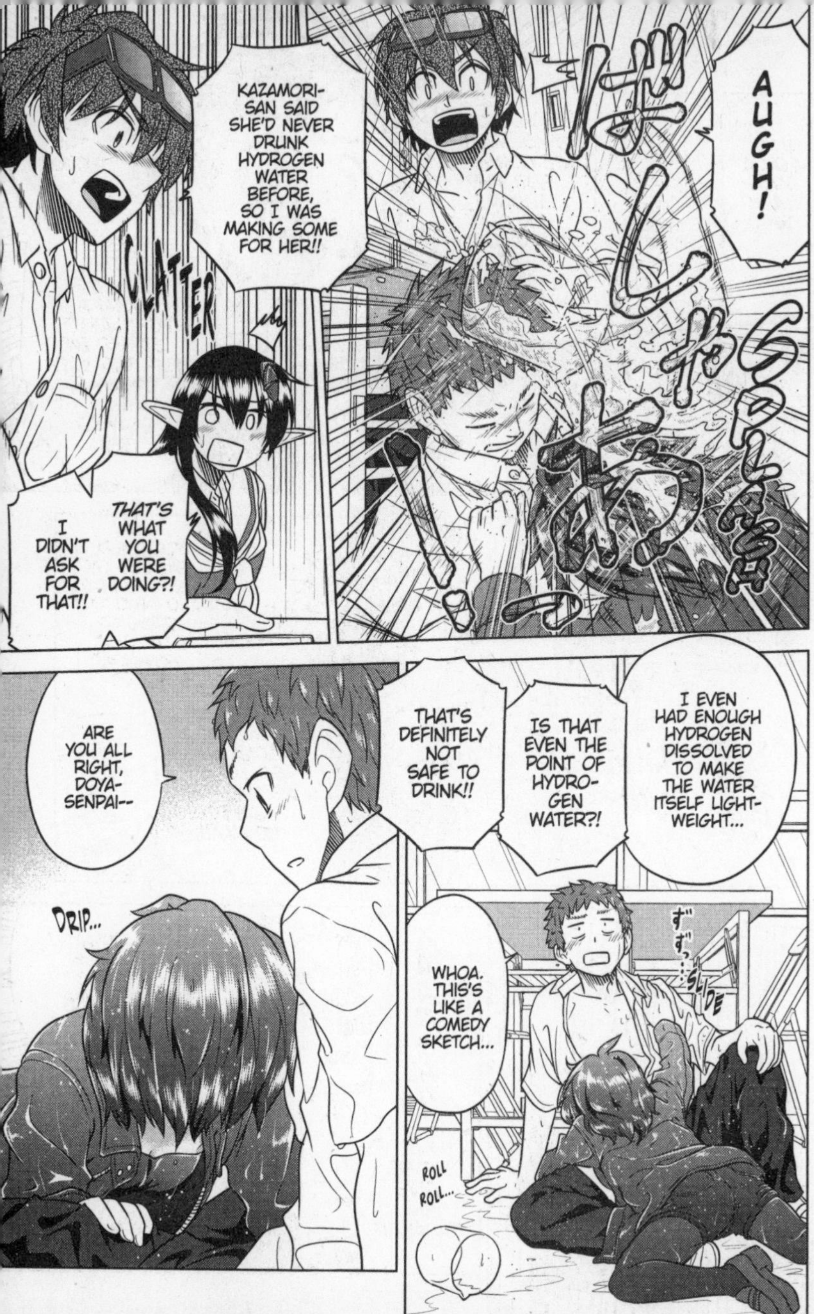
AUGH!
ばしゃあっ
SPLASH
KAZAMORI-SAN SAID SHE'D NEVER DRUNK HYDROGEN WATER BEFORE, SO I WAS MAKING SOME FOR HER!!
CLATTER
THAT'S WHAT YOU WERE DOING?!
I DIDN'T ASK FOR THAT!!
I EVEN HAD ENOUGH HYDROGEN DISSOLVED TO MAKE THE WATER ITSELF LIGHT-WEIGHT...
IS THAT EVEN THE POINT OF HYDRO-GEN WATER?!
THAT'S DEFINITELY NOT SAFE TO DRINK!!
ずずっ
SLIDE
WHOA. THIS'S LIKE A COMEDY SKETCH...
ROLL ROLL...
ARE YOU ALL RIGHT, DOYA-SENPAI--
DRIP...

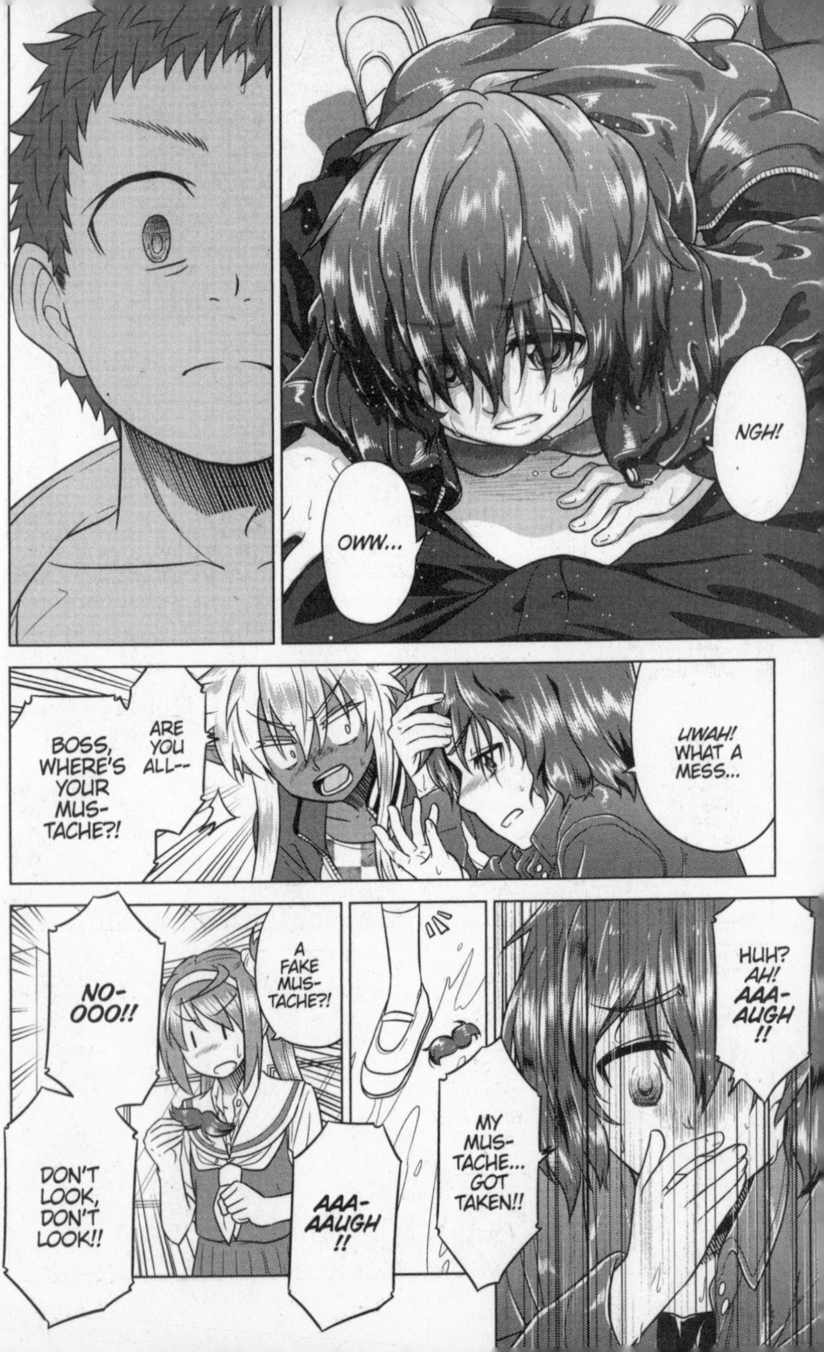
NGH!
OWW...
UWAH! WHAT A MESS...
ARE YOU ALL--
BOSS, WHERE'S YOUR MUS-TACHE?!
HUH? AH! AAA-AUGH!!
MY MUS-TACHE... GOT TAKEN!!
A FAKE MUS-TACHE?!
AAA-AAUGH!!
NO-OOO!!
DON'T LOOK, DON'T LOOK!!

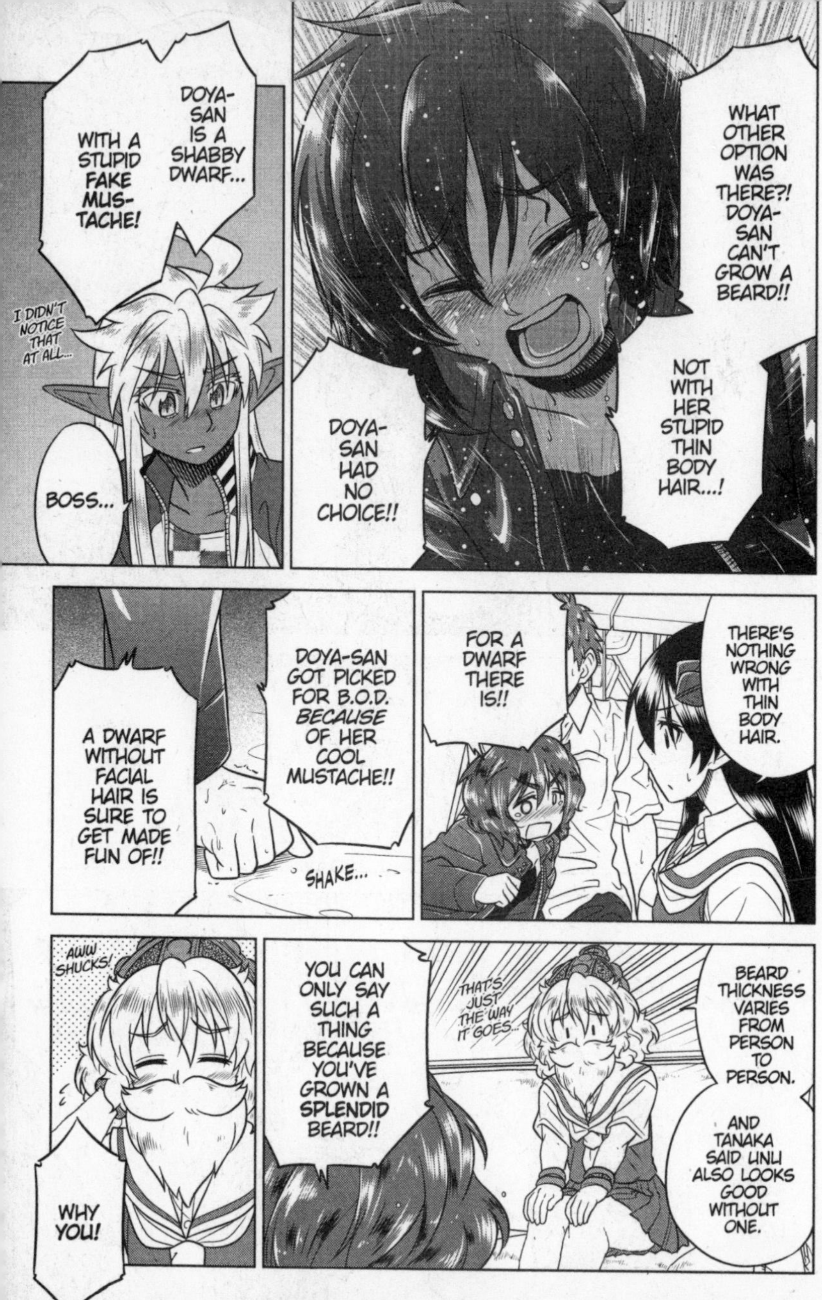
WHAT OTHER OPTION WAS THERE?! DOYA-SAN CAN'T GROW A BEARD!!
NOT WITH HER STUPID THIN BODY HAIR...!
DOYA-SAN HAD NO CHOICE!!
DOYA-SAN IS A SHABBY DWARF...
WITH A STUPID FAKE MUS-TACHE!
I DIDN'T NOTICE THAT AT ALL...
BOSS...
THERE'S NOTHING WRONG WITH THIN BODY HAIR.
FOR A DWARF THERE IS!!
DOYA-SAN GOT PICKED FOR B.O.D. *BECAUSE* OF HER COOL MUSTACHE!!
A DWARF WITHOUT FACIAL HAIR IS SURE TO GET MADE FUN OF!!
SHAKE...
BEARD THICKNESS VARIES FROM PERSON TO PERSON.
AND TANAKA SAID UNLI ALSO LOOKS GOOD WITHOUT ONE.
THAT'S JUST THE WAY IT GOES...
YOU CAN ONLY SAY SUCH A THING BECAUSE YOU'VE GROWN A SPLENDID BEARD!!
AWW SHUCKS!
WHY YOU!

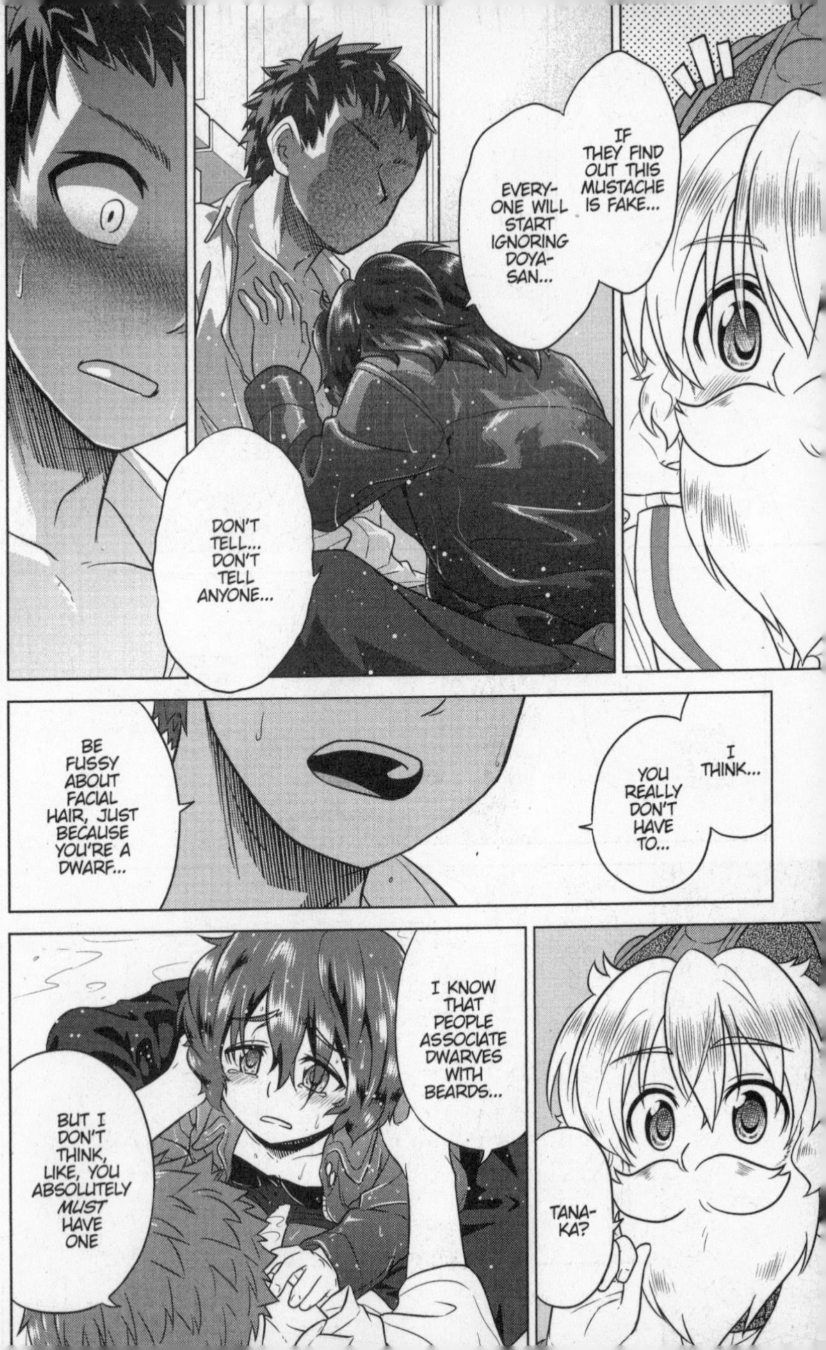
IF THEY FIND OUT THIS MUSTACHE IS FAKE...
EVERY-ONE WILL START IGNORING DOYA-SAN...
DON'T TELL... DON'T TELL ANYONE...
I THINK...
YOU REALLY DON'T HAVE TO...
BE FUSSY ABOUT FACIAL HAIR, JUST BECAUSE YOU'RE A DWARF...
TANA-KA?
I KNOW THAT PEOPLE ASSOCIATE DWARVES WITH BEARDS...
BUT I DON'T THINK, LIKE, YOU ABSOLUTELY *MUST* HAVE ONE

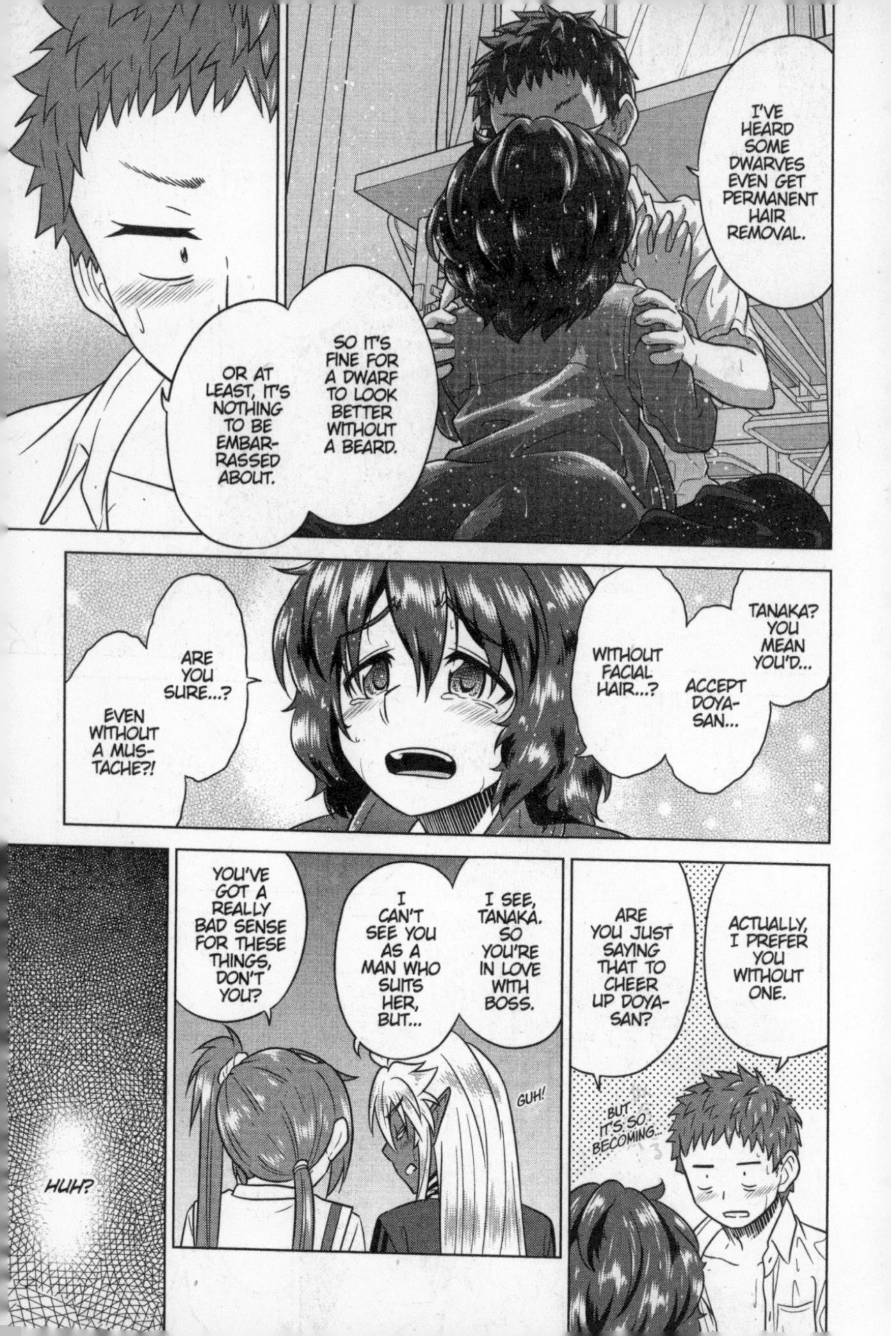
I'VE HEARD SOME DWARVES EVEN GET PERMANENT HAIR REMOVAL.
SO IT'S FINE FOR A DWARF TO LOOK BETTER WITHOUT A BEARD.
OR AT LEAST, IT'S NOTHING TO BE EMBARRASSED ABOUT.
TANAKA? YOU MEAN YOU'D... ACCEPT DOYA-SAN...
WITHOUT FACIAL HAIR...?
ARE YOU SURE...? EVEN WITHOUT A MUSTACHE?!
ACTUALLY, I PREFER YOU WITHOUT ONE.
ARE YOU JUST SAYING THAT TO CHEER UP DOYA-SAN?
BUT IT'S SO BECOMING...
I SEE, TANAKA. SO YOU'RE IN LOVE WITH BOSS.
I CAN'T SEE YOU AS A MAN WHO SUITS HER, BUT...
YOU'VE GOT A REALLY BAD SENSE FOR THESE THINGS, DON'T YOU?
GUH!
HUH?

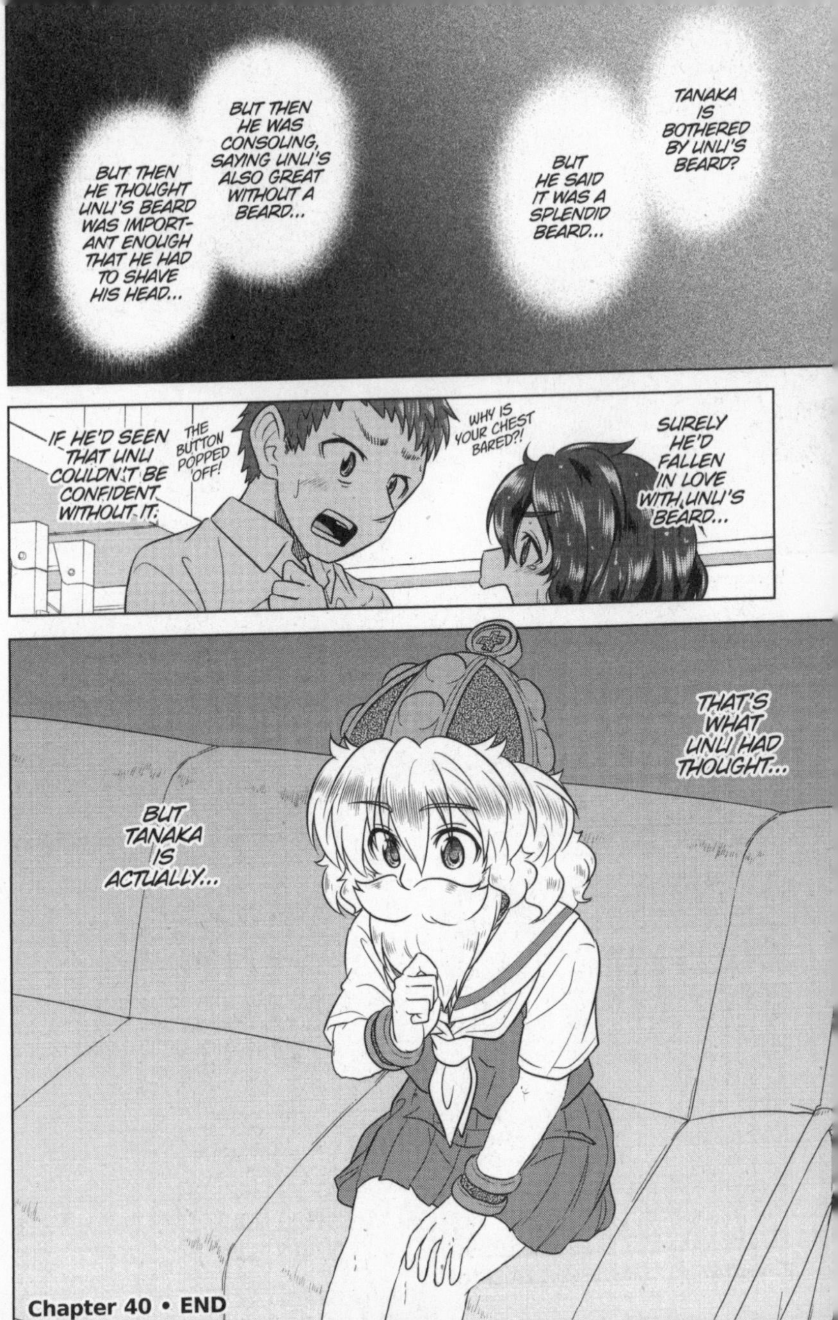
TANAKA IS BOTHERED BY UNLI'S BEARD?
BUT HE SAID IT WAS A SPLENDID BEARD...
BUT THEN HE WAS CONSOLING, SAYING UNLI'S ALSO GREAT WITHOUT A BEARD...
BUT THEN HE THOUGHT UNLI'S BEARD WAS IMPORTANT ENOUGH THAT HE HAD TO SHAVE HIS HEAD...
SURELY HE'D FALLEN IN LOVE WITH UNLI'S BEARD...
WHY IS YOUR CHEST BARED?!
THE BUTTON POPPED OFF!
IF HE'D SEEN THAT UNLI COULDN'T BE CONFIDENT WITHOUT IT.
THAT'S WHAT UNLI HAD THOUGHT...
BUT TANAKA IS ACTUALLY...
Chapter 40 • END

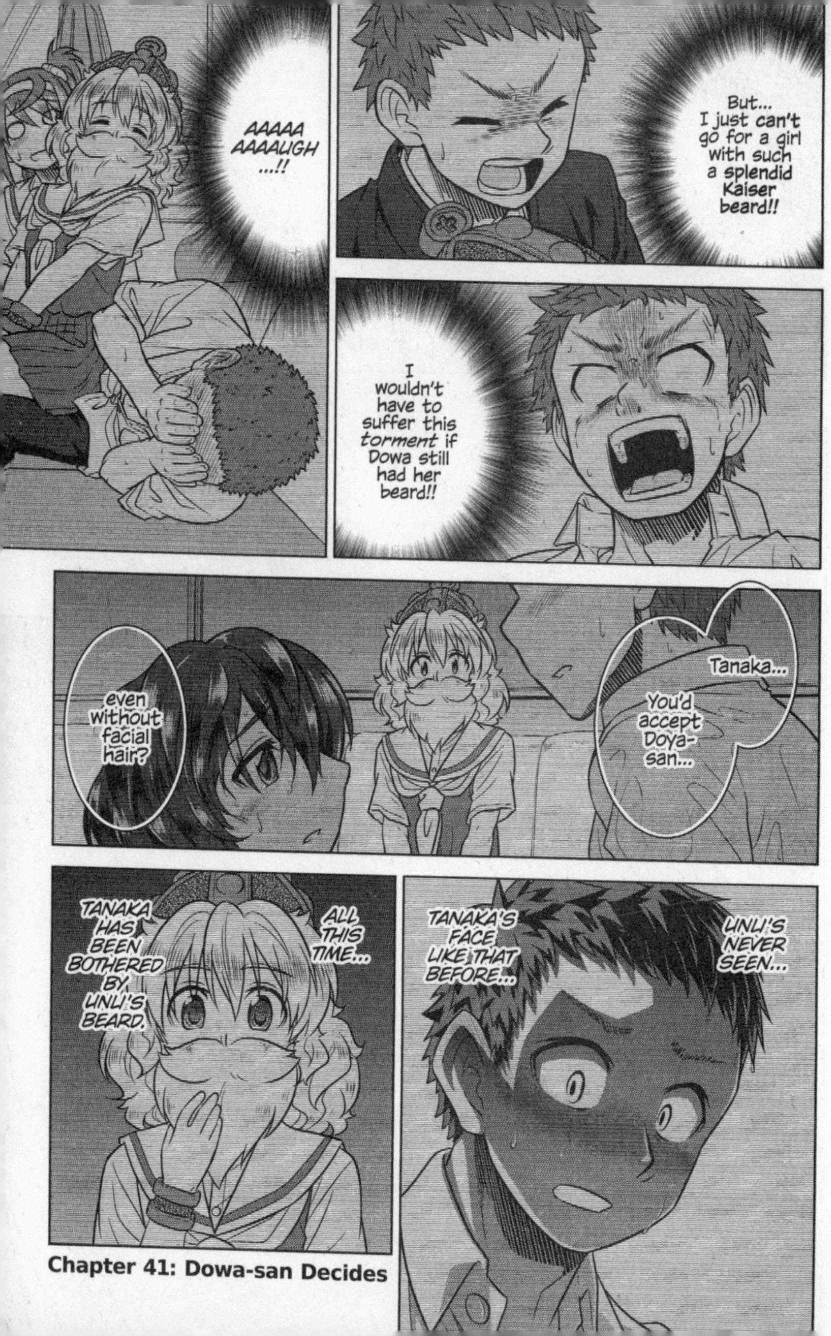
But... I just can't go for a girl with such a splendid Kaiser beard!!
I wouldn't have to suffer this *torment* if Dowa still had her beard!!
AAAAA AAAAUGH ...!!
Tanaka...
You'd accept Doya-san...
even without facial hair?
UNLI'S NEVER SEEN...
TANAKA'S FACE LIKE THAT BEFORE...
ALL THIS TIME...
TANAKA HAS BEEN BOTHERED BY UNLI'S BEARD.

Chapter 41: Dowa-san Decides

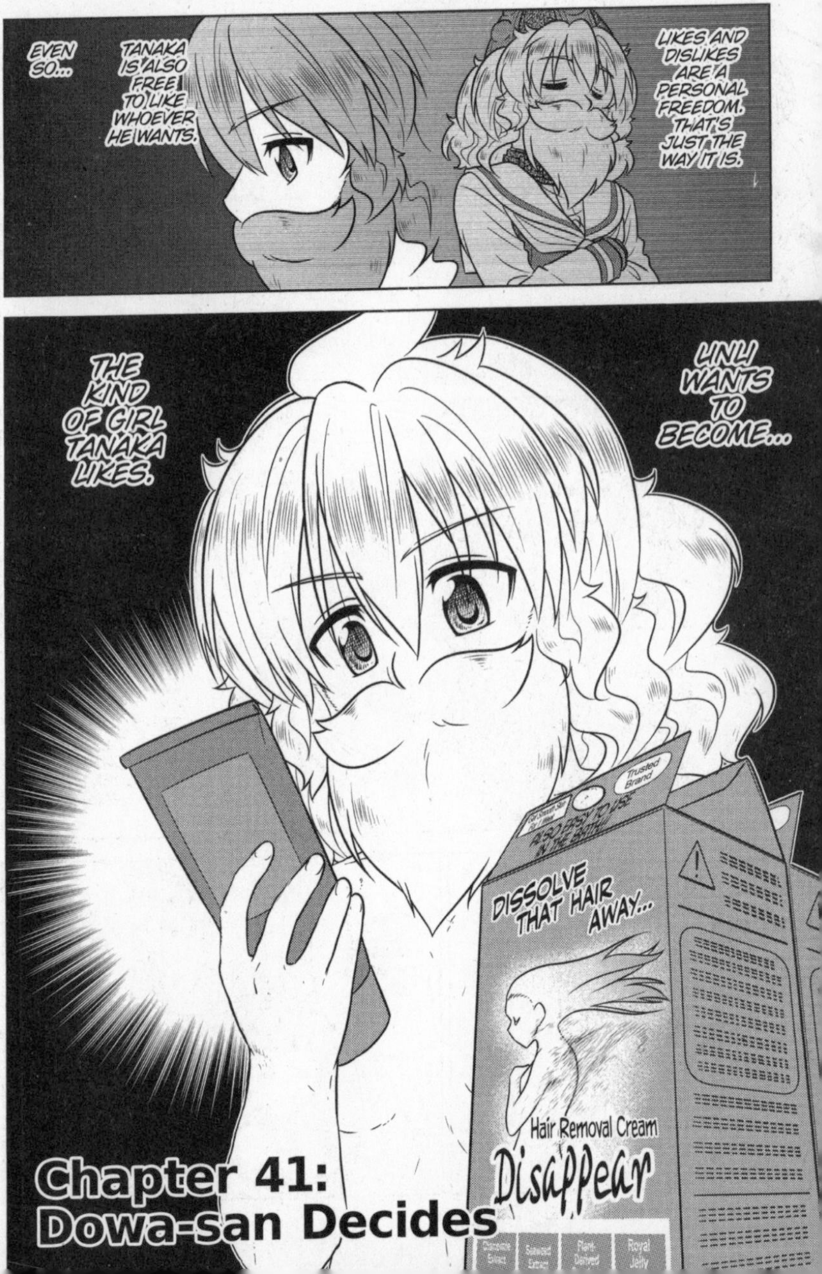
LIKES AND DISLIKES ARE A PERSONAL FREEDOM. THAT'S JUST THE WAY IT IS.
TANAKA IS ALSO FREE TO LIKE WHOEVER HE WANTS.
EVEN SO...
UNLI WANTS TO BECOME...
THE KIND OF GIRL TANAKA LIKES.
Trusted Brand
DISSOLVE THAT HAIR AWAY...
Hair Removal Cream
Disappear
Royal Jelly

Chapter 41: Dowa-san Decides

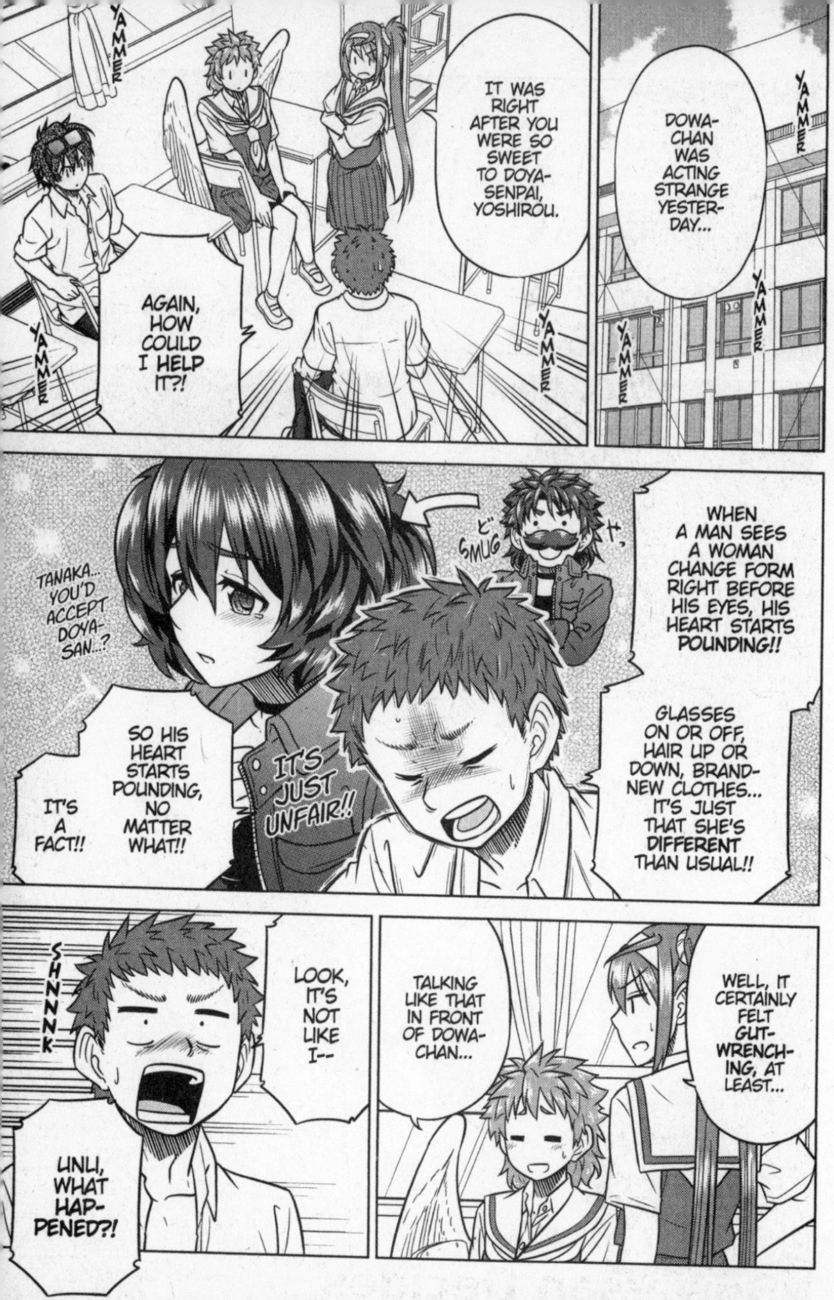
YAMMER
DOWA-CHAN WAS ACTING STRANGE YESTERDAY...
YAMMER
YAMMER
YAMMER
IT WAS RIGHT AFTER YOU WERE SO SWEET TO DOYA-SENPAI, YOSHIROU.
YAMMER
AGAIN, HOW COULD I HELP IT?!
YAMMER
YAMMER
WHEN A MAN SEES A WOMAN CHANGE FORM RIGHT BEFORE HIS EYES, HIS HEART STARTS POUNDING!!
GLASSES ON OR OFF, HAIR UP OR DOWN, BRAND-NEW CLOTHES... IT'S JUST THAT SHE'S DIFFERENT THAN USUAL!!
SMUG
TANAKA... YOU'D ACCEPT DOYA-SAN...?
IT'S JUST UNFAIR!!
SO HIS HEART STARTS POUNDING, NO MATTER WHAT!!
IT'S A FACT!!
WELL, IT CERTAINLY FELT GUT-WRENCHING, AT LEAST...
TALKING LIKE THAT IN FRONT OF DOWA-CHAN...
LOOK, IT'S NOT LIKE I--
SHNNNK
UNLI, WHAT HAPPENED?!

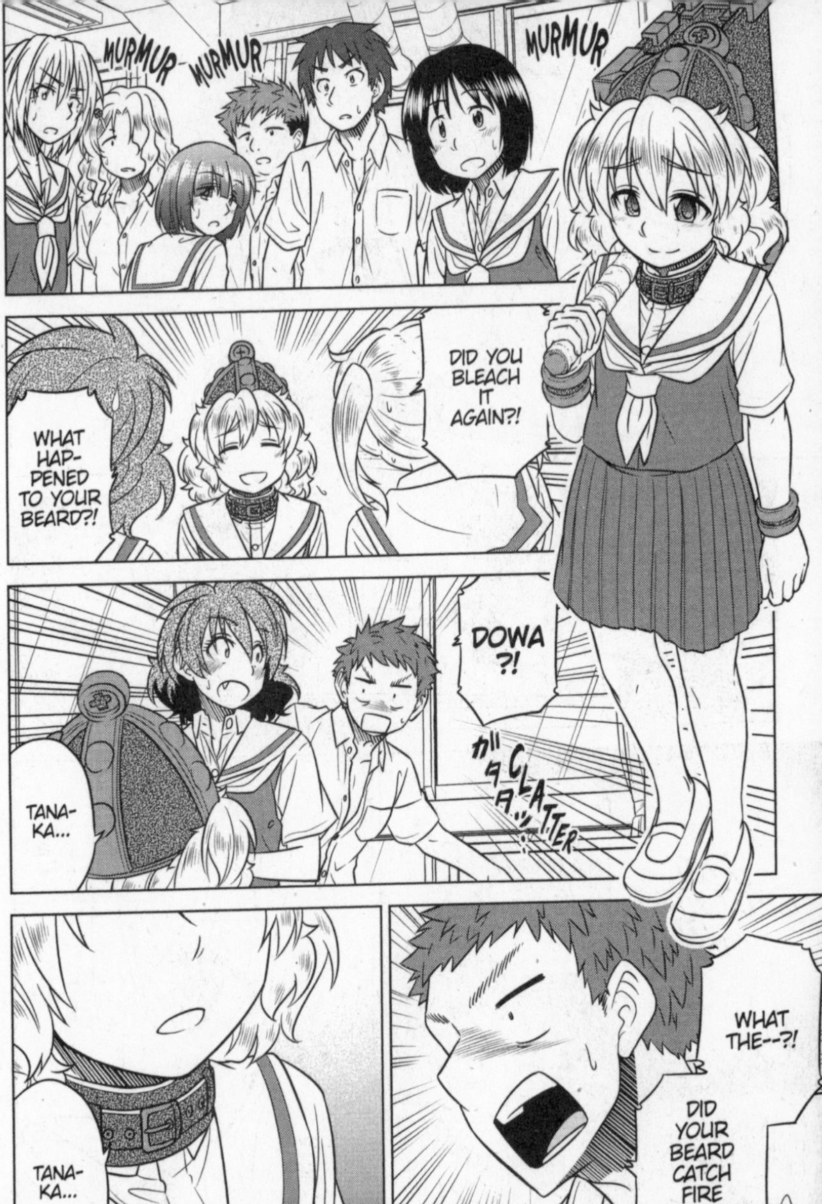
MURMUR
MURMUR
MURMUR
DID YOU BLEACH IT AGAIN?!
WHAT HAP-PENED TO YOUR BEARD?!
DOWA ?!
ガタッ CLATTER
TANA-KA...
WHAT THE--?!
DID YOUR BEARD CATCH FIRE AGAIN?!
TANA-KA...

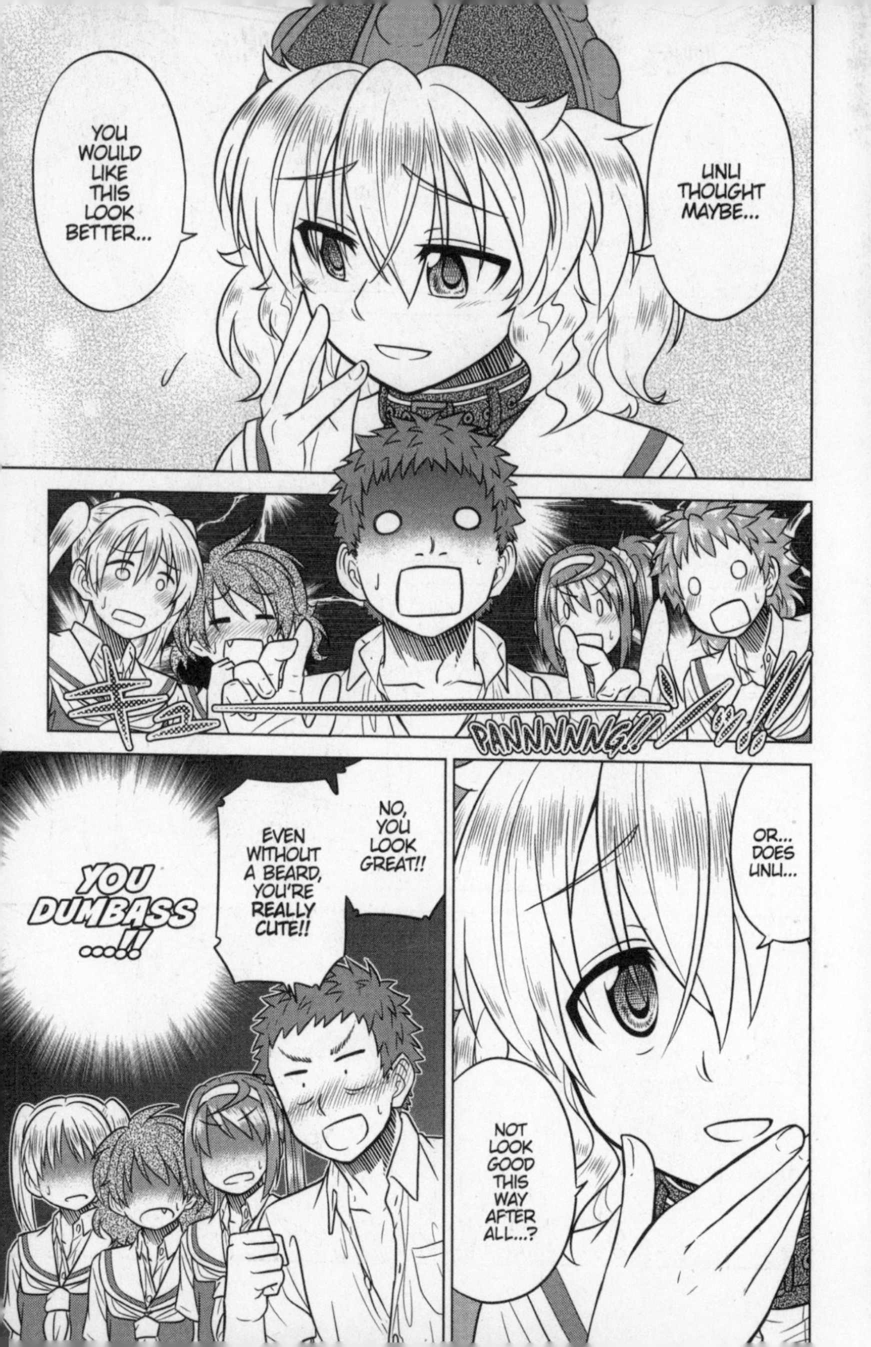
UNLI THOUGHT MAYBE...
YOU WOULD LIKE THIS LOOK BETTER...
PANNNNNG!!
OR... DOES UNLI...
NOT LOOK GOOD THIS WAY AFTER ALL...?
NO, YOU LOOK GREAT!!
EVEN WITHOUT A BEARD, YOU'RE REALLY CUTE!!
YOU DUMBASS ...!!

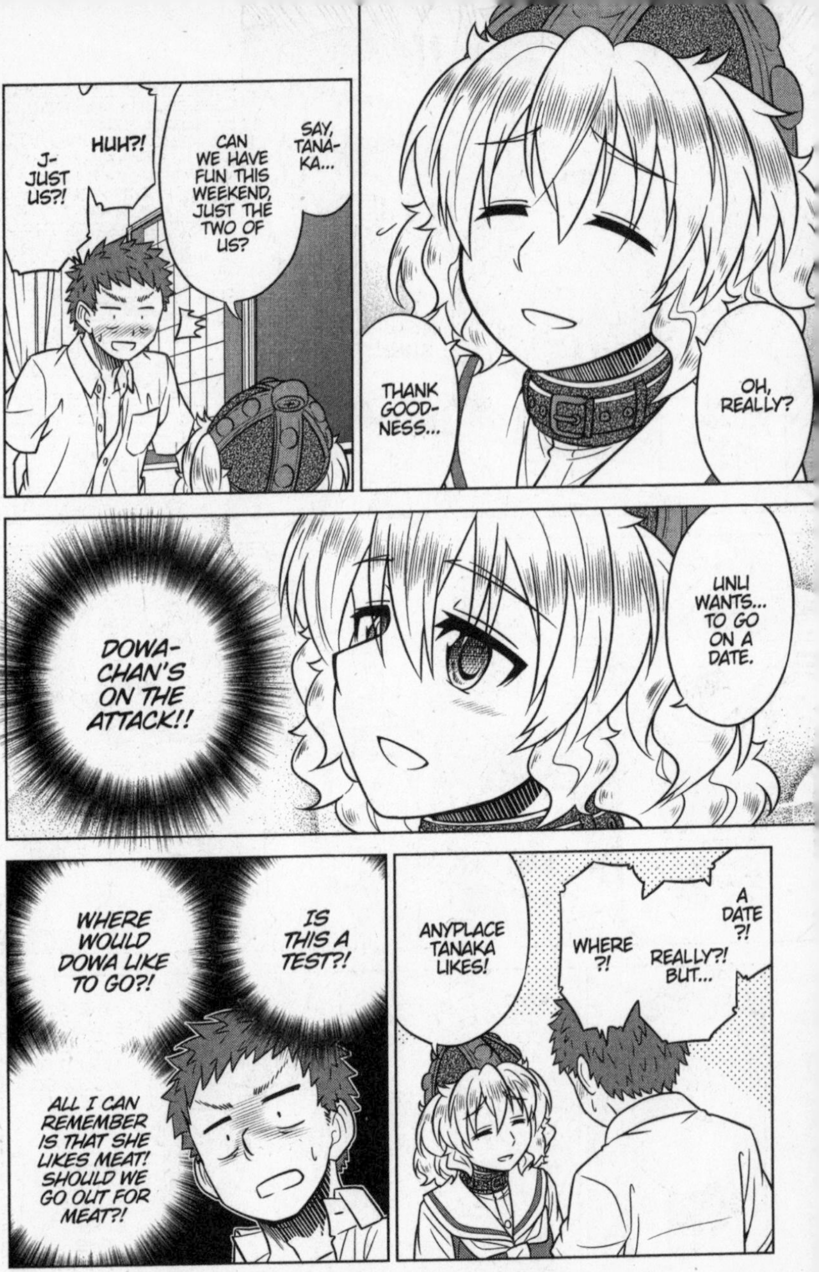
OH, REALLY?
THANK GOODNESS...
SAY, TANAKA...
CAN WE HAVE FUN THIS WEEKEND, JUST THE TWO OF US?
HUH?!
J-JUST US?!
UNU WANTS... TO GO ON A DATE.
DOWA-CHAN'S ON THE ATTACK!!
A DATE?!
REALLY?! BUT...
WHERE?!
ANYPLACE TANAKA LIKES!
IS THIS A TEST?!
WHERE WOULD DOWA LIKE TO GO?!
ALL I CAN REMEMBER IS THAT SHE LIKES MEAT! SHOULD WE GO OUT FOR MEAT?!

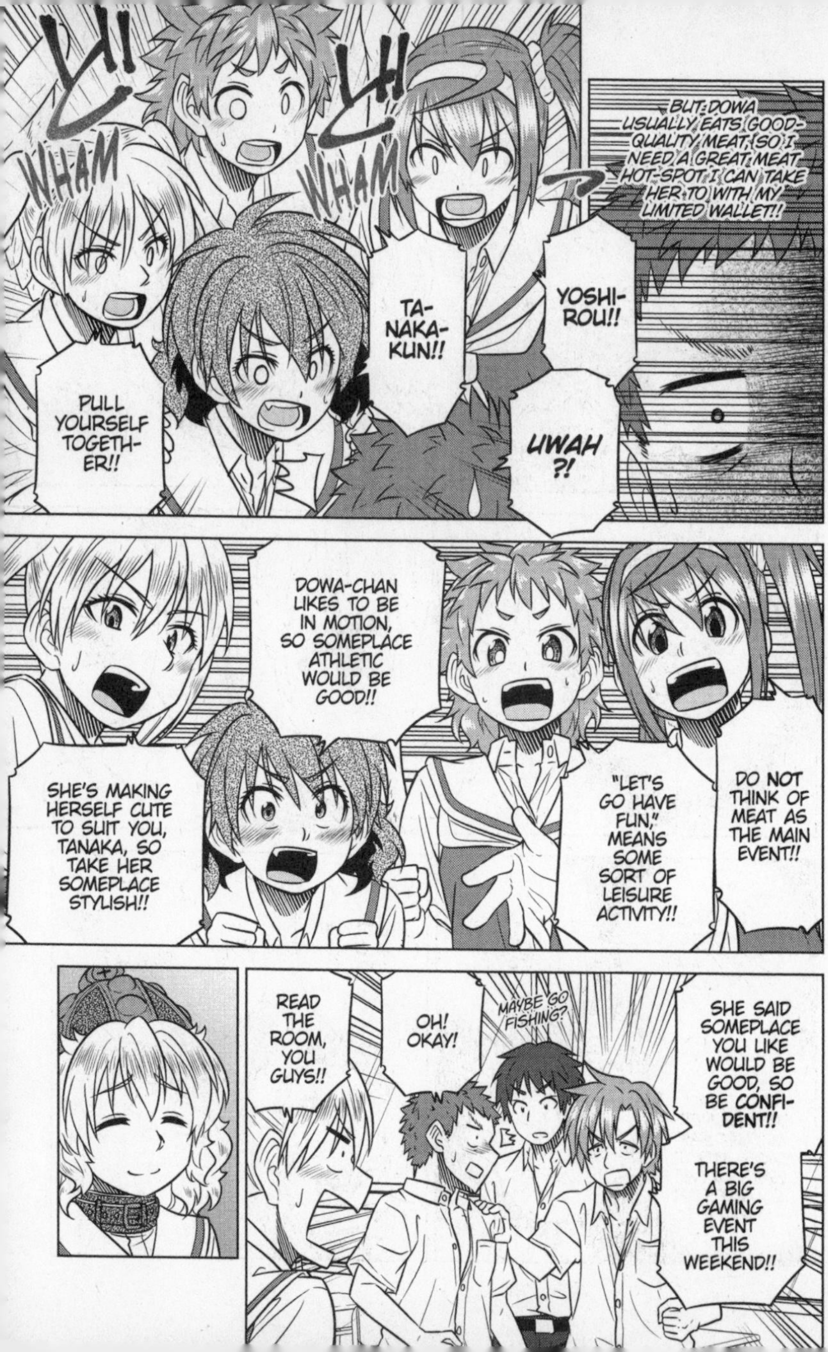
BUT DOWA USUALLY EATS GOOD-QUALITY MEAT, SO I NEED A GREAT MEAT HOT-SPOT I CAN TAKE HER TO WITH MY LIMITED WALLET!!
YOSHI-ROU!!
TA-NAKA-KUN!!
WHAM
UWAH?!
WHAM
PULL YOURSELF TOGETH-ER!!
DO NOT THINK OF MEAT AS THE MAIN EVENT!!
"LET'S GO HAVE FUN," MEANS SOME SORT OF LEISURE ACTIVITY!!
DOWA-CHAN LIKES TO BE IN MOTION, SO SOMEPLACE ATHLETIC WOULD BE GOOD!!
SHE'S MAKING HERSELF CUTE TO SUIT YOU, TANAKA, SO TAKE HER SOMEPLACE STYLISH!!
SHE SAID SOMEPLACE YOU LIKE WOULD BE GOOD, SO BE CONFI-DENT!!
THERE'S A BIG GAMING EVENT THIS WEEKEND!!
MAYBE GO FISHING?
OH! OKAY!
READ THE ROOM, YOU GUYS!!

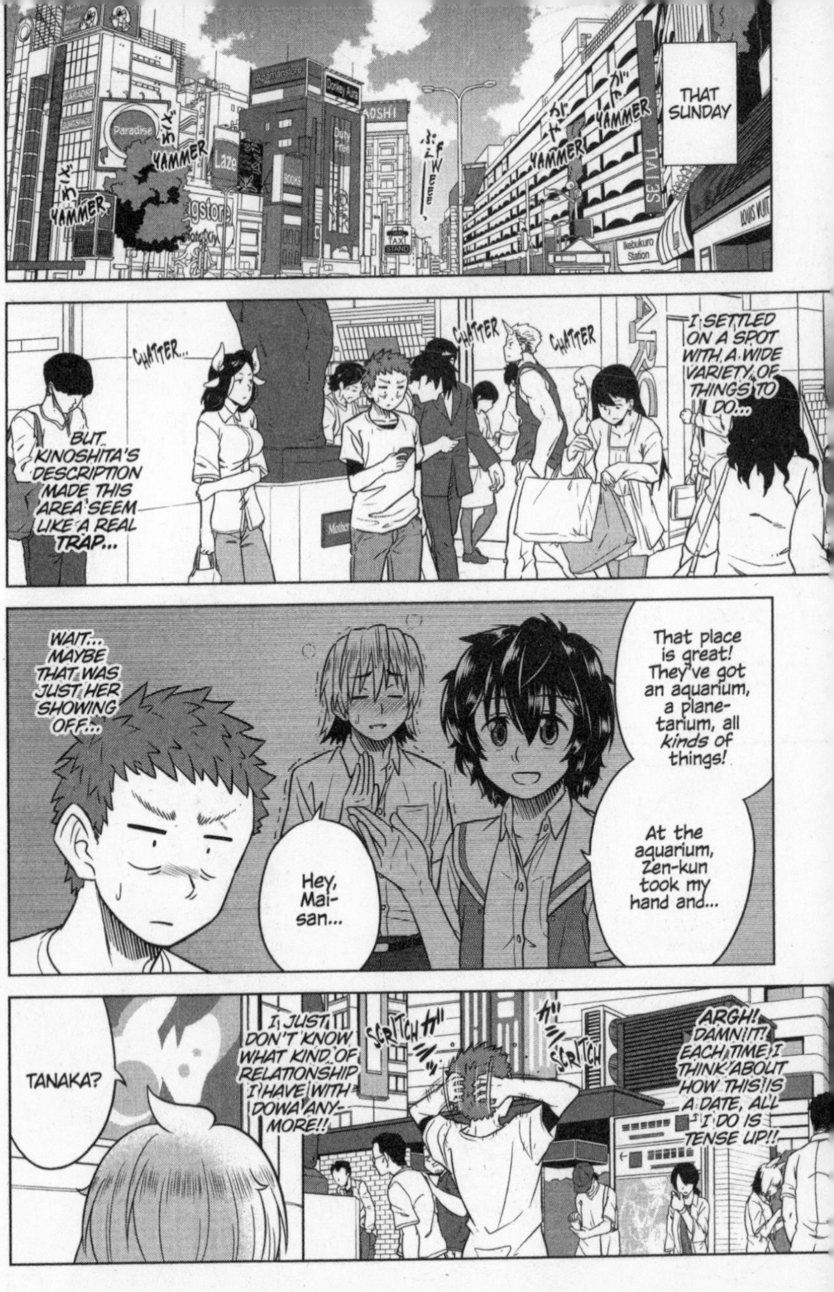
THAT SUNDAY
YAMMER
YAMMER
FWEEE
YAMMER
YAMMER
I SETTLED ON A SPOT WITH A WIDE VARIETY OF THINGS TO DO...
CHATTER
CHATTER
CHATTER...
BUT KINOSHITA'S DESCRIPTION MADE THIS AREA SEEM LIKE A REAL TRAP...
That place is great! They've got an aquarium, a planetarium, all kinds of things!
At the aquarium, Zen-kun took my hand and...
Hey, Mai-san...
WAIT... MAYBE THAT WAS JUST HER SHOWING OFF...
ARGH! DAMN IT! EACH TIME I THINK ABOUT HOW THIS IS A DATE, ALL I DO IS TENSE UP!!
SCRITCH
SCRITCH
I JUST DON'T KNOW WHAT KIND OF RELATIONSHIP I HAVE WITH DOWA ANYMORE!!
TANAKA?

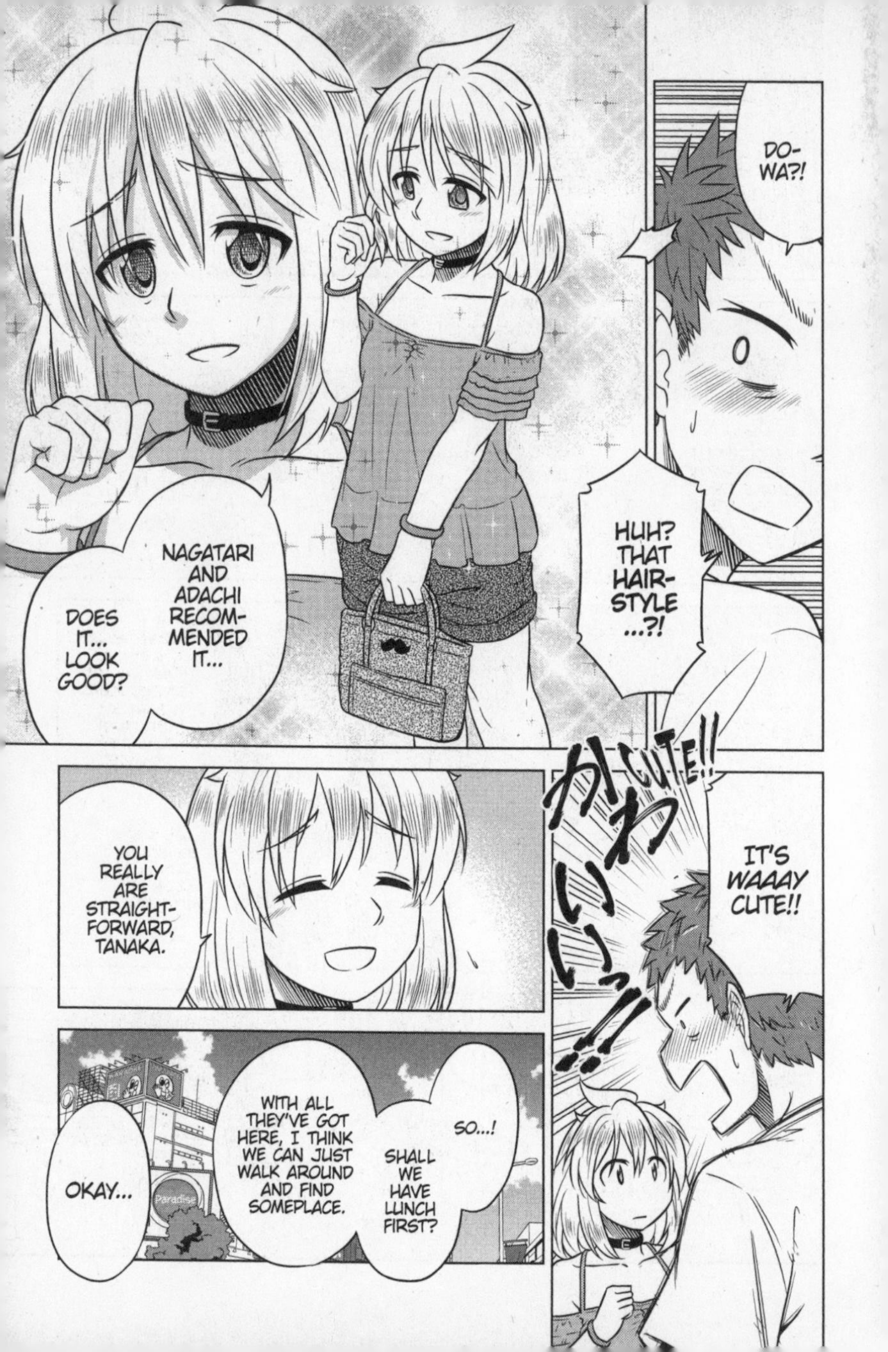
DO-WA?!
HUH? THAT HAIR-STYLE ...?!
NAGATARI AND ADACHI RECOM-MENDED IT...
DOES IT... LOOK GOOD?
かわいいっ!!
CUTE!!
IT'S WAAAY CUTE!!
YOU REALLY ARE STRAIGHT-FORWARD, TANAKA.
SO...!
SHALL WE HAVE LUNCH FIRST?
WITH ALL THEY'VE GOT HERE, I THINK WE CAN JUST WALK AROUND AND FIND SOMEPLACE.
OKAY...
Paradise

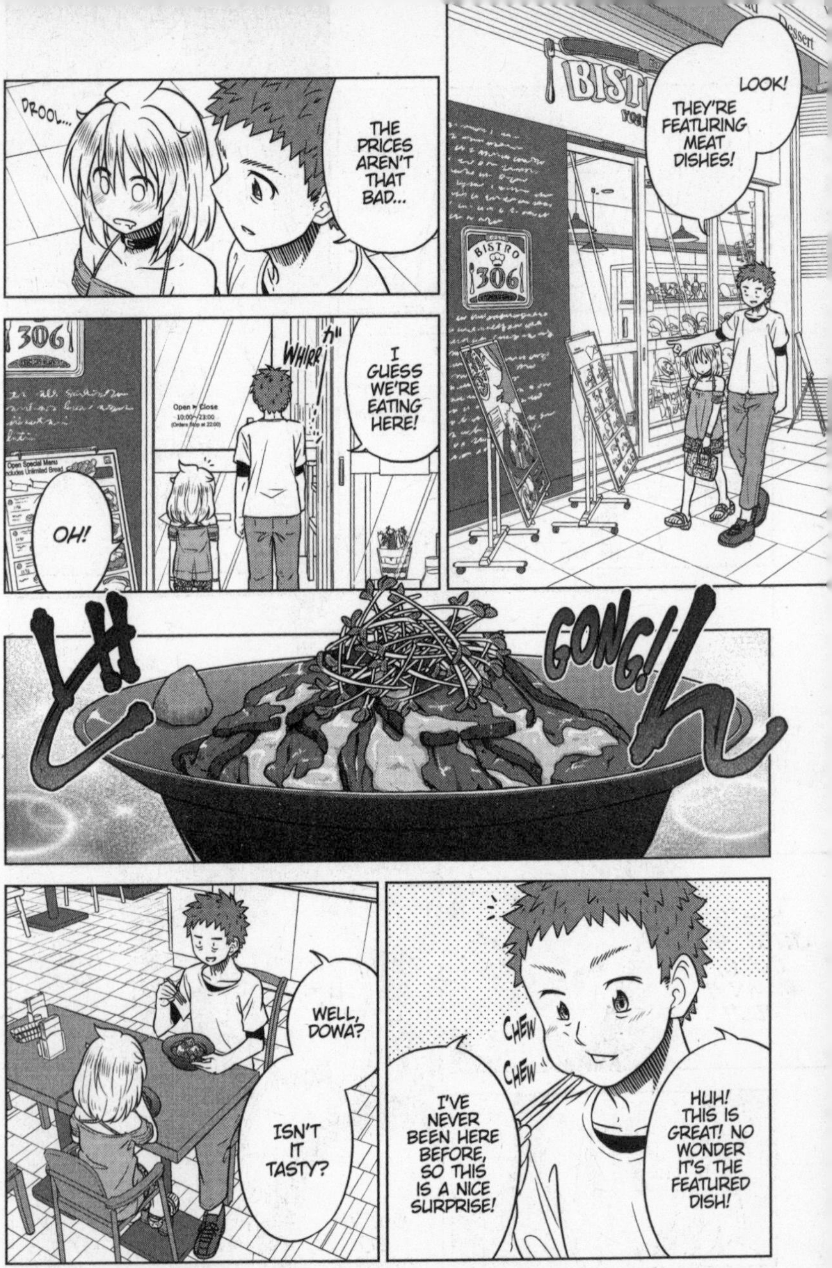
Dessert
BISTRO
LOOK!
THEY'RE FEATURING MEAT DISHES!
BISTRO 306
DROOL...
THE PRICES AREN'T THAT BAD...
306
WHIRR
ガー
Open ▸ Close
10:00~23:00
(Orders Stop at 22:00)
I GUESS WE'RE EATING HERE!
Open Special Menu
Includes Unlimited Bread
OH!
げ
GONG!
ん
HUH! THIS IS GREAT! NO WONDER IT'S THE FEATURED DISH!
CHEW
CHEW
I'VE NEVER BEEN HERE BEFORE, SO THIS IS A NICE SURPRISE!
WELL, DOWA?
ISN'T IT TASTY?

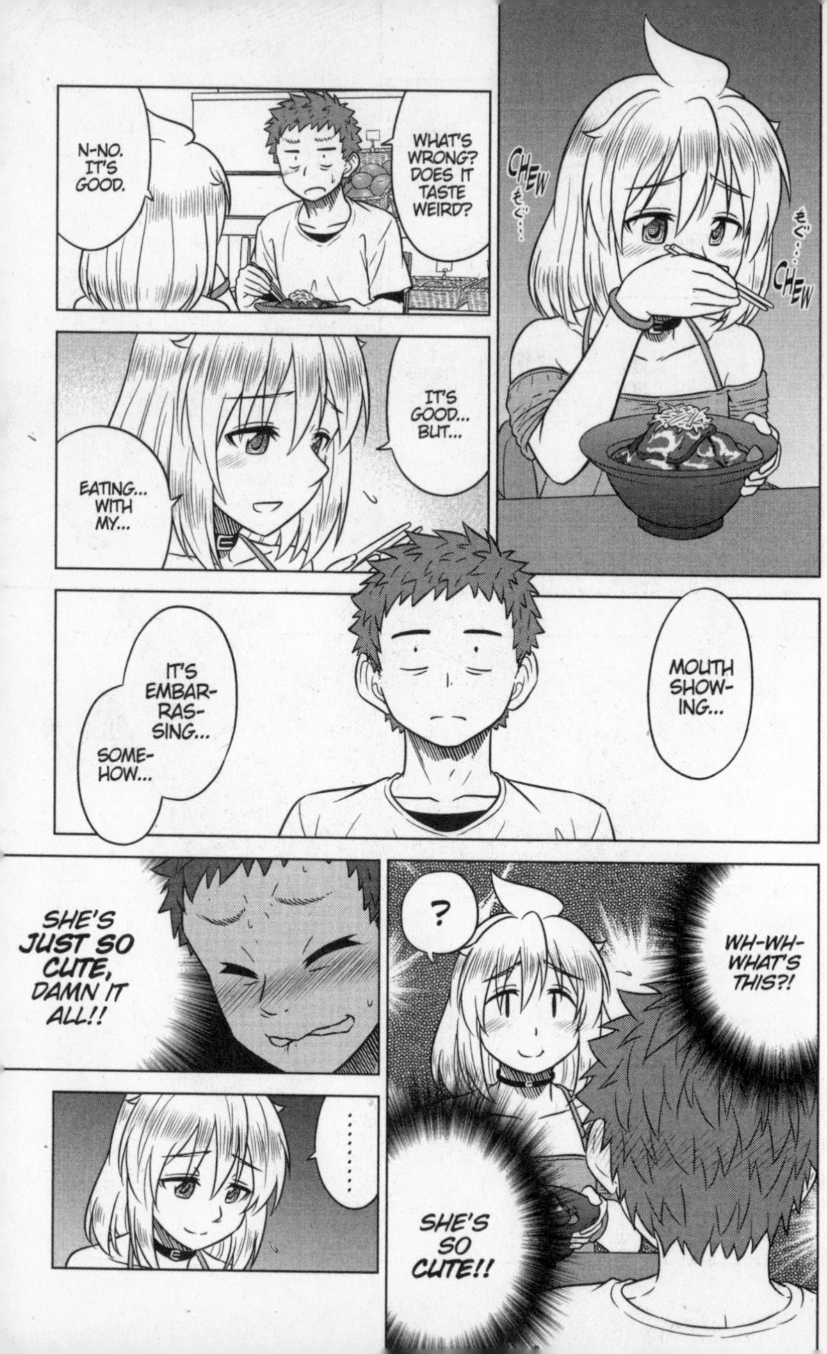
CHEW
もぐ…
もぐ…
CHEW
WHAT'S WRONG? DOES IT TASTE WEIRD?
N-NO. IT'S GOOD.
IT'S GOOD... BUT...
EATING... WITH MY...
MOUTH SHOWING...
IT'S EMBARRASSING... SOMEHOW...
?
WH-WH-WHAT'S THIS?!
SHE'S SO CUTE!!
SHE'S JUST SO CUTE, DAMN IT ALL!!
......

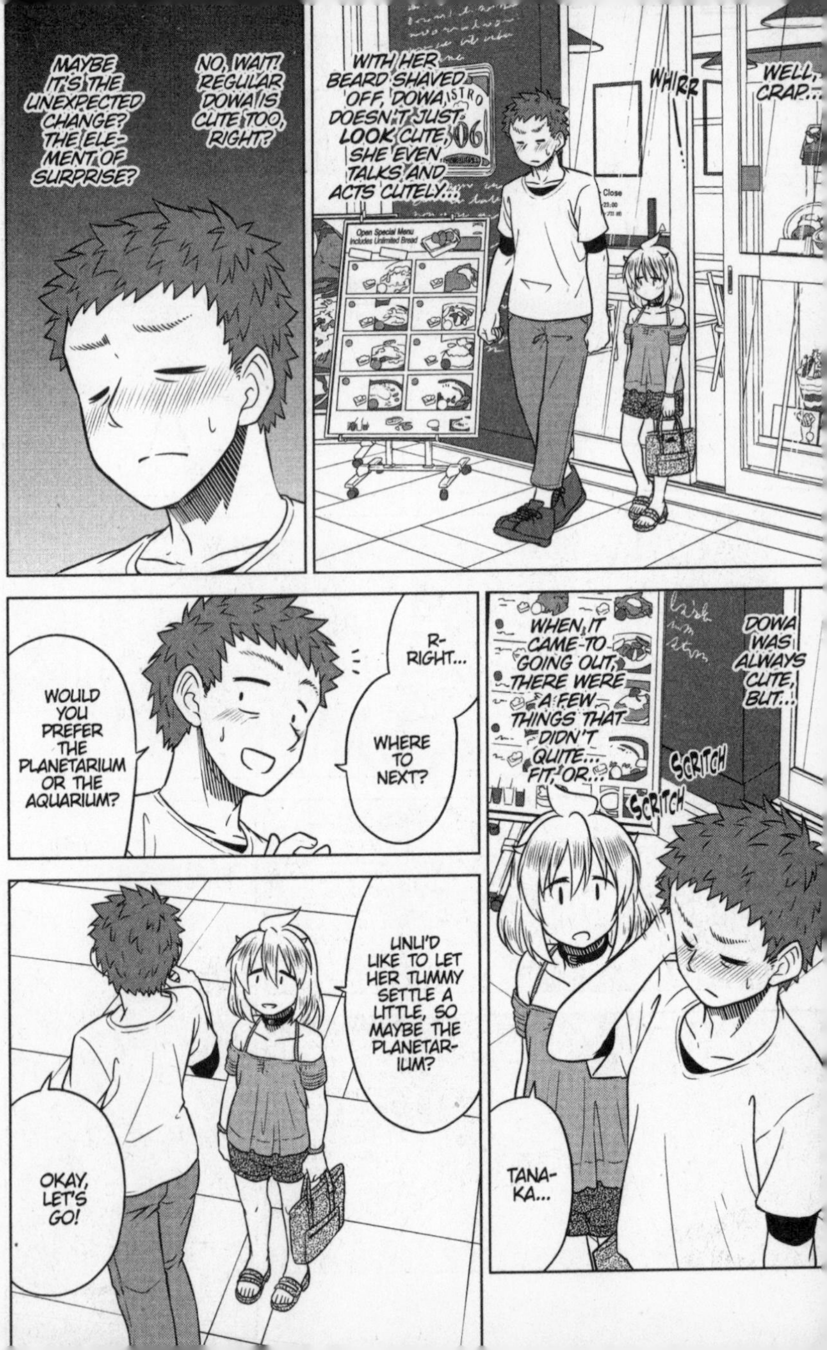
WELL, CRAP...
WHIRR
WITH HER BEARD SHAVED OFF, DOWA DOESN'T JUST LOOK CUTE, SHE EVEN TALKS AND ACTS CUTELY...
Open Special Menu
Includes Unlimited Bread
Close
NO, WAIT! REGULAR DOWA IS CUTE TOO, RIGHT?
MAYBE IT'S THE UNEXPECTED CHANGE? THE ELEMENT OF SURPRISE?
DOWA WAS ALWAYS CUTE, BUT...
WHEN IT CAME TO GOING OUT, THERE WERE A FEW THINGS THAT DIDN'T QUITE... FIT, OR...
SCRITCH
SCRITCH
TANAKA...
R-RIGHT...
WHERE TO NEXT?
WOULD YOU PREFER THE PLANETARIUM OR THE AQUARIUM?
UNU'D LIKE TO LET HER TUMMY SETTLE A LITTLE, SO MAYBE THE PLANETARIUM?
OKAY, LET'S GO!

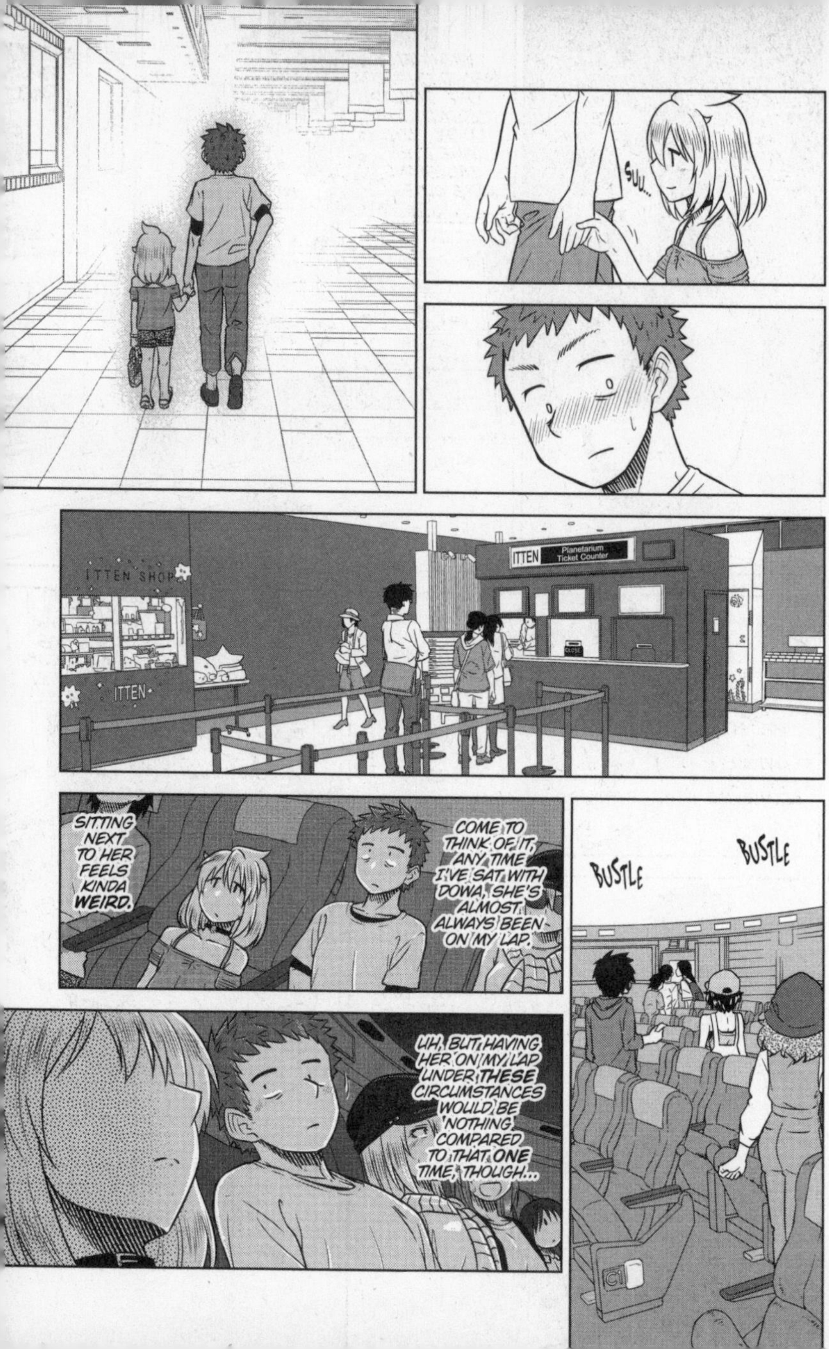
SUU...
ITTEN
Planetarium Ticket Counter
CLOSE
ITTEN SHOP
ITTEN
BUSTLE
BUSTLE
COME TO THINK OF IT, ANY TIME I'VE SAT WITH DOWA, SHE'S ALMOST ALWAYS BEEN ON MY LAP.
SITTING NEXT TO HER FEELS KINDA **WEIRD.**
UH, BUT HAVING HER ON MY LAP UNDER **THESE** CIRCUMSTANCES WOULD BE NOTHING COMPARED TO THAT **ONE** TIME, THOUGH...

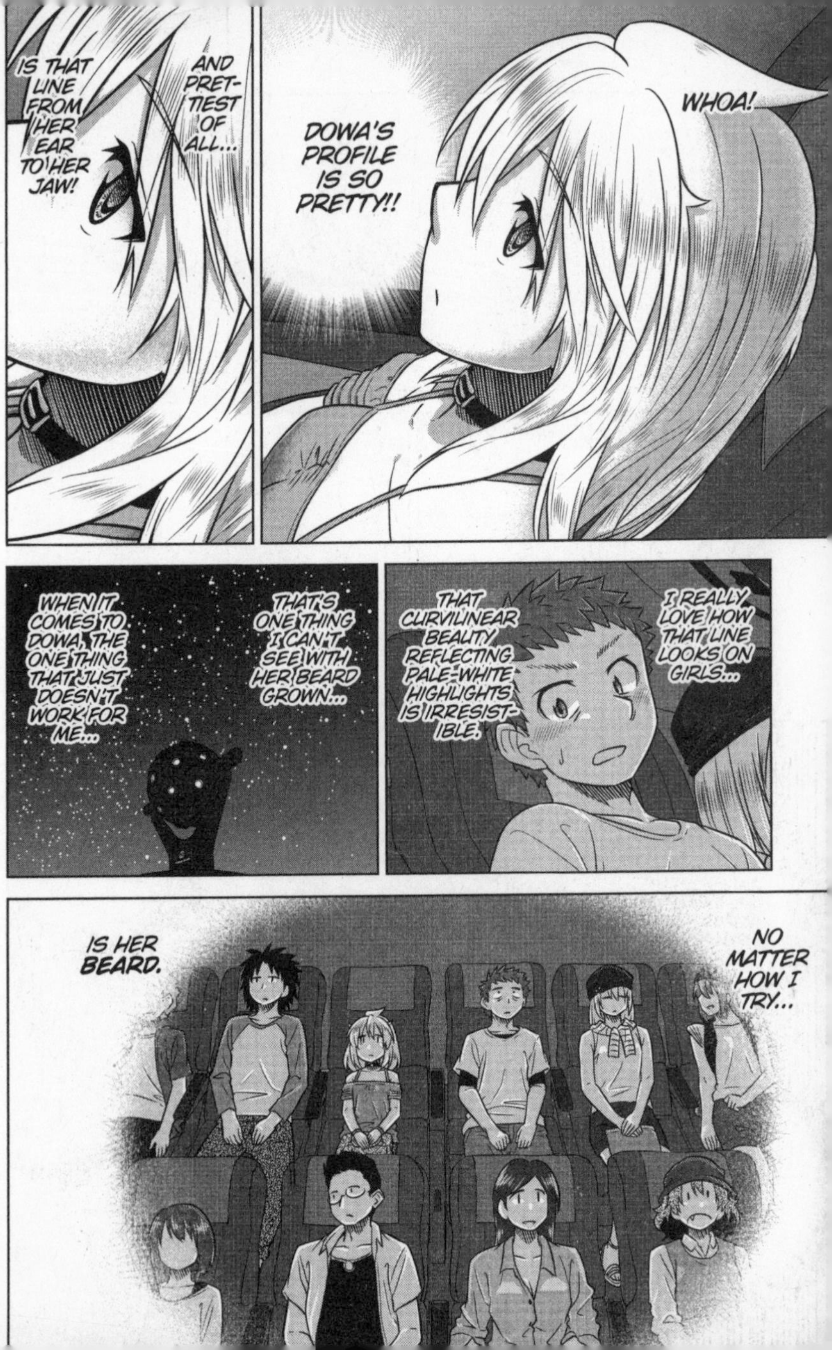
WHOA!
DOWA'S PROFILE IS SO PRETTY!!
AND PRETTIEST OF ALL...
IS THAT LINE FROM HER EAR TO HER JAW!
I REALLY LOVE HOW THAT LINE LOOKS ON GIRLS...
THAT CURVILINEAR BEAUTY REFLECTING PALE-WHITE HIGHLIGHTS IS IRRESISTIBLE.
THAT'S ONE THING I CAN'T SEE WITH HER BEARD GROWN...
WHEN IT COMES TO DOWA, THE ONE THING THAT JUST DOESN'T WORK FOR ME...
NO MATTER HOW I TRY...
IS HER BEARD.

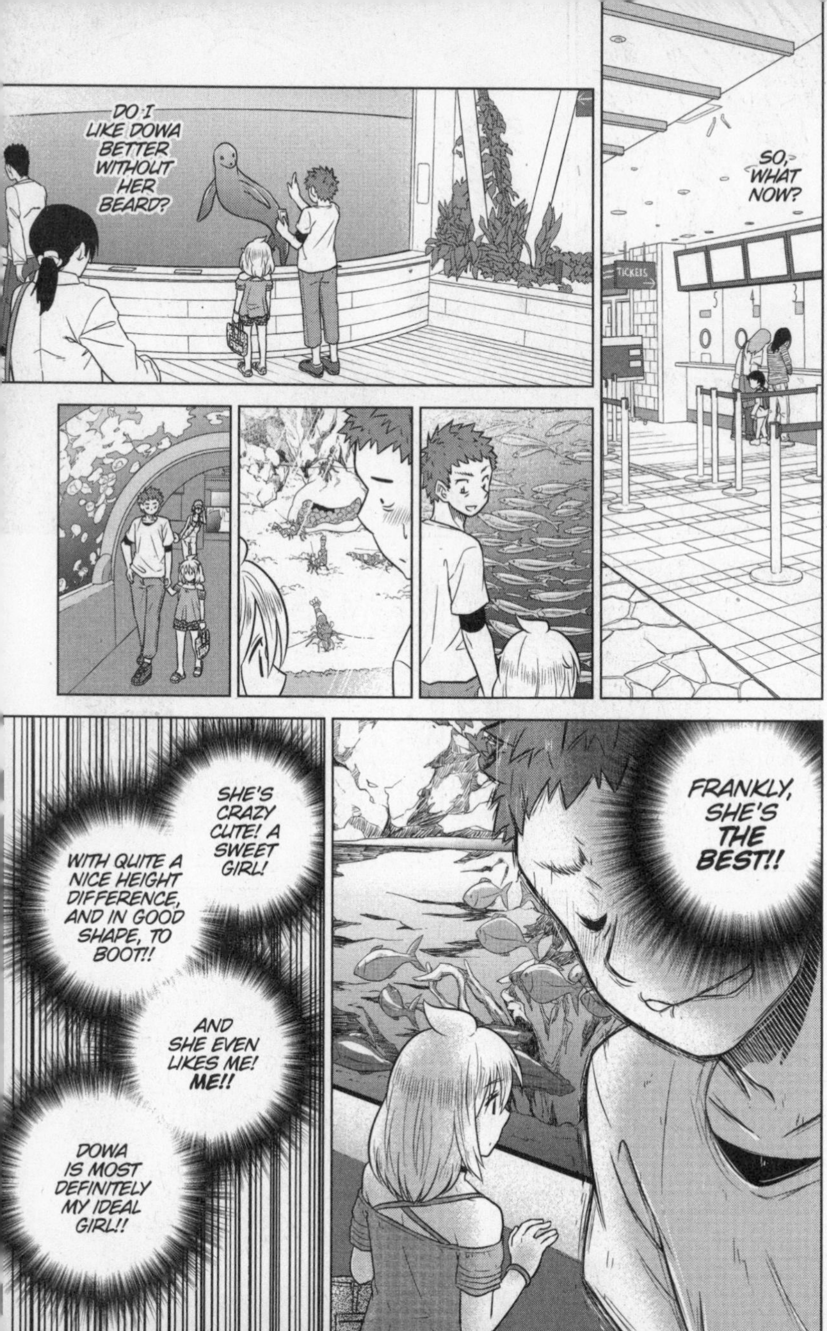
SO, WHAT NOW?
TICKETS
DO I LIKE DOWA BETTER WITHOUT HER BEARD?
FRANKLY, SHE'S THE BEST!!
SHE'S CRAZY CUTE! A SWEET GIRL!
WITH QUITE A NICE HEIGHT DIFFERENCE, AND IN GOOD SHAPE, TO BOOT!!
AND SHE EVEN LIKES ME! ME!!
DOWA IS MOST DEFINITELY MY IDEAL GIRL!!

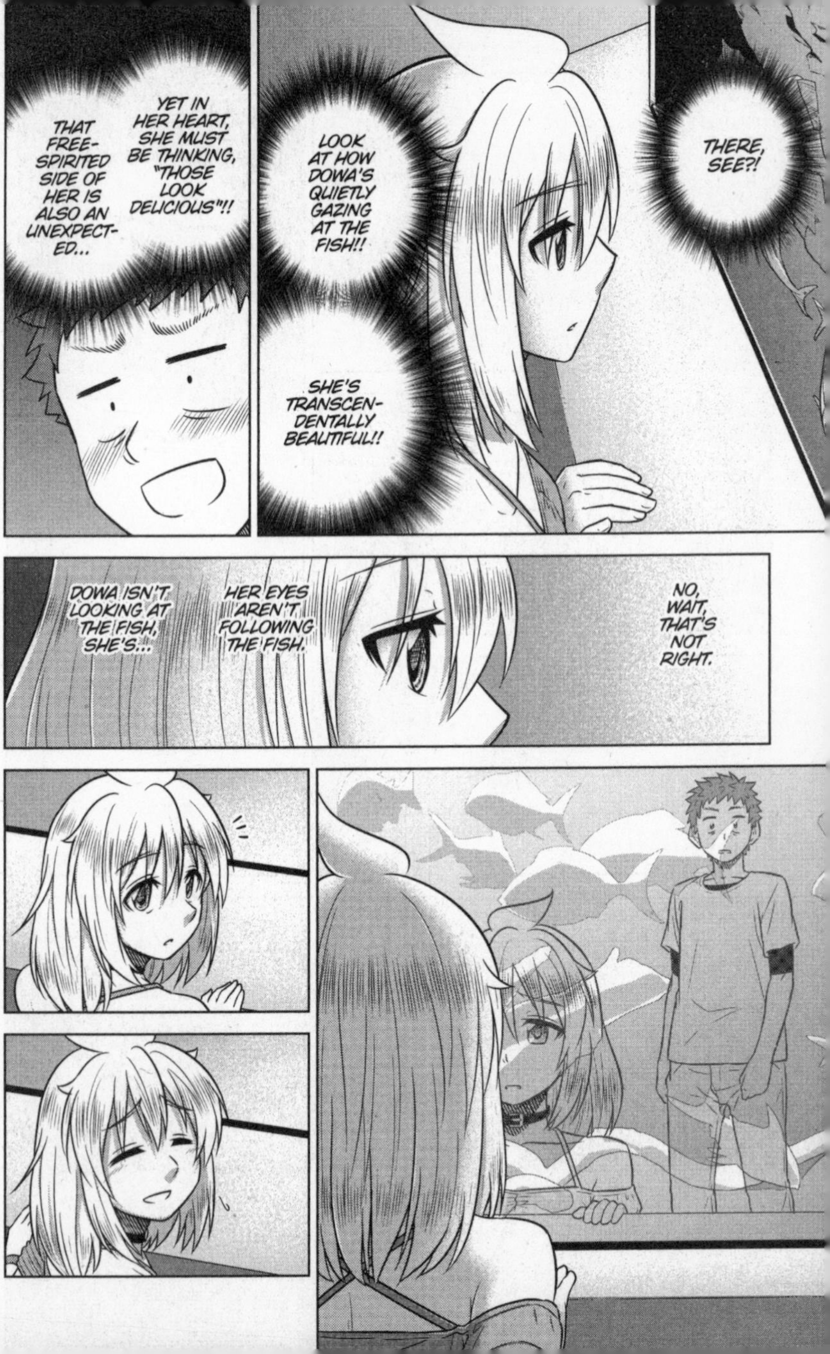
THERE, SEE?!
LOOK AT HOW DOWA'S QUIETLY GAZING AT THE FISH!!
SHE'S TRANSCEN-DENTALLY BEAUTIFUL!!
YET IN HER HEART, SHE MUST BE THINKING, "THOSE LOOK DELICIOUS"!!
THAT FREE-SPIRITED SIDE OF HER IS ALSO AN UNEXPECT-ED...
NO, WAIT, THAT'S NOT RIGHT.
HER EYES AREN'T FOLLOWING THE FISH.
DOWA ISN'T LOOKING AT THE FISH, SHE'S...

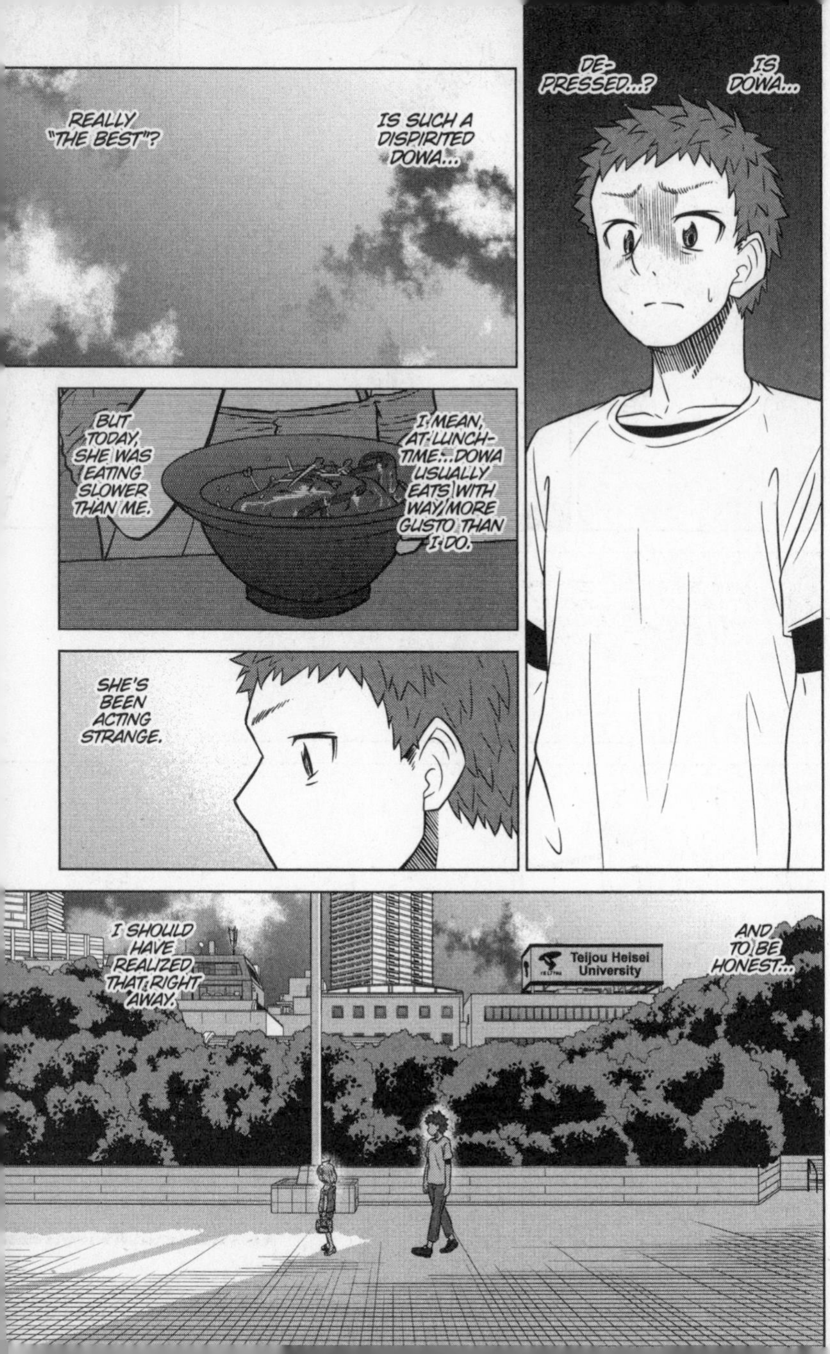
IS DOWA...
DE-PRESSED...?
IS SUCH A DISPIRITED DOWA...
REALLY "THE BEST"?
I MEAN, AT LUNCH-TIME...DOWA USUALLY EATS WITH WAY MORE GUSTO THAN I DO.
BUT TODAY, SHE WAS EATING SLOWER THAN ME.
SHE'S BEEN ACTING STRANGE.
AND TO BE HONEST...
Teijou Heisei University
I SHOULD HAVE REALIZED THAT RIGHT AWAY.

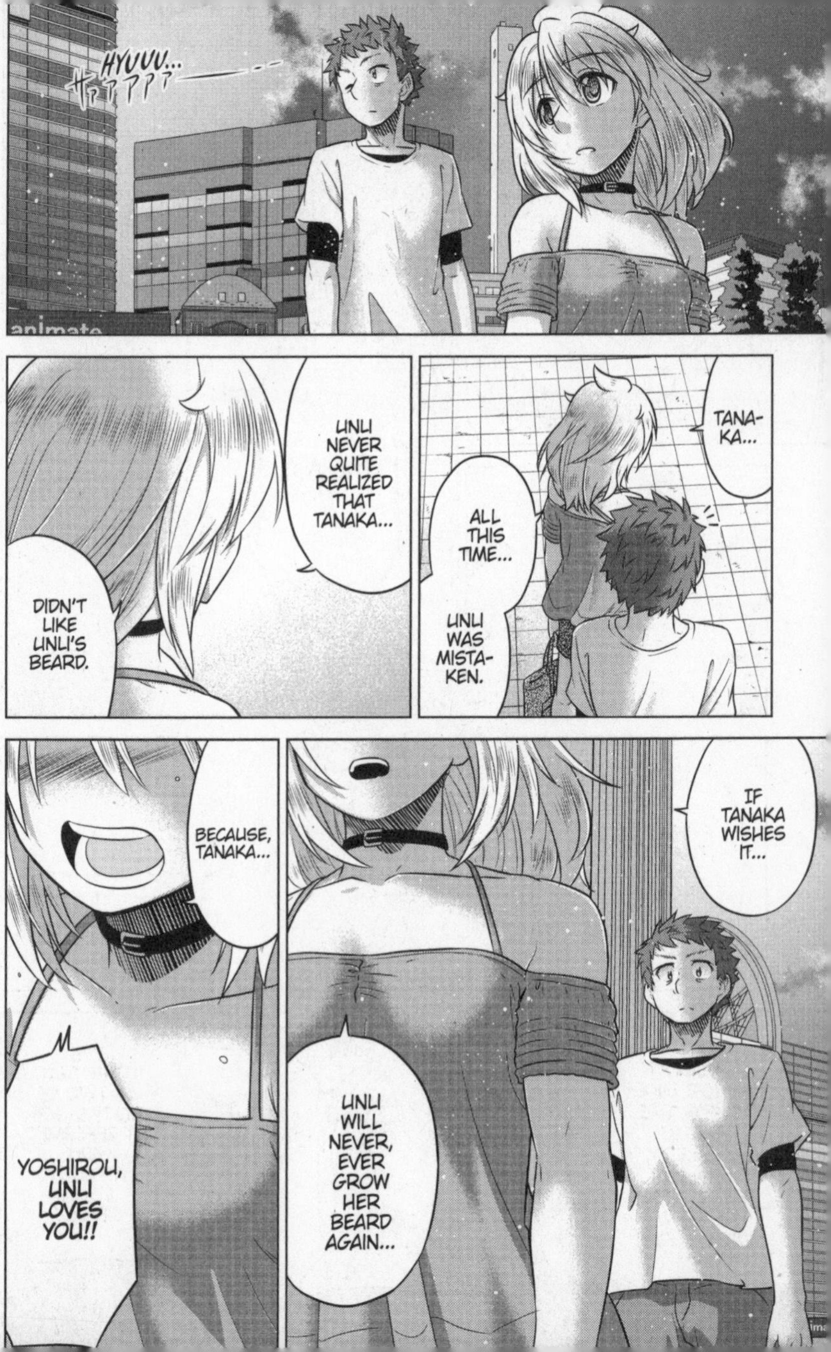
HYUUU...
animate
TANAKA...
ALL THIS TIME...
UNLI WAS MISTAKEN.
UNLI NEVER QUITE REALIZED THAT TANAKA...
DIDN'T LIKE UNLI'S BEARD.
IF TANAKA WISHES IT...
UNLI WILL NEVER, EVER GROW HER BEARD AGAIN...
BECAUSE, TANAKA...
YOSHIROU, UNLI LOVES YOU!!

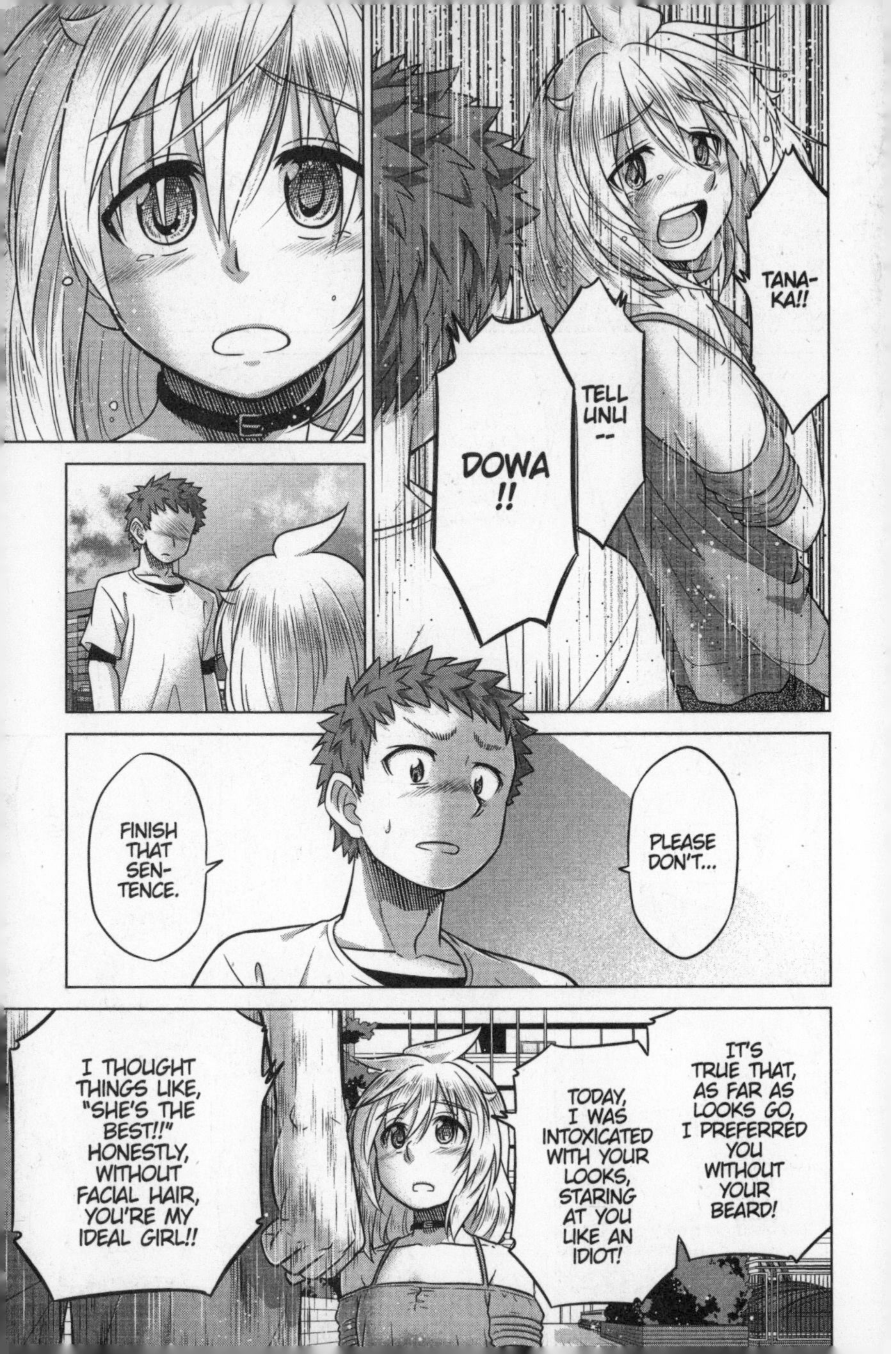
TANA-KA!!
TELL UNLI --
DOWA !!
PLEASE DON'T...
FINISH THAT SEN-TENCE.
IT'S TRUE THAT, AS FAR AS LOOKS GO, I PREFERRED YOU WITHOUT YOUR BEARD!
TODAY, I WAS INTOXICATED WITH YOUR LOOKS, STARING AT YOU LIKE AN IDIOT!
I THOUGHT THINGS LIKE, "SHE'S THE BEST!!" HONESTLY, WITHOUT FACIAL HAIR, YOU'RE MY IDEAL GIRL!!

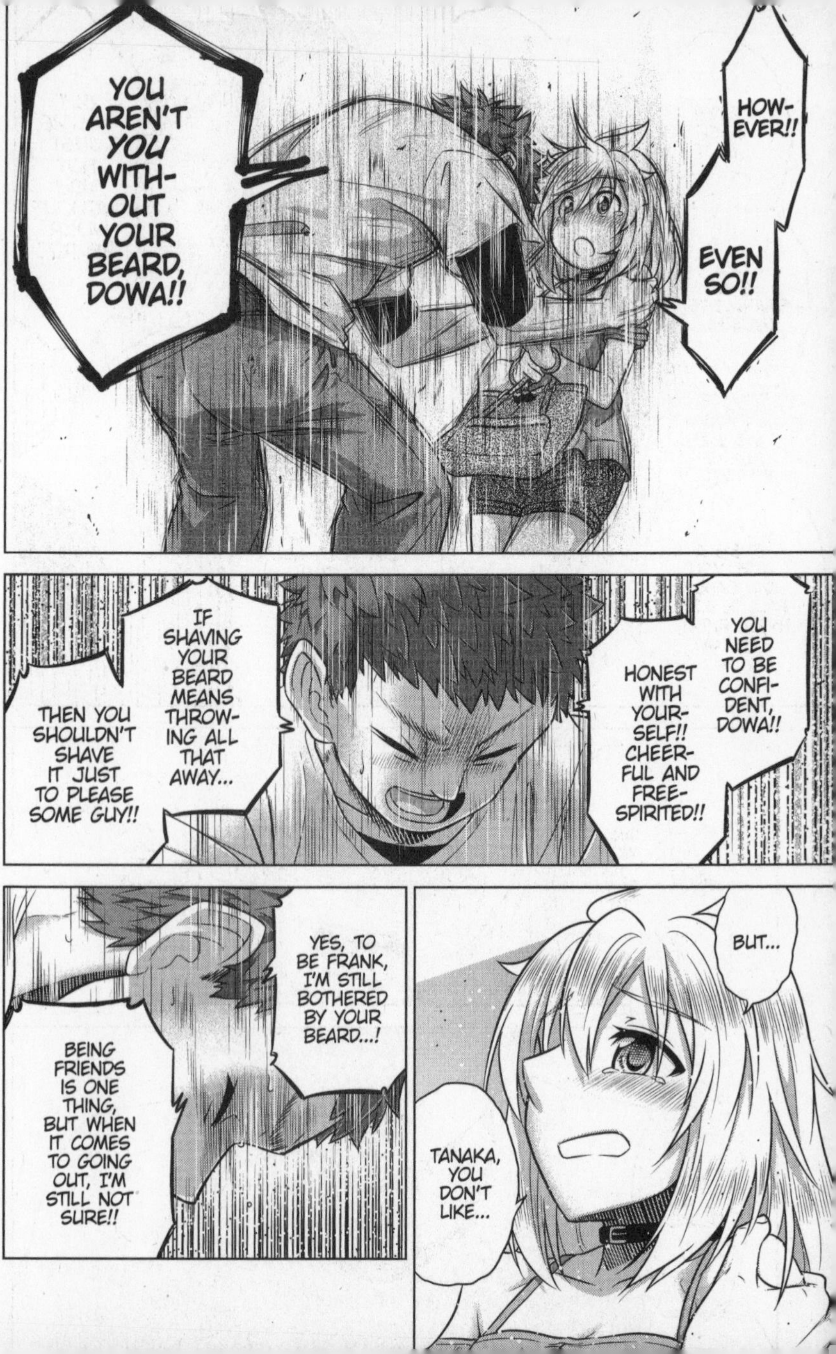
HOWEVER!!
EVEN SO!!
YOU AREN'T YOU WITHOUT YOUR BEARD, DOWA!!
YOU NEED TO BE CONFIDENT, DOWA!!
HONEST WITH YOURSELF!! CHEERFUL AND FREE-SPIRITED!!
IF SHAVING YOUR BEARD MEANS THROWING ALL THAT AWAY...
THEN YOU SHOULDN'T SHAVE IT JUST TO PLEASE SOME GUY!!
BUT...
TANAKA, YOU DON'T LIKE...
YES, TO BE FRANK, I'M STILL BOTHERED BY YOUR BEARD...!
BEING FRIENDS IS ONE THING, BUT WHEN IT COMES TO GOING OUT, I'M STILL NOT SURE!!

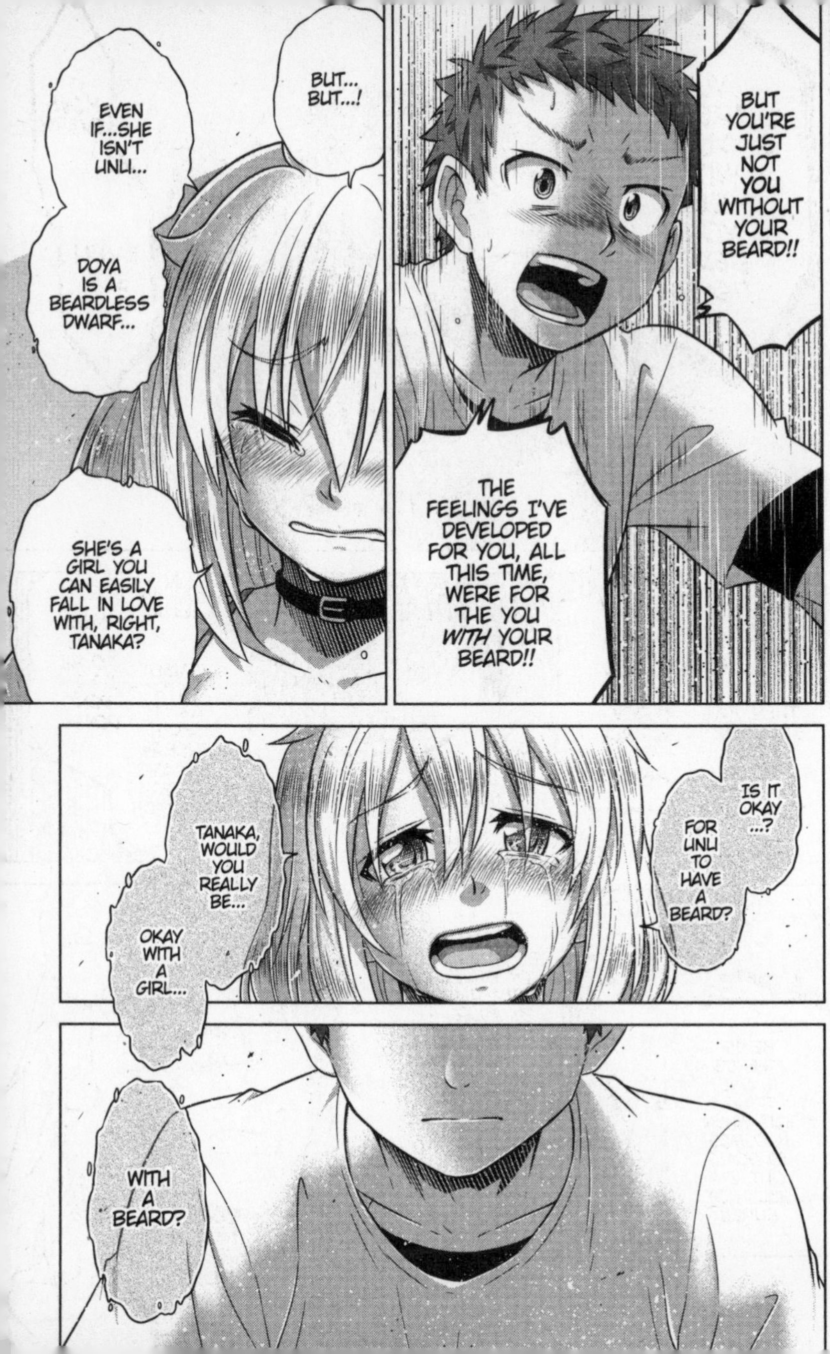
BUT YOU'RE JUST NOT YOU WITHOUT YOUR BEARD!!
THE FEELINGS I'VE DEVELOPED FOR YOU, ALL THIS TIME, WERE FOR THE YOU *WITH* YOUR BEARD!!
BUT... BUT...!
EVEN IF...SHE ISN'T UNLI...
DOYA IS A BEARDLESS DWARF...
SHE'S A GIRL YOU CAN EASILY FALL IN LOVE WITH, RIGHT, TANAKA?
IS IT OKAY ...?
FOR UNLI TO HAVE A BEARD?
TANAKA, WOULD YOU REALLY BE...
OKAY WITH A GIRL...
WITH A BEARD?

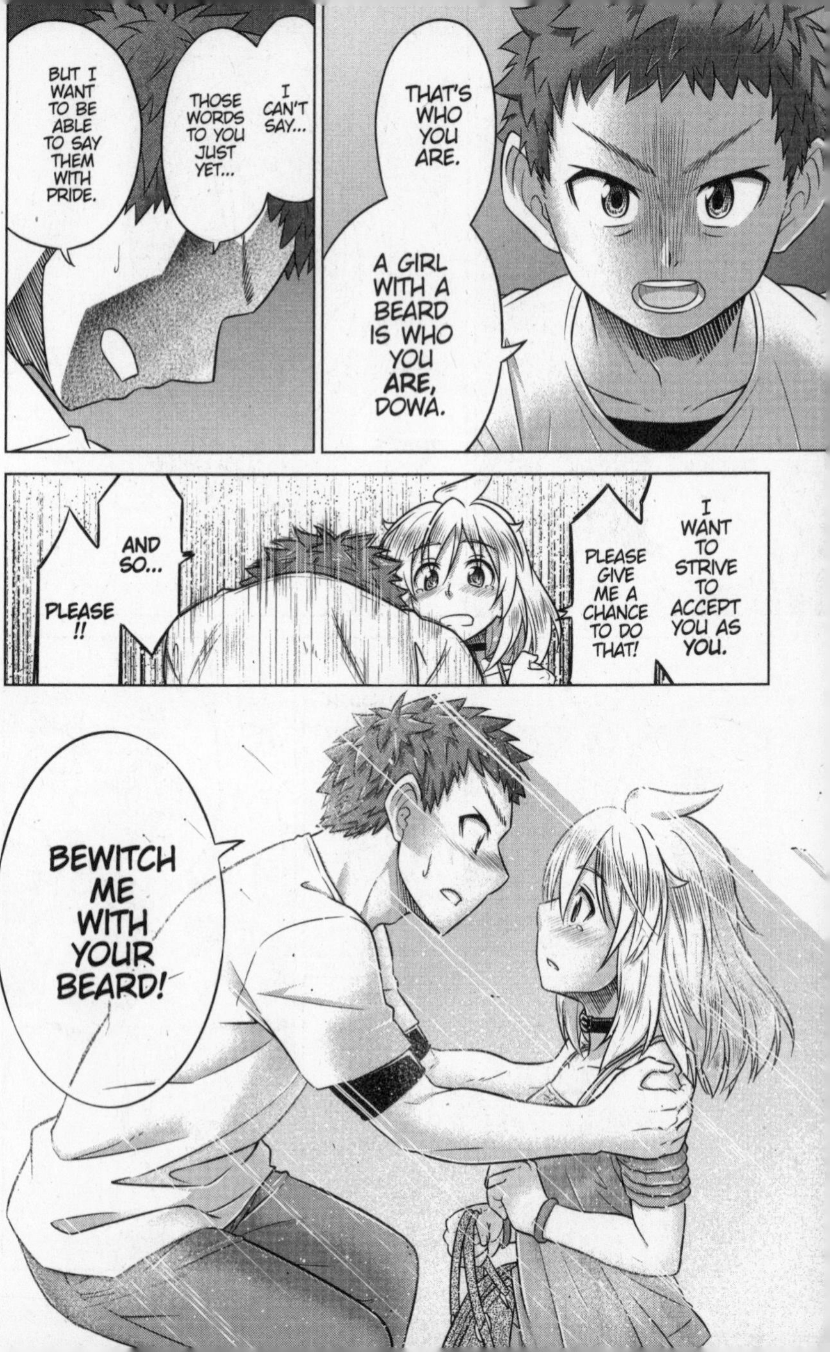
THAT'S WHO YOU ARE.
A GIRL WITH A BEARD IS WHO YOU ARE, DOWA.
I CAN'T SAY...
THOSE WORDS TO YOU JUST YET...
BUT I WANT TO BE ABLE TO SAY THEM WITH PRIDE.
I WANT TO STRIVE TO ACCEPT YOU AS YOU.
PLEASE GIVE ME A CHANCE TO DO THAT!
AND SO...
PLEASE!!
BEWITCH ME WITH YOUR BEARD!

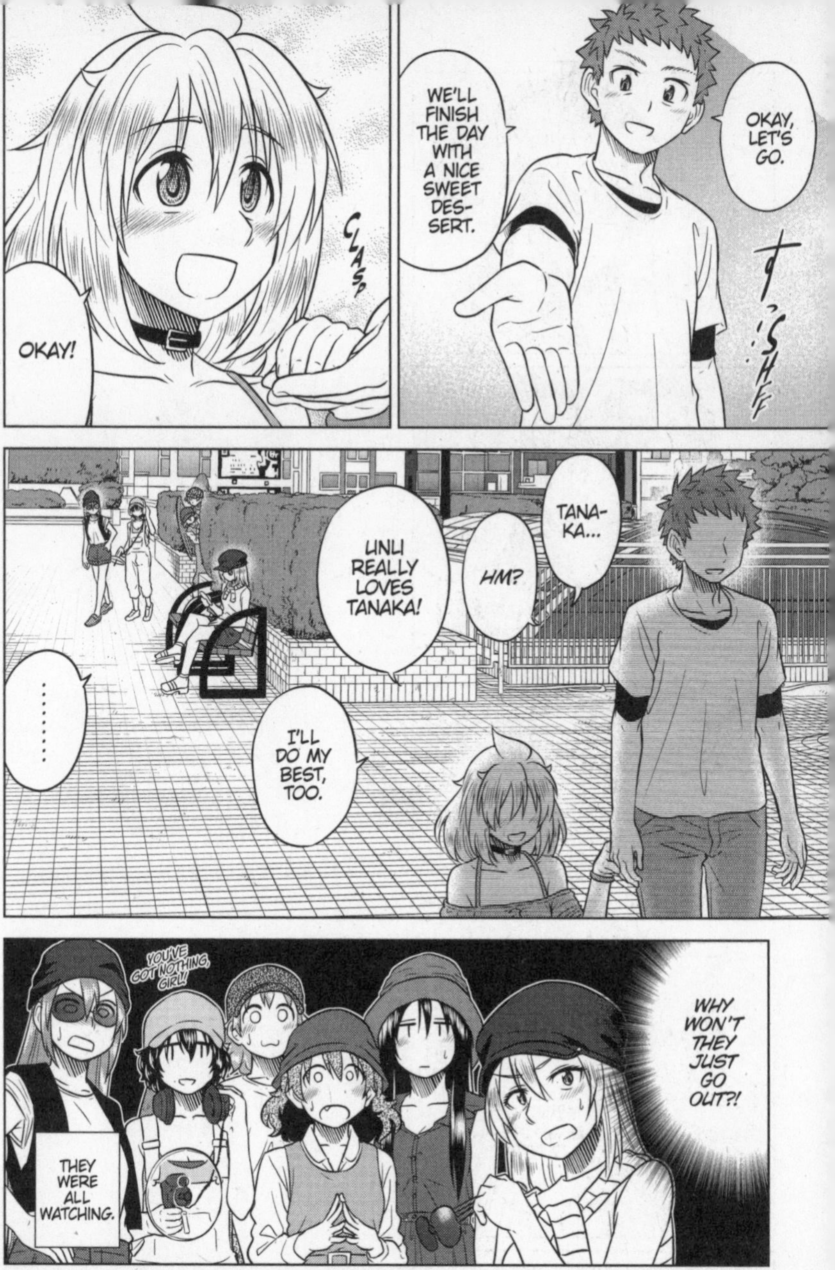
OKAY, LET'S GO.
WE'LL FINISH THE DAY WITH A NICE SWEET DES- SERT.
SHFF
CLASP
OKAY!
TANAKA...
HM?
UNU REALLY LOVES TANAKA!
I'LL DO MY BEST, TOO.
......
WHY WON'T THEY JUST GO OUT?!
YOU'VE GOT NOTHING, GIRL!
THEY WERE ALL WATCHING.

Species Domain Volume 6 / The End

Chapter 41 • END

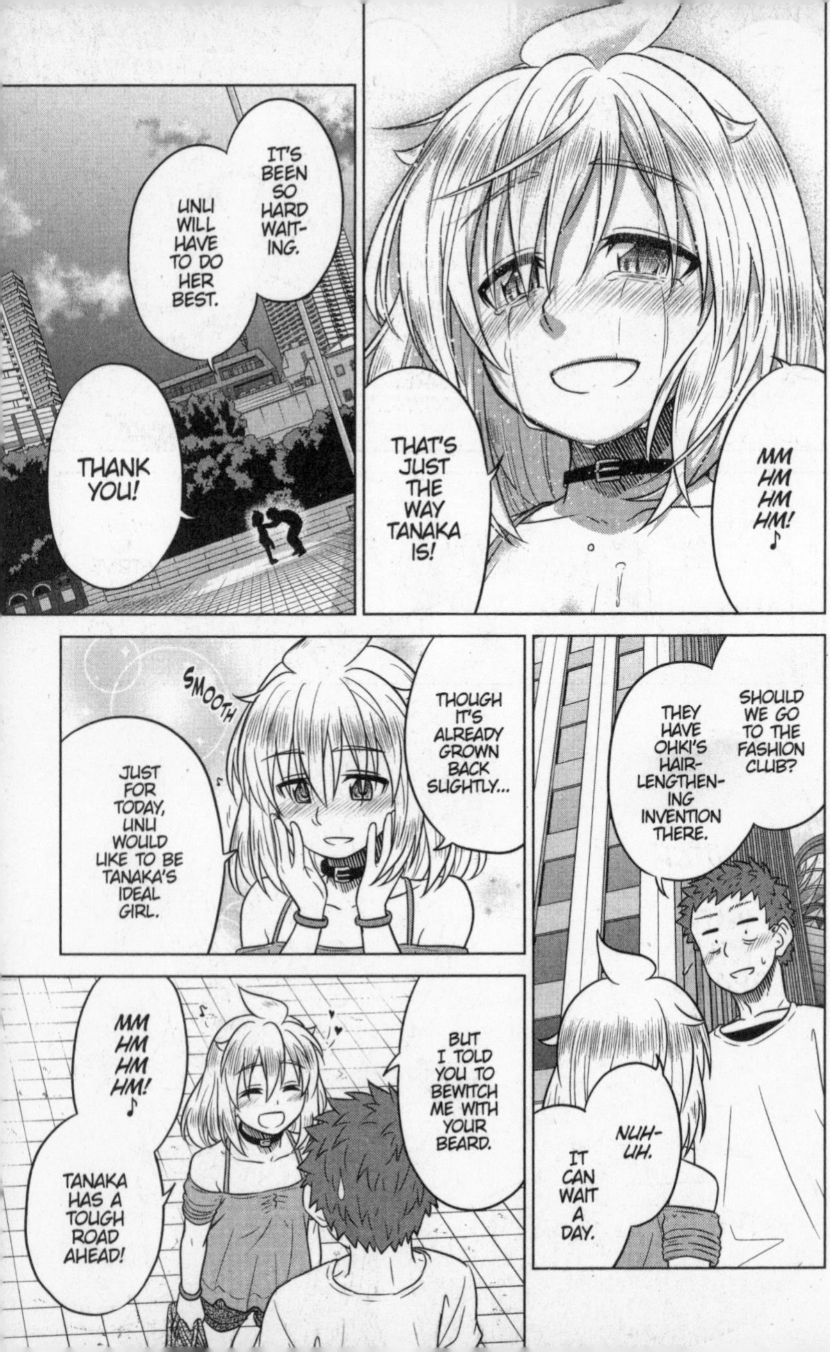
MM HM HM HM! ♪
THAT'S JUST THE WAY TANAKA IS!
IT'S BEEN SO HARD WAIT-ING.
UNLI WILL HAVE TO DO HER BEST.
THANK YOU!
SHOULD WE GO TO THE FASHION CLUB?
THEY HAVE OHKI'S HAIR-LENGTHEN-ING INVENTION THERE.
NUH-UH.
IT CAN WAIT A DAY.
THOUGH IT'S ALREADY GROWN BACK SLIGHTLY...
SMOOTH
JUST FOR TODAY, UNLI WOULD LIKE TO BE TANAKA'S IDEAL GIRL.
BUT I TOLD YOU TO BEWITCH ME WITH YOUR BEARD.
MM HM HM HM! ♪
TANAKA HAS A TOUGH ROAD AHEAD!

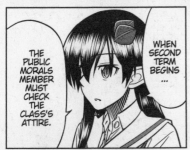

WHEN SECOND TERM BEGINS ...
THE PUBLIC MORALS MEMBER MUST CHECK THE CLASS'S ATTIRE.
FOR NOW, OHKI-KUN, AT LEAST TUCK IN YOUR SHIRT.
NO WAY.
WHY NOT?
THIS WAY IT'S A BIT LIKE A LAB COAT, SEE?
I WANT TO UNBUTTON IT, TOO, ACTUALLY.
YOU REALLY ARE SILLY ABOUT STUFF LIKE THAT.
JUST TUCK IT IN ALREADY!!
BLUUUUSH
NO, I WANT IT HANGING OUT!!
......!!

Fantasy Runs Rampant

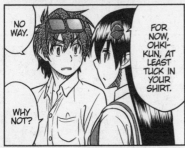

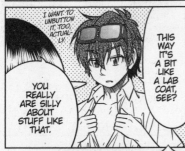

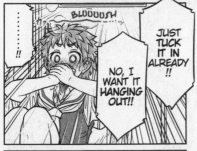

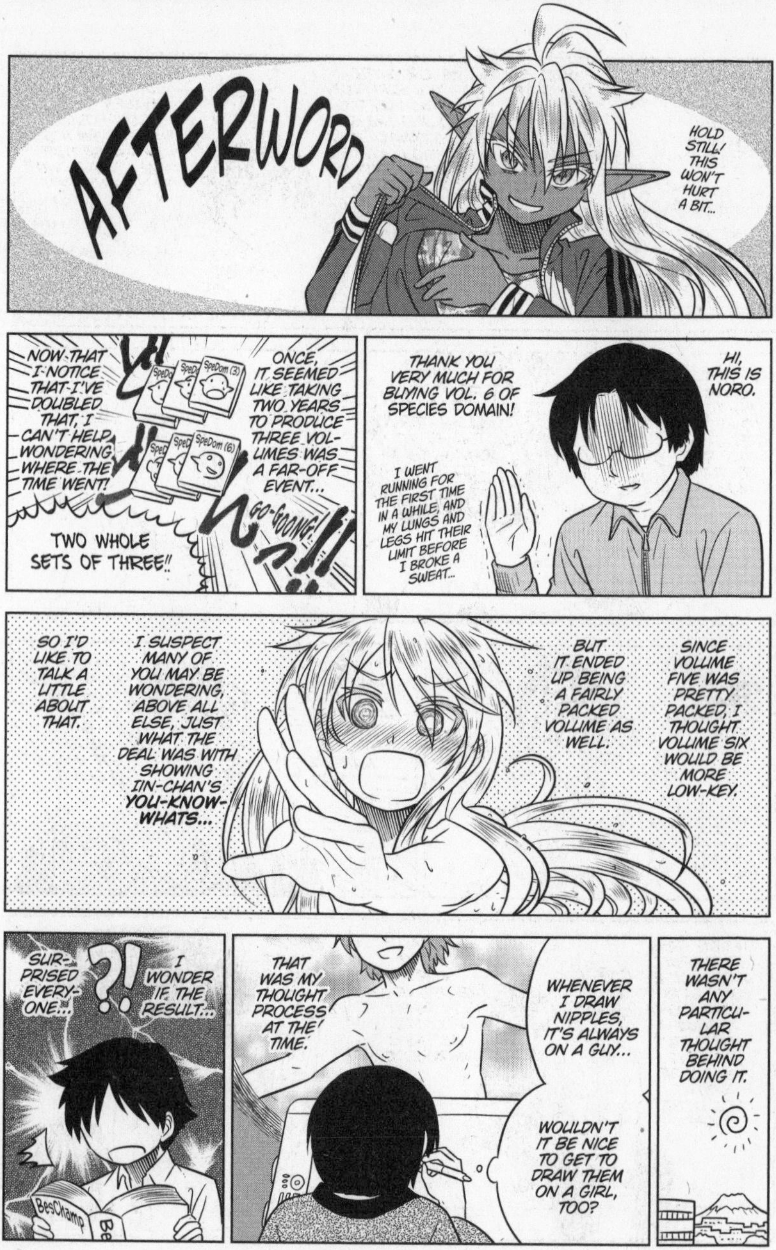
AFTERWORD
HOLD STILL! THIS WON'T HURT A BIT...
HI, THIS IS NORO.
THANK YOU VERY MUCH FOR BUYING VOL. 6 OF SPECIES DOMAIN!
I WENT RUNNING FOR THE FIRST TIME IN A WHILE, AND MY LUNGS AND LEGS HIT THEIR LIMIT BEFORE I BROKE A SWEAT...
ONCE, IT SEEMED LIKE TAKING TWO YEARS TO PRODUCE THREE VOLUMES WAS A FAR-OFF EVENT...
NOW THAT I NOTICE THAT I'VE DOUBLED THAT, I CAN'T HELP WONDERING WHERE THE TIME WENT!
SpeDom (3)
SpeDom (6)
GO-GOONG!!
TWO WHOLE SETS OF THREE!!
SINCE VOLUME FIVE WAS PRETTY PACKED, I THOUGHT VOLUME SIX WOULD BE MORE LOW-KEY.
BUT IT ENDED UP BEING A FAIRLY PACKED VOLUME AS WELL.
I SUSPECT MANY OF YOU MAY BE WONDERING, ABOVE ALL ELSE, JUST WHAT THE DEAL WAS WITH SHOWING IIN-CHAN'S YOU-KNOW-WHATS...
SO I'D LIKE TO TALK A LITTLE ABOUT THAT.
THERE WASN'T ANY PARTICULAR THOUGHT BEHIND DOING IT.
WHENEVER I DRAW NIPPLES, IT'S ALWAYS ON A GUY...
WOULDN'T IT BE NICE TO GET TO DRAW THEM ON A GIRL, TOO?
THAT WAS MY THOUGHT PROCESS AT THE TIME.
I WONDER IF THE RESULT...
SURPRISED EVERYONE...
?!
BesChamp

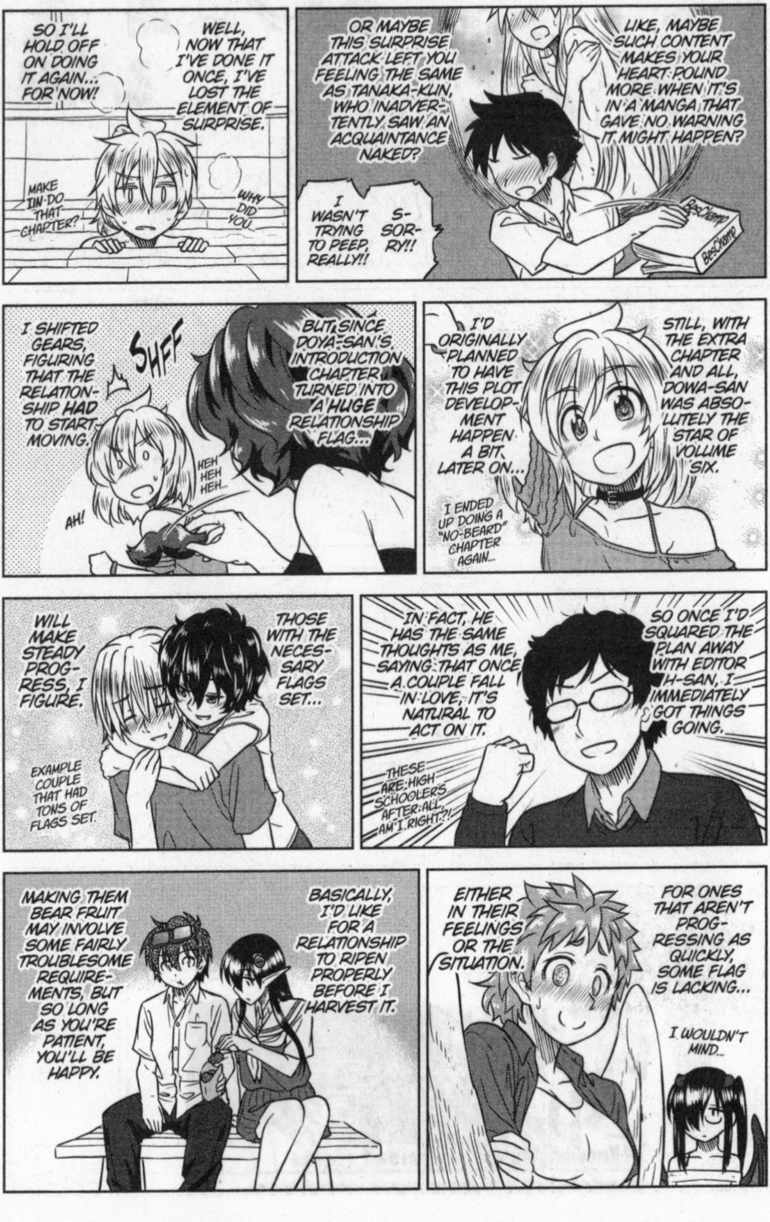
LIKE, MAYBE SUCH CONTENT MAKES YOUR HEART POUND MORE WHEN IT'S IN A MANGA THAT GAVE NO WARNING IT MIGHT HAPPEN?
OR MAYBE THIS SURPRISE ATTACK LEFT YOU FEELING THE SAME AS TANAKA-KUN, WHO INADVERTENTLY SAW AN ACQUAINTANCE NAKED?
S-SORRY!!
I WASN'T TRYING TO PEEP, REALLY!!
BesChamp
BesChamp
WELL, NOW THAT I'VE DONE IT ONCE, I'VE LOST THE ELEMENT OF SURPRISE.
SO I'LL HOLD OFF ON DOING IT AGAIN... FOR NOW!
WHY DID YOU...
MAKE IIN-DO THAT CHAPTER?
STILL, WITH THE EXTRA CHAPTER AND ALL, DOWA-SAN WAS ABSOLUTELY THE STAR OF VOLUME SIX.
I'D ORIGINALLY PLANNED TO HAVE THIS PLOT DEVELOPMENT HAPPEN A BIT LATER ON...
I ENDED UP DOING A "NO-BEARD" CHAPTER AGAIN...
BUT, SINCE DOYA-SAN'S INTRODUCTION CHAPTER TURNED INTO A HUGE RELATIONSHIP FLAG...
SHFF
I SHIFTED GEARS, FIGURING THAT THE RELATIONSHIP HAD TO START MOVING.
HEH HEH HEH...
AH!
SO ONCE I'D SQUARED THE PLAN AWAY WITH EDITOR H-SAN, I IMMEDIATELY GOT THINGS GOING.
IN FACT, HE HAS THE SAME THOUGHTS AS ME, SAYING THAT ONCE A COUPLE FALL IN LOVE, IT'S NATURAL TO ACT ON IT.
THESE ARE HIGH SCHOOLERS AFTER ALL, AM I RIGHT?!
THOSE WITH THE NECESSARY FLAGS SET...
WILL MAKE STEADY PROGRESS, I FIGURE.
EXAMPLE COUPLE THAT HAD TONS OF FLAGS SET.
FOR ONES THAT AREN'T PROGRESSING AS QUICKLY, SOME FLAG IS LACKING...
EITHER IN THEIR FEELINGS OR THE SITUATION.
I WOULDN'T MIND...
BASICALLY, I'D LIKE FOR A RELATIONSHIP TO RIPEN PROPERLY BEFORE I HARVEST IT.
MAKING THEM BEAR FRUIT MAY INVOLVE SOME FAIRLY TROUBLESOME REQUIREMENTS, BUT SO LONG AS YOU'RE PATIENT, YOU'LL BE HAPPY.

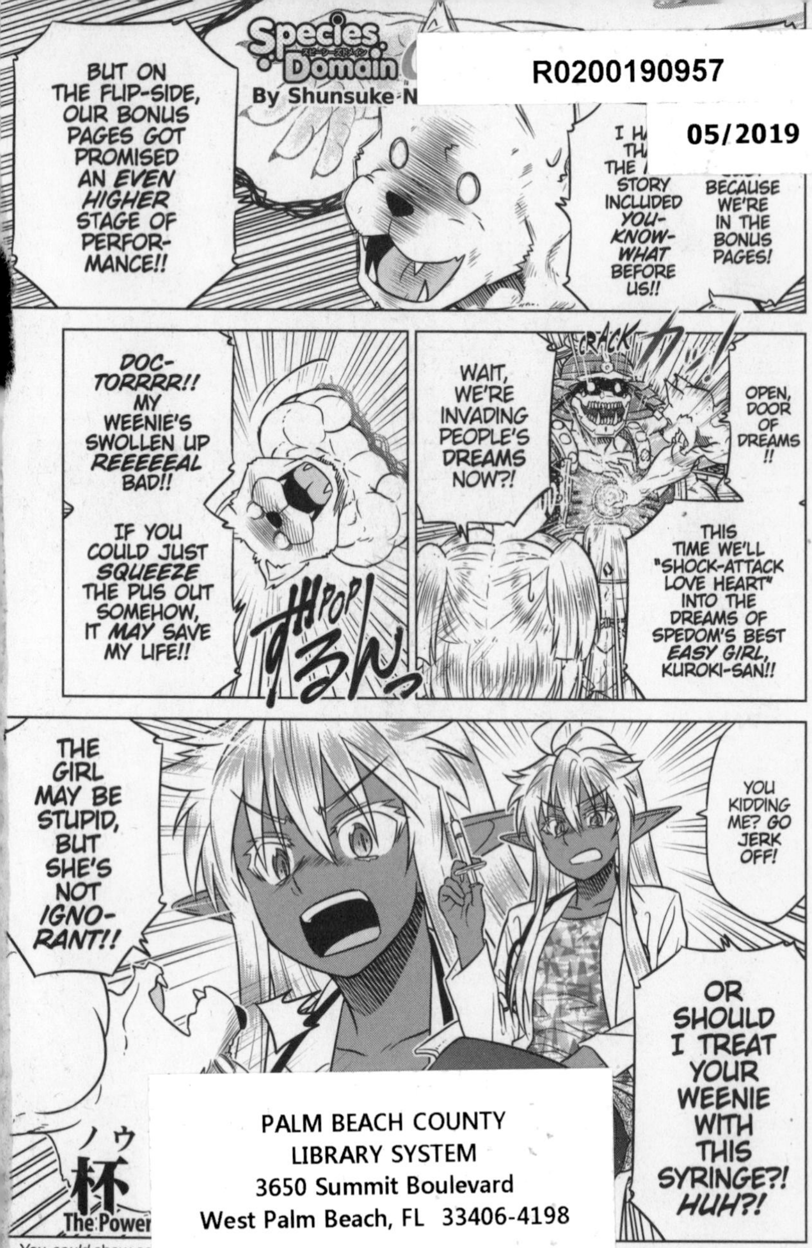
Species Domain
By Shunsuke N
BECAUSE WE'RE IN THE BONUS PAGES!
I HA THA THE STORY INCLUDED YOU-KNOW-WHAT BEFORE US!!
BUT ON THE FLIP-SIDE, OUR BONUS PAGES GOT PROMISED AN *EVEN HIGHER* STAGE OF PERFORMANCE!!
CRACK
OPEN, DOOR OF DREAMS!!
WAIT, WE'RE INVADING PEOPLE'S DREAMS NOW?!
THIS TIME WE'LL "SHOCK-ATTACK LOVE HEART" INTO THE DREAMS OF SPEDOM'S BEST *EASY GIRL*, KUROKI-SAN!!
DOC-TORRRR!! MY WEENIE'S SWOLLEN UP *REEEEEAL* BAD!!
IF YOU COULD JUST *SQUEEZE* THE PUS OUT SOMEHOW, IT *MAY* SAVE MY LIFE!!
POP
YOU KIDDING ME? GO JERK OFF!
THE GIRL MAY BE STUPID, BUT SHE'S NOT *IGNORANT!!*
OR SHOULD I TREAT YOUR WEENIE WITH THIS SYRINGE?! *HUH?!*
ノウ
杯
The Power

You *could* show so